Spaces of International Economy and Management

Spaces of International Economy and Management

Launching New Perspectives on Management and Geography

Edited by

Rolf D. Schlunze

Nathaniel O. Agola

and

William W. Baber

First published 2012 by
PALGRAVE MACMILLAN

Palgrave Macmillan in the UK is an imprint of Macmillan Publishers Limited,
registered in England, company number 785998, of Houndmills, Basingstoke,
Hampshire RG21 6XS.

Palgrave Macmillan in the US is a division of St Martin's Press LLC,
175 Fifth Avenue, New York, NY 10010.

Palgrave Macmillan is the global academic imprint of the above companies
and has companies and representatives throughout the world.

Palgrave® and Macmillan® are registered trademarks in the United States,
the United Kingdom, Europe and other countries.

ISBN: 978–0–230–30022–4

This book is printed on paper suitable for recycling and made from fully
managed and sustained forest sources. Logging, pulping and manufacturing
processes are expected to conform to the environmental regulations of the
country of origin.

A catalogue record for this book is available from the British Library.

A catalog record for this book is available from the Library of Congress.

10 9 8 7 6 5 4 3 2 1
21 20 19 18 17 16 15 14 13 12

Printed and bound in the United States of America

Contents

Tables

Figures

Acknowledgments

This book is a result of the first International Symposium of SIEM launching new perspectives on management and geography. Thus, we are grateful to many geographers and management scientists who contributed with their interdisciplinary effort. We are thankful for the support of Professor Fujio Mizuoka from Hitotsubashi University in Tokyo and Professor Kenkichi Nagao from Osaka City University. At the same time, we wish to express our gratitude to Professor Nobuhiko Hibara, Professor Masaki Kuroki, and Professor Takashi Moriya, our good and supportive colleagues from Ritsumeikan University. We are also particularly grateful to the anonymous reviewers who helped us to select and to improve the quality of the contributions. We would also like to express our gratitude to all contributors. We cannot forget to thank Professor Haruyuki Hasegawa from Doshisha University for his active participation in the discussions at the symposium. We could not have developed the book without a well-organized conference aided by many voluntary working students, among them Ji Weiwei, Kento Yano, Shi Zeng, Hua Ye, Couvois Benoit, Propera Fabien, Yukiko Matsushita, Chen Tian Jing, Zhao Qian, Cheng Linlin, Syoma Toyoda, and Yasuyuki Komai. A special note of thanks goes to Ms. Masayo Miyake from the Human Research Office of Ritsumeikan University for giving us a helpful and steady hand with the accounting and other administrative procedures. We are also grateful to Mr. Yoshio Bono, from the overseas promotion agency of the Osaka City Policy Planning Office, who heartily received us during the after-conference excursion at the Herbis Plaza ENT Tower, to explain the new urban development project at Japan Railway Osaka station. The book and the international symposium of the SIEM research group were sponsored by the Society for the Promotion of Japanese Classical Writings and for Educational Exchanges, Ritsumeikan University, and the Japanese Society for Promotion of Science (Grant No. 19520688).

Foreword

Challenges for management geography: transnational management and global production networks

The development of geographical studies of management is an important one. As economic activities are becoming more globally interconnected and interdependent today, the management of cross-border activities by firms, states, and other institutions is much more challenging and complex. The geographical foundations and specificities of this management in a globalizing era become the crucial research question for the emerging field of management geography. Here, I will focus on two dimensions of such management geography in relation to the nature of management across borders and the globalization of production networks. I argue that in both arenas, space makes a critical difference in the ways in which management and organizational issues should be conceived and understood. Departing from the entrepreneurship and strategic management literature, I argue for an economic–geographical reading of how management in transnational entrepreneurship and global production networks can be attained and studied (see also Yeung, 2009a; 2009b).

Let me begin with two important geographical questions. Does space matter in management and organization theories? And does geography make a difference to the behavior and management of organizations? These are clearly not trivial questions, for several reasons. First, despite the advent of contemporary globalization, there is no conclusive evidence that global corporations from different home countries are converging in their organizational behavior and strategic management. For example, Michael Porter (1990: 614, 807; note 1) argued two decades ago that "[t]he more competition becomes global, ironically, the more important the home base becomes... Yet my research on this book has made it clear that globalization does not eliminate a powerful role for the home nation. The role of location, particularly of the home base, is far greater than I once supposed." It makes sense theoretically to explain why persistent spatial differences in these corporations, presumably the key drivers of globalization, continue to exist.

Second, space and spatial relations remain largely under-theorized in mainstream management and organization theories, a reflection of the predominantly Anglo-American origins of management and organization theories. In their critical reflections on the field of organization theory, Ghoshal and Westney (1993: 6, 11; emphasis added) observed that "studies focusing on organizations and environments in Europe or South-east Asia have been labelled 'area studies', whereas research on organizations in California or Ohio has led to propositions that have been implicitly stated and accepted as universal ... [O]rganization theorists have ignored or underemphasized the case of diversified organizations whose various constituent units are located in different business or *geographic* contexts" (see also Yeung, 2005a; 2005b). For decades, management and organization theorists have conceived organizations as ontological entities separate from two key dimensions of great social significance – time and space. As geographer Bob Sack (1980: 4) noted, "[s]pace is an essential framework of all modes of thought. From physics to aesthetics, from myth and magic to common everyday life, space, in conjunction with time, provides a fundamental ordering system interlacing every facet of thought." While time, as expressed in studies of organizational change and learning, has recently received significant attention in management and organization theories, space remains largely outside the normal orbit of theory-development routines in management and organization studies.

Third, geographical dimensions – distance, location, space, territoriality, geographical scales, and spatial relations – may exert such significant causal influences on the organization and behavior of modern corporations that they may fundamentally challenge our existing conceptions of the strategy, control and management, performance, and impact of these corporations on communities and society. As the late John Dunning (1998: 46) reflected in relation to international business studies, "[t]he emphasis on the firm-specific determinants of international economic activity, while still driving much academic research by scholars in business schools, is now being complemented by a renewed interest in the spatial aspects of FDI [foreign direct investment]." To a certain extent, this interest in the spatial aspects of international investments is related to the greater geographical reach of global corporations in more recent decades. Raymond Vernon (1992: viii) observed some time ago that "[t]he enterprises of the 1990s routinely span distances with an ease that could not have been contemplated two or three decades ago, searching for opportunities and threats in distant places". The global reach of many business organizations, however, has not diminished the important effect of geography in their expansion; we see that geographical differences present a significant challenge to the management, organization, and success of global corporations (see Dicken, 2011).

Despite the above pessimistic observations, however, recent theoretical work in "the new economic geography" (Combes et al., 2008), the analysis of competitive strategy (Porter, 2000) and the geography of international production (Dunning, 2009) has explicitly incorporated location in its analytical frameworks. Econometric studies in "the new economic geography" have shown that geographical agglomeration produces external economies that lead to increasing returns to scale under conditions of imperfect competition and multiple equilibria. In their major review of the economics of agglomeration, Fujita and Thisse (1996: 347) footnoted that "[t]he study of location problems in the international marketplace is still in infancy and constitutes a very promising line of research." In the analysis of competitive strategy, location has been given theoretical prominence through the analytical coupling of the tight relationship between clusters and competitive strategy at the firm level. In this sense, Porter (2000: 272) argued strongly that "geography and location must become one of the core disciplines in management. There is a compelling need to reorient our thinking about corporate strategy in a way that sees location and cluster participation as integral to a firm's success." Finally, location has also been incorporated into John Dunning's revised eclectic framework of international production (Dunning and Lundan, 2008). Spatial transaction costs are theorized to influence the raison d'être of transnational corporations.

These interrelated strands of theorization in management geography, nevertheless, remain partial and static. First, space and location are incorporated into these theoretical frameworks as the backdrop or scaffolding on which economic and organizational processes operate. Although distance (both physical and cultural) and location are conceptualized as exerting some "friction" and influence, firms and organizations continue to be viewed as ontologically independent entities that operate according to some preordained and internalized logic and strategies. Second, such important geographical dimensions as scales and spatial relations are neglected in this theoretical work. Geography is therefore essentially stripped down to "location," which in turn is translated into measurable distance between points in space. This is evident, for example, in Lomi's (1995: 111; my emphasis) observation that "the recurrence of patterns of organizational concentration in *space* across different industries and in a number of national contexts provides indirect evidence that *location* may be a general factor shaping the evolution of organizations." These Euclidean conceptions of absolute distance and space as a "container" tend to dominate the emerging work on the geography of firms, economic development, and international production. Interestingly, over half a century ago the French economist Francois Perroux (1950: 90) made a similar observation about economics: "[a] banal sense of space location creates the illusion of the coincidence of political space with economic and human space". Perroux argued that "it is no longer possible to situate the firm in banal space. It is often composed of establishments geographically dispersed, amongst which are formed bonds of organization of varying strength" (94).

Drawing upon the above conceptual work and the significantly larger body of theoretical literature in the discipline of economic geography, I argue that we should reassert the importance of space and geography in management and organization studies. As argued by Schoenberger (2000: 329)

Spatial form, however, is not merely a by-product of decisions taken according to the more compelling specifics of products, markets, and production processes. Firms produce and use and are shaped by spatial relations as a normal part of doing business and must continually create and seek to validate spatio-temporal processes and understandings as a condition of staying alive. Another way of saying this might be that spatial and temporal processes are very deeply part of the production function and the growth trajectory, not artifacts of them.

In attempting to answer the two opening questions of this Foreword, I argue for a new theoretical framework for examining the geographical foundations of business organizations and for a new direction of research in management geography and organization studies. Instead of taking space and location as the backdrop of organizational behavior and change, we need to theorize the complex relations and interactions between business organizations and geography within the realm of *organizational space*. The conception of organizational space as relational is explained by the ways in which its geometry varies with specific relations constituted by different organizational units. Organizational space thus differs significantly from physical space in which location and distance can be directly observed and measured. Organizational space is also different from the concept of organizational fields in institutional theories that defines the *structural* or population characteristics of organizations as "the totality of relevant actors" (DiMaggio and Powell, 1983: 148).

This theorization can potentially contribute to a *relational perspective* for understanding why and how business organizations are fundamentally spatialized in their formation, management, performance, and impact (Yeung, 2005c; 2008). Pitched at this higher level of abstraction and complexity, this relational approach aims to contribute to the development of more sophisticated theories in management and organization studies that may not be directly operationalizable and measurable. As Rousseau and Fried (2001: 3) cautioned, "the common demands for clean (read: simple) models do not always fit with the messy reality of contemporary work and organizational life." More specifically, my strategy of tackling these theoretical questions is to focus explicitly on one particular type of business organization – transnational corporations and their international business activities. This specific choice reflects my own research preferences, and it underscores the greater likelihood of geography having a significant influence on the organization and behavior of transnational corporations (TNCs) that are defined as large business enterprises operating across national boundaries in an integrated manner. For example, Frost (2001: 121) concluded that "the multinational firm may offer an ideal context for advancing our understanding of the firm-location nexus precisely because of the ability to study a single corporate entity in multiple institutional contexts."

To construct this relational perspective and to clear away "conventional notions to make room for artful and exciting insights" (DiMaggio, 1995: 391), we need to start with a critical review of various theoretical frameworks in the study of firms and transnational corporations that have explicitly incorporated location in their explanatory matrixes. Some of the chapters in this volume have done so well. We need to engage with these frameworks and identify their reluctance to theorize explicitly the role of geographical scales and spatial relations in the international business operations of TNCs. In addition, we must theorize the spatial dynamics of business organizations and their international business activities. To do so, we can draw upon recent theoretical advances in economic geography to illustrate the importance of geographical scales and spatial relations in shaping the dynamics of business organizations and their international behavior in global production networks (Coe et al., 2008; Yeung, 2009b). In short, we need a robust research framework for investigating the geographical foundations of international business firms. This is the crucial agenda for management geography.

The implications of this approach to management geography for business policy and practices are manifold and complex. There are at least two explicit implications that should be laid out briefly here. First, instead of asking whether they have a global strategy to compete for the future, corporate managers should ask themselves whether they have a *spatial* strategy. This question is fundamentally important to corporate performance and success because competition is not necessarily pitched at the global scale only. Corporate competition indeed operates at all spatial scales, and corporate success can be secured only through an understanding of these overlapping scales of competition. By privileging the global scale, the competitive strategy literature might have misled top executives to pursue too much centralization and implementation of corporate decisions on a global scale. This relentless pursuit of a global strategy is often championed at the expense of reaping potential geographical economies through more appropriate scalar configurations and representations of organizational units in this "global" competition.

Second, corporate managers must take stock of how geography is conceived in their organizations – the idea of cognitive representations of space. Understanding and resolving the contradictions and tensions in these cognitive mindsets within an organization will help corporate managers to open better channels of communications within the organization and to strengthen intra-organizational cooperation and solidarity. For example, will it be effective for marketing executives in the parent company to champion a global branding approach if the R&D team takes a highly local orientation in their design of specific products? Alternatively, will a global corporation be efficient if its central purchasing department practices global sourcing and yet managers of its foreign manufacturing plants are so locally embedded to source within the host countries? Ultimately, the success of business organizations depends critically on their willingness and ability to recognize complexity and differentiation in the global *space* economy.

Management geographers and organization theorists who are cognizant of the role of space and geography will not make this global economy less complex, but they can certainly enable it to be more comprehensible and eventually manageable.

Henry Wai-chung Yeung
National University of Singapore
April 2011

References

Coe, Neil, Dicken, Peter, and Hess, Martin (2008), "Global production networks: realizing the potential", *Journal of Economic Geography*, vol. 8(3), pp. 271–95.

Combes, Pierre-Philippe, Mayer, Thierry, and Thisse, Jacques-Francois (2008), *Economic Geography: The Integration of Regions and Nations*, Princeton, NJ: Princeton University Press.

Dicken, Peter (2011), *Global Shift: Mapping the Changing Contours of the World Economy*, Sixth Edition, London: Sage.

DiMaggio, Paul J. (1995), "Comments on 'What theory is not'", *Administrative Science Quarterly*, vol. 40(3), pp. 391–97.

DiMaggio, Paul J. and Powell, Walter W. (1983), "The iron cage revisited: institutional isomorphism and collective rationality in organisational fields", *American Sociological Review*, vol. 48, pp. 147–60.

Dunning, John H. (1998), "Location and the multinational enterprise: a neglected factor?", *Journal of International Business Studies*, vol. 29(1), pp. 45–66.

Dunning, John H. (2009), "Location and the multinational enterprise: John Dunning's thoughts on receiving the *Journal of International Business Studies* 2008 Decade Award", *Journal of International Business Studies*, vol. 40(1), pp. 20–34.

Dunning, John H. and Lundan, Sarianna M. (2008), *Multinational Enterprises and the Global Economy*, Second Edition, Cheltenham: Edward Elgar.

Frost, Tony (2001), "The geographic sources of foreign subsidiaries' innovations", *Strategic Management Journal*, vol. 22(1), pp. 101–23.

Fujita, Masahisa and Thisse, Jacques-Francois (1996), "Economics of agglomeration", *Journal of the Japanese and International Economies*, vol. 10, pp. 339–78.

Ghoshal, Sumantra and Westney, D. Eleanor (1993), "Introduction and overview", in Sumantra Ghoshal and D. Eleanor Westney (eds), *Organization Theory and the Multinational Corporation*, New York: St. Martin's Press, pp. 1–23.

Lomi, Alessandro (1995), "The population ecology of organizational founding: location dependence and unobserved heterogeneity", *Administrative Science Quarterly*, vol. 40(1), pp. 111–44.

Perroux, Francois (1950), "Economic space: theory and applications", *Quarterly Journal of Economics*, vol. 64(1), pp. 89–104.

Porter, Michael E. (1990), *The Competitive Advantage of Nations*, London: Palgrave Macmillan.

Porter, Michael E. (2000), "Locations, clusters, and company strategy", in Gordon L. Clark, Maryann A. Feldman, and Meric S. Gertler (eds), *The Oxford Handbook of Economic Geography*, Oxford: Oxford University Press, pp. 253–74.

Rousseau, Denise M. and Fried, Yitzhak (2001), "Location, location, location: contextualizing organizational research", *Journal of Organizational Behavior*, vol. 22(1), pp. 1–13.

Sack, Robert David (1980), *Conceptions of Space in Social Thought*, London: Palgrave Macmillan.

Schoenberger, Erica (2000), "The management of time and space", in Gordon L. Clark, Maryann A. Feldman, and Meric S. Gertler (eds), *The Oxford Handbook of Economic Geography*, Oxford: Oxford University Press, pp. 317–32.

Vernon, Raymond (1992), "Foreword", in Peter J. Buckley (ed.), *Studies in International Business*, London: Palgrave Macmillan, pp. viii–ix.

Yeung, Henry Wai-chung (2005a), "Organizational space: a new frontier in international business strategy?", *Critical Perspectives on International Business*, vol. 1(4), pp. 219–40.

Yeung, Henry Wai-chung (2005b), "The firm as social networks: an organisational perspective", *Growth and Change*, vol. 36(3), pp. 307–28.

Yeung, Henry Wai-chung (2005c), "Rethinking relational economic geography", *Transactions of the Institute of British Geographers*, New Series, vol. 30(1), pp. 37–51.

Yeung, Henry Wai-chung (2008), "Perspectives on inter-organizational relations in economic geography", in Steve Cropper, Mark Ebers, Chris Huxham and Peter Smith Ring (eds), *The Oxford Handbook of Inter-Organizational Relations*, Oxford: Oxford University Press, pp. 473–501.

Yeung, Henry Wai-chung (2009a), "Transnationalizing entrepreneurship: a critical agenda for economic geography", *Progress in Human Geography*, vol. 33(2), pp. 210–35.

Yeung, Henry Wai-chung (2009b), "Transnational corporations, global production networks, and urban and regional development: a geographer's perspective on *Multinational Enterprises and the Global Economy*", *Growth and Change*, vol. 40(2), pp. 197–226.

Contributors

Tetsuo Abo is Professor of Economics at Teikyo Heisei University with research interest in illuminating the global situation of "hybrid factories," the mixture between Japanese and local management systems, in the major regions of the world, using a management geography approach. His work includes research on Japanese firms and non-Japanese firms and closely connects sociocultural differences with geographical locations and with historical contexts.

Nathaniel O. Agola is Lecturer in the Department of Business Administration and Graduate School of Management of Technology at Ritsumeikan University. He received his Ph.D. in International Development from the Department of Business Economics at Nagoya University. His research interests include technology management-product and service innovation, management of emerging technologies into markets, and innovative transfer of technology products and services across borders. His recent publications include value innovation as an operational strategy in international markets.

William W. Baber has combined education with business throughout his career, teaching business students in Japan and Europe and working in economic development for the State of Maryland. In his work in international business attraction for the State of Maryland, he frequently encountered cross-cultural conflicts and synergies. He studies these issues as an associate professor in the Graduate School of Management at Kyoto University. His research interests include cross-cultural adaptation and interaction of managers.

Anxo Calvo-Silvosa is Professor of Financial Economy at Universidade da Coruña. His studies focus on the regulatory processes of internationalization of economy and energy. Recently, he took over the duties of the dean of the Faculty of Economics and Enterprise. He was previously the General Director of Industry in the Galician Autonomous Government and responsible for the Energetic Galician Public Institute.

Masato Ikuta is Professor in the Department of Geography, College of Letters at Ritsumeikan University. His research interest is in economic geography and focuses on Japanese large cities and mega cities in Southeast Asia, especially Malaysia and Singapore. His interests also include Canadian geography particularly the Western part of the country including Vancouver. He has published several books including *Theory on Consumer Behavior in Japanese*

Metropolitan Regions, Regionalism in Kansai, Japan, Urban Developments in Malaysia, and articles in leading economic geography journals.

Andrew Jones is Professor of Economic Geography and Head of the Geography, Environment and Development Studies Department at Birkbeck College, University of London. His research interests span economic, urban, and sociological issues but have long focused on globalization. A major element of this has been work on management practices, mobility, and organizational form in large transnational firms. His research has focused on financial and business service firms. He is the author of several peer-reviewed journal articles and four books, including *Management Consultancy and Banking in an Era of Globalization* (2003).

Rinas Kashbrasiev conducts his current research on interregional and international trade including important questions such as competition, macroeconomic coordination, outsourcing, industrial cooperation, and regional trade agreements. He takes into consideration the regional variations in cultures because they are encountered by businesses and international managers operating abroad. Apart from being a leading member of SIEM, he has been affiliated with Regional Science Association International (RSAI) since 2000 and International Human Dimensions Program (IHDP) since 2004.

Rubén C. Lois-González is Professor of Economic and Urban Geographyat Universidade de Santiago de Compostela. His research interests target the new spaces of economics activities and urban management. He was previously Dean of the Faculty of Geography and History and a leading member of the Institute of Studies for the Galician development and of the Spanish Commission for evaluation of project Research and Development in Spain.

Sawako Maruyama is Associate Professor at Kobe University reaching back to many empirical insights from her work as a researcher at Osaka Prefectural Institute for Advanced Industry Development. She received her Ph.D. from Nagoya University with a dissertation on intra-industry trade. Her research interest includes international economics and regional economics. She focuses on empirical research in international trade and the activities of multinational enterprises. She also takes a vital interest in the regional economies of Osaka/Kansai and Sweden.

Michael Plattner is currently R&D Manager with a global scope in JT International. He has worked for more than 10 years in academia on the globalization of production and innovation systems with the support of the German Science Foundation (DFG), the Alexander von Humboldt Foundation (AvH), and the Japan Society for the Promotion of Science (JSPS). Through publications, lectures, and presentations at conferences he is an influential key contributor to the field of Management Geography. He holds a Ph.D. with an emphasis on Economic Geography from the Philipps-University of Marburg.

Tim Reiffenstein is Associate Professor at the Department of Geography and Environment, Mount Allison University in Canada. His research focuses on Japanese industrial geography, in particular exploring how evolving intellectual property policy and associated management practices have shaped Japan's international economic relations. Projects include comparative studies of Japanese and American patent law professions, Japanese intellectual property in relation to Vietnam, and linguistic and institutional challenges of patent policy harmonization between Japan and the U.S. He is a member of the Canadian Association of Geographers, the Canadian Regional Science Association, and the Association of American Geographers.

Rolf D. Schlunze is Professor of Intercultural Management in the Department of International Business Administration of Ritsumeikan University. His received his Ph.D. from the University of Tokyo and his post-doctoral research has focused on the locational adjustment of managerial systems. His work has been published in reviewed journals such as *Asian Business & Management* (ABM), *TESG*, the *Japanese Journal of Human Geography,* and the *Annals of the Japan Association of Economic Geographers.* He is adviser to the Euro-Asia Management Study Association (EAMSA) and leads the research group Spaces of International Management and Economy (SIEM) seeking to join research to managerial practices.

Roger Schweizer is Assistant Professor of International Business in the Department of Business Administration, School of Business, Economics and Law at Göteborg University, Sweden. He is also holder of the Broman Fellowship at the Institute for Innovation and Entrepreneurship, Göteborg University. His research interests cover the internationalization processes of firms in knowledge-intensive industries.

Patrik Ström is Associate Professor of Economic Geography in the Department of Human and Economic Geography, School of Business, Economics and Law at Göteborg University, Sweden. He is also holder of The Staffan Helmfrid Pro Futura Fellowship at the Swedish Collegium for Advanced Study, Uppsala, Sweden. His research interest covers the development of a service-based economy in East Asia. He is also interested in regional competitiveness and internationalization of the advanced service industry.

Atsushi Taira is Professor of Geography at Kagawa University in Takamatsu, Kagawa, Japan and a co-founder and leader of the research group SIEM. His research interest concerns spatial characteristics of multinational corporations, especially the local context of business activities of multinational corporations. Currently, he conducts research projects on the internationalization of local industries in Japan.

Ronald S. Wall holds a Master's in urban planning and a Ph.D. in Economic Geography from the Faculty of Applied Economics, Erasmus University Rotterdam. He works for the Rotterdam School of Urban Management (IHS) of the Erasmus University. His research interest includes the impact of global economic networks on urban regional development. In this respect he is developing urban management tools which take into consideration the influence of socioeconomic externalities on urban development. He has published in leading journals such as *Economic Geography, Environment and Planning A*, the *Journal of Social and Economic Geography,* and in books such as *Global Urban Analysis* and the *GaWC Handbook.*

Kenta Yamamoto is Assistant Professor in the Faculty of Economics at Kyushu International University, Fukuoka, Japan. He received his Ph.D. from Tohoku University. His specialties are urban geography and economic geography. His research interests focus on the areas of agglomeration factors for cultural industries, the characteristics of creative spaces, and the divisions of labor in these industries within and between world cities. In addition, he has an interest in and is studying about the structures of cultural industries and how traditional cultures and local policies in regional cities affect these structures.

Katsuo Yamazaki is Professor of International Business at the School of Management at Shizuoka Sangyo University in Japan. He received his doctorate in International Business Administration in 2003 at Nova Southeastern University, Ft. Lauderdale, Florida. His dissertation was "The Management Style of Japanese Automotive Components Companies in North America" and his research interest concerns corporate strategy and management geography. He has participated actively in the Academy of International Business since 2001.

Henry Wai-chung Yeung is Professor Economic Geography in the Department of Geography at the National University of Singapore. His research interests cover broadly theories and the geography of transnational corporations, Asian firms and their overseas operations, and Chinese business networks in the Asia-Pacific region. He has conducted extensive research on Hong Kong firms in Southeast Asia, the regionalization of Singaporean companies, and the emergence of leading Asian firms in the global economy.

Part I
Defining Management Geography

1
Spaces of International Economy and Management: Launching New Perspectives on Management and Geography

Rolf D. Schlunze, Michael Plattner, William W. Baber, and Nathaniel O. Agola

SIEM (Spaces of International Economy and Management) is an innovative, international, and multidisciplinary research group created in 2007. SIEM meetings and presentations have been conducted at the Association of Japanese Geographers (AJG) and the Global Conference on Economic Geography (GCEG) to promote understanding of new spaces of global business and to build a community representing a wide spectrum of perspectives regarding management geography. The community of those interested in what we call "management geography" has grown to 250 members. Organizing the first international symposium, we called for speakers from the science of management geography to present fresh ideas and research results in the spirit of building cross-disciplinary cooperation and to create a breakthrough event displaying all contributions to the discipline of management geography. This book is a collection of selected and revised papers that were presented at the international conference held in March 2010 at Ritsumeikan University, Japan. Recent leaders in economic geography such as Nigel Thrift (2000), Henry Yeung (2010), and Andrew Jones (2007) and management scientists like Tetsuo Abo (2004) and Michael Peng (2009) have presented significant work in the emerging field of management geography and provided potential leads to a new avenue of geographic studies. Their work focuses on international managers and entrepreneurs.

An actor-centered perspective

What contributes to the success or failure of managers? How can managers best adjust to different business environments? Can we observe any patterns that could guide an adjustment strategy of foreign managers charged with succeeding in their firm's business abroad?

A critical review of the literature shows that when managing the embedded multinational corporation, not only network embeddedness, as proposed by Forsgren et al. (2005), but also the transfer of organizational practices and cultural approaches, should be investigated (Abo 1994, 2007; Edwards 2008; Trompenaars 2006). These need to be contrasted with the cultural context in order to determine the degree of managerial adjustment, which in turn reflects an important condition for embeddedness of international managers in a different culture (Schlunze 2003, 2004; Schlunze and Plattner 2007). Beika (1970) emphasized that managers always need to adjust and respond to internal and external conditional changes at the locations where the multinational enterprise (MNE) operates. Accordingly, Totsuka (1990) highlighted that the management of local subsidiaries needs to consider the relationship between global and localization strategies. A multinational corporation needs to meet global standards to compete in globalizing markets. On the other hand, the MNE receives only acceptance from the local business community and consumers through localizing efforts. Therefore, the localizing efforts and adjustments remain important in a phase of globalization.

A company operating in a foreign business environment needs to balance localization and globalization processes in the activities and practices of management. Managerial embeddedness comes into existence when the balance between what is appropriate for the local business environment and the corporate business environment is found. For an international manager, it is easier to grasp what constitutes appropriate action within his or her own corporate environment than it is to figure out what appropriate action to the local business environment might be. Therefore, the tendency exists for expatriates to adjust to the agenda of the headquarters. Those managers apply the managerial business practices from the parent company, rather than adapting to local practices. Additionally, it is much more difficult to sense trends and changes in the local business environment than to anticipate and to react to changes in the global market. To grasp these problems, not only an institution-based view – as favored by many economic geographers – but also a resource-based perspective is important (Peng 2009). While an institution-based view suggests that managers' adaptability is constrained by institutions, the resource-based view suggests that their success and failure are determined by their environments (Florida 2009). The fundamental question of what determines the success and failure of firms and managers around the globe can be answered only when considering both views simultaneously. Traditionally, network analyses investigate from the resource-based view the success and failure of managers who learnt to play according to formal and informal rules of the game.

Granovetter (1985) saw economic actors embedded in the social context and critiques the undersocialized conception of human action. Granovetter's embeddedness argument stressed the role of concrete personal relations and structures or networks of such relations in general trust and discouraging malfeasance. He recognized that business relations spill over into sociability and vice versa, especially among members of the business elite. His argument has import for our vision of management geography, since many of the investigations introduced in this book deal with the business elite and the community of practice. Granovetter viewed patterns of business embeddedness in social relations as explained by cultural peculiarities – especially for Japan. Although his analysis centered on American management, he made clear that for different cultures, such as the Japanese, his argument of embeddedness of economic behavior becomes even more valid. We argue that we need to add to the American experience local aspects of international business globally as a reference for theorizing on global business. The American experience is only one reference point with which to understand global management problems (Gertler 2007). Granovetter`s critique is invaluable for management and geography studies, since on this globe many societies exist in which actors prefer to get to know to each other to some degree before doing business. Citing James Duesenberry's quip (1960, 17) that "economics is all about how people make choices; sociology is all about how they don't have any choices to make", Granovetter pointed out that actors have social obligations and follow customs. Granovetter further noticed that the level of embeddedness of economic behavior has changed less with modernization than many researchers believe. The multinational manager embeds the organization into a wider web of business networks. The international manager in charge of the foreign subsidiary needs to respond to existing business partners such as suppliers and customers within a greater geographical range that relates to his or her market territory.

Recently, Jacoby (2005) showed that embeddedness problems are related to management issues, such as labor relations and human resource management, which are determined by the overall cultural setting of a particular country or location. Thus, the challenges and the success of the corporation are determined by managerial practices that produce internal and external qualities and comparative advantages. This view refers to Granovetter's approach, which was further developed by Uzzi (1996), who investigated the sources and consequences of embeddedness referring to networking activities. The manager networks within the value chain, addressing existing and potential business exchange partners, seeking business opportunities and working for the sake of future business success. We take into account also the discussion of actor networking by Borgatti and Foster (2003), who, based on a review of organizational research, proposed a typology for the network paradigm initially introduced by Forsgren and Johanson (1992). Networking within the MNE can be perceived as a globalizing effort and as an effort toward empowerment within the global organization. Such empowerment can be achieved only through close contact or observation of competing forces within and among MNE networks.

According to Welch (1994), geocentric staffing policy favors the appointment of the candidate with the best qualifications, regardless of nationality and other cultural characteristics. Management practices are a reflection of qualities in social interaction. These techniques determine the degree or range of potential integration within an existing business community, from the local to the global scale. The basic orientation of international management's practices is determined by the market situation. This orientation has been explained by the Integration-Responsiveness paradigm of the international corporate situation (Prahalad 1975; Doz 1979; Prahalad and Doz 1987; Doz and Prahalad 1991). In the Integration-Responsiveness paradigm, local responsiveness aids reflection on localization strategies. Multinationals undertake localizing efforts by entrusting management to host-country nationals with the purpose of embedding the business into the local business environment quickly and successfully. Further, Whitely (1999) certified for international management the necessity of localizing activities to meet the divergent demands of various established and continuing distinctive forms of capitalism. However, embedding efforts do not stop with localization of management.

We enhance the definition of managerial embeddedness as something that is achieved when managerial functions, the flow of practices and information to and from the MNE headquarters and the local operations, are in balance. Only in this case can we expect the business to succeed in the local as in the global business environment. Managerial embeddedness results from the appropriate degree of *hybridization* within the context of tension among corporate and locational settings. Localization and globalization have great implications for geography and management. If the globalization process is advanced in a place, the application of global managerial practices becomes possible. If the influence of globalization processes is low in a place, or if the local or national business culture is resistant to globalization processes, the degree of application of international corporate practices can be expected to be rather low. A dominant local culture is generally characterized by resistance to modernization and strong social exclusion of foreigners and newcomers. If the foreign multinational corporation aims to enter a market characterized by a dominant local business culture, its embedding strategy needs to stress localization efforts. This could mean that local managing directors are assigned or that the foreign manager expatriated from the multinational enterprise needs to adopt a local managerial system in order to avoid friction with employees and misunderstandings with clients and customers.

A multinational firm aiming to control overseas operations tightly will prefer to assign a home-country national as executive manager and therefore favors a location which is up to global standards in many aspects. The pitfall is that such a global business environment does not always encourage an accurate understanding of the local market of the particular host country. Managers often fail to listen in a conflict situation to the local clients because they are preoccupied with images and stereotypes. These stereotypes are often supported by their "community of practice". Especially among the politically powerful managers expatriated directly from their headquarters to foreign subsidiaries, we find so-called global managers who tend to lack appropriate cultural sensitivity. Those managers may overestimate the degree of globalization in a foreign workplace and produce a mismatch of global and local practices by an inappropriate locational adjustment of their organization. In the following we wish to explain this mechanism figuratively.

As seen in Figure 1.1, the management of a multinational corporation is less embedded if the degree of application of international practices is too high for the local business environment. On the other hand, if the company operates within a global or international business environment, the application of global practices should also be high. If the adjustment is inappropriate, managers will realize that they are not meeting their potential. Therefore, we define a firm as a *well-embedded firm* when the adjustment to the particular business environment is advanced and reflected in the appropriate managerial practices for meeting the demands and the challenges of a particular business environment. The prospect of business interaction with the corporate, governmental, and other entities in the local market and business environment is optimal in the embedded firm. A firm incapable of adjusting to the local business environment is defined as a *less embedded firm*. As a result of the inability to embed the firm's managerial activities in the local business environment, the interactions will be

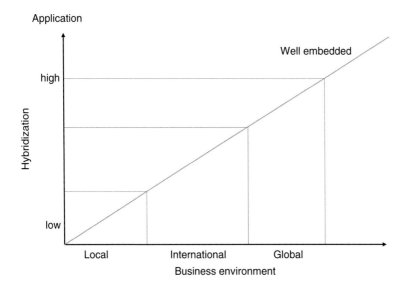

Figure 1.1   Logic of managerial embeddedness

reduced, and therefore there will not be efficient knowledge exchange with external sources.

For example, a *well-embedded firm* could be an international firm that embeds in a global business environment applying managerial practices that are up to the global standard. For a large multinational organization, this is the most desirable situation. In a globalized business environment, the firm is enabled to apply global standards and managerial practices. Interactions with the business environment are most vital. The transfer of knowledge is carried out directly between the collaborating entities and shapes all activities in an efficient way. Ghoshal and Bartlett (1990) approached the multinational corporation as an inter-organizational network phenomenon, investigating global integration and local responsiveness as divergent dimensions of the multinational enterprise's location strategy. Forsgren et al. (2005) explained the embeddedness process as the management of multinationals, investigating the MNE's international network and the internationalization of the firm; two partly congruent dimensions. Both frameworks are centered on the analysis of the MNE's network and do not analyze the international managers' local adjustment nor the organization's hybridization strategy in the context of a systematic evaluation of the particular business environment. A new framework is needed to integrate both analysis of business environments and analysis of management systems!

This framework will incorporate implications of locational dynamics that occur in the real world of a global manager. From our empirical observations, in a workplace unaffected or negatively affected by globalization we expect that a manager needs to reconsider and adapt more to local practices, whereas in a workplace that is positively affected by globalization he or she can connect to the community of global practices. Places that were initially favored by globalization can decline, and places that were once unknown may pop up in the global-city network suddenly. Managers must also adjust to such sometimes sudden changes caused by the swinging pendulum of globalization. Many of the following chapters will deal with such management problems in the rapidly changing global business environment. SIEM researchers will give us evidence to build up a theory of international management that does not neglect the geographical dimension of doing business internationally.

A networking perspective

International managers coordinate, organize, and (re)locate globally linked business operations, closely connected to certain management practices and executives' decisions. The personal networks involved contribute fundamentally to the empowerment of the multinational enterprise. In an international business environment, this field of interaction is crossing cultural boundaries linking host and home cultures, attitudes, and behaviors (Vance and Paik 2005). The field is multi-place-oriented, covering several cultural dimensions in economic space. Therefore networking and acculturation go hand in hand. In this sense, social capital theory has to be acknowledged, but there is a need to add on collocation of intermediary individuals and groups as a core concept where cultural norms deploy their socialization effects (Noteboom 2006). Regarding the relational constructivism approach of the social network analysis, it is crucial to know in which comprehensive social structure international managers create knowledge and how acculturation takes place.

International managers are the social capital of multinational enterprise. Their cultural values and norms have a crucial impact on the social networks (Borgatti and Foster 2003; McGrath and Krackhardt 2003; Mitchell 1969). The international manager's social capital is situated around specific business communities, and the work is performed within and between those communities. Capable of exercising global action, these agents can be seen as gatekeepers in the circulation of information on intra- and inter-firm levels because of their multiple activity dependencies between the local and the global level of business. According to the knowledge transfer model, transaction occurs as socializing and internalization from explicit to tacit in collocation, or at least temporary co-presence, of trusted managers (Nonaka and Konno 1998, 43). Transaction cost may be reduced by the phenomenon that like-minded people build influence bearing links to each other, blending attitudes and norms. In sum it can be inferred that socialization refers to culture norms as a precondition for the international manager's interaction in groups such as communities of practice (Wenger 2004; Amin and Cohendet 2005).

Regarding their intensive expertise, international managers need to conduct local and global business in a network of professionals with competences in a particular domain. Each manager need therefore consult with one or more local as well as global experts who have deep knowledge of the cross-national issues involved. As "fast subjects" those managers span a variety of networks as knowledge-rich in-groups (Haas 1992, 2; Grabher 2006; Storper and Venables 2003, 356; Thrift 2000).

As Enns et al. (2008) suggest, is there a shrinking gap of cultural distance and proximity in international business networks? Social network analysis serves here as an appropriate tool, but most empirical work considering network rules in the sense of the "small-world" phenomenon has been done under the mathematical approach of relational determinism (Watts and Strogatz 1998; Watts 1999, 2004) and actor- and resource-based relational instrumentalism (Gould 1993; Bathelt and Glückler 2005; Glückler 2007). Both approaches have their shortcoming regarding their quantitative bias. Relational determinism focuses on the general description of the network to draw descriptive and static formulas, and the dynamics of a network are not well incorporated. The disadvantages of relational instrumentalism are the focus on the attributes of actors and their contexts while downsizing the measures of relations between actors. Thus, the synergistic relational constructivism approach of the social network analysis would be the appropriate way to go (Watts 2003; White 1992, 2002). The approach takes the temporal dynamics into account and is focusing on the aspects of socioeconomic relations of the personal interaction rather than the structural. Further pros result from the ability to acknowledge co-presence between the actors in spatial, cultural, institutional, and organizational entities.

An international business communication perspective

An international business communication perspective is beneficial to industry practitioners and researchers to understand how successful actors develop in the context of their local and particular business environment. Here, communication can be seen as part of the cultural adjustment and development of the actor in the business world. From academic journals to popular media, it is widely acknowledged that cross-cultural communication is of increasing importance. In today's globalized business world, English is entrenched as the language of use in international networks and at the nodes where local networks connect with international networks. Yet a lingua franca is not a panacea for the travails of day-to-day business, and even native speakers may experience considerable difficulties. Deeper perhaps than linguistic issues posed by cross-cultural business communication are issues regarding culture, cultural identity, corporate culture, and adaptation that play direct and indirect communications roles which must be understood in order to see the actor as central to business interaction and business success.

Our approach is to shift the focus of research from organizational-level behavior to that of the actor in the context of his or her surroundings; therefore the roles in question include personal abilities and traits. Before enumerating these roles, it is important to note that we do not directly reject studying organizational behavior; shedding light on individual actors is a primary goal, but not to the exclusion of any other factors that impact how business occurs across geography.

What is to be included in studying the communications and successes of actors in the business environment as it relates to local and international economic spaces? One aspect will be the home and host cultures of actors. Hall (1976), Hofstede (1986, 2001), Hofstede and Hofstede (2005), and Trompenaars and Hampden-Turner (1998) provide value-based frameworks which can be applied numerically or as benchmarks of general expectations regarding macro-level culture and large populations. Despite apt critiques of these authors (Baskerville 2005; Szkudlarek 2005; Nakata 2010), we can productively borrow the frameworks of Hofstede and Trompenaars for comparisons of the traits and dimensions they describe in order to help us understand the behaviors of an individual actor; however, we reject the notion that they may be taken as the defining strokes of those individuals, nations, or ethnicities. Decidedly the opposite, it appears to us that it is necessary to look into micro-level issues of environment as in the examples of Gudykunst and Nishida (1994), experience and socialization (Feldman and Bolino 1999), one-to-one transfer of knowledge (Baber, below), situational context such as location and personal surroundings (Schlunze 2007), identity (Moore 2009), personality (Peltokorpi 2008), and perceived psychic distance (Prime et al. 2009) in order to understand in depth the here and now of an actor and possibly the wider community of practice (Wenger 1998) within which that actor moves. The multitude of aspects mentioned above suggests a range of study remains to be done seeking to comprehend the expatriate as a corporate actor within a web of constructs, inputs, networks, and context that give meaning to the actor's behavior, success, and potential.

At the same time, notions built somewhat simplistically on Hofstede's framework, such as cultural distance (Kogut and Singh 1988) and psychic distance, as described by the various writers of the Scandinavian school, will be avoided, as they equivocate the important differences between individual actors and macro-scale entities such as nations, ethnicities, and corporations.

A technology innovation perspective

In addition to the various perspectives already offered, it is important to consider a technology innovation perspective and its direct bearing on management geography. Location-based services (LBS) technology innovations are increasingly transforming not only the scope of what can be done, but also how things can be done within geographical space, distance, and time. The scope and depth of economic activities ranging from industrial economic undertakings to consumer services have so far been captured and analyzed in disparate disciplines like computer science, information technology, technology management, law, and to some limited extent LBS case studies within the general field of management and economics mainly focusing on market opportunities and size of the LBS market. All these studies commenced and have progressed within almost the same space of time; thus an overlap can be noted. We cannot therefore note a chronologically progressive time sequence for the diverse LBS studies.

The first studies started with the analysis of network architectures and standards for LBS (see Adams et al. 2003; Peng and Tsou 2003; Ahn et al. 2004). Almost at the same time, there were studies covering the techniques used in delivering LBS, such as positioning methods and how documentation could be done for activities tenable within locations, space, and time (see Worboys and Duckham 2004). With proliferation of LBS of all sorts – some of them truly innovations and others mere improvements to convenience – there was also an emergence of studies on business opportunities backed by case studies as a logical development in the studies on LBS (see Barnes 2003). Currently, LBS studies are focused on how the technologies and services can be precisely tailored to the needs of each user, with decision support being a critical element. At the same time, as efforts become more targeted at accurate personalization, the issue of privacy has continued to rage. The recent discovery that Apple, through its iPhones and iPads, systematically tracked users' locations and kept an archive of such information has raised anger and privacy concerns amongst users and consumer watchdogs. It is also notable that Google has also been harvesting user location data on Android handsets, potentially for marketing purposes. Thus through LBS technologies, location, space, and time have gained heightened consideration in the conduct of daily economic transactions.

Hence the field of study of management and economic geography cannot fail to embrace location-based service innovation technologies as a critical part of its evolving knowledge frontier. Their huge economic potential also makes a potent case for a worthy consideration of these innovations with regard to how economic activities are being transformed at both macroeconomic and microeconomic levels. However, for the field of economic and management geography to manage a worthy catch-up effort on how technological advances in the area of LBS are transforming our global socioeconomic landscape, a multidisciplinary approach is necessary. It is necessary to understand the architecture of the LBS technologies together with value offering to users within the framework of challenges of location, space, and time, while at the same time considering the legal implications of how activities are conducted in the course of deployment of LBS technologies.

This book is therefore a bold and first attempt to incorporate LBS technology innovations into management and economic geography. Accordingly, it will facilitate expansion of the knowledge frontier of economic and management geography. In this book, the subject matter of LBS is appropriately served, mainly in an introductory format, making it easier for those not familiar with LBS technologies to gain insight. We have focused on the case of LBS in Japan with a view to opening the window of general and in-depth understanding of LBS and its place in the field of economic and management geography. We intend to cover LBS in economic and management geography further in terms of both depth and scope in future work in management geography.

In the post-war era, the global market has undergone immense changes, with managers becoming key actors conducting business internationally. Entrepreneurs and managers have taken advantage of the remarkable progress in communication and transport systems, accumulating profits and power. The places and spaces that belong to their multinational network are related to this growth process and are affected by the way business is conducted.

Our ambition is to make this clearly important subject more accessible to an international audience of interdisciplinary scientists by providing theoretical foundations, methodological tools and empirical evidence. Studies presented at the SIEM symposium and in our conference book include one or more of the following aspects: Theory of management practices in geographic space using approaches related to leadership, international human resource management (IHRM), global versus local practices and networking of entrepreneurs and managers. The symposium and this book introduce new methodologies for investigating managerial practices and strategies, capability, and capacities for decision making, and manager appraisal of changing agents in private and governmental organizations moulding international spaces. Further, we present empirical evidence on the cross-border expansion of managerial practices that contribute to the formation of new communities in metropolitan spaces. In particular, studies included here investigate how new career and location patterns and apply to decision-making needs of international managers in global and local contexts. Implications for local and regional government are also found that enable cities to encourage international entrepreneurship and management talent.

The first part of this volume works towards a definition of management geography based on reflections about the following two different approaches of actor-centered investigations analyzing international management issues at individual levels with consideration of locational conditions. Both approaches are part of one management appraisal that can be synthesized. Rolf Schlunze investigates international managers' intercultural competence from a contextual perspective. Michael Plattner investigates the locational preferences of international managers. The two authors jointly develop a synthesis of these approaches. Therefore these chapters provide an introduction and analysis of the concept of "mobile elite in the global city" based on a case study of Tokyo. The authors show that relocation and concentration of globally linked business operations are closely connected to the lifestyles of foreign executive managers. Schlunze's analysis investigates foreign executive managers' working and living styles by investigating four dimensions. The approach developed here distinguishes various types of executive managers by evaluating their potential for creating cultural synergy. Plattner's study applies conjoint analysis to quantify executive locational preferences of international managers. By doing so, he evaluates whether they focus on globalizing or localizing efforts, and to what extent their preferences to succeed in the foreign business environment are balanced. The analysis by Schlunze shows significant differences in the working and living styles of expatriate and so-called hybrid managers, a type of manager who succeeds in the foreign business environment through a high degree of acculturation. Plattner shows that executives' preferences regarding first- and second-tier global-city locations show significant correlation with their creation of synergies.

Outline of Part II

"Spaces of International Economy" delves into analytical frameworks for analyzing spaces of international economy using new economic geography approaches focusing on mapping business networks, harmonization of global competition principles and practices and managerial and locational decision making.

Ronald S. Wall empirically demonstrates the role cities play in the global economy by revealing their network positions in relation to other cities and the interdependencies that they exhibit with one another. The centrality and structure in these networks is analyzed by a geographical information system (GIS). The work maps world cities using three levels of corporate ownership of the world city network for international business. The results here show that New York and Tokyo are primarily regionally connected cities, London and Paris are more globally oriented and Hong Kong and Singapore play a strong subsidiary role in the business world.

Rinas V. Kashbrasiev analyzes the development of competition in the BRIC countries (Brazil, Russia, India and China) with a view to a unified international economic space. Case studies of the BRIC countries are used. These four large countries are outstanding in their recent history of economic growth and progress. Cooperation in economic growth and development is important for them to maintain fast growth. Therefore, this part of the book analyzes the BRIC countries' attempts to harmonize national competition principles and antitrust measures, as well as business rules, as an essential condition for intensification of international trade and attractiveness of foreign direct investment. Kashbrasiev also analyzes opportunities and challenges for future long-term growth in the BRIC countries and infers from the research results that these countries have everything necessary for long-term growth.

Anxo Calvo-Silvosa and Ruben C. Lois-González provide analysis of how to manage regulatory risk in energy investment developments in South America. Multinational energy firms usually make global plans with local and regional consequences. Normally, their investments deal with the supply of basic services or infrastructures, are usually linked to the presence of negative externalities and have significant impact on local welfare. These local effects attract host-government interest in the firm's activity and, consequently, generate a new factor of risk that should be considered by the investor: regulatory risk. The analysis here therefore provides how energy firms could introduce that source of risk in their methods of international investment valuation. Financial management as a "hard variable" and regulatory and country risks as "soft variables" are considered in the model, exposing managerial practices for decision making in an environment mutually influenced by private and governmental decisions.

Masato Ikuta discusses the western part of Japan (Kansai area) from the perspective of the locality debate previously seen in the United Kingdom. Considering the region's role in the Japanese national economy, the author controversially argues about two contradicting concepts: general relationships between regions versus local conditions within the region. Kansai area consists of three central cities – Osaka, Kobe, and Kyoto – which compose a large metropolitan region. During their growth, the three cities created distinctive values for the actors operating in the regional economy. Actors in peripheral areas maintained economic activities while utilizing geographical proximity to the centers of the metropolitan area. After economic prosperity in the phase of the industrial revolution and high economic growth after World War II, the regional economy began to deteriorate, and many major companies relocated their headquarters or manufacturing functions to Tokyo or – as the recent case of Panasonic shows – overseas. Industrial change has affected mainly employment in the manufacturing sector but promoted the growth of various new service industries. As a reaction to these changes, the local business community and government are preparing to introduce the decentralized province system as in Italy and France. Local energy and transport companies helped to develop public relations that favor the establishment of a system with more freedom from the central government. The analysis here ends by recommending that if the Kansai region would obtain more political power from the central government, then the regional economy would be positively affected and attract international business again.

Sawako Maruyama gives a case analysis of the trading area and locational decision of foreign affiliates in Osaka Prefecture. Since the 1990s, the Japanese government has recognized the significance of inward investment and eased regulations in order to promote foreign direct investment. The author indicates that many foreign direct investment studies lack an analysis of the relationship between locational decision and transactions of foreign affiliates. Thus, the author seeks to reveal the background of location of foreign affiliates focusing on trade relations. Therefore, the author analyzes the trade relations in contrast to the locational background of foreign affiliates in Osaka. The survey results show that most foreign affiliates' trade relations extend nationwide. Thus, the results also reveal that Osaka is valued for accessibility to existing domestic business partners. The conclusion is that relationships with domestic companies were integral to many foreign firms' decision to locate in the Japanese market. Nonetheless, deeper understanding of the process by which individual decision makers become knowledgeable of the host location's business culture and general society is needed.

Outline of Part III

In "Spaces of International Management", actor-centered approaches are used to analyze the spaces of international management, focusing on logistical practices of the animation industry in East Asia, Americanization of legal practices in Japan, a leading Japanese general electronics manufacturer's decision making, and the cultural adjustment efforts of individual foreign managers in Japan.

Tim Reiffenstein seeks to answer the question of how US educational experience shapes the everyday work environment of Japanese legal professionals. This provides an opportune moment to bring a geographical perspective to bear on the Japanese context. Through analysis of interviews with Japanese lawyers who sojourned to the United States in order to enhance their international legal skills, the author explores the motivations for and experiences of these migrations while revealing their subsequent relevance in the lawyers' professional careers. The key findings suggest that in the case of Tokyo-based lawyers working for both Japanese and international law firms, the credentials earned abroad appear to command greater utility than the actual skills acquired en route. The reason for this is that Japan's international legal market is still very much bifurcated, with distinctive roles assigned to nationals and expats. The results point toward a number of unique management challenges that must be overcome if the incipient internationalization of the Japanese legal sector is to proceed.

Tetsuo Abo includes an introduction of the concept of hybrid factories, using the example of Japanese Multinational Enterprises' hybrid factories in the global economy. The author suggests that various business or management models based on socioeconomic differences are closely connected to those of geographical locations along with historical contexts. At the center of this analysis is the locational fit of various types of Japanese hybrid factories in the particular business environment. The approach also has strategic merit for Japanese and other multinational firms in global management endeavors. Additionally, Katsuo Yamazaki presents case studies from North and South America explaining how the style of Japanese management practices changes in foreign locations. The author shows that within the last decade of drastic changes in the world economy, Japanese management styles came under pressure and managers needed to consider new adjustment strategies. Companies in the automotive industries are therefore investigated regarding their potential to transfer their production and management systems effectively. At the level of the transplants, the efficiency of Japanese-style management is examined while screening the dynamic interplay between the forces of application of the Japanese management and adaptation to the local management system. Case studies drawn from experiences in the United States and Brazil are used in the study, and a comparison is then made. The comparison shows that one company changed its labor relations by the application of Japanese management practices, and the second company kept a Japanese-style work organization and administration. However, as time progressed, management of both companies adapted to the local management system. Finally, the author argues that future research should also look at financial issues to evaluate the effectiveness and adjustment strategies of such firms.

Atsushi Taira introduces a case study of the glove-related industry in Eastern Kagawa, Japan. The author shows the survival strategies of a local industry within the context of overseas operations. This case study is used to analyze the survival strategy of local industries located outside the major metropolitan regions of Japan. The glove-related industry in Kagawa traditionally focuses on the domestic market. These small- to medium-sized companies were able to maintain a leading position in Japan due to the existence of a highly skilled and innovative workforce. Their survival strategy centers on the attempt to make new gloves for various sports and ultraviolet protection and to produce new products using special techniques invented by the Japanese glove industry. Recently, they produce increasingly for the domestic market due to severe competition in overseas markets. At the same time, one company has actively expanded its overseas operations for production in East and Southeast Asia and R&D to Europe and the US. The author concludes that the success of the glove industry in Kagawa was due to the creation of a global–local network linking the domestic base with foreign operations that sustain the competitiveness of the firm.

Kenta Yamamoto presents a survey of the key actors within the Japanese digital animation industry. This is followed by an analysis of the production allocation strategies and spatial structure of international division of labor in Japanese animation studios, which itself is very novel information. The author examines international management strategies and spatial structures of the international division of labor in the animation industry. Japanese studios select different production allocation strategies. The international division of labor in the Japanese animation industry therefore comprises inter-regional relations such as simple one-on-one trade relations and complex competitive/cooperative relations among clients and subcontractors.

William Baber investigates international managers' cultural adjustment efforts, showing how they adjust to a culturally distant space such as Japan while seeking support from an interculturally fluent key person. Japan is represented in the literature as a difficult place for foreign managers. For the purpose of gaining knowledge about the local business environment, a deeper understanding of the process by which these individuals become knowledgeable of the host location's business culture is needed. Specifically, the existence of a cultural informant passing local knowledge on to foreign managers is seen as important. Managers' special interest in seeking such cultural insights is closely related to the will to succeed in the foreign cultural context and demands special abilities. The author presents data from interviews with foreign managers active in the Kansai Corridor highlighting the presence of interculturally fluent individuals in the adjustment process of the managers and analyzing the mechanisms of cultural adjustment.

Outline of Part IV

"A New Perspective" on management geography is finally introduced by scholars of management science and geography. The novel research introduced here discusses new areas such as LBS innovation, the conceptualization of complexity of managerial decision making, and the concept of "globality" of firms due to the emergence of a community of global practices in international management.

Andrew Jones introduces the novel concept of "corporate globability" while discussing the new geographies of global managerial practices, bringing evidence from a survey on the case of business services. Economic globalization is radically transforming the ways in which firms in all sectors organize themselves and operate in the global economy, not only in terms of the physical locations of offices and employees, but also with respect to organizational form, corporate strategy and the way in which work itself is undertaken. Managerial professionals are thus at the forefront of a major transformation of the way in which key wealth-generating activity is now taking place in the global economy. However, the author argues that the management literature has been relatively slow to engage with these transformations, tending to remain focused on conventional concepts of the geographic space occupied by firms and their employees. In order to develop this proposition, the author provides a critical overview of the key transformations of global managerial practice that are developing in the contemporary global economy. This section draws on more than a decade of research of transnational business service firms in banking, management consultancy, legal services, accountancy, and advertising. The author consequently examines how international managerial professionals have responded and adapted their work practices to an increasingly interconnected global market for their services, which has been accompanied by a radical transformation and internationalization of their work practices. In particular, the author examines how knowledge transfer, innovation, and the practices of corporate control are bound into new and dynamic corporate geographies that present significant challenges for existing place-focused concepts of global corporate operation.

Nathaniel O. Agola focuses on the innovations of location-based technologies and their commercial applications in Japan through a survey and critical analysis that will find the interest of many readers. Location-based service innovation technologies have the distinctive characteristic of unrivalled lifting of limitations of time and geographical distance not only within national territories, but across national borders as well. Little extant research has focused on providing a critical analysis of location-based service innovation technologies with regard to the sources of the innovation, the value creation impact and perhaps the bottlenecks facing the progress of the technology. This research provides a survey and a critical analysis of location-based service innovation technologies in Japan to further the understanding of the technologies. The findings of this research are that whereas the location-based service innovation technologies have great economic value creation potential, the lack of major platforms on which services falling under similar categories can be launched and sustained limits the progress of these technologies. Again, social, legal, and institutional bottlenecks are highlighted as barriers to progress of the location-based service innovation technologies.

Patrik Ström and Roger Schweizer offer a novel approach to managerial decision making by discovering what the authors call "space oddity". The authors argue that complexity in decision making has hitherto not been adequately mirrored in the prevailing research streams dealing with various aspects related to a firm's international expansion in space. Indicating that there are "watertight bulkheads" between research in the fields of economic geography and international business, the authors provide a new conceptualization. The analysis here is framed within traditional neoclassical trade theory, internalization theory, transaction-cost theory, and the eclectic paradigm, though the authors favor a behavioral approach to internationalization and the process of increasing involvement in international operations. Based on the anticipations of the Uppsala Model, the authors anticipate that a firm's accumulated knowledge influences its possibility to recognize foreign business opportunities. The authors see internationalization not merely as the action of crossing borders, but rather as an outcome of the efforts undertaken by entrepreneurs, or managers performing entrepreneurial activities, to improve their companies' operations and investments. The authors also assert that internationalization is best understood as a by-product of efforts taken to improve a company's position in its networks. Hence, the approach used here is in sync with much of the research done within internationalization theory, but the scope is broadened through discussions about clusters, the concept of embeddedness, organization within space and national or regional competitiveness.

Michael Plattner's research focuses on work in multinational corporations, which is increasingly located in differing cultural environments. Business networks have changed from being dominated by expatriate managers to ones in which local staff and new intermediary hybrid managers interface in flexible relationships. The key question is the extent to which international hybrid managers function as translators of knowledge while contributing to the reduction of transaction cost. To answer that question, a social network analysis was applied to measure the similarity among related network actors with divergent cultural norms. The structural change of a multinational business network was tested during three periods of internationalization, between 1983 and 2005. The analysis uses the illustrated novel of *Kosaku Shima* business manga to review a 267-node network. This manga was believed to be fiction, but from an interview conducted with the author it became evident that most of the stories and characters are indeed reality-based. Findings include that hybrid managers break down barriers of cultural distance. They are brokers of knowledge between local and global levels of business, thereby reducing transaction costs.

The book provides a new overview of the field of management geography. Various perspectives on management geography are introduced. Important aspects such as globalization, embeddedness and globality of MNEs, adjustment strategies and networks, and location-based technology innovations analyses are included.

The book brings contributions from leading international experts on their particular areas of expertise; thus it is an authoritative multidisciplinary push to a new frontier in the field of management geography. This multidisciplinary team of researchers came together thanks to the SIEM group activities in general to bring more attention to new research ideas and activities in the field of management geography. SIEM seeks to create and strengthen working relations between researchers and practitioners in the field of international management to improve the understanding of modern corporations and ambitious managers who wish to succeed as agents of change in the fast-changing world.

We are grateful to Henry Wai-chung Yeung from NUS, who provided an encouraging foreword for this book. During the SIEM conference, he explained in a keynote speech transnational entrepreneurship and global production networks: challenges for management geography. He asserts that while economic activities are becoming more globally interconnected and interdependent today, the management of these cross-border activities by firms, states, and other institutions is much more challenging and complex. The central argument presented here is that in both arenas, space makes a critical difference in the ways in which management and organizational issues should be conceived and understood. The contribution constitutes frontier research about transnational entrepreneurship and global production networks, as he provided details of the nature of entrepreneurship across borders and the globalization of production networks which will inspire other researchers and readers keen on furthering their understanding on spaces of international economy and management.

References

Abo, T. (ed.) (1994) *Hybrid Factory: The Japanese Production System in the United States*. New York: Oxford University Press.

Abo, T. (2004) An integrated theory of management geography: Japanese hybrid factories in the three major regions. In V. Gupta (ed.), *Transformative Organizations: A Global Perspective*. New Delhi: Response Books.

Abo, T. (2007) *Japanese Hybrid Factories: A Comparison of Global Production Strategies.* London: Palgrave Macmillan.

Adams, P.M., G.W.B. Ashwell, and R. Baxter (2003) Location-based-services – An overview of standards. *BT Technology Journal* 21(1): 34–43.

Ahn, Y.S., S.Y. Park, S.B. Yoo, and H.Y. Bae (2004) Extension of Geography Markup Language (GML) for mobile and location-based applications. *Lecture Notes in Computer Science* 3044: 1079–88.

Amin, A. and P. Cohendet (2005) Geographies of knowledge formation in firms. *Industry and Innovation* 12: 465–86.

Barnes, S.J. (2003) Developments in the M-commerce value chain: Adding value with location-based services. *Geography* 88(4): 277–88.

Baskerville-Morely, R.F. (2005) A research note: the unfinished business of culture. *Accounting, Organizations and Society* 30(4): 389–91.

Bathelt, H. and J. Glückler (2005) Resources in economic geography: From substantive concepts towards a relational perspective. *Environment and Planning A* 37(9): 1545–63.

Beika, M. (1970) Keiei Kankyoron (Business environment theory), Tokyo: Maruzen

Borgatti, S.P. and P.C. Foster (2003) The network paradigm in organizational research: A review and typology. *Journal of Management* 29: 991–1013.

Doz, Y. and C.K. Prahalad (1991) Managing MNCs: The search for a new paradigm. *Strategic Management Journal*, Special Issue (Summer 1991): 145–64.

Edwards, J.M. (2008) *Hybrid Organizations: Social Enterprise and Social Entrepreneurship.* N.p.: Lulu.com.

Enns, S., T. Malinick, and R. Matthews (2008) It's not only who you know, it's also where they are: Using the position generator to investigate the structure of access to embedded resources. In N. Lin and B.H. Erickson, *Social Capital: An International Research Program*, 255–81. Oxford: Oxford University Press.

Feldman, D.C. and M.C. Bolino (1999) The impact of on-site mentoring on expatriate socialization: A structural equation modeling approach. *International Journal of Human Resource Management* 10(1): 54–71.

Florida, R. (2009) *Who's Your City? How the Creative Economy Is Making Where to Live the Most Important Decision of Your Life.* New York: Basic Books.

Forsgren, M., U. Holm, and J. Johanson (2005) *Managing the Embedded Multinational – A Business Network View.* Cheltenham: Edward Elgar.

Forsgren, M. and J. Johanson (1992) Managing in international multi-centre firms. In M. Forsgren and J. Johanson (eds), *Managing Networks in International Business.* Philadelphia: Gordon and Breach.

Gertler, M.S. (2007) Tacit knowledge in production systems: how important is geography? In K.R. Polenske (ed.), *The Economic Geography of Innovation*, 87–111. Cambridge: Cambridge University Press.

Glückler, J. (2007) Economic geography and the evolution of networks. *Journal of Economic Geography* 7: 619–34.

Gould, R.V. (1993) Collective action and network structure. *American Sociological Review* 58: 182–96.

Grabher, G. (2006) Trading routes, bypasses, and risky intersections: Mapping the travels of 'networks' between economic sociology and economic geography. *Progress in Human Geography* 30: 163–89.

Granovetter, M. (1985) Economic action and social structure: the problem of embeddedness. *American Journal of Sociology* 78(3): 3–30.

Gudykunst, W. and T. Nishida (1994) *Bridging Japanese/North American Differences.* Thousand Oaks, CA: Sage Publications.

Haas, P. (1992) Introduction: epistemic communities and international policy coordination. *International Organization* 46: 1–37.

Hall, E.T. (1976) *Beyond Culture*. Garden City, NY: Anchor/Doubleday.

Hofstede, G. and J.H. Hofstede (2005) *Cultures and Organizations: Software of the Mind*. New York: McGraw-Hill.

Hofstede, G. (1986) Cultural differences in teaching and learning. *International Journal of Intercultural Relations* 10: 301–20.

Hofstede, G. (2001) *Culture's Consequences*. Thousand Oaks, CA: Sage Publications.

Jacoby, S.M. (2005) *The Embedded Corporation: Corporate Governance and Employment Relations in Japan and the United States*. Princeton, NJ: Princeton University Press.

Jones, A. (2007) More than managing across borders? The complex role of face-to-face interaction in globalizing law firms. *Journal of Economic Geography* 7: 223–46.

Kogut, B. and H. Singh (1988) The effect of national culture on the choice of entry mode. *Journal of International Business Studies* 19(3): 411–32.

McGrath, C. and D. Krackhardt (2003) Network conditions for organizational change. *Journal of Applied Behavioral Science* 39: 324–36.

Mitchell, J.C. (1969) The concept and use of networks. In J. C. Mitchell (ed.), *Social Networks in Urban Situations*, 1–50. Manchester: Manchester University Press.

Moore, T.M. (2009) The sojourner's truth: exploring bicultural identity as a predictor of assignment success in American expatriates. Unpublished manuscript. North Carolina State University.

Nakata, C. (ed.) (2009) *Beyond Hofstede: Culture Frameworks for Global Marketing and Management*. UK: Palgrave Macmillan.

Nonaka, I. and N. Konno (1998) The concept of Ba: building for knowledge creation. *California Management Review* 40(3): 40–54.

Nooteboom, B. (2006) Social Capital, Institutions and Trust. CentER Discussion Paper, 35, 1–22.

Peltokorpi, V. (2008) Cross-cultural adjustment of expatriates in Japan. *International Journal of Human Resource Management* 19(9): 1588–1606.

Peng, M. (2009) *Global Business, International Edition*. 2nd Edition. Ohio: Cengage.

Peng, Z.-R. and M.-H. Tsou (2003) *Internet GIS: Distributed Geographic Information Systems for the Internet and Wireless Networks*. Hoboken, NJ: John Wiley.

Prahalad, C.K. (1975) *The Strategic Process in a Multinational Corporation*. Boston: Harvard University.

Prahalad, C.K. and Y. Doz (1987) *The Multinational Mission: Balancing Local Demands and Global Vision*. New York: Free Press.

Prime, N., C. Obadia, and N. Vida (2009) Psychic distance in exporter–importer relationships: A grounded theory approach. *International Business Review* 18(2): 184–98.

Schlunze, R.D. (2003) Locational adjustments of the European manufacturing management in Japan. *Annals of the Japan Association of Economic Geographers* 49(4): 109–10. (J)

Schlunze, R.D. (2004) Managerial embeddedness of European manufacturing firms in Japan. *Japanese Journal of Human Geography* 56(5): 64–82.

Schlunze, R.D. (2007) Spurring the Kansai economy: embedding foreign corporations. *Ritsumeikan International Affairs* (Ritsumeikan kokusai chiiki kenkyu), 5(6): 17–42.

Schlunze, R.D. and M. Plattner (2007) Evaluating international managers' practices and locational preferences in the global city: an analytical framework. *Ritsumeikan Business Review* 36(1): 63–89.

Storper, M. and A.J. Venables (2003) Buzz: Face-to-face contact and the urban economy. *Journal of Economic Geography* 4: 351–70.

Szkudlarek, B. (2005) Book review: building cross-cultural competence: how to create wealth from conflicting values. *Management Learning* 36(4): 518–23.

Thrift, N. (2000) Performing cultures in the new economy. *Annals of the Association of American Geographers* 90(4): 674–92.

Totsuka, H. (1990) 'Kokusai bungyo no shintenkai to Nihonkigyo' (A new turn of international division of labor and Japanese firms), *Shakai Seisaku Gakkai Nenpo* (Annals of the Society for the Study of Social Policy) 34: 3–22. (J)

Trompenaars, F. (2006) *Riding the Waves of Culture: Understanding Cultural Diversity in Business.* 2nd ed. London: Nicholas Brealey Publishing.

Trompenaars, F. and C. Hampden-Turner (1998) *Riding the Waves of Culture: Understanding Diversity in Global Business.* New York: McGraw-Hill.

Uzzi, B. (1996) The sources and consequences of embeddedness for the economic performance of organizations: the network effect. *American Sociological Review* 61(4): 674–98.

Vance, C.-M. and Y. Paik (2005) Forms of host-country national learning for enhanced MNC absorptive capacity. *Journal of Management Psychology* 20: 590–606.

Watts, D.J. (1999) Networks, dynamics, and the small-world phenomenon. *American Journal of Sociology* 105(2): 493–527.

Watts, D.J. (2003) *Six Degrees: The Science of a Connected Age.* New York: W.W. Norton & Company.

Watts, D.J. (2004) The 'new' science of networks. *Annual Review of Sociology* 30: 243–70.

Watts, D.J., and S.H. Strogatz (1998) Collective dynamics of 'small world' networks. *Nature* 393: 440–2.

Welch, D. (1994) HRM: Implications of globalization. *Journal of General Management* 19(4): 52–6.

Wenger, E. (2004) Communities of Practice: A Brief Introduction. Retrieved October 2008 from: http://www.ewenger.com/theory/index.htm.

White, H.C. (1992) *Identity and Control: A Structural Theory of Social Action.* Princeton/NY: Princeton University Press.

White, H.C. (2002) *Markets from Networks: Socioeconomic Models of Production.* Princeton/NY: Princeton University Press.

Whitley, R. (1999) *Divergent Capitalisms: The Social Structuring and Change of Business Systems.* Oxford, New York: Oxford University Press.

Worboys, M. and M. Duckham (2004) *GIS: A Computing Perspective.* Boca Raton, FL: CRC Press.

Yeung, H.W. (ed.) (2010) *Globalizing Regional Development in East Asia: Production Networks, Clusters, and Entrepreneurship.* Regions and Cities 41. CITY: Routledge.

2

"Hybrid" Managers Creating Cross-Cultural Synergy: A Systematic Interview Survey from Japan

Rolf D. Schlunze

Introduction

Buckley (1997) found that barriers to foreign direct investment in Japan include government restrictions, cultural barriers, xenophobia, and long-termism. One decade later, the government has changed its attitude with the official mandate to agencies such as Japan External Trade Organization (JETRO) to promote inward investment, and many government restrictions have disappeared. Strikingly, corporations have little demand for long-termism since American standards now prevail in the financial market. What remains are cultural barriers and xenophobia. Many stories of Western managers in Japan being refused the necessary resources to do a good job in Japan have been heard (Buckley 1997). As a result, Japan has gained the image of being a difficult business environment due to the frustration of Western managers who were unable to accomplish their goals. Nevertheless, there is sparse scientific work on such issues as the foreign manager's work style and lifestyle in Japan. According to data from my survey on human resource management at foreign affiliate corporations in Japan, not the resources but the character of Western managers is the main problem. Therefore, this character is the key to understanding why foreign managers are often incapable of succeeding in Japan. In other words, international business demands certain mental skills in working with people from other cultures (Adler et al. 1986).

One frequently given excuse for early repatriation has been that the spouse of the foreign executive manager was unable to adjust to the Japanese living environment. Dolles and Morlock (2005a, 2005b) investigated the acculturation problems of the spouses of German managers. Their results showed that a preparation phase is important not only for the expatriated manager but also for the accompanying spouse/family. The success, as defined later in this chapter, of German managers is determined not only by their working environment but also by the living environment of their family.

The Japanese Labor Research Institute (2001) surveyed the living conditions of foreign expatriates in Japan. The study shows that more than half of the top managers believe that the Japanese language is important for their work and life in Japan. Most of them came with their family to Japan, and they tend to stay less than three years. They indicated that those interacting favorably with Japanese colleagues, as well as outside the company, are using the Japanese language. However, the contradiction is obvious: Foreign managers do not succeed in making such language achievements when staying with their family less than three years! Foreign managers need to make a conscious effort and adapt to local systems and managerial practices, particularly for succeeding with their leadership and their human resource management in another cultural context. Therefore we can assume that the ability to create synergy effects is affected by the international manager's strategic intent and acculturation. The hypothesis will be examined using the data and method described below. This survey is part of a series of investigations on foreign management in Japan (Schlunze 2004, 2006, 2007, 2008) and attempts to shed light on both: the significance of the work style and lifestyle of foreign businesspeople who successfully adjusted to the Japanese working and living environment. The aim of this investigation is to explain how the foreign manager's work style and lifestyle influences the creation of synergy effects. We will investigate where such "hybrid managers" succeeded to create cultural synergy through their strategic intent, succeeding in a foreign business environment and efforts to adjust to the local culture. The following literature review will show the importance of this investigation, emphasizing insights and shortcomings of previous research and promoting a deeper understanding of doing business in Japan.

Recent literature on cultural management and synergy

A review of the recent business literature – including multinational enterprise (MNE) theory (Dunning 1988; Buckley and Ghauri 1999), and culturally based approaches to the analysis of Japanese MNEs (Koike 1988; Abo 1994; Mead 2006; Trompenaars 2006) show that there is no acceptance of the best-practice orientation of global-management gurus and therefore of the conversion thesis. Accordingly, Gertler (2004) recognizes that within the global production system, manufacturing cultures differ. Also, Whitley (1999) strongly supports the divergence thesis, suggesting that despite the growth of international investment and capital flow, distinctive business systems remain different from each other.

Cultural management studies became popular after Adler (1983) indicated the need for development of this branch within management studies. Nowadays, cultural studies have full coverage of management-relevant issues extending to corporate social responsibility and sustainability (Habisch et al. 2005; Husted 2005). Thus, Habisch et al. showed how the application of the European Commission's CSR approach varies by the institutional and cultural environments of each European nation. Husted showed that cultural variables do play a role in environmental sustainability. His findings on culture and ecology support the national culture hypothesis proposed by Hofstede (1997, 2001), who constructed five different work-environment-related values that help to distinguish different cultures around the globe.

Referring to the existing literature, Javidan and Carl (2005) introduced a taxonomy of managers to investigate leadership across cultures. In their taxonomy, *visionary managers* develop a sense of direction based on their analysis of opportunities and threats and the firm's competencies, along with their own deep personal beliefs and values. *Symbolizer managers* live the vision and effectively communicate their plans. The *innovator* is willing to take risks and generate new ideas, rewarding success and tolerating failure. The *mobilizer* pools intellectual and emotional energy within the organization. The *auditor* has high performance expectations and makes himself available and in touch, and encourages self-monitoring among subordinates. Meanwhile, *ambassador* managers understand intra- and inter-organization interdependencies and develop mutually satisfactory relationships with various stakeholders (Javidan and Carl 2005). Javidan and Carl (2005) found that Canadian (Western) managers tend to focus on a visionary leadership because they are concerned with advancement and are more individualistic; meanwhile Taiwanese (Eastern) managers, taking a mobilizer role, focus on the creation of a strong work environment that centers on cooperation and organizational belongingness. Javidan and Carl indicated the limitations of their findings, stating that they were "not clear, ... what specifically it means in each culture and how it is enacted by leaders". Further, there is evidence that Asian managers or managers working in the Asian cultural context do actually have a vision, even though they prefer to appear as a mobilizer. What distinguishes Western and Eastern managers is the way they negotiate their visionary thinking and strategic intent.

The result of the investigation by Parboteeah et al. (2005) of US and Japanese accounting firms does not support the national culture hypothesis. Their study suggests that institutional forces may exist to counterbalance cultural forces that are potentially dysfunctional to accounting practices. One explanation is that the Japanese accounting system is becoming more similar to the US accounting system. They find that US employees have stronger principle-cosmopolitan climates than the Japanese, and they concluded that "the lower principle climate for the Japanese is consistent with

Japanese culture and their preference to base decisions on situations or circumstances rather than principles" (Parboteeah et al. 2005, 478). This work demonstrates that inherent cultural characteristics such as strong particularism in Japan can be overwhelmed by universalistic approaches born by a neo-liberalist agenda. Thus, it appears that pressure from the outside (*gaiatsu*) affects the corporate and market environment in Japan. However, it is often neglected that globalization effects arrive in particular places differently (Sadler 2007) and that Japanese corporations have become themselves a promoter of neo-liberal activities.

Peltokorpi (2006) finds that differences in communication roles lead to reduced cross-cultural communication and sometimes to the isolation of foreign expatriate managers in Japan. According to his investigation, it is sometimes frustrating for foreign expatriate managers to work in Japan because they do not get the feedback they expect from their subordinates, who tend to restrain from voicing their opinions. He concludes that differences in communication rules increase miscommunication and lead to a reduction of cross-cultural interaction. In the worst cases, it may lead to isolation of expatriate employees. Interestingly, Peltokorpi indicates that this can happen not only to foreign but also to Japanese employees with a long overseas experience or females with a more liberal gender attitude (Peltokorpi 2006). Negative outcomes of intercultural communication are often in evidence, but the process that leads to such outcomes is often not fully understood. Indeed, the different approach to socializing and human interaction in the Japanese workplace makes it difficult to apply foreign or international managerial practices. However, as long as the female or foreign manager shows enthusiasm, he or she will be supported by the team or group. Critique must be mentioned informally and yet carefully in a collaborative way in order to make possible formal decisions regarding improvements in the corporate environment.

McCaughey and Bruning (2005) recommend strategies to enhance the acculturation and adjustment of an expatriate. According support strategies such as pre-assignment support, assignment support, and repatriation support influence the ability of an expatriate to acculturate and adjust to his or her assignment. These organizational actions do increase job satisfaction and decrease incidents of premature repatriation. However, they also warn that organizations should be aware of the isolating influence of being abroad and finally consider alternative staffing options such as impatriates and flexpatriates.

Thanks to the contribution of the researchers, we recognize differences between Oriental and Occidental mind-sets; but to gain a deeper understanding on cultural management in Asia and to state on implications for international managerial action, we need to incorporate the work of Asian scholars as well.

Academic background: international managers' adjustment practices

Japanese scholars contributed early to the intersection of geography and management. Beika (1970) emphasizes that managers always need to adjust actively or passively to internal and external conditional changes. Totsuka (1990) suggests that the meaning of locational adjustment in the process of globalization remains important. Kawabata (1996) suggests that in the information age it is increasingly the optimal location and the efficient corporate network that creates synergy effects. Using an original analytical approach, the Japanese Multinational Enterprise Study Group (JMNESG) has investigated more than 300 Japanese overseas factories since the 1980s in order to analyze transferability of Japanese management models. Initially called the dilemma approach, JMNESG's "hybrid model" is based on the relationship between application and adaptation and focuses on the evaluation of application degree. The fundamental idea of the "hybrid model" is the dynamism that the Japanese management and production system creates when mixed with the local management system or other local managerial elements in overseas factories. This serves as a theoretical framework for the investigation and analysis centering on the formation of a hybrid management system. According to Kawamura (2005), this hybridization varies by country, region, industrial sector, individual corporate strategies and so on. Interestingly, the study group developed the "hybrid model" based on the fundamental insight or basic observation that the dilemma of the application of the Japanese management system can be also perceived as dynamism and a core strategy of Japanese transplants. The foreign business environment not only restricts conditions for the application of Japanese methods and practices but helps to form new "hybrid" factories. Recently, the founder of the study group, Professor Tetsuo Abo, proposed a "preliminary concept of management geography" (Abo 2002). He emphasizes that cross-cultural difference in human interaction and networking need to be incorporated into the geography of management. Since he used characteristics typical of Japanese production management as a measure for his analysis, his framework is useful to investigate the degree of application of Japanese managerial techniques and practices within Japanese transplants. Nevertheless, there remains a need to upgrade the framework by incorporating fundamental dimensions of culture that would make it possible to distinguish cross-cultural differences in human interaction of the international and local actors involved.

While the above-mentioned research group analyzes management systems of particular corporations, our focus shifts to a more actor-centered approach. As Adler (1983) already emphasized, the behavior of people within a work system appears to be greater than the cultural impact on systems themselves. Granovetter's embeddedness approach (1985) is based on the central fact that all economic behavior is fundamentally socially embedded. No manager's work is performed in isolation.

International managers need to adapt to various cultural environments within the global-city networks, but they are believed to have the consumption and lifestyle pattern evident among international managers in global cities (Thrift 2000; Sassen 2001).

Jones (2002) sees the "global city" misconceived, discovering the myth of "global management" by making the international manager or "change agent" the subject and the multinational firm in the global-city network the object of his study. This actor-centered approach is distinguished from previous approaches focusing on environmental determinants affecting the international manager's decision making (Krumme 1981; Nishioka and Krumme 1993). Nowadays, managers are seen as "change agents", coordinating and modifying interests in overlapping spheres of work and life. Due to the increasing competition between firms, managers may be set on current exigencies. They need to become change agents who are the fastest and best managers by adjusting to and creating new practices and skills (Czinkota et al. 1999). Experienced international managers are equipped with sensitivity to several spaces and are capable of showing "situated rationality" intuitively (Livingstone 2000). Organizations do not simply weather their environment; they actively select, interpret, choose and create their environments (Trompenaars, 2006). The change agent in a company needs to adapt to and modify the corporate, market, and living environments constantly by embedding strategies and implementing business practices. Those executive managers are often described as being disembedded from the cities in which they work. It remains unknown which practices work for which types of foreign executive manager in terms of a particular business environment. We assume that business environments in first-tier and second-tier global cities are different and thus, depending on where the business takes place, international managers' success practices are significantly different.

Methodology

The analytical approach introduced here is an actor-centered approach. A triangulation was undertaken to estimate the synergy effects of foreign managers in Japan. First, their style of working and living was evaluated. Second, the degree of acculturation and finally the clearness of the strategic intent of the foreign executive manager were assessed in order to estimate the potential of synergy creation in the cross-cultural workplace. The sample of the survey included all 141 foreign executive managers listed in the directory of the German Chamber of Industry and Commerce in Japan (DIHK) and affiliates.

I sent these managers a detailed questionnaire about their working and living style based on the work of Dolles and Morlock (2005a, 2005b); 81 of them responded (return rate 57%), and 58 of these participated in an interview. During the interview the information from the questionnaire was then verified; however, the data from that self-assessment was not as important as the reasoning and additional information the foreign executive gave in the course of the interview. The questionnaire was also used to gather additional data confirming interview results. The results from the database analysis and interviews have been double checked. In cases where we found deviation, we deepened the investigation through follow-up interviews. Where it was necessary we conducted additional interviews; 43 valid cases, 30 percent of the total population, have been used for analysis.

First, we introduce an approach to differentiate expatriate and hybrid executive managers; second, we will show how their potential for creating cultural synergy was investigated. During the interview we discussed with the interviewees a typology to assess work and living style of foreign executive managers built in line with our four dimensions, risk, adjustment, sense of challenge, and sensitivity. The managers had to assess themselves according to the four dimensions. Since managers tend to self-indicate that they rate rather high in the dimensions of risk or discovery and rather strong for adaptability or sensitivity, for our scientific assessment we analyzed not their self-assessment but their reasoning. All interview information was arranged on a sheet showing the self-assessment for each dimension. Framed by these four dimensions, we provided a typology enabling the manager to identify him or herself as change agent or maintenance agent on the risk dimension, or application-oriented and adaptation-oriented on the adaptability dimension. In a similar manner, we introduced a typology to assess the living style of the manager. The manager had to state whether he or she perceived him or herself as disembedded or as embedded in the business community and whether the manager saw him or herself as a contributor to or only a participant in the local community. The typology was well understood and received by the interviewees. We were in fact astonished that managers often confessed their weaknesses. The research team's living and working experiences in Japan provided clues as to whether a manager was realistic about him or herself or not. Strong cultural adjustment, the manager's history and experiences in Japan, advanced language proficiency, the will to be involved in the local decision-making process and a partnership with a culturally fluent host national were the most important criteria in distinguishing the hybrid manager from the normal expatriate manager. These particular data points contain no emotional bias from the investigators or interviewees. Rather, they are objective facts that document an objective reality of an expatriated manager's adjustment practice.

Synergy created by the hybrid manager

Synergy is actively created by foreign executive managers. To achieve synergy, McCaughey and Bruning (2005) suggest strategies to enhance the acculturation and adjustment of expatriate managers. According to their work, support strategies such as pre-assignment support, assignment support, and repatriation support influence the ability of an expatriate to acculturate and adjust. These organizational activities increase job satisfaction and decrease incidents of premature repatriation. However, McCaughey and Bruning also warned that organizations should be aware of the isolating influence of being abroad and concluded with considering alternative staffing options. Accordingly, expatriated managers are often described as being disembedded from their working and living environment. Since expatriates are believed to have little understanding of the local business environment and employee relations, a dual structure with a Japanese representative at the top exists in many foreign companies in Japan. However, we did observe that the success of MNEs in Japan increasingly depends on the availability of foreign executive managers educated and trained within Japan. These *hybrid managers* are socially embedded and evince more sensitivity to local norms and values. As an outcome, they are often more efficient and successful in the Japanese market than the typical expatriate executives. They have the ability to select the optimal location and proper human resources. According to Skyrme (1996, 2007) the term "hybrid" was originally coined by Peter Keen in the mid-1980s and later refined by Michael Earl, who identified a hybrid manager as "a person with strong technical skills and adequate business knowledge." To mimic this definition in the cross-cultural management context, we identified a hybrid manager as a person with strong cultural adjustment skills and adequate business knowledge or vice versa. Hybrids are people with skills achieved during an acculturation process. They are able to *work together* with local subordinates as a local would, but meanwhile developing and implementing international managerial practices and ideas in a fashion that makes synergy effects possible. "Synergy" comes from the Greek words meaning "working together," and according to Harris and Moran (2000), synergy represents a dynamic process that involves adapting, learning and joint action. The total effect is greater than the sum of effects when acting independently. Synergy creates an integrated solution. With true synergy, nothing is given up or lost. According to Abraham Maslow (cited by Harris and Moran 2000, 114), Japan is a high-synergy society where there is a strong emphasis upon cooperation and the society seeks win/win solutions. This suggests that foreign managers from low-synergy societies can actually learn a good deal in the process of adjusting to the Japanese business environment. Nevertheless, cultural synergy develops new solutions that respect all cultures involved.

We wish to answer the following research questions with the proposed framework:

1. In order to be successful in the foreign business environment, what kind of working style and what kind of living style do foreign executive managers choose?

2. Can we identify different types of foreign executive managers, and do they differ in their potential to create cultural synergy?
3. Is the location important for creating synergy?

Therefore, a typology will be employed estimating the optimal conditions for creation of synergy effects in cross-cultural management. Here, work and living style of foreign executive managers will be evaluated, including such elements as career patterns, interaction with subordinates and customers, and their individual lifestyle.

Favorable decision making in cross-cultural management centers on the creation of synergy effects. Synergy effects can be achieved when cross-cultural communication is conducted appropriately and the actors implement strategies and execute projects efficiently. As seen in Figure 2.1, two dimensions are seen as important in contributing to the creation of such effects: cultural adjustment and strategic intent of the foreign executives with regard to the local operation and his or her overseas assignment. According to Turner and Trompenaars (2000), "strategic intent is an 'animating dream' that provides the emotional and intellectual energy to take a journey guided by the 'strategic architecture' of the brain," or a manager's professional intuition. Successful foreign executives need to have a "sense of discovery" that the future is "out there", not "in here", when managing abroad. Mintzberg (1987) previously showed that direct strategies often ignore changes and differences in the business environment. Corporate strategies designed by the parent company or foreign executives (inner direction) might not match the reality of the particular overseas market when emergent strategies are demanded (outer direction). Together with the local managers, a crafted strategy needs to be formed. If international managers succeed in proceeding in an agreed direction, learning and knowledge become cumulative and synergy can be expected (Hamel and Prahalad 1994). The degree of cultural adjustment achieved can be seen as an outcome of the professional adaptability to the Japanese working environment and psychological sensitivity in human interaction in daily life. Sensitivity to or tolerance toward other cultural values can be better exercised and achieved through personal contacts in private life than at the workplace, because the workplace hierarchy often prevents immediate feedback. In private life this can be achieved among friends and partners who have the necessary cultural knowledge. Not only in business, but also in private life, people with business success have a vision or strategic goals. Their positive attitude toward risk taking in the corporate environment and their curiosity for other cultures go hand in hand. Therefore, strategic leadership and a high degree of cultural adjustment are necessary conditions for creating synergy effects in cross-cultural management (Type B in Figure 2.1). Thus the hypothesis states that synergy effects in cross-cultural management will be created only if the cultural adjustment is strong and the foreign executive manager advertises his or her strategic intentions.

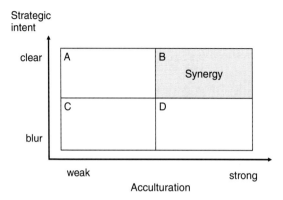

Figure 2.1   Strategic intent and acculturation: necessary conditions for synergy

We assume that only clear strategic intent and successful cultural adjustment make synergy effects in intercultural management possible. Taking into account the individual working styles and lifestyles of a foreign executive, we can distinguish the degree of potential for synergy in cross-cultural management.

Important for the acculturation process is the depth of experience, which grows with the length of the stay. The best way to prepare for a country is to have lived there. Language proficiency can accelerate the depth of experience since more information becomes available and a greater understanding of the foreign culture can be achieved with fewer pitfalls and in a more favorable fashion. Work style is important because cultural environment often demands different approaches than does a foreign executive's home culture. For example, if not efficiency, but persistence and regular appearance at the working place are demanded, the willingness when necessary to accept long working hours indicates cultural adjustment to customs and attitudes. To overcome cultural differences, communication strategies to avoid risk, misunderstanding and miscommunication are also important. Since communication strategies are usually based on corporate guidelines for interpersonal interaction in culturally diverse workplaces, they can be summarized as conflict management. We can consider the expatriate assignment of a foreign executive manager to be successful only if he or she influences the decision-making process. Therefore participation in meetings of the local subsidiary and the corresponding meetings at the regional or global headquarters is crucial. Gaining influence in a foreign workplace depends on the manner of information sharing and knowledge exchange. Is the foreign executive manager able to interpret information from local sources him or herself, or does he or she depend on local subordinates to analyze local business data? These are questions and important issues that determine the working style. Further, living style contributes to the acculturation process. A good marriage or partnership is very valuable for the assignment abroad. Is the partner supportive or not? Bringing the family abroad can be also a burden for the foreign executive manager and therefore put risk on his or her assignment and the success of his or her mission in the foreign workplace. A marriage or partnership with a national often helps to accelerate the acculturation process. Instant feedback, often not provided in the workplace, can be given by a partner or friend with the local cultural background. This is especially helpful for foreign executives with open-ended assignments or local contracts.

Having a strategic intent is important not only for the individual manager's motivation but also for encouraging and managing subordinates. Decisions that prepare a company for growth motivate company leaders as well as subordinates. Career aims such as becoming an area specialist, a marketing expert, or an international or global manager contribute to keeping a high motivation profile, which often earns the respect of the local subordinates and therefore makes managing people easier. Individual motivation is highly related to identification with corporate aims. Enthusiasm about new business opportunities, successful product adjustment or locational expansion of the corporate network indicates that strategic intent exists. Involvement in corporate decisions also has a spatial dimension: extensive travel activity within the host country and region, in some cases even around the globe. These are important indicators of the questionnaire for assessing an international manager who is involved with the MNE's corporate strategy and trusted to translate strategic intent to the staff of the overseas subsidiary.

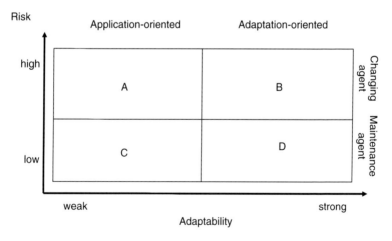

Figure 2.2 Types of working style

As shown in Figure 2.2, working styles *[W-STYLE]* are characterized by attitude toward **risk** and the **adaptability** of a manager. Those managers who function as change agents tend to be risk-takers. They have the power and authority to guide the start-up phase of an operation or undertake major organizational changes in a later stage of the overseas operation. Those who function as *maintenance agents* have a different attitude toward risk and do not have the same degree of freedom, empowerment and support from the parent company. Their work is to control and *maintain* the sustainable growth of a fully established business operation. Only a manager with strong adaptability will succeed with *adaptation-oriented* practices. A foreign executive manager with weak adaptability tends to be rather *application-oriented*. An application-oriented manager tries to apply managerial practices and methods from the home country. On the other hand, an adaptation-oriented manager tries to adapt to the host country's practices and customs. In order to work efficiently, a balance of both methods is favorable, but here we categorize manager performance by evaluating adaptability. Thus, during the interview managers were asked about their behavioral orientation; a manager perceiving him or herself as a change agent was assessed as strong in risk-taking. A manager assessing him or herself as a maintainer implies that he or she avoids risk and therefore was assessed as low in risk-taking. In a similar fashion, the team assessed a manager's adaptability as weak if he or she applies home-country practices and as strong if he or she adapts to host-country practices to succeed in the foreign workplace.

In a similar manner I assessed the foreign executives' living style *[L-STYLE]* (see Figure 2.3). Therefore we attempt to explore their degree of **sensitivity** and sense of **discovery** or willingness to interact with the local culture. The

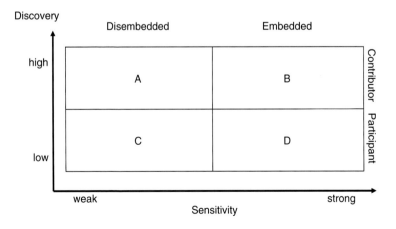

Figure 2.3 Types of lifestyle

population of foreign executives can be divided into managers who stick with the foreign community and those who undertake an effort to discover the local culture in their free time. The *disembedded* type (A, C) is expatriated by the parent company to Japan. He or she usually does not speak any Japanese and often has not received proper cultural sensitivity training for expatriate life in Japan. The *embedded* type (B, D) has developed cultural sensitivity through frequent interaction with locals. This manager type is often married to a local and/or received academic or professional education within the country of assignment. This manager is often employed locally by the foreign firm. Type A and B have in common active socializing and being *contributors* to the business community. Therefore they are involved in the foreign and/or local community. Participation not only in the workplace but also in private life is essential to enacting successful intercultural communication. The *participant* (C, D) is not excessively ambitious. In private life this type of manager prefers a quiet family life and does not actively contribute to the business community. Since the work of international managers is quite demanding, many tend to seek mere relaxation within their private space in their nonworking hours. Thus during the interview we asked whether the expatriate manager feels embedded or disembedded. Accordingly, we assessed the manager's sensitivity as high if he or she could indicate that he or she succeeded in integrating with people of the host country. From our perspective, the fact that a manager advertises frustration about not being embedded refers to a low cultural sensitivity – an inability to sense the embracing emotions and mechanism of the human network in the host-country environment.

Results

The interview data containing 43 cases has been evaluated corresponding to the analytical framework shown in Figures 2.1 to 2.3. The aim was to investigate the working style and living style of foreign executive managers and their potential to create synergy in the cross-cultural workplace.

Based on the questionnaire and the interview information, I classified the interviewees into two groups: hybrid and normal expatriate managers (in Table 2.1, Hybrids and Expats). Their attitude toward *risk* and sense of *discovery* was assessed simply as low or high, their *adaptability* and *sensibility* as weak or strong. To investigate differences in the behavioral orientation of normal expatriate and hybrid managers, nonparametric tests were conducted. The Two-Independent-Samples Tests procedure of SPPS+ compares the two groups of managers on one variable for each dimension investigated. The hybrid manager is expected to perform better in each aspect of his or her work life in Japan. To find out whether the hybrid manager performs better, the 20 hybrid managers were compared to the 23 normal

Table 2.1 Differences between expat and hybrid managers (Mann–Whitney Test)

Ranks				
	MTYPEC	**N**	**Mean Rank**	**Sum of Ranks**
Risk	Expat	23	19.61	451.00
	Hybrid	20	24.75	495.00
	Total	43		
Adaptability	Expat	23	18.59	427.50
	Hybrid	20	25.93	518.50
	Total	43		
Discovery	Expat	23	15.24	350.50
	Hybrid	20	29.78	595.50
	Total	43		
Sensitivity	Expat	23	17.72	407.50
	Hybrid	20	26.93	538.50
	Total	43		

Test Statistics[a]				
	Risk	**Adaptability**	**Discovery**	**Sensitivity**
Mann-Whitney U	175.000	151.500	74.500	131.500
Wilcoxon W	451.000	427.500	350.500	407.500
Z	−1.599	−2.611	−4.372	−3.086
Asymp. Sig. (2-tailed)	.110	.009	.000	.002

[a]Grouping variable: MTYPEC

expatriate managers. From the Mann-Whitney U test one can find that, on average, hybrid managers do rank higher than normal expatriate managers in adaptation, discovery and sensitivity. Consequently, on average the hybrid manager is more acculturated than the normal expatriate manager.

However, no significant differences concerning the attitude toward risk were found. One reason could be that in business, risk always exists. Managers must know when they can take risk and when they should refrain from undertaking experiments. When opportunities exist but others refrain from taking them, only the manager able to calculate the risk of failure wins the opportunity to make extraordinary profits. Concerning risk in the intercultural workplace, both expatriate and hybrid managers take risk when they apply home practices or adapt to local management practices. Success in a foreign cultural setting is difficult. A successful international manager needs to achieve the flexibility to manage in different cultural settings without losing his or her individual culture and trust.

The analysis showed that normal expatriate and hybrid managers differ clearly in their living style. Especially, their "sense of discovery" is different. Often, normal expatriate managers are seeking relaxation at home or comfort provided by their colleagues at clubs or within enclaves of foreigners. On the other hand, hybrid managers have the skills to build linkages to nationals in their professional and their private life. As a result of frequent interaction with local nationals – not limited to the workplace – they achieve more insights into the local society. Therefore, hybrid managers develop a strong sensitivity to cultural issues and attain appropriate knowledge for intercultural communication. Consequently, it was verified that expatriate managers and hybrid managers show significantly different degrees of acculturation. Acculturation efforts directly impact managers' potential to create synergy. Therefore, hybrid managers show a strong potential to create synergy in the intercultural workplace; meanwhile, normal expatriate managers are relatively weak, but sometimes succeed in creating synergy by implementing their strategic intent. Nevertheless, cultural experience is needed to overcome deficits of acculturation when translating the strategic intent to local managers and staff members. Normal expatriate managers are able to interpret cultural signals in a less turbulent business environment.

Analyzing the interview data, we could verify that acculturation of foreign executive managers based in Osaka-Kobe is slightly stronger than that of those based in Tokyo-Yokohama. The table shows that the managers based in Osaka-Kobe are more acculturated than the managers interviewed in Tokyo. This result let us infer that the business environment in Osaka-Kobe remains, relatively, more traditionally Japanese. Or, to make it clear, Tokyo-Yokohama has been more affected by globalization processes. There is a strong population of Japanese and foreign managers with rich international experience. Because of the mixing of cultures in the first-tier global city, it is difficult for a relatively inexperienced expatriate manager to extract what is particularly Japanese.

To conclude, hybrid managers adapt more to the local business environment. They have a high "sense of discovery" and show strong sensitivity to cultural issues in their private and work life. As an outcome, hybrid managers are more advanced in their acculturation. Since the business environment in Osaka-Kobe is more homogeneous and therefore easy to interpret, some expatriate managers based in Osaka succeeded in greater acculturation than their counterparts in Tokyo. One reason for this observation is that those expatriate managers based in Osaka-Kobe are expatriated for longer

Table 2.2   Synergy creation differs by location

		Acculturation * GCC Crosstabulation		
		GCC		
Count		Tokyo-Yokohama	Osaka-Kobe	Total
Acculturation	weak	12	5	17
	strong	10	16	26
Total		22	21	43

		Symmetric Measures	
		Value	Approx. Sig.
Nominal by	Phi	.314	.039
Nominal	Cramer's V	.314	.039
N of Valid Cases		43	

[a.] Not assuming the null hypothesis.
[b.] Using the asymptotic standard error assuming the null hypothesis

periods. Hybrid managers tend to have strong acculturation. As an outcome, their potential to create synergy in the intercultural workplace was found to be higher than that of the average expatriate manager. It appeared that they tend to have the advantage of a relatively strong acculturation and succeeded in implementing their strategic intent regularly. However, according to the analysis of our interview data, we could not testify to significant differences regarding their strategic intent. One reason could be that the strategic intent of various managers had diametrically opposite dimensions when reacting to global and local pressure. The interview results showed that favorable efforts in acculturation create cross-cultural synergy. Because the hybrid manager spends more effort, he or she is likely to feel more highly compensated by cross-cultural synergy created.

A clear pattern regarding strategic intent was evident only for the attitude toward risk. However, our observations throughout the interview process led us to the qualitative conclusion that a clear strategic intent to compete with local companies might lead to synergy effects in the first-tier global city; however, in the case of most expatriate managers, such effects cannot created without the help of local managers. The executive manager based in a second-tier global city, such as Osaka-Kobe, needs to undertake greater efforts in acculturation, emphasizing the strategic intent to collaborate with the local business community. The discussion of cases will show in detail how foreign executive managers facilitate those characteristics and potentials in the local business environment for the creation of cross-cultural synergy.

Discussion: balancing practices for synergy

The results let us infer that indeed leveraging sources can be seen as a process that initiates and drives the acculturation of an individual which also influences the character and the way in which the strategic intent is communicated. The results let us assume that the degree of acculturation determines how and with what effect the strategic intent can be communicated. Such individual synergy potentials transcend cultural boundaries by creating new entities that develop *hybrid cultures* of their own.

The results showed that synergy cannot be created merely by a clear strategic intent and a strong effort to adjust to a different cultural environment. Instead, it is necessary to balance foreign and local managerial practices. Therefore, not extreme adjustment, but a balanced approach enables the foreign executive manager to create synergy effects. Successful managers were conscious that they needed to show flexibility when switching between their own and the local approach. Acculturation, if successfully conducted, is mutual with regard to the host and the home cultures. However, as we can see in Figure 2.5, too little or too much effort in cultural adjustment will lead to friction. Friction with local staff members occurs when the adjustment of the foreign executive manager is not sufficient. Human resource management problems occur if the strategic intent is packaged in a fashion that does not suit the host culture (see Figure 2.5, Situation A).

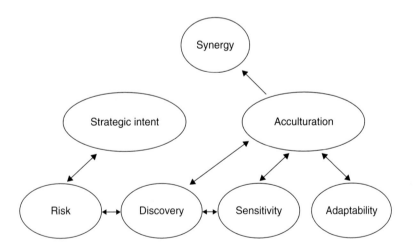

Figure 2.4   Leveraging of sources of synergy

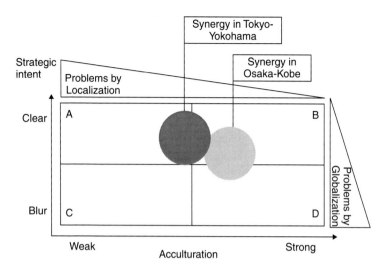

Figure 2.5   Balancing strategic intent and acculturation for synergy

Even if the manager's strategic intent is clear and his or her cultural adjustment is strong, a risk of producing parent-subsidiary conflicts still exists. The manager needs to learn how to switch between the cultures. Most of the hybrid managers learned how to become good intercultural negotiators (Situation B). A loss of leadership may result from weak cultural adjustment and unclear strategic intent (Situation C). If the strategic intent of the manager is unclear and the foreign executive manager adjusts too much, he or she risks losing the trust of the parent company (Situation D), because his or her activities and efforts are not well understood at company headquarters. These situations can be documented by case studies. To achieve synergy in the second-tier global city in this study, Osaka-Kobe, comparatively more effort was required. Here, lock-in effects can be avoided since the international manager is more exposed to the local environment. We found that expatriate managers based in Osaka-Kobe showed more cultural sensitivity than their counterparts in Tokyo-Yokohama.

Ultimately, the results of our interviews led us to conclude that important differences remain: more than hybrid managers, the typical expatriate manager tends to advertise clear strategic intentions. This led us to infer that globalization and localization problems must be balanced to create synergy in the intercultural workplace. While executive managers in Tokyo-Yokohama frequently address globalization problems, more efforts are undertaken to cope with localization problems in Osaka-Kobe. Individual synergy potentials transcend cultural boundaries by creating new entities that develop *hybrid cultures* of their own.

Cultural synergy in the context of our investigation entails implementing business practices that produce the best work from every employee. However, this requires effective intercultural communication because the foreign executive's strategic intent depends on how he or she is facilitated by communication. Communication underpins all managerial functions (Saee 2005). Foreign executives should be equipped to communicate their strategic intent. In doing so, and to be heard by subordinates in the local subsidiary, they should show a certain amount of acculturation. To lead people means to know people! Therefore, cultural experiences in the workplace as well as in daily life are an important resource for building competence to lead people in a culturally different environment. In contrast to typical expatriate managers, the hybrid managers who participated in our interview survey seem to have deeper understanding of relationships within Japanese society, psychological adaptation processes, and uncertainty reduction. Nevertheless, living and working in the global city, some hybrid managers did not always put their "knowledge" to work when operating in a first-tier global city.

In some cases, foreign executives have stayed for a long period and developed some identity problems. Apparently, hybrid managers in the global city try to reconnect to the expatriate managers' community and their practices. By emphasizing that they are not willing to adjust too much to Japanese business practices, some of them even create an artificial distance from the local business environment. On the other hand, we found that this approach does not often occur in the second-tier global city. Here, even the expatriate managers show similarities to the managerial approach of hybrid managers and therefore tend to be more balanced in their locational preferences as well. An English manager working for a German automotive company told us that he needs to adjust to the cultures of the East Asian market and the European headquarters. To conclude, the acculturation process has two directions: Managers need to adjust simultaneously to the West and the East. They need to learn how to balance application of global practices and adaptation of local practices. The finding of this research is limited to the experience of Western managers, but it would be beneficial to investigate how Asian managers perform in Japan. In comparison, Japanese managers' efforts at synergy creation should be investigated to learn more about successful team management in the intercultural workplace.

Acknowledgment

The author acknowledges the generous Grant-in-Aid for Scientific Research support provided by the Japanese Ministry of Education, Science and Culture (No.:17520548). It was beneficial to present and discuss the here introduced author's original framework at the 2006 annual meetings International

Geographers Union and of the European-Asian Management Conference. Many thanks go to Harald Dolles, Michael Plattner and William Baber who participated in the interview survey providing reflections that helped to interpret the cases.

References

Abo, T. (2002) An approach for management geography: In the case of Japanese hybrid factories in the three major regions. Academy of International Business 2002 Annual Meeting, San Juan, June 28–July 1.

Adler, N.J. (1983) Cross-cultural management research: The ostrich and the trend. *Academy of Management Review* 8(2): 226–32.

Adler, N.J., R. Doktor, and S.G. Redding (1986) From the Atlantic to the Pacific Century: Cross-cultural management reviewed. *Journal of Management* 12(2): 295–318.

Beika, M. (1970) *Keiei Kankyoron* (Business environment theory), Maruzen. (J)

Buckley, P.J. (1997) Foreign direct investment in Japan: Theoretical explanation and evidence from European direct investors. In N. Kobayashi (ed.), *Management: A Global Perspective*, 85–93. Tokyo: The Japan Times.

Buckley, P.J., and P.N. Ghauri (1999) *The Internationalization of the Firm*. London: International Thomson Business Press.

Czinkota, M.R., I.A. Ronkainen, and M.H. Moffett (1999) *International Business*. Orlando: Harcourt Brace.

Dolles, H., and E. Morlock (2005a) Die Auslandsentsendung aus Sicht der mitreisenden Familie – Teil 1: Umzug nach Japan. *Japan Markt*, January, 22–5.

Dolles, H., and E. Morlock (2005b) Die Auslandsentsendung aus Sicht der mitreisenden Familie – Teil 2: Verbesserungswuensche und Empfehlungen. *Japan Markt*, February, 22–5.

Earl, M.J. and D.J. Skyrme (1990) Hybrid managers: What should you do? *Computer Bulletin*, May, 19–21.

Earl, M.J., and D.J. Skyrme (1992) Hybrid managers: What do we know about them? *Journal of Information Systems* 1(2): 169–87.

Granovetter, M. (1985) Economic action and social structure: The problem of embeddedness. *American Journal of Sociology* 91: 481–510.

Habisch, A., J. Jonker, M. Wegner, and R. Schmidpeter (2005) *Corporate Social Responsibility across Europe*. Berlin, Heidelberg, New York: Springer.

Hamel, G., and C.K. Prahalad (1994) *Competing for the Future*. Boston: Harvard Business School Press.

Harris, P.R. and R.T. Moran (2000) *Managing Cultural Differences: Leadership Strategies for the New World of Business*. Houston: Gulf Publishing.

Hofstede, G. (1997) *Culture and Organization: Software of the Mind*. New York: McGraw-Hill.

Hofstede, G. (2001) *Culture's Consequences: Comparing Values, Behaviors, Institutions, and Organizations across Nations*. 2nd ed. Beverly Hills: Sage Publications.

Husted, B.W. (2005) Culture and ecology: A cross-national study of the determinants of environmental sustainability. *Management International Review* 45: 349–71.

Japanese Labor Research Institute (2001) *Zainichi gaishikei kigyo ni okeru gaikokujin haken kinmusha no shokugyo to seikatsu ni kansuru chosa* (Survey on work and life of foreign expatriates at foreign companies in Japan). Tokyo: Hobunsha.

(J) in Japanese.

Javidan, M., and D.E. Carl (2005) Leadership across cultures: A study of Canadian and Taiwanese executives. *Management International Review* 45: 23–44.

Jones, A. (2002) The 'global city' misconceived: The myth of 'global management' in translation service firms. *Geoforum* 33: 335–50.

Kawabata, M. (1996) Jyohoka jidai no "kukan keiei" shiron (Essay on "spatial management" in the information age). In Faculty of Business Administration at Ryokoku University (ed.), *Gendai Nihon Kigyo no Jyoho to Kaikei (Information and Accounting of Modern Japanese Corporations)*, Bunshindo, 29–43. (J)

Kawamura, T. (ed.) (2005) "Gurobaru keizaika no amerika Nikkei kojo (Japanese factories in America in global economy)", Toyokeizai Shimposha.

Koike, K. (1988) *Understanding Industrial Relations in Modern Japan*. Basingstoke: Macmillan.

Krumme, G. (1981) Making it abroad: The evolution of Volkswagen's North American production plants. In F.E.I. Hamilton and G.J.R. Linge (eds), *Spatial Analysis, Industry and the Industrial Environment, Vol. 2: International Industrial Systems*, 325–56. Chichester: John Wiley.

Livingstone, D.N. (2000) Putting geography in its place. *Australian Geographical Studies* 38: 1–9.

METI (2005) *Dai38kai gaishikeikigyo no doko: Heisei 16nen gaishikeikigyo doko chosa* (38th Trend of foreign companies: Survey on the trend of foreign firms in 2004). National Printing Bureau. (J)

McCaughey, D., and N.S. Bruning (2005) Enhancing opportunities for expatriate job satisfaction: HR strategies for foreign assignment success. *Human Resource Planning* 28: 21–9.

Mead, R. (2005) *International Management: Cross-Cultural Dimensions*. Malden: Blackwell Publishing.

Mintzberg, H. (1987) Crafting strategy. *Harvard Business Review* 2: 66–75.

Nishioka, H., and G. Krumme (1993) Location conditions, factors and decisions: An evaluation of selected location surveys. *Land Economics* 14: 195–205.

Parboteeah, K.P., J.B. Cullen, B. Victor, and T. Sakano (2005) National culture and ethical climates: A comparison of U.S. and Japanese accounting firms. *Management International Review* 45: 459–81.

Peltokorpi, V. (2006) The impact of relational diversity and socio-cultural context on interpersonal communication: Nordic subsidiaries in Japan. *Asian Business Management* 5: 333–56.

Sadler, D. (2007) Neo-liberalising corporate social responsibility. Conference paper presented at the Second Global Conference on Economic Geography, Beijing, 25–28 June 2007.

Saee, J. (2005) *Managing Organizations in a Global Economy: An Intercultural Perspective*. Eagan, MN: Thomson South-Western.

Sassen, S. (2001) *The Global City: New York, London, Tokyo*. 2nd edition. Woodstock: Princeton University Press

Schlunze, R.D. (2004) Managerial embeddedness of European manufacturing firms in Japan. *Japanese Journal of Human Geography* 56(5): 61–79.

Schlunze, R.D. (2006) Working and living in the mega cities: Foreign managers in Japan. In R.C.L. González (ed.), *Urban Changes in Different Scales: Systems and Structures*, 503–18. Universidade de Santiago de Compostela Publicacións.

Schlunze, R.D. (2007) Spurring the Kansai economy: Embedding foreign corporations. *Ritsumeikan International*, 5: 17–42.

Schlunze, R.D. (2008) Location and role of foreign firms in regional innovation systems in Japan. *Ritsumeikan International Affairs* 6: 1–15.

Skyrme, D.J. (1996) The hybrid manager. In M.J. Earl (ed.), *Information Management: The Organizational Dimension*, 436–55. New York: Oxford University Press.

Skyrme, D. J., The Hybrid Manager. http://www.skyrme.com/insights/6hybrid.htm (Retrieved February 28, 2007)

Thrift, N. (2000) Performing cultures in the new economy. *Annals of the Association of American Geographers* 90(4): 674–92.

Totsuka, H. (1990) Kokusai bungyo no shintenkai to Nihonkigyo (A new turn of international division of labor and Japanese firms). *Shakai Seisaku Gakkai Nenpo* (Annals of the Society for the Study of Social Policy) 34: 3–22. (J)

Trompenaars, F., and C. Hampden-Turner (2006) *Riding Waves of Culture: Understanding Cultural Diversity in Business.* London: Nicolas Brealey Publishing.

Whitley, R. (1999) *Divergent Capitalisms: The Social Structuring and Change of Business Systems.* Oxford: Oxford University Press.

3
Mobile Elite in the Global City: International Managers' Locational Preference

Michael Plattner

Introduction: coordination and control in the global city

The globalization process is resulting in an acceleration of the concentration of corporate functions of foreign firms in first-tier global cities. In the last decade, Japan has received inward investment in large amounts. This investment is mainly flowing to Tokyo, which functions as Japan's most important market entry point and business environment. The number of foreign firms has risen drastically in this first-tier global city in recent years. In 1974 only 150 non-manufacturing firms and 129 manufacturing firms had invested in Tokyo. Thirty years later, according to the Ministry of International Trade and Industry (MITI), the number had increased to 1440 foreign companies, among them 1085 non-manufacturing firms. By comparison, the second-tier city Osaka did not achieve the same growth rate for international businesses. With 136 companies, this second-tier global city lags behind even Yokohama-Kanagawa, which has attracted 201 foreign firms (MITI 2005). Additionally, since the 1960s and still ongoing, domestic and foreign companies have been shifting their headquarters functions to Tokyo (Hirai 2004). Although costs there tend to be the highest within Japan, most new investors consider locating only in the first-tier city of Tokyo. The concentration of globally linked economic functions goes hand in hand with the expensive lifestyle of the new top corporate officials, including foreign executive managers. This process is embodied by new landmarks such as Ark Hill and Roppongi Hills. Here, we can observe quick circulation of managerial knowledge among new members of the international corporate elite that integrates local and foreign business leaders.

The core question is, which factors cause executive managers to prefer to work and reside in Tokyo? Thus management practices and the preference for certain features of the spatial environment in which to carry out good management practices need to be analyzed. In the following section of this chapter I discuss the current state of research. After that, I present the research framework and the result of the analysis on international managers' locational preferences in Tokyo, a first-tier global city, and Osaka, a third-tier global city, compared. Conclusively, the typology of global managers' activity pattern in the global city is presented.

International managers: fast subjects in the global flow of information

No manager's work is performed in isolation. Each manager's work is embedded in a local and global web of industrial and social activities (Håkansson and Johanson 1993, 40). Capable of exercising global action, these agents are gatekeepers in the circulation of information on intra- and inter-firm levels because of their multiple activity dependencies between global cities. According to Thrift (2000), those "fast subjects" span global-city networks with knowledge-rich, epistemic business communities. International managers have the consumption and lifestyle pattern evident among international managers in global cities (Sassen 2001). As a consequence, "the best practices" culled from national management systems were seen as converging, but recently it has become obvious that such ideas of a "standardized world" are misleading. Thus, Whitley (1999) strongly supports the divergence thesis, suggesting that despite the growth of international investment and capital flow, distinctive business systems force different locational preferences. According to the GAWC Inventory of World Cities, the impact of globalization is the same among alpha, beta, and gamma world cities while the quality of control and information connections differs (Beaverstock 1996; Taylor et al. 2002, 98). Therefore it can be expected that international management practices will continue to converge, but with adaptation to specific locations.

Jones (2002) critiqued Sassen's concept of global city as too narrow in epistemological scope, imbuing places and spaces indirectly and confusing corporate power and control as located in the multinational enterprise's (MNE) headquarters. In contrast, he proposed emphasizing the nature of the social practices that constitute transnational corporate power. He argues that power and control in transnational business activities need to be understood in much more spatially diffused terms (Jones 2002, 337). According to this analysis, management hierarchies and systems do not always correspond with highly centralized systems of control centered on head offices in the global cities. In contrast, control is spreading through a decentralized network of social actors across transnational firm networks. Thus, I will focus on the general structure of corporate and spatial organization of MNEs which is indeed embedded in the global-city network. From a relational point of view, managerial communication through the above-mentioned network connection is crucial for business success.

In economic geography, decision making of MNEs often is depicted as the key factor shaping global information flows and knowledge creation through the global-city network (Nonaka and Takeuchi 1995, 1997; Dicken 2003; Suzuki et al. 2005; Taira 2005). The fact that high-income professional and managerial employees are more vulnerable to dismissal enables the foreign MNE to implement global strategies and managerial practices relatively independent of the local business culture. However, for importing and implementing best practices proven elsewhere, the cross-cultural management process is important. From the geographers' literature we know only that international managers prefer to live in the global city – the linkages between success practices and locational preferences are almost unknown. The question is, what global and local practices are applied to lead international managers to success?

The managers in the regional headquarters of foreign firms have crucial impact on coordination and control. As decision makers, they select the human resources and shape the corporate environment for international business. Therefore an actor-centered approach can fit the needs of the research. In the regional head offices and overseas subsidiaries, international business managers are under increasing pressure as they lead their MNEs to success. These supposedly "fast subjects" necessarily unfold their activities in a city network that embodies circulation and provides the basis for the creation of new business practices (Thrift 2000).

Recently within geographical literature, managerial behavior has been recognized as an analytical tool to evaluate the quality and potential of spaces in the competition of globalization. Schlunze and Plattner (2007) proposed a framework with the intention to promote geography of management concentrating on only a few managerial dimensions that will help to differentiate a range of management practices to create synergies for local, national, and international operations. Those mentioned international managers are often described as being disembedded from the cities in which they work. Granovetter's embeddedness approach (1985) is based on the central fact that all economic behavior is fundamentally socially embedded. According to Oinas (1998), the embeddedness school is divided into two groups: one centering on the network paradigm (Forsgren and Johanson 1992), the other strongly following the implications of the "new flexibility" for organizational strategies and structures. Both groups have contributed to the corporate network discussion but have neglected the management of MNEs as a key driver. As an outcome of the activity of these key drivers, alpha global cities like Tokyo, New York, London, and Frankfurt are becoming more significant as translators and mediators of information flow in the global-city network, while beta and gamma global cities such as Osaka, Düsseldorf, and Manchester may become less strategically important.

The global city is a center of translation and calculation in a worldwide network of heterogeneous flows. In addition, the global city itself

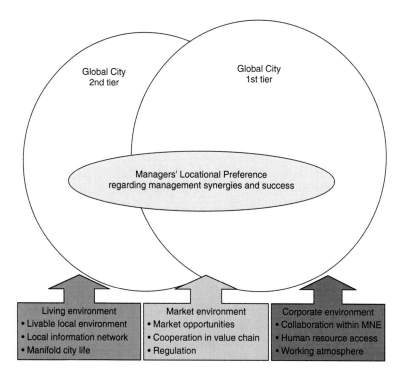

Figure 3.1   Framework to measure sources of international management success

is a heterogeneous assemblage of practices, materials, and actors drawn from within and without the city limits. As mentioned before, it remains unknown which practices work for which types of foreign executive manager in terms of a particular business environment. It can be assumed that business environments in alpha and gamma global cities are different and thus, depending on where the business takes place, international managers' success practices and their locational preferences are significantly different. Further analysis will therefore compare managers in both locations regarding the specifics of the business environment: corporate, market, and living environment. The following research questions will be answered with the proposed framework (see Figure 3.1). First, to what extent does the international manager respond to the three environments? Are those resources most available in the alpha global city? Second, what type of international manager is using which environments?

Accordingly, the research framework evaluates an international manager's performance in terms of distinctive environmental circumstances. Methodologically, the analytical framework is based on an actor-centered approach and a quantitative conjoint analysis of international managers' locational preferences. The sample consists of executives listed in the directory of the German Chamber of Industry and Commerce in Japan (DIHK) and affiliates (N = 141). Fifty-eight cases, or 41 percent of the total population, replied. Forty-three cases, or 30 percent, of the cases are valid for the conjoint analysis. The part-worth utility values are normally distributed.

Locational preferences of the mobile elite

A business environment consists of three spheres: corporate, market, and living environment. Facilitated by these environments, an executive manager creates synergies. First, conjoint analysis unfolds hidden locational preferences regarding synergies in first- and second-tier global cities. Secondly, principal component analysis distinguishes the executives regarding their activity pattern.

Methodology

The originality of this work lies in the development of an analytical framework and accompanying software program to test the environmental preferences of international managers. According to McCann and Mudambi (2004, 516), a "careful mapping of corporate information and decision making structures and inter-firm relations within a explicitly geographical setting" should be done. Using conjoint analysis executives' preferences in working environment, market environment and living environment can be investigated. The reason for selecting conjoint analysis is that this instrument offers a more realistic combination of explicit and implicit demands on the decision maker than other approaches. Psychologists and marketing researchers have successfully applied the instrument to a number of different problems (Green et al. 2001). Another important advantage is that international managers are familiar with conjoint analyses, since they use it as a decision-making tool for marketing purposes. Conducting test interviews, interviewees exhibited great interest in the application and were highly motivated to learn about the results. This stems from the point that the conjoint analysis is conducted with the interview and provides instant feedback. Then, factor analysis of the conjoint data uncovers activity patterns of international managers' synergy and success.

Conjoint analysis provides a feasible method of measuring management locational preferences (Plattner 2005). Instead of evaluating single characteristics, conjoint analysis reveals information hidden in the combination of characteristics. Rather than directly asking managers what they prefer in a location, or what attributes they find most important, conjoint analysis employs the more realistic context of those managers evaluating potential location profiles. These profiles are a combination of different locational characteristics. Moreover, the complexity of creating a preference ranking by the respondent is reduced. Thus, methodologically the characteristics

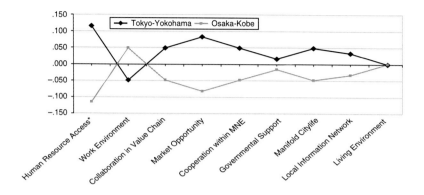

Figure 3.2   Results from the principal component analysis: Tokyo vs Osaka

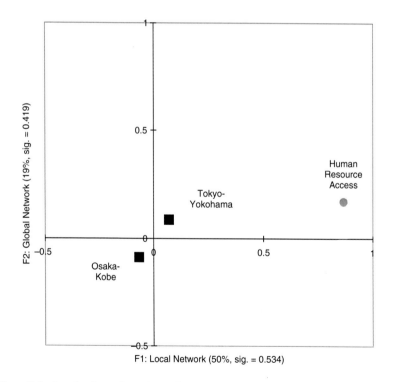

Figure 3.3   Results from the principal component analysis: global vs local network by city-location

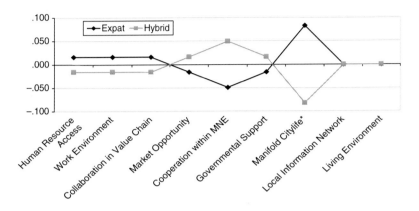

Figure 3.4   Results from the principal component analysis: expat vs hybrid manager

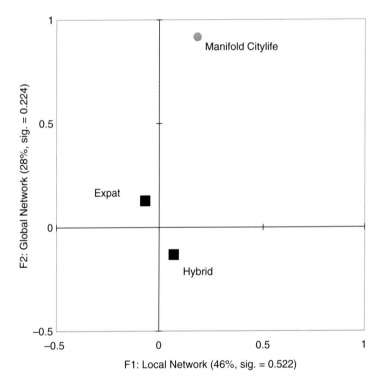

Figure 3.5   Results from the principal component analysis: global vs local network by manager type

must be independent of each other and there must be a complementary relation between the attributes. With regard to the research approach, three independent attributes were selected: the corporate environment, the market environment, and the living environment (see Table 3.1). These three environments are the context in which managers operate. Focusing on the main characteristics, the effect on locational preferences is measured via conjoint analysis.

Next, a full profile design creates a selection of two profiles, each containing three characteristics. The two profiles were presented to the manager. The manager selected a locational profile that fit his or her success needs best. Using conjoint analysis implies that the decision maker ranks each profile according to his or her preferences by paired choices. Having realistic profiles in mind, the managers select always the best set of characteristics instead of single locational features. An ordinal ranking of the profiles is generated, and after the implicit selection process an explicit evaluation and re-ranking can take place. Thereafter, the preference structure is analyzed by calculating the part-worth utility for the locational characteristics in the ranked profiles. Assuming that the distance between the ranks is equal, the order made by the international managers can be interpreted metrically. At the end of the analysis, a least square regression estimates the part-worth utility (Addelman 1962; Jacroux 1992; Klein 2002). The part-worth utility function is a quantitative expression of the locational preferences. The outcome of the above-mentioned methodologies is a clear comparative classification based on both quantitative as well as qualitative methodology. Based on the literature in the field of business environments and cross-cultural management, three success attributes were distinguished in preliminary interviews. As a result of these interviews, we reduced the number of variables to the three most important ones (see Table 3.1).

The attributes are defined as follows:

Table 3.1 Attributes and variables to distinguish locational preferences

Attributes	Variables		
Corporate Environment	Collaboration within the MNE	Human resource access	Working atmosphere
Market Environment	Cooperation with suppliers and customers in the value chain	Market opportunities	Governmental supportive setting
Living Environment	Livable local environment	Local information network	Manifold city life

Source: Key variables distinguished by a pre-test of foreign executive managers in June 2006

According to Schein (2005), the **corporate environment** is defined by three cognitive levels of organizational culture. We therefore distinguish three key components of the corporate environment abroad: the working atmosphere, the human resource access, and the collaboration in the MNE.

The *working atmosphere [WORK]* consists of a material and an informational level. Material elements include visible things such as facilities, offices, furnishings, displayed awards and recognition, and dress code. Informational elements include nonvisible elements such as the verbal and nonverbal interaction practices of employees with each other and with clients, suppliers, and partners. Both levels are necessary to analyze the impact of an individual workplace on the performance of a foreign executive manager. A mismatch can explain why change agents fail to achieve their goals. Underlying tacit cultural norms are generally not understood by expatriate managers before would-be change agents begin their actions in the foreign subsidiary. Hybrids have much more experience and they are embedded in the local context.

Next, *human resource access [HUMAN]* is crucial for management success. Especially in international business, expatriates need translators and mediators in the process of communicating with the local workforce more than do hybrid managers who possess in-depth language and cultural skills. Moreover, the latter are much asked after in negotiations along the value chain with local suppliers and customers. Thus, expatriates and hybrids need a different variety of human resources to help develop the culture established between foreign executives, local employees, and cooperation partners. Expressions of organizational identity, company slogans, mission statements, local, and personal values are embodied in the available work styles of the human resources. This can explain why a mismatch may lead to failure on the management side as well as the employee side.

Last but not least, the *collaboration within the MNE [COLLAB]* refers to the organization's tacit assumptions. These are unseen elements not cognitively identified in everyday interactions among organizational members. These collaborations are essential for successful coordination of the international production system. Here, expatriates are representatives of the corporate culture formulated in the headquarters. International managers see themselves as change agents implementing corporate strategy and educating the local staff members about corporate culture. Having too much cultural sensitivity can result in mission failure. Nevertheless, outside the first-tier global cities, sensitivity and tacit assumptions are required.

The **market environment** consists of market opportunities, cooperation with suppliers and customers in the value chain, and governmental supports. A market is an institution that links buyers and sellers to allow the exchange of goods or services. Therefore firms' *market opportunities [MARKT]* to buy or sell goods and services are a necessary condition for business success in the foreign market. Foreign executive managers have often a different point of view on the local markets than their counterparts. Expatriates come from international business, and they have to manage products already successful in other markets or develop new products under the actual market circumstances. In the latter, localizing managers are probably more suitable. New, locally adjusted products create potential advantages for the global product portfolio of the MNE as well. Lastly, in order to be successful, a foreign executive manager has to communicate the specific needs within the firm's network to achieve market shares and profit margins.

The advantages arising from *cooperation with suppliers and customers in the value chain [COOP]* can be realized by localizing managers more easily. Some parts of the chain may be local and others global. Specific customer needs and supplier abilities lead to adopted production methods and goods specification. As a result, the foreign executives' attitudes and cultural sensibility on cooperating in changing market environments is the second main factor in success. Notably, the *governmental supportive [SUPPORT]* setting influences market advantages with support for assets, financial as well as legal. There are converging technological circumstances such research, engineering, and production methods, but the main feature distinguishing markets are the legal systems. In addition, local standards as well as international requirements have to be met. For expatriate managers this can be an auxiliary expense, while for localizing managers it is a chance to optimize products. The methods used by a foreign executive determine business success or failure.

The key elements of the **living environment** consist of livable local environment, manifold city life, and the local information network. Foreign executive managers are under tremendous pressure to meet business targets. In order to rest and recover, a *livable local environment [LIFE]* is needed. There is no one environment that fits all; a suitable environment depends on the cultural background of the foreign executive and his or her individual skills related to socialization. For foreign executives, a livable local environment comprises mainly the location and characteristics of his or her residence and related goods which make living in a foreign country more comfortable. Expatriate managers and their families fashion their refuge as a small piece of their home country, while locals tend to adopt the foreign lifestyle in general and create a combination of the two worlds. However, each strategy is important to recovery from office work and for finding a work-life balance.

In addition, a *manifold city life [CITY]* supplies expatriate and local managers with a wealth of spaces such as restaurants, bars, museums, cinemas, and theaters. It also makes available high-quality health care and education, as well as access to other nodes in the global-city network. The feeling of being part of a dynamic environment is an intangible factor leading to business success. Differences between expatriates and hybrids arise out of the time dimension. Expatriates are distinguished by the demands they place on their environment, as they have limited time to stay, and their cost of living is covered. On the other hand, the hybrids think long term and become more integrated in the local society.

Within the livable local environment and the manifold city life a *local information network [NETWORK]* emerges. Private contacts and business contacts are overlapping parts of this network. This is an open source for information about business and issues of personal life. Moreover, it provides a source of direct feedback regarding a manager's actions that is usually missing in the workplace. Information circulates among the members of such a network very quickly with low barriers to communication. Nowadays information of this sort is locally available through electronic media even if the members of the individual network are physically active in other parts of the world. This network often enables an international manager to make the right decision at the right time.

Results

The outcome of the conjoint analyses shows that the international manager located in alpha global cities has a positive impact on demand for human capital and a negative impact on vertical cooperation. The last could be a side effect of the weak adaptability of executives in alpha global cities.

a) Executives with weak adaptability have a significantly (t-test, sig. < 0.01) stronger preference for human capital access than do executives with a strong ability to adapt;
b) executives with weak adaptability have a significantly (t-test, sig. < 0.05) weaker preference for cooperation in the value chain.

In the alpha global city, access to human resources is crucial. The investigation of foreign executive managers' locational preferences showed that the variable human resource access scores significantly higher than in the gamma global city. It seems that human resources or internationally skilled local subordinates are used to compensate for a lack of adaptation by the executives to the host culture. Those local employees are needed and facilitated to communicate in the local business context with suppliers and customers. This is reflected on

a) negative chi-square relation between human resource access and adaptability (Phi -0.290, Sig. < 0.067, C'V 0.290 Sig. $< .067$, CC 0.279 Sig. < 0.067).
b) three positive chi-square relations between
  cooperation in the value chain and adaptability (Phi 0.346 Sig. < 0.05, C'V 0.346 Sig. < 0.05, CC 0.327 Sig. < 0.05),
  cooperation in the value chain and discovery (Phi 0.3 Sig. $= 0.058$, C'V 0.3 Sig. < 0.058, CC 0.287 Sig. < 0.058), and
  cooperation and acculturation (Phi 0.354 Sig. < 0.05, C'V 0.354 Sig. < 0.05, CC 0.334 Sig. < 0.05).
Clearly, international managers and local managers have different locational preferences. They will be called expatriates and hybrid managers (see

Schlunze 2011, xx). Hybrid managers tend to cooperate significantly more with suppliers and customers than the expatriated managers (t-test, sig. < 0.05). This result lets us assume that localizing managers have advanced skills for socializing and intercultural communication.

According to the above-mentioned principal component analysis, preference patterns regarding successful management practices distinguish expatriate and hybrid managers as "Localizing", "Embedding", "Networking", and "Globalizing" (see Tables 3.2–3.4).

These four types of manager respond differently to market, corporate, and living environment. They also demand different environmental settings in order to achieve their business success.

The *localizing pattern* is characterized as international manager's personal communication in the living community. Managers' preferences for the livable local environment and the local information network are high, while the interest in the manifold city life is antipodal.

Second, the *embedding pattern* is characterized as international managers' operative communication at the workplace. Good working atmosphere is most important next to livable local environment, while collaboration in the MNE is in diametrical opposition.

Third, the *networking pattern* is characterized as international managers' operative communication in the business network. Those executives use the cooperation possibilities in the value chain as well as the local information network to be successful in business. For them, the general market opportunity is contrarious as an explicit factor.

Fourth, the *globalizing pattern* is characterized as managers' strategic communication of headquarters' commands to subsidiaries. The success of those managers is based on close collaboration within the MNE considering the governmental supportive setting in market regulation. The human resource

Table 3.2 Coefficients of the principal component analysis by city-location

Attributes	Tokyo-Yokohama	Osaka-Kobe	sig.
Human Resource Access*	.115	−.115	.048
Work Environment	−.049	.049	.402
Collaboration in Value Chain	.049	−.049	.360
Market Opportunity	.082	−.082	.193
Cooperation within MNE	.049	−.049	.402
Governmental Support	.016	−.016	.598
Manifold Citylife	.049	−.049	.309
Local Information Network	.033	−.033	.569
Living Environment	.000	.000	1.0

Table 3.3   Coefficients of the principal component analysis by manager type

Attributes	Expat	Hybrid	sig.
Human Resource Access	.016	–.016	.780
Work Environment	.016	–.016	.780
Collaboration in Value Chain	.016	–.016	.761
Market Opportunity	–.016	.016	.796
Cooperation within MNE	–.049	.049	.402
Governmental Support	–.016	.016	.598
Manifold Citylife*	.082	–.082	.088
Local Information Network	.000	.000	1,000
Living Environment	.000	.000	1,000

Table 3.4   Result of the rotated component matrix[a]

	Component			
	1 Localizer	2 Embedder	3 Networker	4 Globalizer
CE Human Resource Access	.266	–2.02E-02	4.80E-02	–.831
CE Good Working Atmosphere	–.123	.824	.139	–.165
CE Collaboration in the MNE	–9.47E-02	–.581	.291	.471
ME Market Opportunities	–7.17E-02	.173	–.762	3.42E-02
ME Cooperation Possibilities in the Value Chain	–.142	.119	.7235	6.57E-03
ME Government Supportive Setting	.272	–.166	4.26E-02	.565
LE Manifold City Life	–.845	7.36E-02	.141	.115
LE Local Information Network	.587	.199	.502	5.54E-02
LE Livable Local Environment	.488	.597	–7.10E-02	.262

Extraction Method: Principal Component Analysis
Rotation Method: Varimax with Kasier Normalization

[a]Rotation converged in 9 iterations

Source: Own Survey 2007.

access is complementary. However, they do not always succeed to create synergy in the intercultural workplace. They fail if their locational preferences are not balanced and when they are not congruent with the real locational characteristics of their corporate, market, and living environment.

Typology of international managers in the global city

The conclusive thesis is that international managers and especially expatriate managers concentrate mainly in alpha global cities. Human resource access, market opportunities, and livable living conditions are more important for their managerial success than other corporate, market, and life environmental characteristics. Due to their specific control practices and embeddedness in the local/national business environment, international managers do have different advantages in the extent to which they adjust to first- and second-tier global cities. Indeed, global strategies and systems have had greater impact on management practices within first-tier global cities, whereas in second-tier cities the degree of internationalization lags increasingly.

The results showed that managerial success cannot be created merely by adjusting to a different cultural environment. Instead, a balanced approach enables the foreign executive manager, whether expatriate or hybrid, to be successful. Those managers were conscious that they need to have flexibility when switching between their own and the local approach. Acculturation, if successfully conducted, is mutual with regard to the host and the home cultures. Further, foreign executives in the first-tier global city do not feel that the local staff wants them to adjust. Various explanations are possible.

One reason might be that the main role of the foreign managing director or president is to ensure the input from the parent company. Another, negative reason, would be that the foreigner manager remains outside the flow of information, and decision making therefore is basically entrusted to the local management. Workplace problems, however, also have a spatial dimension. International managers need to embed their leadership practices into the host country's work culture. It can be assumed that only managing executives who have mastered the switch between the MNE's global style and the local or Japanese style of leadership are effective and perform well. Nonetheless, in first-tier global cities more similarities than differences among local and foreign leaders are expected.

Obviously, the hybrid manager tends to have different locational preferences than the typical expatriate manager. The expatriate manager will emphasize access to human resources; the hybrid manager – since he or she is capable of analyzing the local market him or herself – is more balanced in his or her locational preferences but prefers significantly more to make use of the local information network in order to achieve business success. Based on his or her local expertise, the hybrid manager's vision, for example maintaining local markets and improving product quality, will be understood by the local employees. The hybrid manager will, however, sometimes find it difficult to communicate with headquarters where the focus is on growth rates and other strategic intent of expansion. Not following up such growth plans will endanger the empowerment granted by headquarters. In this case, the hybrid manager will ultimately face difficulties achieving success.

In some cases, the expatriate manager may be totally trusted by the parent company, even if the parent company does not understand the management process in Japan. If the company employs a decentralized control strategy, an expatriate manager with networking abilities who enjoys the necessary cultural knowledge is most valuable to guide the management process. Especially in the alpha global city, expatriate manager contributions become invaluable since the market and living environment are less international.

Acknowledgment

I gratefully acknowledge the funding and support I have received from the Alexander von Humboldt Foundation and from the Japan Society for the Promotion of Science (P05716). Thanks are due to Professor R.D. Schlunze, with whom I discussed and presented preliminary results at the 2007 Second Global Conference on Economic Geography. Moreover, thanks are due to William W. Baber and Dylan Southard, who carefully read and helped to improve the clarity of this research piece. The analytical approach on locational preferences was presented at the 52nd Annual Conference of the North American Meeting of the Regional Science Association. The research framework has been introduced at the OAG and at the Tokyo conference of the Association of Japanese Geographers in March 2007 and Leeds 2007 as well as at the 2010 1st SIEM Conference on Managerial Geography, Kyoto.

References

Addelman, S. (1962) Orthogonal main-effect plans for asymmetrical factorial experiments. *Technometrics* 4(1): 21–46.
Beaverstock, J.V. (1996) Migration, knowledge and social interaction: Expatriate labour within investment banks. *Area* 28(4): 457–70.
Dicken, P. (2003) *Global Shift: Reshaping the Global Economic Map in the 21st Century.* 4th ed. London: Sage Publications.

(J) in Japanese

Forsgren, M., and J. Johanson (1992) Managing in international multi-centre firms. In M. Forsgren and J. Johanson (eds), *Managing Networks in International Business*, 19–31. Philadelphia: Gordon and Breach.

Green, P. E., A. M. Krieger, and Y. Wind (2001) Thirty years of conjoint analysis: Reflections and prospects. *Interfaces* 31(3): 56–73.

Hamel, G., and C.K. Prahalad (1994) *Competing for the Future*. Boston: Harvard Business School Press.

Håkansson, H., and J. Johanson (1993) The network as a governance structure: Interfirm cooperation beyond markets and hierarchies. In G. Grabher (ed.), *The Embedded Firm: On the Socioeconomics of Industrial Networks*, 35–51. London: Routledge.

Hirai, T. (2004) *Corporate Headquarter Function in Osaka: Is It Still Shifting to Tokyo?* . http://www.pref.osaka.jp/aid/kisokennkyuu/ronsyu18–06.pdf (Retrieved February 28, 2007).

Jacroux, M. (1992) A note on the determination and construction of minimal orthogonal main-effect plans. *Technometrics* 34(1): 92–6.

Jones, A. (2002) The 'global city' misconceived: The myth of 'global management' in translation service firms. *Geoforum* 33: 335–50.

Klein, M. (2002) Die Conjoint-Analyse: Eine Einführung in das Verfahren mit einem Ausblick auf mögliche sozialwissenschaftliche Anwendungen. *ZA-Information* 50: 7–45.

McCann, P., and R. Mudambi (2004) The location behavior of the multinational enterprise: Some analytical issues. *Growth and Change* 35(4): 491–524.

MITI (2005) *Dai38kai gaishikeikigyo no doko: Heisei 16nen gaishikeikigyo doko chosa* (38th Trend of foreign companies: Survey on the trend of foreign firms in 2004), National Printing Bureau. (J)

Nonaka, I., and H. Takeuchi (1995) *The Knowledge-Creating Company: How Japanese Companies Create the Dynamics of Innovation*. Oxford, New York: Oxford University Press.

Nonaka, I., and H. Takeuchi (1997) *Die Organisation des Wissens*. Frankfurt: Campus Verlag.

Oinas, P. (1998) The embedded firm: Prelude for a revived geography of enterprise, Helsinki: Helsinki School of Economics and Business, *Acta Universitatis Oeconomicae Helsingiensis* A-143.

Plattner, M. (2005) Mobility of Industrial Locations – A Conjoint Analytical Approach. *Proceedings of the Final Open Conference COST A-17 Small and Medium Enterprises, Economic Development and Regional Convergence in Europe*, Barcelona.

Sassen, S. (2001) *The Global City: New York, London, Tokyo*. 2nd edition. Woodstock: Princeton University Press.

Schein, E.H. (2005) *Organizational Culture and Leadership*. 3rd ed. San Francisco: Jossey-Bass.

Schlunze, R.D, and M. Plattner (2007) Evaluating international managers' practices and locational preferences in the global city. *Ritsumeikan Business Review* 36(1): 63–89.

Suzuki, Y., Y. Sakurai, and A. Sato (2005) *Takokusekikigyo no ricchiron* (Location theory of Multinational Enterprise). Hara shobo. (J)

Taira, A. (2005) *Nihonkigyo no kaigai ricchi tenkai to senryaku: toshiken/ chiikiken sukeru ni okeru chirigakuteki bunseki* (Overseas locational development and strategy of Japanese firms: Geographical analysis on city and regional scale). Kokon shoin. (J)

Taylor, P.J., D.R.F. Walker, and J.V. Beaverstock (2002) Firms and their global service network. In S. Sasssen (ed.), *Global Networks: Linked Cities*, 93–115. New York: Routledge.

Thrift, N. (2000) Performing cultures in the new economy. *Annals of the Association of American Geographers* 90(4): 674–92.

Whitley, R. (1999) *Divergent Capitalisms: The Social Structuring and Change of Business Systems*. Oxford, New York: Oxford University Press.

Part II
Spaces of International Economy

4
Managing Global Cities through Corporate Network Analysis
Ronald S. Wall

Global city networks

Today, academics and policymakers generally concentrate on subnational regions as the essential unit of economic activity, and most studies fail to adequately conceptualize urban regional development in an era of globalization (Dicken and Malmberg 2001). It is arguable, however, that global production networks and regional assets need to be coupled, mediating activities across different geographical and organizational scales (Coe et al. 2004; Dicken et al. 2001). This concept is not entirely new. Friedmann and Wolff (1982) conceptualized global cities as "command centers", regulating the "international division of labor", and Gereffi et al. (1994) defined global commodity chains as interorganizational networks of products that increasingly tie enterprises and states together within the world economy. These initial approaches have led to various studies on cities and globalization (e.g. Sassen 1991; Amin and Thrift 1992; Castells 1996; Cohen 1981; Meijer 1993; Abbott 1997; Godfrey and Zhou 1999), but the number of empirical global-city network studies remains quite limited. It is said that this is due to scarcity of "relational" data (Smith and Timberlake 1995; Taylor et al. 2002). To date, only a handful of relational studies exist – for example, on international banks (Meyer 1986), advanced producer firms (Taylor 2004), multinational corporation (MNC) governance (Rozenblat and Pumain 2006; Alderson and Beckfield 2004; Wall 2009), and corporate directorates (Carroll 2007). These studies attempt to understand the significance of corporate ownership without privileging one particular geographic scale (Coe et al. 2004).

Multinational corporations and location choice

The gradual integration of nations within our globalizing world is strongly characterized by the economic networks formed by multinational headquarters and their various subsidiaries located across the globe (Barba

Navaretti and Venables 2004; Brakman and Garretsen 2008). A multinational corporation (MNC) is a firm that has the ability to coordinate production across national boundaries from a central point of strategic decision making (Cowling and Sudgen 1987). These cross-border operations lead to a complex organization of economic activities at different geographical scales, such as decisions to concentrate or disperse a firm's functions. MNC networks therefore represent distinct loci of power that have a significant impact on the contemporary global economy. For instance, the top 200 global corporations (1999) accounted for approximately 30 percent of world GDP (Anderson and Cavanaugh 2000), and the top 500 multinationals (2004) accounted for 90 percent of world foreign direct investment and 50 percent of global trade (Rugman 2005). Much of this corporate activity consists of transnational exchanges which are typically controlled by corporate headquarters that determine the magnitude of foreign investment, the transfer of technology, access to international markets, the repatriation of profits, the number of employees, and so on.

It is often argued that MNCs locate their production plants all over the globe and so geography is irrelevant (Cairncross 2001; Friedman 2007). However, the world is certainly not flattening (Linders et al. 2008; McCann 2008), and instead MNCs carefully choose headquarter and subsidiary locations, based on the qualitative characteristics of nations (Brakman and Van Marrewijk 2008). Although some nations are clearly larger and geographically less remote than others, economic and geographic differences alone cannot justify the disproportionality in the corporate network. In his book *The Competitive Advantage of Nations*, Porter (1990) shows that corporate and national successes are interdependent, based on the development of skills and knowledge in particular industries, and on connections between clusters of businesses and the attributes of their national home bases. Therefore, it is interesting to demonstrate how attributes related to competitiveness, such as GDP, technological development and business openness, relate to the corporate connectedness of nations and the number of connections between nations. In the *first* analysis, using national indicators from various sources (e.g. the World Economic Forum), it is the aim to show that competitiveness is critical to the corporate connectivity of nations. National indicators are used in this study, due to the unavailability of reliable worldwide urban indicators.

City competition based on corporate connectivity

Because economic competition takes place at increasingly larger geographical scales than those of the traditional city (Kloosterman and Musterd 2001; Van Oort et al. 2008), administrative boundaries have become insufficient devices of control (Friedmann 1986). Therefore, urban competitiveness is considered as a function of its network, in which cities are highly influenced or disturbed by other cities in the interaction network (Pred 1977) and where urban development can no longer be understood without considering the networks and systems to which cities belong (Rozenblat and Pumain 2007). Interest in the concept of urban performance and competitiveness has led to many urban ranking lists, in which cities are compared on the basis of economic performance (Kresl and Singh 1999), multinational presence (Taylor 2004), creativity and innovativeness (Florida 2005), access and quality of services (Kaufman et al. 2005), or environmental sustainability (Dutzik et al. 2003). However, although most studies on competitiveness assume that cities compete vis-à-vis one another, little attention is paid to actually measuring the intensity of competition between cities. Most national planning policies (e.g. Randstad 2006) still consider the spatial proximity of cities as being decisive to their economic performance, hereby neglecting their transnational networks (Van Oort et al. 2006; Taylor et al. 2008). This is odd, considering that many studies (e.g. Camagni and Salone 1993; Batten 1995; Davies 1998; Carroll 2007) stress the need for an "intellectual transition" in the conceptualization of urban external relations (Meijers 2007).

In order to validate urban competitiveness, it is important to understand the extent to which cities compete, and where this competition comes from. Shifting the focus to a networked understanding of collaboration and competition between cities can loosen the assumption that all cities are connected and compete with each other (Markusen and Schrock 2006). In this way, academics and policymakers can start to understand why certain cities are more capable of attracting and sustaining global corporations, or as Ann Markusen (1996) terms it, the puzzle of stickiness in an increasingly slippery world. Along these lines, network analysis can serve as a useful device to reveal the economic interaction between cities and determine their relative levels of development and competition. Therefore, the *second* analysis, based on insights from niche overlap theory (Hannan and Freeman 1977), employs a unique model for measuring the intensity of competition between cities, based on their functional linkages. Competition is operationalized as an attribute of the relationship between two cities, which is regarded as the lowest unit of analysis at which competition can be measured (Sohn 2004). In this context, it is argued that cities are in competition to the extent that they serve the same geographical market, for particular functions within the urban system. As there are many dimensions in which cities compete (Lever and Turok 1999), the focus will predominantly be on economic competition between cities in terms of attracting and retaining firms.

Toward a theory of city network management

Rather than being perceived as a mechanistic production function, the firm can be seen as a contested site for discursive and material constructions at various organizational and spatial scales. In this manner, the firm can be considered as a constellation of network relations governed by social actors. Rather than being a mechanistic production function, it is a contested site for discursive and material structures at different organizational and spatial scales (Yeung 2005). According to De Filippis (2001), networks encompass hierarchies of power; otherwise, they would not be networks in the first place. There would be no incentive for powerful actors to remain in a network if they did not disproportionately gain from the benefits of network participation (Lin et al. 2001; Christopherson and Clark 2007). In this light, it is interesting to understand how corporate power in the global corporate network affects the fate of cities (Alderson and Beckfield 2004). Although corporate boundaries are increasingly difficult to empirically determine (Sanchez 1999), it is important to map the relations of firms in the context of other actors and institutions in society and space. In this manner, we need to identify the various actors which determine corporate networks, such as business units, labor unions, and municipalities, and start to understand the intentions and motives of these social actors and the related power in their networks and how these are embedded in particular spaces (Yeung 2005). Furthermore, all social actors are not bound together in the same territories. Instead, there are distinct spaces for actors to engage in network relationships. These spaces can be at the local level, like business centers and intercity spaces, such as contractual webs of mergers and acquisitions. In this way, firms can again start to focus on their organizational capacity and the benefits to actors in society and space (McNee 1960). Based on this, the *third* aspect of this chapter concerns the conceptualization of how actors can benefit from knowledge of their contending nodes (firms, cities or nations) and use this to manage the future development of their economic networks.

Data and methodology

The data used in this research concerns ownership relations (51 percent or more share) between headquarters and subsidiaries worldwide, based on Fortune and LexisNexis databases (2005). Although MNCs have global reach, they differ by economic size and geographic location, which subsequently determines the total number of corporate connections and strengths of the ties between cities. The resulting global network holds a total of 9243 corporate ties between headquarters and subsidiaries, connecting 2259 unique cities worldwide. The data is original because cities are not preselected, as is usually the case, but instead include all cities that exhibit headquarter or subsidiary ties. Based on this data, the corporate *centrality* and *structure* of cities has been defined for each scale. *Centrality* is a measure of total corporate ownership ties that a city has with other cities. This can be measured in two ways: outdegree and indegree. *Outdegree* is a measure of the number of headquarters that a city holds and the number of linkages these have with subsidiaries in other cities. It is a measure of a city's economic power over other cities (Alderson and Beckfield 2004). *Indegree* is a measure of the number of subsidiaries located within a city, and the number of linkages these have to headquarters in other cities. It measures how dependent other cities are on a particular city. *Structure* is a measure of the linkage strengths that a city has with other cities, but also to which cities in the network it is connected. Also, geographic information system (GIS) analysis has been used to give insight into the global distribution of the corporate networks.

By aggregating the data to the national level, a worldwide corporate network between countries is constructed between 43 home countries with at least one outgoing corporate connection and 110 host countries that have at least one incoming corporate connection. Using this initial data, the *first* analysis could be carried out. In the first analysis, both home- and host-country determinants were collected to estimate the centralities (nodal values) and structures (linkage values) of the network. For home and host countries, this concerns *GDP, GDP per worker, remoteness of the country, openness to business, technological exports, stock market capitalization, credit provision, fuels exports, quality of institutions* and *corporate taxes*. For the linkage model, *physical distance, regional integration agreement (RIA) dummy, common language dummy, sectoral distance* and *GDP difference* have been used. Because standard OLS regression models result in inefficient and biased estimates when used on count data, a negative binomial regression model is used to better estimate the network. Considering the space constraints of this chapter, the argumentation behind these variables and techniques is excluded. The working paper can be requested from the author (Wall et al. 2008).

Concerning the second analysis, a subset of the original global corporate network has been used – namely the advanced producer services network. This is because cities which hold large counts of service firms are considered to be key command points in the organization of the world economy (Sassen 1991; Taylor 2005). First, GIS has been used to map the geographic distribution of the producer services network. Network competition is explained using the provided diagram (Figure 4.1). (1) Cities A and G are linked to different cities (to cities B and C and cities E and F, respectively). For this reason, the similarity between their geographical markets is 0 percent, meaning that there is no urban competition between cities A and G. (2) Cities B and C have exactly the same linkage structure, because both cities are linked only to cities A and D. Hence, the similarity between their networks is 100 percent, meaning that the geographical markets of cities B and C maximally overlap. (3) Cities A and D have a partly overlapping linkage structure. Although cities A and D are both linked to cities B and C, city D is also linked to cities E and F. Hence, the intensity of competition between cities A and D is intermediate, as their geographical markets only partly overlap. The relative Manhattan distance model is used to measure the relative distance or dissimilarity in niche between two cities in the city network. The full paper on this technique can be downloaded (Burger et al. 2008).

Table 4.1 Negative binomial pseudo maximum likelihood regression on the number of corporate connections between countries

	Model (1) - C_{ij}	Model (2) - C_{ij}	Model (3) - C_{ij}	Model (4) - C_{ij}
Home Country				
GDP	1.34 (.069)**	1.36 (.076)**		
GDP per worker	0.23 (.076)**	0.24 (.074)**		
Remoteness	-1.56 (.154)**	-1.52 (.146)**		
Openness	0.99 (.198)**	1.04 (.141)**		
Technology exports	0.37 (.102)**	0.39 (.100)**		
Stock market capitalization	0.59 (.103)**	0.59 (0.97)**		
Credit provision	0.34 (.181)	0.35 (.175)*		
Host country				
GDP	0.62 (0.47)**		0.60 (0.35)**	
GDP per worker	-0.22 (.055)**		-0.23 (.047)**	
Remoteness	1.31 (.161)**		0.95 (.129)**	
Openness	0.35 (.104)**		0.32 (.080)**	
Technology exports	0.05 (.056)		0.05 (.046)	
Fuels exports	0.02 (.037)		0.02 (.031)	
Quality of institutions	0.45 (.091)**		0.46 (.078)**	
Corporate taxes	-0.49 (.451)		-0.73 (.038)	
Bilateral				
Physical distance	-0.70 (.073)**	-0.71 (.073)**	-0.48 (.064)**	-0.41 (.059)**
RIA dummy	-0.13 (.108)	-0.31 (.115)**	0.23 (.101)*	0.15 (.099)
Common language dummy	0.32 (.106)**	0.34 (.175)**	0.35 (0.98)**	0.36 (.098)**
Common history dummy	0.22 (.146)	0.14 (.133)	0.70 (.157)**	0.54 (.134)**
Sectoral distance	-0.02 (.050)	0.06 (.110)	-0.03 (.047)	0.06 (.133)
GDP difference	-0.15 (.046)**	-0.15 (.066)*	-0.17 (.033)**	-0.19 (.036)**
Observations	4687	4687	4687	4687
Home country fixed effects	NO	NO	YES	YES
Host country fixed effects	NO	YES	NO	YES
Log pseudolikelihood	-2251	-2170	-1921	-1809
AIC	4547	4587	3957	3936
LR test of overdispersion	1028.2**	685.4**	402.9**	142.8**

**p<0.01, *p<0.05; robust standard errors in parentheses. All variables are in natural logs, except for dummy variables, quality of institutions, and corporate taxes.
Source: Wall et al. 2009.

Results on network performance and competition

Network performance

In the GIS map (Figure 4.2) the distribution of intercity corporate networks, aggregated to the national level, is shown. It is clear that North America, Europe and Pacific Asia form the cores of the world economy. The data is also mapped (Figure 4.3) using UCINET software (Borgatti et al. 2002), in which the most important nations and their linkages are illustrated. Models 1–4 (Table 4.1) present the estimates for the negative binomial regression model. Turning to the main results, it can be inferred that home-country-specific ownership advantages (Models 1 and 2) play an important role in explaining the geography of corporate networks. First of all, the size and wealth of the home country have a positive and significant effect on the corporate connectivity between countries. An increase in home country GDP by 1 percent increases the expected corporate connectivity by over 1.3 percent, while an increase in GDP per worker by 1 percent increases the expected corporate connectivity by about 0.23 percent. This signifies not only that the size of the pool of potential investors is an important determinant of the geography of global corporate networks, but also that the availability of economic resources matters. Besides size and wealth, other home-country-specific ownership advantages appear to be important, such as a home country's degree of openness, remoteness, level of technology, and stock market capitalization. With respect to the host-country effects (Models 1 and 3), it can be observed that market size, GDP per worker, remoteness, openness, level of technology and quality of institutions have an statistically significant effect on the expected corporate connectivity. This signifies that a mixture of market-seeking, efficiency-seeking and strategic-asset-seeking motivations of firms shapes the geography of global corporate networks. The expected corporate connectivity increases with the market size, openness, and quality of the institutional environment of the host country and decreases with the wage level of the host country. With respect to bilateral variables (Model 4), it is found that physical distance, cultural proximity and difference in GDP all have a statistically significant effect on the expected number of corporate connections, while having a Regional Integration Agreement does not. Taking the effects of the host-country and bilateral variables together, it can be inferred that most foreign direct investment is indeed horizontal and not vertical. First of all, the market and strategic asset seeking motives (exemplified by GDP, remoteness, openness, and technology exports variables) appear to be more important than the efficiency-seeking and natural-resource-seeking motives (mainly exemplified by the GDP per worker and fuels exports variables).

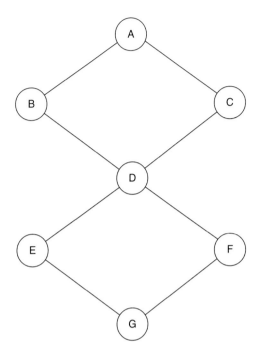

Figure 4.1   Functional linkages in a hypothetical urban system
Source: Wall et al. 2009.

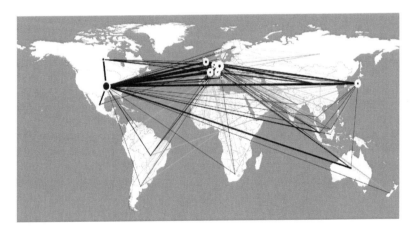

Figure 4.2   GIS map of the distribution of corporate connectivity (ownership shares) between nations.
Source: Wall et al. 2009.

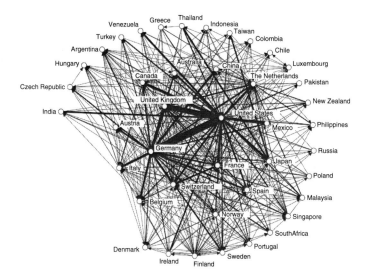

Figure 4.3   UCINET network diagram of the distribution of corporate connectivity between nations.

Source: Wall et al. 2009.

Network competition

First, the global distribution of the producer service network is shown in the GIS map (Figure 4.4). Again it is evident that advanced producer services are concentrated in North America, Europe and Pacific Asia. A clear north/ south divide is seen. Applying the resulting competition measure derived from the previously discussed Manhattan Model, a matrix of the intensity of competition between these 20 financial centers in the global-city network is derived using UCINET software (Figure 4.5). Overall, the competition coefficient ranged from 0 percent (e.g. Berlin–Osaka) to 41 percent (Frankfurt–Zurich). The nodes in the network represent the different global cities, where the shade and shape of the node represents the continent on which the city is situated (Europe, North America or Asia). The node sizes represent the position of a city in the corporate intercity network of advanced producer services based on the total number of outward linkages the city has. This position can range from that of a primary global city (London, New York, Paris) to that of a global city with relatively few commanding relations to other cities (Hong Kong, Madrid, Toronto). If there is no linkage drawn between two cities (e.g. Toronto–Madrid), the competition coefficient is lower than 5 percent. This means that there is hardly any geographical market overlap between the two cities for the urban function under consideration. In other words, both cities command totally different

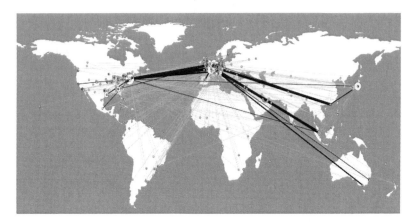

Figure 4.4   GIS map of the intercity distribution of advanced producer service connectivity (ownership relations).

Source: Wall et al. 2009.

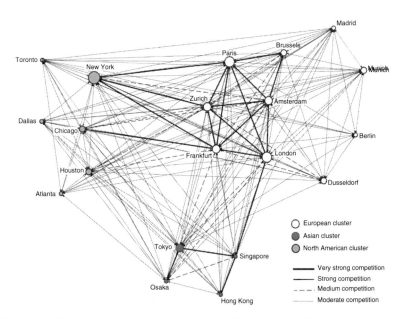

Figure 4.5   Competition in the corporate intercity network of advanced producer services

Source: Wall et al. 2009.

cities in the advanced producer services network. A thin intercity linkage (e.g. Munich–Amsterdam) indicates that the competition coefficient ranges between 5 percent and 15 percent, which means that the degree of geographic market overlap between the two cities ranges from low to average for this urban function. A dashed intercity linkage (e.g. London–Tokyo) indicates an average degree of geographical market overlap between the two cities with a competition coefficient that lies between 15 percent and 25 percent. The second-thickest linkage (e.g. Amsterdam–Brussels) signifies that the competition coefficient falls between 25 percent and 35 percent, which indicates an average-to-strong degree of geographical market overlap. Finally, the thickest intercity linkage (e.g. Frankfurt–Paris) indicates that the competition coefficient is over 35 percent, which points to a strong degree of geographic market overlap for advanced producer services between these two cities and indicates that both cities command similar cities to a large extent. For this reason, the intensity of competition between these cities is fiercest.

It is seen that producer service competition between cities has a strong geographical dimension. Competition between cities that are geographically proximate tends to be stronger than competition between cities that are geographically distant. In general, the intensity of competition between cities situated on different continents is low to average. Moreover, if there is a strong intensity of competition between cities situated on different continents, there is also at least one primary global city (London or New York) involved. This is not surprising, as these primary world cities serve a more diverse geographical market with larger geographical scope than do other cities in the global-city network (see also Derudder and Witlox 2008). Applying a hierarchical cluster analysis (Johnson 1967) to the competition coefficients, two major clusters of contending cities are identified, namely (1) Northern Transatlantic Seaboard (London, Frankfurt, Zurich, Paris, Amsterdam, Brussels, New York) and (2) Pacific Asia (Tokyo, Osaka, Hong Kong, Singapore). From this, it can be inferred that the intensity of competition that Tokyo receives from the other large global cities (London, New York, Paris) as command center (of advanced producer services) is rather limited. Whereas Tokyo's commanding intercity relations are primarily directed toward Asian cities (for over 70 percent), the commanding intercity relations of New York and Paris are predominantly directed at European and North American cities. London is in this respect the most globally oriented city, as it is not only strongly connected to cities in Europe and North America, but also has linkages to cities in Pacific Asia (particularly Hong Kong and Singapore). These findings once more stress that not all global cities serve the same "hinterworld" (cf. Taylor 2001; Taylor and Walker 2004). Moreover, competition is fiercest between cities at the top of the urban hierarchy. Smaller cities such as Atlanta, Berlin, Toronto, Dallas and Madrid face relatively little economic competition from the other global cities in the sample. This is related to the fact that the commanding relations of these cities have a primarily regional scope. In other words, such cities have a relatively regionally oriented hinterworld. For example, over two-thirds of the commanding relations of Madrid remain within southern Europe and go to cities like Barcelona and Milan. Likewise, over 90 percent of the commanding linkages of Toronto do not leave Canada. This is in line with the research conducted by Derudder and Witlox (2008), who find that the intercity relations of the most important global cities in terms of network connectivity are predominantly global in scope, while the intercity relations of the less well-connected cities in the global-city network have a more regional scope.

Conceptualizing urban network management

So far it has been shown that there is a strong relationship between territorial development and corporate connectivity and that network analysis can be used to identify a city's true competitors. The results show generic trends common to the entire system. It is also evident that specific trends can be identified, for instance for home and host countries. However, these analyses are still elementary, and more specific analyses need to be done on different types of regions of the world (e.g. developing and developed regions, or individual countries or cities). For this, more elaborate datasets are required. However, based on the hypothetical model (Figure 4.6), a conceptualization of future urban management can be made. The nodes could represent firms, cities or nations, depending on the scale at which the corporate network is aggregated. Let us imagine that A–D are the most competitive nodes derived from a much larger set of nodes and that they are competing in a common industry. A–D are each connected to an array of nodes. These linkages could represent trade, foreign direct investment or corporate ownership. It means that actors situated in these nodes exchange some form of economic activity across time and space. These activities can be different or the same, depending on the industry. As discussed earlier, nodes are in competition to the extent that they (1) hold the same functional exchange (e.g. manufacturing or business services) and (2) serve the same geographic market for the particular functions within the system. In the diagram, the dark gray nodes represent the functional and geographic overlap of nodes A–D. Hence, this area represents the "niche market" of these nodes. Furthermore, as demonstrated in the first analysis, the exchange taking place between nodes is dependent on the resources found within the nodes (e.g. GDP, level of technology, stock market capitalization). In reality, a mixture of market-seeking, efficiency-seeking and strategic-asset-seeking motivations of firms shape the geography of global corporate networks. In this, the expected corporate connectivity increases with the market size, openness and quality of the institutional environment of the host country and decreases with the wage level of the host country.

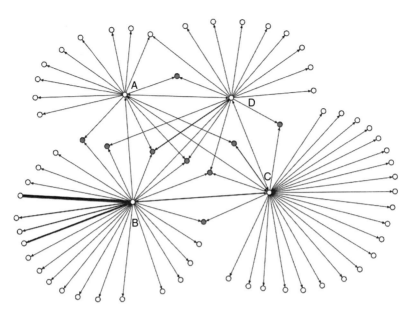

Figure 4.6 Hypothetical model to explain urban management in relation to network performance and competition

Source: Wall 2010.

As shown earlier, bilateral variables (e.g. physical distance, cultural proximity) also have a statistically significant effect on the expected number of corporate connections. Based on the above, it is argued that actors can utilize this knowledge to improve the collaborative and competitive relationships of their nodes (firms, cities, or nations). Let us say that node A ranks lowest of the four competitive nodes, due to its weaker connections. Actors in node A (e.g. corporate or urban managers) can first identify the specific actors in the market overlap nodes (gray nodes) and find out which resources in node B are causal to this relationship. This can provide essential knowledge to node A on how to improve required resources which can enable it to better compete against node B. Secondly, node A could investigate why, for instance, node B and node C are connected to more individual nodes (white nodes) and why certain linkages are more powerful (thickness of tie). This kind of knowledge would enable node A to investigate and gain access to these markets. By knowing which nodes these are (firms, cities or nations), investigations can be carried out to establish the determinants that are causal to node B and node C's ties with these individual nodes. By developing these resources in node A, it can be expected that in future, node A can better compete against node B and node C. Based on this hypothetical model and the empirical analyses discussed earlier, it is imaginable that a network methodology can be developed over time which can serve as an interesting device for different levels of management.

Conclusion

In this chapter it is argued that because economic competition takes place at increasingly larger geographic scale than that of the traditional city, a new form of urban management is needed which accommodates and utilizes knowledge of these higher scales – a new form of urban management that combines knowledge of the city as a place to the city as a network. The relationship between territorial development and corporate network connectivity has been demonstrated, as well as a method to identify which cities are common competitors. Based on the explorative analyses, an initial conceptual model has been posited which could start to tie the separate disciplines of economic geography, social network analysis, corporate management and urban management together. In this light, the most essential contribution of this model is that it enables actors in nodes to become more specific about which competitors, resources and markets they are associated with. The model needs much conceptual and methodological improvement, and the relationship with management needs to be thoroughly developed. A weakness of the results discussed is that they represent only cross-sectional data – a momentary snapshot of the network in time. Future analyses should acquire longitudinal datasets, in which the transformation of the network over time can be observed. This can be useful to estimate future developments of the global-city network and hereby add essential value to a future network management model.

Literature

Abbott, C. (1997). The international city hypothesis: An approach to the recent history of U.S. cities. *Journal of Urban History* 24: 28–52.

Alderson, A.S., and J. Beckfield. (2004). Power and position in the world city system. *American Journal of Sociology* 109: 811–51.

Amin, A., and N. Thrift. (1992). Neo-Marshallian nodes in global networks. *International Journal of Urban & Regional Research* 16: 571–87.

Anderson, S., and J. Cavanaugh. (2000). *Field guide to the global economy*. New Press.

Barba Navaretti, G., and A.J. Venables. (2004). *Multinational firms in the world economy*. Princeton, NJ: Princeton University Press.

Batten, D.F. (1995). Network Cities: Creative urban agglomerations for the 21st Century. *Urban Studies* 32: 313–27.

Borgatti, S.P., M.G. Everett, and L.C. Freeman. (2002). UCINET 6 for Windows: Social network analysis Software. Analytic Technologies, Needham, MA. http://www.analytictech.com/ucinet/ucinet.htm.

Brakman, S., and H. Garretsen. (2008). Foreign direct investment and the multinational enterprise: An introduction. In S. Brakman and H. Garretsen (eds), *Foreign direct investment and the multinational enterprise*, 1–10. Cambridge, MA: MIT Press.

Brakman, S., and C. Van Marrewijk. (2008). It's a big world after all: On the economic impact of location and distance. *Cambridge Journal of Regions, Economy and Society* 1: 411–37.

Burger, M.J., R.S. Wall, and G.A.V.D. Knaap. (2008). Measuring urban competition on the basis of flows between cities: Some evidence from the world city network. *GaWC Research Bulletin* 273 (A).

Cairncross, F. (2001). *The death of distance: How the communications revolution is changing our lives.* Cambridge, MA: Harvard Business School Publishing.

Camagni, R., and C. Salone. (1993). Network urban structures in Northern Italy: Elements for a theoretical framework. *Urban Studies* 30: 1053–64.

Carroll, W.K. (2007). Global cities in the global corporate network. *Environment and Planning A* 39: 2297–323.

Castells, M. (1996). *The rise of the network society.* Oxford: Blackwell.

Christopherson, S., and J. Clark. (2007). Power in firm networks: What it means for regional innovation systems. *Regional Studies* 41: 1223–36.

Coe, N. M., M. Hess, H.W-C. Yeung, P. Dicken, and J. Henderson. (2004). 'Globalizing' regional development: A global production networks perspective. *Transactions of the Institute of British Geographers* 29(4): 468–84.

Cohen, R.B. (1981). The new international division of labor, multinational corporations, and urban hierarchy. In M. Dear and A. Scott (eds), *Urbanization and urban planning in capitalist society*, 287–315. New York: Methuen.

Cowling, K., and R. Sudgen. (1987). Market exchange and the concept of the transnational corporation. *British Review of Economic Issues* 9: 57–68.

Davies, W. K. D. (1998). Urban systems research: Unfulfilled promises? *Canadian Journal of Regional Science* 11: 349–56.

De Filippis, J. (2001). The myth of social capital in community development. *Housing Policy Debate* 12: 781–806.

Derudder, B., and F. Witlox. (2008). World integration through global city networks: Specification, measurement, and analysis. Paper presented at the *conference of the regional science association international*, Sao Paulo, 17 – 19 March.

Dicken, P., and A. Malmberg. (2001). Firms in territories: A relational perspective. *Economic Geography* 77: 345–63.

Dicken, P., P.F. Kelly, K. Olds, and H.W-C. Yeung. (2001). Chains and networks, territories and scales: Towards a relational framework for analyzing the global economy. *Global Networks* 1: 89–112.

Dutzik, T., J. Baumann, and M. Purvis. (2003). *Toxic releases and health: A review of pollution data and current knowledge on the health effects of toxic chemicals.* Washington DC: United States Public Interest Research Group Education Fund.

Florida, R. (2005). *Cities and the creative class.* New York: Routledge.

Friedman, T.L. (2005). *The world is flat: A brief history of the twenty-first century.* New York: Farrar, Straus & Giroux.

Friedmann, J. (1986). The world city hypothesis. *Development and Change* 17: 69–147.

Friedmann, J., and G. Wolff. (1982). World city formation: An agenda for research and action. *International Journal of Urban and Regional Research* 6: 309–44.

Gereffi, G., M. Korzeniewicz, and R.P. Korzeniewicz. (1994). Introduction: Global commodity chains. In G. Gereffi and M. Korzeniewicz (eds), *Commodity chains and global capitalism*, 1–14. Westport, CT: Praeger.

Godfrey, B.J., and Y. Zhou. (1999). Ranking world cities: Multinational corporations and the global urban hierarchy. *Urban Geography* 20: 268–81.

Hannan, M.T. and J.H. Freeman. (1977). The population ecology of organizations. *American Journal of Sociology* 82: 929–64.

Johnson, S.C. (1967). Hierarchical clustering schemes. *Psychometrika* 32: 241–53.

Kaufmann, D., F.A. Leautier, and M. Mastruzzi. (2005). Globalization and urban performance. In F.A. Leautier (ed.), *Cities in a globalizing world: Governance, performance and sustainability*, 27–68. Washington DC: World Bank Publications.

Kloosterman, R.C. and S. Musterd. (2001). The polycentric urban region: Towards a research agenda. *Urban Studies* 38: 623–33.

Lever, W.F., and I. Turok. (1999). Competitive cities: Introduction to the review. *Urban Studies* 36: 791–3.

Lin, N., K.S. Cook, and R.S. Burt. (2001). *Social capital: Theory and research*. New York: Aldine de Gruyter.

Linders, G.J.M., M.J. Burger, and F.G. Van Oort. (2008). A rather empty world: The many faces of distance and the persistent resistance to international trade. *Cambridge Journal of Regions, Economy and Society* 1: 439–58.

Markusen, A. (1996). Sticky places in slippery space: A typology of industrial districts. *Economic Geography* 72: 293–313.

Markusen, A., and G. Schrock. (2006). The distinctive city: Divergent patterns in growth, hierarchy and specialization. *Urban Studies* 43: 1301–23.

McCann, P. (2008). Globalization and economic geography: The world is curved, not flat. Cambridge *Journal of Regions, Economy and Society* 1: 351–70.

Mcnee, R. (1960). Towards a more humanistic geography: The geography of enterprise. *Tijdschrift voor Economische en Sociale Geografie* 51: 201–6.

Meijer, M. (1993). Growth and decline of European cities: Changing positions of cities in Europe. *Urban Studies* 30: 981–90.

Meijers, E. (2007). From central place to network models: Theory and evidence of a paradigm change. *Tijdschrift voor Economische en Sociale Geografie* 98: 245–59.

Meyer, D. R. (1986). The world system of cities: Relations between international financial metropolises and South American cities. *Social Forces* 64: 553–81.

Oort, F.G. van, J. van Brussel, O. Raspe, M.J. Burger, J. van Dinteren, and G.A. van der Knaap. (2006). *Economische netwerken in de regio*. The Hague/Rotterdam: Netherlands Institute for Spatial Research and NAi Publishers.

Oort, F.G. van, M.J. Burger, and O. Raspe. (2008). Economic networks and urban complementarities. *GaWC Research Bulletin* 243.

Porter, M.E. (1990). *The competitive advantage of nations*. New York: Free Press.

Pred, A. (1977). *City systems in advanced economies: Past growth, present processes and future development options*. London: Hutchinson.

Randstad Regio (2006). *Randstadmonitor – economic strategy Randstad (ESR)*. Brussels: Huis van de Nederlandse Provincies.

Rozenblat, C., and D. Pumain. (2006). Firm linkages, innovation and the evolution of urban systems. In P.J. Taylor, B. Derudder, P. Saey, and F. Witlox (eds), *Cities in globalization*. London: Routledge.

Rugman, A. (2005). The regional multinationals. Cambridge: Cambridge University Press.

Sassen, S. (1991). *The global city: New York, London, Tokyo*. Princeton, NJ: Princeton University Press.

Smith, D.A., and M. Timberlake. (1995). World cities: A political economy/global network approach. *Research in Urban Sociology* 3: 181–207.

Sohn, M. (2004). Distance and cosine measures of niche overlap. *Social Networks* 23: 141–65.

Taylor, P.J., G. Catalano, and D.R.F. Walker. (2002). Measurement of the world city network. *Urban Studies* 39: 2367–76.

Taylor, P.J. (2001). Specification of the world city network. *Geographical Analysis* 33(2): 181–94.

Taylor, P.J. (2004). *World city network: A global urban analysis*. London: Routledge.

Taylor, P.J. (2005). Leading world cities: Empirical evaluations of urban nodes in multiple networks. *Urban Studies* 42: 1593–1608.

Taylor, P.J., M. Hoyler, and R. Verbruggen. (2008). External urban relational process: Introducing central flow theory to complement central place theory. *GaWC Research Bulletin* 261.

Taylor, P.J. and D.R.F. Walker. (2004). Urban hinterworlds revisited. *Geography* 89: 145–51.

Wall, R.S. (2009). *Netscape: Cities and global corporate networks*. Rotterdam: Haveka.

Wall, R.S., M.J. Burger, and G.A.V.D. Knaap. (2009). National competitiveness as a determinant of the geography of global corporate networks. *GaWC Research Bulletin* 285 (A).

Yeung, H.W.-C. (2005). The firm as social networks: An organizational perspective. *Growth and Change* 36: 307–28.

5
Competition Development in the BRIC Countries: Toward a Unified International Economic Space

Rinas V. Kashbrasiev

Introduction

Traditionally, in economic growth theory much attention is devoted to the factors and conditions for long-term economic growth (Wan, 1971; Todaro, 1994; Barro and Sala-i-Martin, 1995). However, in recent economic studies, we can observe a shift to the concepts of competitive advantages of countries, regions, and companies (e.g. Porter, 1990; Lewis, 2004; Cook et al., 2009) where geographic location and international economy and management issues are taken into consideration.

Competitive advantage is related to strategic market choices in terms of pioneering behavior, niche strategies, and the development of skills and knowledge in particular industries and connections between clusters, as well as "national champion" policy. In analyzing the strength of nations, Porter (1990) mentions that a country's production and demand conditions are related to social, cultural, and historical factors in a specific national context. It is important to underline the geographical factor here: A nationally well developed functional division of labor is essential in creating dynamic learning externalities and in utilizing economies of scale and scope.

Competitive advantages of countries, economic growth, and competition development are interconnected concepts. Protecting home industries from foreign competition and allowing a few firms in such industries to command most of a nation's resources can speed up economic growth. Nonetheless competition spurs innovation and efficiency. As Lewis (2004) asserted, economic progress of nations depends on increasing productivity, which depends on undistorted competition. When government policies limit competition, more efficient companies cannot replace less efficient ones. As a result, economic growth slows and nations remain poor. Thus, an investigation into issues of competition development addresses questions such as: Why are some countries rich and others poor? Which countries are successful and which countries fail?

The aim of this chapter is to examine opportunities and challenges for future long-term growth in the BRIC countries (Brazil, Russia, India, and China), their competitive advantages, and conditions needed for stable economic development.

For that purpose in this chapter:

- Current issues of economic development of the BRIC countries are investigated.
- The fundamental importance of interaction among the four countries to maintain fast economic growth (in the field of competition development) is explored.
- BRIC's possibilities of joining the international economic space are discussed.
- The main features of country competitive advantages are described.
- The BRIC countries' attempts to harmonize national competition principles are analyzed.

Why BRIC?

BRIC is an acronym for the four biggest, in terms of territory, countries having a collective successful history of economic growth and progress.

The first distinctive characteristic is the high economic growth rates of these countries (see Figure 5.1). From 1999 to 2008, the combined average

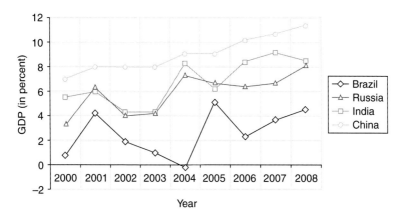

Figure 5.1 Economic growth rates of BRIC countries, 2000–2008
Source: http://indexmundi.com/g/g.aspx?v=66&c=br&l=en

GDP of the BRIC countries outpaced other emerging countries as well as developed countries including the US and European nations.

The BRIC countries certainly have everything necessary for long-term growth. Their economies are based upon their unique resources, huge labor forces, and crucial financial resources. These factors, combined with proper economic growth strategies,[1] demonstrate the potential for these countries to become leading players in the global economy. Wise utilization of competitive advantages and stimulation of domestic consumption, combined with competitive and antitrust policies, will guarantee them further high growth and continued high performance.

The 2008–9 economic crisis was a serious challenge for the BRIC countries. The global downturn had hit all developed and emerging economies. One of the consequences of the crisis was that the BRIC countries diverged in terms of economic growth. In 2009, China and India were expected to record growth of 8.6 and 6.0 percent, respectively, but Brazil expected only 0.3 percent growth, and Russia's GDP plunged as much as 8.5 percent (Aslund, 2009). However, the BRIC countries have all survived. They raised $6.7 billion in 26 initial public offerings in 2010, and recorded the highest amount ever for the month of January (Weaver, 2010).

What about the future for the BRIC countries? According to Goldman Sachs, in less than 40 years, the BRIC countries' economies together could be larger than those of the G6 (in US dollar terms). Of the current G6, only the United States and Japan may be among the six largest economies in US dollar terms in 2050 (Wilson and Roopa, 2003: 2).

However, the main challenge to this future (in terms of international economy and management) is in international trade, in which the BRIC countries currently have relatively little activity. This is a common attribute of big countries: Large territories usually provide advantages by possessing greater reserves of natural resources and potentially large domestic markets. At the same time, however, many BRIC companies very much depend on markets abroad. Therefore, it is in the national interest of each country to promote manufacturers and traders into the global markets of raw materials, semi-finished and finished goods and also to support them with their exploration of international markets.

Toward a unified international economic space

The world economy is becoming increasingly homogenous; goods and services, capital, and labor all flow across borders. Modern communications and transportation technologies have worked to promote global economic integration. All governments of Western nations reduced their trade barriers during the twentieth century and recent years. With the transition to a market economy, many companies of Eastern nations have also become globally oriented. Today the question of economic cooperation and integration occupies a central position in the development of any country. Therefore we can conclude that the world is moving toward a unified economic space.

Solving economic and technical cooperation problems has turned out to be essential not only for economic reasons, but also for the promotion of political issues. Some technical programs such as space research, biotechnology, and nuclear power engineering require economic and political coordination. A global economic space is expressed in the form of a free exchange of goods and services, capital and labor, investments, and innovations.

This is done according to principles of mutual advantage for all countries:

- Encouraging the international division of labor
- Promoting comparative advantages
- Developing mutual trade on the basis of long-term agreements

However, this process has been limited by existing political, economic, and social constraints. The most important constraints may be identified as the following:

- Each country has its own legislation. Laws regulating manufactures, trade, and consumer protection are different. Goods and services must comply with these national regulations.
- Each country has its own currency. This factor can have important consequences for financing international trade. When the exchange rates changes, the terms of trade will change.
- These countries have different levels of average income and inequalities in the distribution of family income. What are the characteristics of the market? Will there be a demand for the goods exported to this country?
- The countries belong to different cultures, and the social behavior traits and beliefs of the main groups of societies are essentially different. This notion includes traditions, values, laws, language, and religious institutions. Business follows the cultural norms in each country. Also, there are habits and ethics in the business community. How does your business partner behave? How appropriate is your behavior as perceived by your business partner?

The internationalization of trade and economic relations is connected with ensuring predictable conditions for running businesses and creating a sound competitive environment. The effective implementation of competition policy globally promotes economic and trade liberalization, as well as allows consumers around the world to take advantage of the global market and international economic space.

Let us next discuss BRIC's opportunities to join the international (already existing) economic space.

BRIC as a new phenomenon in the world

The BRIC format initially posited great opportunities for the four countries, outclassing in size and growth much of the developing world. The financial media have written in depth about the immense opportunities for global companies (especially investment companies) to make both direct and portfolio investments to maximize earnings.

According to Weaver (2010), the coming years also promise to be successful. Since the beginning of 2010, the four BRIC countries have issued a record amount of equity equal to $6.7 billion. It is estimated that at least 140 BRIC offerings are on the list for 2010, with a collective value of more than $29 billion. This surpasses expected issuances this year of $21.6 billion from the United States and $15.4 billion from Western Europe. Thus, the BRIC countries have rushed to take advantage of the financial and economic recovery.

However, it is impossible to believe that BRIC may be construed simply as an economic market. The purpose of political leadership and the aim of economic development should be to sustain each other. To promote BRIC as a political union may provide the democratic and effective institutions to maintain high economic growth rates and to improve standards of living.

There are varying opinions regarding this bloc's place in international politics, economy, and finance, ranging from skeptics who believe that BRIC is an amorphous organization (the countries are very different) and has no future prospects, to optimists who are convinced that the group can be formed as a political institution to play a growing role in the global economy. What are the prospects for this organization?

Russia is actively developing its trade and economic relations with Brazil, India, and China, but it does not seek (and does not try to accelerate) any definite status for this bloc. Development of all kinds of economic activity and bilateral trade is considered a priority for Russia, because it helps to implement its current competitive advantages. Meanwhile, political processes are intensifying, as seen in the political dialogue within BRIC that started in September 2006 in the meeting of the BRIC countries' foreign ministers during the UN General Assembly in New York. Now their meetings are regular. Also, there was a "mini-summit" of the leaders of the BRIC countries and two meetings of BRIC finance ministers, including their meeting in London in March 2009 on the eve of the London G20 meeting.

Recently, the main dialogue of the BRIC countries was held in Yekaterinburg, Russia. On June 16, 2009, the leaders of the four countries met there for the first full-format BRIC summit. It was a significant historic event, with serious discussions focused on practical roads to follow and finding solutions to the biggest problems facing the countries.

Despite the economic destruction of 2009, BRIC is continuing its development: The second summit of the BRIC leaders will be held in Brazil in 2010 – the countries are coming together because in collective cooperation they increase their individual strengths.

Thus, we can define BRIC as a semiformal organization. Alongside economic issues, financial recovery, food, and energy security are on its agenda today. In terms of development issues, to further their economic progress the BRIC countries have to promote principles of competition.

Competition and monopoly issues

Competition is one of the most important terms in economics. It is considered that the best situation for a market economy is fair competition: All businesses must engage in some form of competition as long as other businesses produce similar goods or services. When a market includes many sellers of a particular good or service, each seller accounts for a small part of the total market. As a result, there is no control over price. The price that consumers pay for such products is a correct signal about the value of that product in society. Perfect competitive industries yield economic efficiency.

However, in the real economic life and practice of any country, each business attempts to capture as large a share of its market as possible. As a result, they may sell (or buy) a good or service in amounts large enough to affect price.

Competition policy has become an integral component of the development policy within BRIC as a result of the increasing recognition of its role in facilitating economic growth. It is considered today that the main task of competition authorities is to achieve balance of interests among the participants of the competition relations through (1) stimulating the creation and functioning of competitive, efficient companies, (2) protecting the interests of consumers of produced goods, and (3) the full satisfaction of the market requirements of quality goods at accessible prices.

But economic globalization has brought about increasing controversy regarding the competition policy at the national level. On the one hand, countries continue to acknowledge the benefits of competitive markets and are focused on improving their competition models. On the other hand, a growing number of countries facilitate development of so-called national champions: companies that are competitive globally due to their large scale and high concentration of economic resources.

Amid the conditions of fast economic growth and rapidly growing bilateral trade (Russia–China, China–Brazil, China–India, India–Russia, Brazil–Russia, Brazil–India), working out the following issues has become increasingly important, namely closer (even harmonized in the future) national competition principles, identical business rules, competition advocacy and anti-cartel activity.

Enforcement of competition law is good for growth and development for many reasons. When firms can freely enter a market, they increase the pressure on firms already in the market, forcing them to be more efficient in order to maintain their market share and profits. The less-efficient firms will be compelled to drop out of the market as the number of firms increases. This way, a competitive environment motivates firms to attain the minimum level of costs for a given level of output. The process of entry and exit from the market is beneficial for growth and development, because it induces increases in the competitiveness of firms and delivers improvements in efficiency, innovation, and productivity.

Enforcement of competition law is good also for international trade relations. The law may ensure that the intended benefits of international trade reform are achieved. As well, a well-structured and enforced competition law makes an economy more attractive as a location for foreign investment and maximizes the benefits that flow from such investment.

Globalization of economic relations is closely connected with the movement of states toward the liberalization of world trade and investment regimes. These processes, in general rendering positive influence toward economic efficiency and consumers' welfare at national levels, obviously affect the nature of competition, making it sharper and increasingly international in character.

Economic globalization calls for increasing cooperation among competition authorities.

BRIC, its competitive advantages, and global competition

To realize the opportunities for future long-term high growth rates (unique resources, huge labor force, and crucial financial resources), the BRIC countries have to create certain conditions. The main condition is competition. This necessary condition follows more than 70 years (for Russia – other countries had shorter periods) during which the trend was for monopolization of political power and economic resources. Perfect competition is highly welcomed in these countries. However, competition is a contradictory issue today: Nations want to use their absolute and comparative advantages and need globally competitive national or transnational corporations – that is, monopolies (alongside perfect competition).

Is BRIC able to damage the current global economic order which is based on competition?

The economies of the BRIC countries are characterized by high concentration ratios. It is due to the influence of geographic factors such as huge territory and unique resources, as well as a heritage from the period prior to economic liberalization in these countries. Nonetheless, it remains important to measure the degree of this concentration.

To measure industrial (resources) power of the countries, we suggest using the Herfindahl-Hirschman Index (HHI). Usually, the HHI is calculated to evaluate mergers and monopoly power. For evaluating geographic concentration of industries, experts at regional studies prefer indicators of regional specialization and geographic concentration (Traistaru et al., 2002) or concentration ratio.

We use the HHI because it has some benefits:

1) The major benefit of the HHI is that it gives greater weight to those firms (industries) which have large market shares measuring the concentration ratio.
2) The index shows the degree of competition among industries.
3) The HHI as an economic concept is applied in competition law in many countries.
4) The index has clear classification criteria. The guidelines classify industries as follows (The Herfindahl-Hirschman index, 2010):

- HHI < 1000: industry is unconcentrated
- 1000 < HHI < 1800: industry is moderately concentrated
- HHI > 1800: industry is highly concentrated

A low index indicates a competitive industry with no dominant players. The guidelines are working well in cases of merger control. Indices give a good prediction of government challenges to mergers, and indeed most firms that want to merge will ensure their companies fit within the specified guidelines.

The HH Index is derived using:

$$HHI = S_1^2 + S_2^2 + S_3^2 + \ldots + S_n^2,$$

where $s_1, s_2, \ldots, s_n$ are the percentage market shares of each firm in the industry. The result is proportional to the average market share, weighted by market share. In a four-firm industry, for example, in which each firm enjoys a 25 percent market share, the HHI is:

$$HHI = 25^2 + 25^2 + 25^2 + 25^2 = 2500$$

The HHI can range from roughly 0 to 10,000, moving from a huge number of very small firms to a single monopolistic producer (trader). Increases in the index generally indicate a decrease in competition and an increase of market power, whereas decreases indicate the opposite.

We would like to use this index to evaluate the industrial power of countries:

$$HHI = S_1^2 + S_2^2 + S_3^2 + S_4^2 ,$$

where s_1, s_2, s_3, s_4 are the percentage market shares of each country in the global industry: *1* – Brazil, *2* – Russia, *3* – India, *4* – China.

The HHI was calculated to evaluate concentration of selected natural resources (oil, coal, gas, iron, bauxite, copper, nickel, manganese, and tin). Some indexes are the following:

$HHI_{oil} = 3.1^2 + 9.25^2 + 1.53^2 + 3.57^2 = 110.26$
$HHI_{coal} = 0.37^2 + 6.42^2 + 8.34^2 + 37^2 = 1479.91$
$HHI_{gas} = 0.5^2 + 27^2 + 3.24^2 + 3.12^2 = 749.48$

What does it mean? $HHI_{oil} = 110.26 < 1000$; the industry is unconcentrated. $HHI_{coal} = 1479.91 < 1800$; the industry is moderately concentrated. $HHI_{gas} = 749.48 < 1000$; the industry is unconcentrated.

If all BRIC countries are considered as a single economic unit, even in this case HHI_{oil} would be equal to $(3.1 + 9.25 + 1.53 + 3.57)^2 = 304.5$; $HHI_{coal} = 2717.54$; $HHI_{gas} = 1146.5$.

The conclusion is the countries have no ability to damage global competition (and the current global economic order).

Of course, this is a hypothetical example. The BRIC countries should not be considered to be a single economic unit, nor even a political alliance (like the European Union) nor a formal trading association. But the HHI indices characterize the potential of the competitive and cooperative power of countries. According to my calculations, the BRIC countries have the potential to form a powerful economic bloc.

Nevertheless, the HHI analysis may be used in formulating the spatial development strategies of companies. Today it is clear that national and corporate strategies are interdependent. The BRIC countries (especially Russia and China) must create a sound business environment and foster the modern multinational corporation. These companies will then be able to draw up the modern locational, hybrid, and other managerial strategies of their development. Porter's "diamond" of national competitive advantages, as well as concepts of national competitive development policy, offers a clear framework in the determination of the main strengths and weaknesses of a country's competitive position in the world economy.

BRIC's activity in the field of competition

Cooperation on various aspects of economic growth and development is important for the BRIC countries to maintain fast growth. The BRIC

International Competition Conference (September 1–3, 2009, Kazan, Russian Federation) has shown that competition enforcement is considered a priority in fostering such cooperation. Today it is clear that the BRIC countries must promote principles of competition policy if they wish to further their economic progress.

The Kazan conference was the first BRIC conference devoted to economic issues, and it highlighted perspectives on cooperation, sustained economic growth, poverty reduction, and well-functioning markets of these countries. Participation of the heads of state of the Russian Federation and the Republic of Tatarstan at the conference gave emphasis to the role of competition policy in economic regulation and the importance of economic cooperation among the BRIC countries.

The BRIC International Competition Conference in Kazan focused attention on the challenges for competition policy development in the BRIC countries. Specific attention was paid to the formation of an effective anti-cartel system, because anti-competition agreements create economically unjustifiable preconditions for increase of price on the relevant product markets. This, in turn, does not promote stimulation of the domestic demand and impedes recovery from crises.

Some BRIC countries have more developed systems of competition authorities. For example, Brazil has a clear division of functions among departments. One department carries out monitoring and control functions; a second, investigation; a third, punishment and leniency; and so on. In Brazil, the office of the attorney general plays a special role, as it is entitled to request judicial orders to conduct investigations, phone tapping, and searches and seizures. In India, there is the Competition Commission of India (CCI), alongside the Competition Appellate Tribunal (CAT). All these help competition authorities to achieve their goals more effectively.

Other countries have experienced more practical processes. Numerous interesting cases regarding antitrust activity, especially reforming natural monopolies, have been observed in Russia's history of competition policy, and instances of merger control are to be found in China's history of anti-monopoly policy. The study of this experience and generalization of the cases would be very useful for India and Brazil.

Russian competition authorities work to curb anti-competitive practices at all levels and contribute to the establishment of transparent mechanisms and processes in its markets. Below are some of the functions of the competitive authority of Russia (*Proceedings*, 2009: 3–12):

- Suppression of abuse of dominance
- Suppression of anti-competitive actions of the state authorities
- Provision of observance of sector legislation (forest, land, living, water, natural resources)
- Combating cartels

- Merger control
- Control of the activity of natural monopolies
- Prevention of unfair competition
- Control of legislation regarding advertising
- Control over foreign investment in economic entities having strategic value to the state security
- Provision of enforcement of competition legislation for foreign economic activity

International cooperation in competition policy, setting priority on combating cartels, is extremely important for Russia. Steps undertaken recently by the Russian government on strengthening anti-cartel activity testify to its readiness to eradicate international cartelization.

Indeed, the character of the BRIC countries' economies – high rate of production concentration, stable corporate ties, and institutional imperfection – makes them fertile ground for domestic and international cartels. To resist cartels it is proposed that the countries harmonize approaches of implementation of competition policy at the national level (by each competition authority) and create effective mechanisms of interaction not only on the bilateral basis, but also within the four-sided format.

From Brazil's point of view, competition development within BRIC was taking place at a very suitable moment when BRIC was acquiring increasing influence in the world economy, and the current context of international economic crisis had hastened the process for remodeling the balance of power of states in global governance. For Brazil the main challenge today is a new competition policy law and proposed institutional restructuring. Brazilian competition authorities made every effort to obtain an approval by the senate, of Competition Bill by June 2009. This Competition Bill is expected to significantly increase efficiency and also to modernize the national competition system (*Proceedings*, 2009: 29).

Notably, all BRIC competition authorities are dealing with challenges related to initiatives for the improvement of their own competition systems. The Russian Federal Antimonopoly Service (FAS) has been focusing on cartel enforcement and last year created a specialized division for this purpose. India is closer to completing the implementation of its 2002 Competition Act. China has released further guidance to provide clarification and increase compliance on the application of its Anti-Monopoly Law, which went into force in August 2008.

China's competition authorities consider that the Chinese anti-monopoly law reflects the need to improve the socialistic market economy system and take full advantage of basic functions of the market in allocation of economic resources and promote the healthy and fast development of the economy, as well as the need for Chinese enterprises to participate in economic globalization according to international business rules and conduct fair market competition (*Proceedings*, 2009: 21–7). China as a developing country is still facing a number of pressing issues concerning improvement of competition legislature and law enforcement. Therefore China is pleased to share with other countries its successful experience on anti-monopoly legislature and law enforcement, and it is particularly willing to enhance cooperation and exchanges on competition law enforcement with the competition law enforcement agencies of other BRIC countries.

India's competition authorities also would like to share experiences regarding common interests and identical or similar problems, to exchange opinions and dialogues for creating a culture of fair competition. Such a culture of sharing will encourage innovation and higher productivity, leading to accelerated economic growth. For the consumers it will bring the advantage of lower prices, increased choice, and improved services. The preamble of the Indian Competition Act of 2002 contains reference not only to the objectives of promoting and sustaining competition, preventing practices that have adverse effects on competition, and ensuring freedom of trade in markets, but also to protecting the interests of consumers. In emerging economies, the challenge in implementation of competition policy is twofold: Not only must the policy aim at ensuring faster development of these jurisdictions, but it should also be able to meet the objectives of growth with more equitable distribution of income (*Proceedings*, 2009: 39–40).

Thus, international competition conferences may be considered as a platform for mutual learning and sharing of experience, as well as a place of discussion and sharing views to fulfill the object of effective enforcement, coordination, and improvement of competition law at local, national, and global levels. Creation of a normal competitive environment and predictable business conditions is one of the main conditions for internationalization of trade and economic relations and mutual investments between the BRIC countries.

Conclusion

In a few decades Brazil, Russia, India, and China may become the world's largest economies. The idea of BRIC, unifying the four countries as a political and economic entity, is essential for them to be a part of the global market, as well as to be strong enough to solidify their positions in the world.

Today, BRIC companies are increasingly active in international business, which is important to provide them up-to-date information on world markets, competition legislation, and prospective customers. Also it is important to help world companies with investments in BRIC, locating these companies in emerging markets.

Competition policy in the BRIC countries is one of the rapidly expanding directions of their governments' policies. They have focused their activities on certain fields that are the most topical: anti-cartel, abuse of dominance, merger control, and reforming of natural monopolies.

There are some achievements in certain directions which create a field for interaction among BRIC countries and promote exchange of the best practices on anti-monopoly and competitive development. All these developments bring these countries closer to world business standards and to the unified global economic space.

Note

1. A prime example is "Russian 2020."

References

Aslund, A. (2009) Take the R out of BRIC (What on Earth is Russia doing on the list of top emerging economies?) *Foreign Policy* http://www.foreignpolicy.com/articles/2009/12/02/kick_russia_out_of_bric [Accessed February 15, 2010].

Cook, P., R. Fabella, and C. Lee (eds.) (2009) *Competitive Advantage and Competition Policy in Developing Countries*. Edward Elgar Publishing.

Barro, R., and X. Sala-I-Martin (1995) *Economic Growth*. New York: McGraw-Hill.

Lewis, W. (2004) *The Power of Productivity: Wealth, Poverty, and the Threat to Global Stability*. Chicago: University of Chicago Press.

Porter, M. (1990) *The Competitive Advantage of Nations*. New York: Free Press.

Proceedings of the International Competition Conference BRIC 2009 (2009). Kazan, Russia.

The Herfindahl-Hirschman index http://www.justice.gov/atr/public/testimony/hhi.htm [Accessed February 27, 2010].

Todaro, M. (1994) *Economic Development*. New York: Longman.

Traistaru, I., P. Nijkamp, and S. Longhi (2002) *Regional Specialization and Concentration of Industrial Activity in Accession Countries*. ZEI Working Paper B16.

Wan, H. (1971) *Economic Growth*. Cornell University, Harcourt Brace Jovanovich.

Weaver, C. (2010) BRICs raise $6.7bn amid demand for EM assets. *Financial Times* http://www.ft.com/cms/s/ [Accessed February 15, 2010].

Wilson, D., and P. Roopa (2003) *Dreaming With Brics: The Path to 2050*. Goldman Sachs Global Economics Paper No. 99.

6
Regulatory Risk and Foreign Investments Developed in Latin America

Anxo Calvo Silvosa and Rubén C. Lois-González

Introduction

In recent decades the well-defined contexts of the social sciences have shown a tendency to disappear. This is particularly relevant for geography and economics, two disciplines that have discovered a set of common inter-disciplinary interests. In this process, the growing consideration of space and territory as essential variables to be considered has permitted the elaboration of new perspectives for the analysis of the economic system and of international financial regulation. As a result, and within the interesting debate regarding the renovation of economic geography, we have set ourselves to the study of a subject raising unquestionable implications regarding space and the productive system: regulatory risk and country risk.

Each national state presents particular models of inner institutional organization and faces individually its insertion into the global market. Geography (political) has shown this repeatedly since the end of the nineteenth century, and at present it permits the improvement of the concrete focuses of work and of the indicators employed for financial economy. It is a branch of economic knowledge that has received enough relevance when deepening its investigations concerning the behavior of the transnational capital concerned. At the same time, its relevance is due to the globalization process and to the emergence of a new and singular political map, which should be known a priori for the evaluation of the security and profitability of financial operations.

Country risk and regulatory risk

Before analyzing regulatory risk, it is necessary to make a conceptual comparison between *country risk* and *regulatory risk*. Country risk (Lessard, 1993; Erb et al., 1996; Zopounidis et al., 1998; Oetzel et al., 2001; Hoti and

MacAleer, 2004; Iturralde et al., 2010) is one of the most significant risks international investors have to face. For this reason, its investigation, delimitation, measure, control and management have been the object of attention not only from the academic point of view but also from business and government. Generally speaking, country risk is conceived as a multidimensional concept originating from a set of factors whose measure is established through indicators combining different relevant variables of the problems (Iturralde et al., 2010).

San Martin and Rodríguez (2008) have formulated a wider definition of country risk by making reference to what occurs when working with or in a specific country, even in the case of imports and/or exports. When clarifying this concept, they identify its components: *economic-financial risk, political risk* – divisible into socio-political risk and regulatory risk – and *country risk*[1].

Rodríguez (1997) identifies political risk with the possibility of loss of property resulting from governmental intervention and/or the intervention of political and social forces of the host society, or of nearby countries that can affect it. In turn, and as a part of political risk, regulatory (or administrative) risk would be associated with the possible decrease in profits deriving from increasing restrictions on the performance of foreign corporations as a result of non-specific interventions by the host country's authorities: more interventionist regulations, greater demands and requirements, new and higher taxes, increases of various types of controls and operating difficulties, and so on (Figure 6.1).

According to Conthe (2004), it is necessary to consider the fact that investments addressed to the provision of basic services and infrastructure (electricity, telecommunications, highways, sanitation, harbors, airports, etc.) present three specific characteristics that make them susceptible to regulatory risk. First, they require a large volume of implicated financial resources that become profitable only through a long-term service provision. Second, due to the fact that after the initial investment has been made the marginal

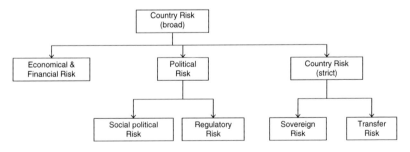

Figure 6.1 Regulatory risk as a component of political risk and, in turn, of country risk (adapted from Rodríguez, 1997)

cost of supplying clients with an additional unit of service is reduced, and, consequently, the average cost of supply decreases with greater units sold, the activity usually offers "economics of scale" (in certain cases, it will be a natural monopoly). Finally, the service supplied tends to be essential for the proper development of economic activity and for the welfare of the populace as a whole. Taking all these facts into account, many of these services are well-regarded by the public and are supplied directly or by means of public entities – private companies holding public concessions or some other formula of private management. In the latter cases, governments are free to choose their licensee and public provider and to submit the activity to certain regulations. The above-mentioned author identifies regulatory risk with the possibility that the public administration might substantially change the economic basis affecting an activity submitted to regulation. This would alter the long-term profitability of a project once it has been ascribed and the initial investment has been made.

Due to the lack of infrastructure in emerging countries, their governments try to attract foreign investments by privatizing the public services. At first, the benefits of such privatization were explained by the achievement of higher incomes as a consequence of the sale of the companies that supplied these services, by the lower need for public investment destined to infrastructure, and by a greater expected efficiency and quality in supplying these services as a consequence of private management.

Among the main factors generating regulatory risk is a change in the behavior of governments after the private foreign companies have committed the required investments. As stated by Conthe (2004), Vernon used the expression "obsolescing bargain" to explain the difficulties experienced by American multinational companies that had invested in emerging countries. Briefly, this situation consists of the governments of countries receiving investments assuming a double attitude: before the investments have been made, and with the intention of attracting foreign investors, governments often offer highly attractive conditions to do business within their territory; but once the investments have been committed, these same authorities impose greater requirements upon the investors and, on certain occasions, can alter the conditions initially accorded and even precipitate the renationalization of the company.

In general, there are various causes for this behavior. The opinion of Spanish business executives with significant investments in Latin America can be illuminating. According to Ontiveros et al. (2004), there is a big "social disappointment" regarding the results of the privatization process of basic services companies. Moreover, numerous executives believe that many of these countries do not possess the basic conditions ensuring a universal access to essential public services which can be financed by private initiatives. In the case of the countries with major risk, the profits required by the stockholders of the foreign companies make the level of service tariffs for these services politically unviable and unsustainable. On the other hand, in some sectors it is not easy to find the required investments for universal access to basic public services. This is due to their volume and to the lack of culture of payment for these services (water, sanitation, electricity, etc.). Consequently, if governments want to obtain the universalization of services, it will be necessary to take into consideration the implication (at least partially) of the public powers of these countries when financing investments. Likewise, it will be opportune to implement a mechanism to subsidize the access to basic services for low-income users.

For the Latin American case, Ontiveros et al. (2004) mention a number of favorable experiences which contribute to reducing the level of regulatory risk for foreign companies. Among the most notable cases are the creation of a High Counsellor to facilitate the resolution of disputes with the private sector (Colombia), the granting of coverage for fluctuations of the local currency exchange rate (Chile), and the drawing up and implementation of income distribution mechanisms to compensate for eventual declines in activity (Chile).

An approach to regulatory risk in Latin America

As stated at the beginning, the present study attempts to combine two disciplinary focuses for the analysis of a theme that is most relevant for the investigation. On the one hand, as previously stated in the definitions of regulatory risk and country risk, we proceed from concepts that are strictly economic and financial. On the other hand, space is not considered an indifferent variable, and we will try to reflect upon this in the following pages. In a context of globalization such as we have at the present time, each region of the world can offer a perfectly individualized set of particular evolutionary dynamics and illustrate a combination of economic, political, and social factors that will have an impact upon development (Castells, 1989). Geography restates its analytical capabilities within a framework of temporal-space comprehension and must help the economic sciences answer questions regarding the various international dangers pertaining to individual countries and to well-identified world areas (Peet and Thrift, 1989).

The space we are going to investigate has been denominated as Latin America, but let us provide a more precise definition regarding this expression. Latin America is generally identified with territories that were colonized by the Spanish, Portuguese, and French, and which also received large numbers of immigrants from those countries (as well as from Italy). These territories extend from the Rio Grande, the border between the United States and Mexico, down to the tip of South America. Latin America, therefore, includes Mexico, the countries of Central America and the Caribbean, and all of South America. It is true that some small nation-states (such as Belize, Guyana, and Jamaica) were once British or Dutch colonies (The Netherlands and France still maintain some of their possessions in this region), but their scant entity and reasons of vicinity explain their incorporation into the joint study on the Latin American reality (Domínguez, 2003; Biardeau, 2004; Chiriyankandath, 2008). In our study, we will employ a restrictive interpretation of Latin America, which is more functional for our objective. We have, therefore, excluded the analysis of Mexico, due to the influence of the United States upon its economy and society, to whom it is bonded through a Free Trade Agreement (which includes Canada as well). We have also excluded the whole of Central America and the Caribbean, where the proliferation of small-sized nation-states might seriously distort our work. For this reason, in our study Latin America will be identified with South America, where large countries with abundant natural resources, societies not historically egalitarian, and a tendency for political instability form a good field of observation for regulatory risks and country risks in terms of international investments. We have decided to focus our attention on South America, but within this area we will not take into account the smaller territories which barely exceed 150,000 km² (for example, Surinam and Uruguay), as compared to the 8.5 million km² of Brazil. Similarly, we avoid studying countries with populations of less than 5 million: Surinam (520,000 inhab.), Guyana (760,000 inhab.) and Uruguay (3,330,000 inhab.).

Within the specialized academic literature and in countless press references, Latin America (and concretely South America) has been considered the "backyard" of the United States. This image was established at the beginning of the nineteenth century by the Monroe Doctrine, which was in part aimed at obtaining Panama's independence from Colombia and the building of the canal at the beginning of the twentieth century. Numerous direct and indirect US military interventions in the region have helped consolidate this image (Adams, 1977; Calvocoressi, 1987). The United States has traditionally exercised economic, social, and political authority over Latin America, and this is fundamental for understanding the region's history. In the economic sector, the direct foreign investments of the United States and the commercial transactions originating from and ending in this country have excelled in the context of the total fluxes of transactional capital.

Some economies of Central America have been considered simple satellites of their northern neighbor, thus popularizing the expression "banana republic" to explain the dependence of entire governments upon the decisions of some large North American company (in the early days, United Fruits). On the social level, the existence of a populace under a weak government, in general not much concerned with the principles of the welfare state, have resulted in populations characterized by a large inequality, much of it determined by ethnic criteria (secular prostration of the indigenous and black communities; less of the mulatto and mestizo). In this regard, the countries of Latin America have copied the example of the United States, but within a context of general poverty. Concerning politics, the United States guaranteed itself obedient, pro-Western and anticommunist regimes, this being the best example of the control exercised over the region. This objective justified the generalization of bloody military dictatorships during the 1960s and 1970s, which would progressively be substituted in the 1980s and 1990s by liberal democracies that are deregulative at the economic level.

This scenario, however, has changed notably during recent years, and this introduces very innovative elements to the present analysis. On the one hand, the participation of US foreign investments in South America has been continually decreasing compared with the increases recorded for the European Union and the rising participation of Chinese and Japanese companies (the latter sustained by large colonies of immigrants in Brazil and Peru). In fact, bank, energy, and telecommunication corporations from Spain, resorting to a historical and cultural proximity with Latin America, have entered in force into many countries of the region. France has distinguished itself for its intense relations with Brazil. Germany has increased its presence all over the subcontinent (Ontiveros et al., 2004). At a political level, the neo-liberal regimes of many nation-states have been displaced due to crises of legitimacy, being substituted by a new generation of left-wing leaders who are more interventionist and prone to the regulation of the financial sector. A new breed of political groups with strong indigenous components have come into power in Ecuador, Bolivia, and Paraguay. The classical left-wing political forces striving for more social justice have won elections in Brazil and Uruguay. The left-wing populism of Hugo Chávez is still alive in Venezuela, and more moderate but regulative and socially sensitive governments have obtained dominance in Argentina, Peru, and Chile.

In this generalized process taking place between the end of the twentieth and the beginning of the twenty-first centuries, there are two main events that attract attention. The first is the fact that the unionized working class, the indigenous movements, and the representatives of the poorest social groups have for the first time reached the executive and legislative powers of their countries, trying to impose a program of greater social redistribution and public control of national resources. The second significant event is the fact that this general left-wing turn all across South America is taking place during one of the region's most stable periods of economic growth – a growth sustained by the discovery of new and significant energy reservoirs (in Venezuela, Bolivia, and Brazil), but also because of a decrease of social and labor conflicts (many of their supporters are now in power), a more serious public administration, a stronger hold of democracy, and the reform of institutions which have traditionally been related to corruption and inefficiency (police and military forces, justice system, etc.).

Starting out from this situation of change that has taken place in recent years, we propose the elaboration of a synthetic index of regulatory risk and country risk with a number of limited variables. We will attempt to classify South American countries internally into groups distinguished by their economic and business potentialities. To do this, we have been especially careful to employ indicators which are not strictly financial, but rather those of a political and social nature that might facilitate or complicate business operations (Meny, 1981; Urwin, 1982). Thus, we consider the factors deriving from an authentic division of power to be extremely important, particularly the autonomy of the judicial system and the trust citizens have upon it. In nations that have suffered periods of military dictatorships, or have found themselves affected by corruption (with dismissal from office of a number of presidents in Ecuador, Venezuela and Brazil under charges of corruption), the creation of an efficient justice system is one extra guarantee for foreign investors – who are always afflicted by a certain level of distrust regarding the legal possibilities offered by a recently consolidated democratic system.

The political variables are also important; in fact, the consolidation of democracy in this region of the world has been associated with a decrease in violence and certain events regarding the extra limitation of public power. Consequently, the indicators of political stability and absence of risk represent further variables to consider (Burnell and Randall, 2008). There is no doubt that examples of historically deeply rooted democracies, and of the overcoming of military governments by strong popular mobilizations such as those in Chile or Uruguay, offer an adequate context for investments. This is also the case in states such as Brazil where the division of power among the different administrations (federal, state, and local) functions properly. On the other hand, situations of permanent inner tension such as those of Venezuela, Bolivia, and Argentina do not contribute to the creation of a positive climate for sustained economic development. Other variables chosen also place emphasis on the importance of the proper functioning of the structures of each country, either because external organizations have the ability to control the functioning of political and economic indicators, or because there are many types of infrastructure of acceptable quality (or recent progress has been achieved in this context), and because democratic stability has its correlate in an elevated level of trust in the public administration. To summarize, our hypothesis applied to the Latin American context goes through the valorization of the political-administrative modernization process, improvements in the division of power, and the correction of social injustices as factors directly affecting economic and financial security.

Model

Objective and methodology

The objective of the present study is the classification of different Latin American countries according to their perceived level of regulatory risk. Since this variable is not directly observable, we will employ the dimensions or components indicated in the previous graph (figure 6.1), starting out from the definitions and instruments of measurement subsequently proposed. The countries to be classified are Argentina, Bolivia, Brazil, Chile, Colombia, Ecuador, Peru, and Venezuela.

To develop this classification we will employ cluster analysis, an analytical technique of interdependence. The objective of the analysis is the creation of groups with certain common characteristics such that the differences in content within one particular group are lowest, and those between that group and the other groups are highest (Iglesias et al., 2003). The analysis is accomplished in three steps: (1) estimating the similarities between the objects by measurements of correlation, distance or association of the different variables; (2) comparing the similarities to create the groups; (3) determining the number of groups to be created, finding equilibrium between the simplicity of the structure and homogeneity within the conglomerates.

According to Iglesias et al. (2003), although factorial analysis is similar to cluster analysis in that both study interdependence, the first is employed only for grouping variables, while the second fundamentally permits the creation of groups of objects or observations, as well as of variables. Nevertheless, it could be stated that both techniques can be used complementarily for the identification of factorial analysis: first, by using a set of factors based upon a greater number of variables, and afterward using cluster analysis of the previously mentioned factors for identifying groups of individuals. The present study opted to perform the classification of the eight countries without the need to resort to the obtainment of previous factors. In other words, we started out from the original set of variables, taking their number and nature into account.

Due to the characteristics of this descriptive technique, it will be employed primarily with an exploratory purpose, without pretending to perform inferences for a particular population based on one sample, since the objective of the study is wholly defined by the eight countries over which the classification is performed. Thus, the present study does not pretend to verify the existence of a causal relationship between membership in a specific group and the values adopted by the variables used for that classification. This is the reason discriminant analysis is not used in a stage following the creation of the groups.

We will undertake a post hoc segmentation according to the method of hierarchical clusters by means of the SPSS statistical program. Consequently, the number of groups, size and description will result from the application of this technique, as there are no previous hypotheses. Once the groups have been created according to the similarity of profiles with reference to the variables under consideration, a description of the characteristics of each group will be given, and there will be an attempt to give an approximation of the regulatory security perceived in each one of them. In conclusion, optimal groups are being created from a statistical point of view since they correspond to the criterion of greater internal homogeneity and greater heterogeneity among each other (Picón et al., 2003).

Variables and measures

Independence of the judicial system

This indicator is obtained from surveys of business executives based on subjective information and perceptions. It refers to the opinion of whether or not the judicial system is independent of the influences of governments, private citizens, and corporations. The measurement scale ranges from 1 (significantly influenced and not independent) to 7 (completely independent). This question is part of the Opinion Survey of the World Economic Forum developed by the Global Competitiveness Report. An average of 94 company presidents or other high-level executives have been surveyed in each country from a sample of corporations working in foreign markets, branches of foreign corporations, and corporations with a significant percentage of state ownership (where applicable).

Political stability and absence of violence (Source: IDB)

This combines into one aggregated index various available indicators related to political stability, including those concerning the presence of violent conflicts, tensions, and racial problems, the probability of dramatic institutional changes, unconstitutional changes in the governments and so forth. This aggregation of indicators is derived from numerous sources and has been performed by means of a unique model of components. Some of the indicators considered for this index are based on surveys, while others are based on the opinions of experts. The index value can range from –2.5 to 2.5. A value of 0 indicates the average of the world sample.

This is one of the six composed indexes that measure dimensions of governability formulated by the World Bank according to hundreds of indicators, derived for the 2006 edition from 31 different databases, put together by 25 different institutions. The creation of a single index, derived from multiple and different sources of information, is useful for increasing the content of a concept that the aggregate measure wants to represent.

Trust in the judicial system (IDB)

This index indicates the total percentage of those surveyed answering that they trust fully or partially in the judicial system. *Latinobarómetro* (Latin Barometer)[2] is an annual survey of public national opinion performed in 18 Latin American countries. On average, it surveys 1000 people in each country. This indicator, based on subjective information or perceptions, is obtained from public opinion surveys.

Democracy at risk

This indicator is taken from the AmericasBarometer survey of the Latin American Public Opinion Project (LAPOP)[3]. It represents the percentage of the adult population entitled to vote who express low support for the political system and low tolerance of minority rights (based on two scales, with a total of nine items in the survey, each one with a measure of 7 and 10 points). The survey of the AmericasBarometer involves face-to-face surveys in 21 nations of Latin America and the Caribbean, phone surveys in Canada, and one Internet survey in the United States.

Monitoring by external organizations (IDB, 2008)

This indicator measures the effectiveness of monitoring performed by external organizations. It is based on a questionnaire completed by experts and users concerning budgetary information, experts' analysis regarding the practical conditions of the budgetary process, and a framework unifying the perceptions of the survey with the practical questionnaire. The indicator consists of the following attributes:

1. The external controller is reliable.
2. The recommendations made by the external controller have contributed to curb corruption.
3. The external controller verifies the complaints of executives with the actual objectives of the program budgets.
4. The external controller has the capability of carrying out effective monitoring of federal expenses.

The theoretical range of each indicator runs from 0 percent to 100 percent, the highest values indicating a greater capability of control on the part of the external organizations. This indicator, based on subjective information and perceptions, is derived from the answers to a survey addressed to experts on national budgets in various Latin American countries.

Trust in the public administration (IDB, 2008)

This indicator, based on subjective information and perceptions, represents the total percentage of those who answered stating they have much or at least some trust in the public administration, as compiled by the *Latinobarómetro.*

General quality of infrastructure

This variable brings together the opinions of business executives concerning the general quality of the infrastructure in their respective countries. It is calculated on a scale of seven points ("1": poorly developed and inefficient; "7": among the best in the world). This question forms part of the

Opinion Survey of the World Economic Forum performed by the Global Competitiveness Report.

Results

As stated previously, the analysis of the clusters has been performed employing a hierarchical procedure without predetermining the numbers of groups (post hoc analysis). In this method of applied agglomeration, each observation (each country) begins the process within its own cluster. During the following stages, the two nearest clusters join together to create a new, aggregated cluster. This process is repeated in each of the following stages, and the number of clusters is reduced until all the items are within one cluster. In the present case, we would go from an initial number of eight clusters, each composed of only one country, to one sole cluster at the end of the process. Table 6.1 shows the assignment of the different countries to groups according to the number of clusters chosen for the analysis: 3, 4 or 5.

Figure 6.2 shows the dendrogram resulting from the application of the Ward Method[4]. This graph clearly represents the case history of the clusters, beginning with the eight initial countries up till the "final single cluster". It can be stated that there are groups which are precisely defined and whose behavior can be simply and coherently explained according to the seven variables taken into account for the classification. These groups are Argentina and Venezuela (Group 1); Ecuador, Peru, and Bolivia (Group 2), and Chile, Colombia, and Brazil (Group 3). The dendrogram shows that Group 2 was the first one to be established.

This indicates a great similarity among its components, and a moderately strong difference with respect to the other clusters, as this group remains unchanged until an eventual fusion with Group 1 at a later stage. This is the third group to constitute itself and to integrate rapidly into a new cluster

Table 6.1 Clusters

Case	5 Clusters	4 Clusters	3 Clusters
1 Argentina	1	1	1
2 Bolivia	2	2	2
3 Brazil	3	3	3
4 Chile	4	3	3
5 Colombia	4	3	3
6 Ecuador	2	2	2
7 Peru	2	2	2
8 Venezuela	5	4	1

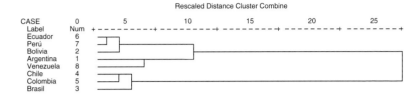

Figure 6.2   Dendrogram using the Ward Method

with another group (Group 2) in a later stage. Meanwhile, Group 3 (established relatively early) reveals itself as the most dissimilar and presents great internal proximity among its components because its inclusion into the final cluster takes place during the last step of the process.

By means of the corresponding box plots shown in Figures 6.3 and 6.4, the behavior of each of the three groups identified by the reference variables is explained.

It could be stated that Group 1 (Argentina and Venezuela) is characterized by an average political stability, though with a level which is slightly superior to that of Group 2 and clearly inferior to that of Group 3. This is due to the following four reasons: (1) a relative trust in the judicial system, even if this is the group in which the judicial system is perceived to have the lowest level of autonomy from influence of governmental and private sectors; (2) the lowest perception of danger to the democratic system among the three reference groups; (3) an intermediate positioning, although relatively near to the level of Group 2, regarding the trust generated by the administration, and the perception of the quality of its infrastructure; (4) being the group which records the lowest possibility of control from external organizations.

Group 2 (Ecuador, Peru, and Bolivia) has the lowest indices concerning political stability, trust in the public administration and in the judicial system – even if this group registers an intermediate value in the perception of autonomy of its judicial system from the influence of the governmental and private sectors. This is the group in which the lowest level of infrastructure quality is perceived. As far as the capacity of control by external organizations, it situates itself slightly above Group 1. This is the cluster in which risk to the democratic system is perceived as being the highest.

Group 3 (Brazil, Chile, and Colombia) shows the highest levels of political stability, trust in and autonomy of the judicial system, trust in the administration, possibility of control by external organizations, and quality of infrastructure. Regarding the perception of risk affecting its democratic system, it records a level similar to that of Group 1 (minimum), even if slightly higher.

Regulatory risk is a variable not directly observable in the present work. In spite of this, according to what has been explained, it can be stated that

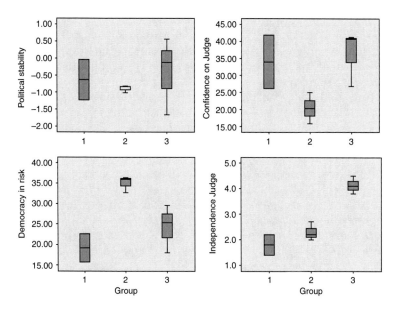

Figure 6.3 Variables (1)

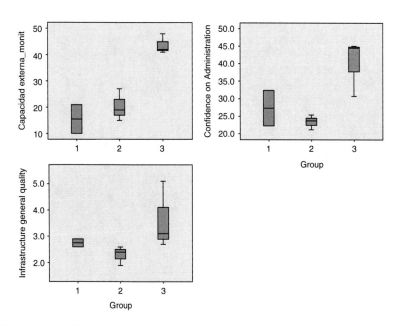

Figure 6.4 Variables (2)

there is a lower perception of regulatory risk when there is greater trust in the public administration and in the judicial system. Similarly, the autonomy of the judicial system and the possibility of control from external organizations reduce the perception of regulatory risk. Political stability also seems to have the same effect. Likewise, the general perception that existing infrastructure is of high quality might be interpreted as a sign that there is some stability in the regulation and that, consequently, there is a level of investments capable of maintaining public services (water, electricity, transport, etc.) within an acceptable level of efficacy and efficiency. Finally, the idea that the democratic system might be in danger contributes to an increment in distrust and, consequently, the risk derived from regulation.

It is evident that what has been indicated in the previous paragraph describes a model of causes and consequences of regulatory risk that should necessarily be submitted to empirical contrast. Nevertheless, the results obtained from the analysis of the clusters will permit the identification of three different profiles of regulatory risk, which are associated to the three groups that have been identified. In this sense, Group 3 (Brazil, Chile, and Colombia) would comprise a geographical space of regulatory stability, which is able to attract international investments. In the opposite extreme, Group 2 (Ecuador, Peru, and Bolivia) might represent the group of countries with the weakest institutions and lowest political stability, which is translated into greater risk generated by regulation. Finally, Group 1 (Argentina and Venezuela) represents an intermediate position fluctuating between the other two groups according to the variables considered. This poses reasonable doubts when the time comes for assigning them a precise level of regulatory risk. Such questions are doubtlessly an obstacle for capturing foreign investments for infrastructure.

Conclusions

In the present work we have reviewed the concept of regulatory risk, deeming it a component of political risk, which forms part of the so-called country risk. The analysis of regulatory risk is a fundamental aspect to be considered for the evaluation of international investment projects carried out within a regulated context. This category would primarily include the infrastructure required for the supply of public and essential services (electricity, water, energy, communications, telecommunications, etc.).

Considering the enormous amount of financial resources required for these investments, the long periods of time necessary to guarantee their profitability, the economies of scale, and in some cases the existence of natural monopolies, plus the effects these projects may have upon the welfare of the population, it is natural that governments hosting international projects within their territory should play a key role in increasing or decreasing the risk derived from regulation.

Latin America is one of the geographical spaces with greater potential for attracting companies from the European Union, the United States, Japan, and China. In spite of this, the continent should not be treated as completely homogeneous regarding the possibility of regulatory risk. Different administrative traditions, singular political structures, and different points of view regarding the role played by regulation on economic activity coexist. The present work, therefore, has identified three groups of Latin American countries in terms of the level of regulatory risk based on certain variables (political stability, trust in the administration, trust in the judicial system, independence of the latter from political and/or business influences, belief that the democratic system is in danger, possibility of exerting external controls, and overall quality of the infrastructure).

Ecuador, Peru, and Bolivia form a cluster with the greatest registered level of regulatory risk. Generally speaking, we are dealing with state administrations having serious difficulties in historic consolidation. In these countries, the majority of the population is below the poverty level (especially the indigenous communities), and there are all sorts of hindrances to economic development (deficient inner connectivity, a poorly remunerated workforce and a tendency to governmental instability that has only started to be overcome in recent years, to name a few). Even though the situation in these countries has shown a tendency toward improvement, there is still a high level of insecurity for investment and a high level of regulatory risk for foreign investors due to limited trust in the public administration and in the judicial system, and the perception of a lack of political stability.

The group integrating Brazil, Colombia, and Chile positions itself as the one with the lowest regulatory risk of the three groups, and it is therefore the most attractive for foreign investments. This is due to a long and lasting economic development stage and relative democratic political stability (with the exception of the civil war against insurgents which persists within some of the Colombian provinces). In these countries we see a division of power, trust in the institutions, the possibility of control, the improvement of infrastructure, and the consolidation of independent means of mass communications. Furthermore, the increasing purchasing power of their internal markets shows that these countries offer the safest options for the development of infrastructure by companies from the European Union, the United States, Japan, and China.

Finally, Argentina and Venezuela form a third group with a level of regulatory risk which is situated between the two former groups, although it is closer to that of the group comprising Bolivia, Ecuador, and Peru. It should be stated that the political stability and the relative trust in the judicial system derive from apparently consolidated democratic systems. In Venezuela, the last military dictatorship ended in 1958, and even if the peculiar regime of Chávez shows militarism, populism, and a tendency to the restriction of certain liberties, the system of representative democracy has not yet been questioned. Argentina has had a democratic government for almost 30 years, and the parliamentary and presidential political system is not presently questioned. Both countries have a per capita income that has traditionally been higher than average for Latin America, and this has brought about quality infrastructure (historical capability for larger public expenses). Nevertheless, the continuous economic and political ups and downs of recent years, the tendency towards an increasing statistical opacity, the aggressive nationalism of Latin American rulers, and the perceived danger of a social or political crisis, explain why reliably low risk countries do not take into consideration the possibility of making investments in these regions at the present time.

In future works it will be necessary to perform a more thorough study of the regulatory risk model of analysis. For this purpose, two differentiated parts will be established: one regarding causes and antecedents, and another regarding the consequences of foreign investments. It will be obviously necessary to determine new variables and to introduce measures alternative to the ones employed in the present study.

Notes

1. Strictly speaking, country risk refers to the risk assumed when subscribing or acquiring fixed-income or variable titles issued by entities of a foreign state, or by granting loans or credits to residents of that country. Its most typical manifestation lies in the eventual delay or in the impossibility of charging dividends and interest and/or recovering the original investment.

2. The *Latinobarómetro* (Latin Barometer) is the main standardized source of information of public opinion in Latin America regarding the development of democracy, as well as social and economic issues. The surveys are performed annually in collaboration with a recognized research organization in each country. The sample size is relatively large, thus reducing measurement errors and providing many observations for statistical analysis. Nevertheless, the *Latinobarómetro* presents certain limitations, including lack of transparency regarding details of the methodology employed to evaluate of the level of representation of the sample and to control the reliability of the survey process.

3. The AmericasBarometer of the Latin American Public Opinion Project (LAPOP) is a survey concerning democratic attitudes and behaviors comprising the Americas from Canada in the north to Argentina in the south, as well as various Caribbean countries, for a total of 24 nations in 2008/2009, involving more than 40,000 surveyed subjects. The survey of the AmericasBarometer employs a common design to build a stratified probabilistic sample (with quotas of levels of homes) of approximately 1500 individuals, with the exception of Bolivia (N = 3000), Ecuador (N = 3000), Paraguay (N = 1200), and Canada (N = 2000). In the case of countries with significant indigenous-speaking populations, the questionnaires are translated into those languages (for example, Quechua and Aymara in Bolivia). There are also versions in English for the English-speaking countries, in French for Haiti, and in Portuguese for Brazil.

4. The Ward Method identifies the sum of the squares between two clusters summed up for all the variables, represented as a distance among them. In each step of the

agglomeration process, the sum of the squares is minimized within the cluster for all the partitions obtained through the combination of two clusters during a previous step. Generally speaking, this method has a tendency to combine the clusters with a reduced number of observations and produces groups with approximately the same number of individuals (Hair et al., 1999).

References

Adams, W.P. (1977): *The United States of America*. Fischer Taschenbuch Verlag, Frankfurt.

Alcántara Sáez, M. (2004): "El estado de la política en América Latina", en J.Mª. Cadenas (Comp.), *América: unidad en la pluralidad*, pp. 79–97. Universidad Central de Venezuela, Caracas.

Beato, P. and Merino, P.A. (2008): "Las necesidades de inversión en el sector energético en un contexto de crecimiento económico", en *Energía y regulación en Iberoamérica*. Thomson, Pamplona, vol. I, ed. Aranzadi, pp. 39–74.

Biardeau, J. (2004): "América Latina es una construcción imaginaria", en J.Mª. Cadenas (Comp.), *América: unidad en la pluralidad*, pp. 41–7. Universidad Central de Venezuela, Caracas.

Burnell, P., and Randall, V. (eds) (2008): *Politics in the Developing World*. Oxford University Press, Oxford.

Calvocoressi, P. (1987): *World Politics since 1945*. Longman Group Ltd, London.

Castells, M. (1989): *The Informational City: Information Technology, Economic Restructuring and the Urban-Regional Process*. Basil Blackwell, Cambridge.

Chiriyankandath, J. (2008): "Colonialism and Post-Colonialism Development", in Burnell, P., and Randall, V. (eds), *Politics in the Developing World*, pp. 35–53. Oxford University Press, Oxford.

Conthe, M. (2004): "Inversiones en infraestrutura y Riesgo regulatorio", *Universia Business Review – Actualidad Económica*, Tercer trimestre, pp. 124–36.

Domínguez, J. (Comp.) (2003): *Conflictos territoriales y democracia en América Latina*. Siglo XXI Eds. y Universidad de Belgrano, Buenos Aires.

Erb, C., Harvey, C., and Viskanta, T. (1996): *Political Risk, Economic Risk and Financial Risk*, Working Paper, Duke University.

Gans, J. (2007): "Taking into Account Regulatory Risk", presentation http://www.mbs.edu/home/jgans/presentations/Reg-Rik-07–07–23.pdf.

Hair, J.F., Anderson, R.E., Tatham, R.L., and Black, W.C. (1999): *Análisis Multivariante*, 5ª Edición. Prentice Hall Iberia, Madrid.

Hoti, S., and MacAleer, M. (2004): "An Empirical Assessment of Country Risk Ratings and Associated Models", *Journal of Economic Surveys*, 18 (4), pp. 539–88.

Iturralde, T., Lasso, C., Urrutia, A., and Rodríguez, A. (2010): "Country Risk Inequality and Polarization in the World: An Empirical Analysis", *Journal of Money, Investment and Banking*, issue 13, pp. 44–54.

Lessard, D.R. (1993): "Country Risk and the Structure of International Financial Intermediation", in Das, D.K. (ed.): *International Finance: Contemporary Issues*, pp. 451–70. Routledge, London.

Lyon, T., and Mayo, M. (2005): "Regulatory Opportunism and Investment Behavior: Evidence from the U.S. Electric Utility Industry", *RAND Journal of Economics*, 36 (3), Autumn, pp. 628–44.

Meny, Y. (1981): "Crises, régions et modernisation de l'etat", *Pouvoir*, núm. 19, pp. 5–18.

Oetzel, J.M., Bettis, R.A., and Zenner, M. (2001): "Country Risk Measures: How Risky Are They?", *Journal of World Business*, 36 (2), pp. 128–45.

Ontiveros, E., Conthe, M., and Nogueira, J.M. (2004): "La percepción de los inversores de los riesgos regulatorios e institucionales en América Latina", *Análisis*, Nº 115, primer trimestre, pp. 5–13.

Peet, R., and Thrift, N. (1989): *New Models in Geography: The Political-Economy Perspective*. Umwin Hyman Ltd, London.

Rodríguez, A. (1997): "El riesgo país: concepto y formas de evaluación", *Cuadernos de Gestión*, nº 19, pp. 41–65.

San Martín, N.; Rodríguez, A. (2008): "¿Reflejan los índices de riesgo país las variables relevantes en el desencadenamiento de las crisis externas? Un análisis sobre el período 1994–2001", *Cuadernos de Gestión*, vol. 8 Nº 2, pp. 65–80.

Urwin, D. (1982): "Territorial structures and political development", in Rokkan, S., and Urwin, D. (eds.), *The Politics of Territorial Identity*, pp. 425–36. Sage Publications.

Zopounidis, C., Pentaraki, K., and Doumpos, M. (1998): "A Review of Country Risk Assessment Approaches: New Empirical Evidence", in Zopounidis, C., and Pardalos, P.M. (eds): *Managing in Uncertainty: Theory and Practice*, pp. 5–22. Kluwer Academic Publishers.

7
Restructuring in Regional Economies and Introducing a Province System in Japan: With Special Reference to the Kansai Region

Masato Ikuta

Introduction

Regional integration has progressed significantly in Europe and North America since the 1990s. This phenomenon is called "regionalism" in international political science. Another type of regionalism, at the domestic level within nation-states, has gained vitality as well because of increasing transborder economic activity. Meanwhile socioeconomic development is leading to a relative increase in the political relevancy of regions and transnational agencies at the expense of nation-states. To distinguish the two types of regionalism, the progress of domestic regionalism is referred to as "new regionalism". This new regionalism has characteristics that differentiate it from provincialism as it developed in Western Europe in the twentieth century (Keating 1998, 73, 115).

Japanese regionalism bears great differences compared to European and North American nations. At the same time, Japan has a situation greatly different from other Asian developing nations, though at present these countries are closely related economically. Most Asian nations are in a period of forming and expanding their national economies at a rapid pace. They are trying to utilize regional integration across national borders as a means of economic growth. In order to consider the Kansai region amid this complex of international relations, it is necessary to explore a methodology for examining the regional economy within the notion of new regionalism.

The Japanese national standard of living has reached a comfortable level, though there are still regional differences in employment opportunities and consumption. It has come to the stage in which regions – for example,

Kansai, with the most mature economy of Asia – should pursue an internally acceptable living standard that will allow sustainable development in the future. For this purpose, decentralization of decision-making ability to regions appears wholly different from the current centralized political and economic system. It should, however, be recognized that a regional economy has complexly interrelated national economy and politics. The province system that Japan's central government intends to introduce would have a strong influence on the regional economy.

In considering a regional economy from a policy viewpoint, it is necessary to suppose a mechanism of consensus building within a region and the manner of action of the various elements of the region such as large and small private enterprises, local governments, administrative branches of central government, workers, and consumers.

The geographic area of Kansai contains more than 20 million people, and a variety of additional entities, the sum of which can be considered equivalent to a nation (Ikuta 2008). In viewing this large and complicated regional economy, the author reviewed prominent contributions concerning the locality debates in the United Kingdom since the 1980s, found in Massie (1984) and Johnston (1991). These two geographers considered how a specific region could be accurately evaluated in a nation. These geographers' methodologies for placing a region in a country have similarity, though their views toward society seem to be quite different. They suggested that a region has two important characteristics – namely, a common character relating to nearby regions and unique qualities that do not exist in other regions. In this chapter, the expression of the common character (Johnston 1991) is taken as a necessary relationship. Even if the expression of necessary relationships cannot be understood easily, they constitute the basic character of a region in a country. It indicates each region has common interests concerning the economic and other social activities as one part of a nation. An enterprise established in one region can easily expand into other regions to obtain new markets, while an enterprise established in other regions can move forward into that region. The degree of freedom of location for enterprises seems to be relatively high within one nation in market economies. Although moving and establishing branches is closely restricted by law and governmental bodies, locational freedom within Japanese regions remains relatively high.

A region, additionally, has unique features that cannot be found in other regions, and hence these are called "local conditions." The concept of local conditions includes characteristics peculiar to a region. Summarizing these concepts, the necessary relationship reflects commonness among regions, whereas local conditions mean peculiarities in a region. The peculiarities can generate indigenous value and also create a new kind of economic activity when a society has entered into a mature stage after rapid economic growth, such as the Kansai region has. This article will progress based on these two concepts.

Japanese economic geographers considered theories of drastic changes within regional economies during the high economic growth period which continued for some 20 years from the middle of the 1950s (Kato 2003). One is called "regional structure theory" and may be applicable for examining changing spatial patterns of regional economies within a nation during times of rapid economic growth. This theory seems to be effective for evaluating regional reorganizations of present Asian nations, which are still continuing to grow in spite of the current economic situation. A nature of this theory, however, demonstrates that regional economies that compose one nation can be restructured as a part of the national economy. The regional outline of the national economy is judged in this theory; thereby it does not pay attention to regional economies itself, which has complicated internal circulations within the region. This theory, accordingly, does not contemplate an interrelation between regional economies and the national economy. Young and Lin (2003) have called for a theory for explaining Asian growth in the field of economic geography and pointed out only the Flying Geese hypothesis as the Japanese contribution, criticizing their poor contributions. Their critiques of Japan's reduced output is unfortunately true; even so, an idea of regional structure theory has a possibility to assess issues on regional restructuring in a national economy in Asian developing nations (AJEAG 2005).

Relocation of the manufacturing industry

The Kansai region in Japan

Japan experienced a great transformation of regional economies after the World War II. There were two periods of rapid growth, including one of high economic growth and the asset-inflated economy, or bubble economy, in the latter half of the 1980s. The economic changes caused brutal upheavals in all aspects of regional economies: industries, local governments, workers, and consumers. The manufacturing industry had a principal role in that economic growth. Large enterprises producing manufactured goods developed among a large number of small and medium-sized enterprises in three metropolitan areas including Tokyo, Osaka, and Nagoya city. These major metropolitan areas, home to half of the total Japanese population, have dominated the national economy.

The regional development of manufacturing industries has been restructuring Japan's urban system (Ikuta 1998). Major components of the system are large and prefectural cities, which play decisive roles in the jurisdiction. The most important cities, outside metropolitan areas, include central cities of regions such as Sapporo, Sendai, Hiroshima, and Fukuoka, as shown in Figure 7.1. These cities developed as centers for both industrial production and distribution in the region in the high economic growth period and have exercised governmental and economic influence across

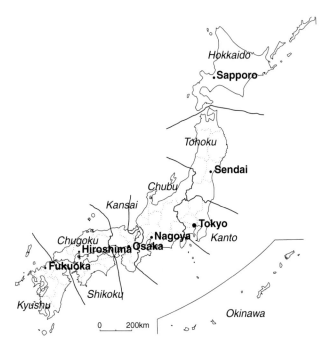

Figure 7.1   Japanese regions

prefectural borders in the region. While there are many branch offices dispersed throughout Japan in consumer-goods industries like pharmaceuticals, there are few branches concentrated in large cities in intermediate and capital-goods industries like textiles (Suda 1993); however, many companies with headquarters in Tokyo or Osaka had branch offices in these cities (Hino 1995). Land developers constructed a number of office buildings to accommodate these offices until the 1990s. The vacancy rate of these buildings has recently soared following corporate restructuring. The problem has become even serious in Sendai city in the Tohoku region.

The Kansai economy has been losing its relative importance as a core area for manufacturing industries in Japan. The urban function, however, has not decreased broadly and is supported by growing wholesale and trading industries. The economic status of Kansai within the nation has descended relatively in the post-war period with the rapid growth of Kanto and other regions. If we take a closer look at metropolitan areas, three metropolitan areas grew simultaneously during the high economic growth period, whereas in the bubble economy, only Tokyo and its Kanto region were expanding. The latter was called the period of concentric growth in Tokyo compared to the rest of the country. Spatial patterns of regional growth have fundamentally changed between the two periods accompanied by restructurings of the national economy. Kansai's shifting position had been pointed out as early as in the 1970s. Policy measures could not prevent the deterioration of Kansai economies, although the central government had implemented various measures to recover the declining economic situation.

A new type of retail business, the supermarket, had begun to open on shopping streets in cities with the start of high economic growth in the 1950s. The supermarket eventually started to relocate to places along major roads in suburban metropolises with the growth of suburban populations (Ikuta 1991). Retail location was accurately reflected by population redistributions within market areas. Because of rapid growth of new retail facilities, a series of disputes between supermarkets and small stores in existing shopping streets intensified not only in metropolitan areas but also in local cities across the nation in the 1960s. To manage these conflicts in regional economies, national government introduced a so-called large-scale retail-store law in 1973 that aimed to prevent the locating of supermarkets in existing shopping streets.

Restructuring in waterfront areas

Unlike Western nations, Japanese metropolitan areas have heavy agglomerations of manufacturing industries as do current metropolises in other Asian nations. Japan had intended to catch up with Western nations within a short time period by accelerating economic growth by concentrating industrial investments in three metropolitan areas. The waterfront area from Kobe to Osaka city had led the Japanese industrial revolution since the 1880s. A large-scale coastal industrial area was formed based on the munitions industry in the 1930s. Manufacturing industries grew rapidly, accompanied by serious pollution, in densely populated metropolitan areas during the period of high economic growth. A regional policy was introduced to relocate factories from metropolises to the countryside in the 1960s. Heavy industry operations like shipbuilding, steel, and petrochemical industry started to relocate due to severe industrial restructuring during the time of high economic growth.

Nonetheless local governments commenced reclaiming new industrial sites along waterfront areas to locate the heavy and chemical industries that had promoted Japanese economic growth in the 1960s. In this period, one of the most important regional policies for Kansai was creating special districts for industrialization around metropolitan areas by the central government. One of them was created adjoining the western part of the Osaka Metropolitan Area (OMA). The special district played a vital role for increasing manufacturing production in the region. Heavy and chemical industries along the waterfront between Osaka and Kobe had decreased production with this locational restructuring (Figure 7.2).

A new employment policy was required to create new job opportunities, especially in Kobe, because employment on the waterfront had decreased with the relocation of production facilities to other places including the special district. Similar locational trends were realized in Osaka, though ramifications of the difficulty were clearly different between the two cities. Osaka had a larger number of job opportunities and different types of manufacturing, whereas Kobe had historically depended on only some major manufacturing enterprises in the waterfront area was well as sea transportation activities. City Hall had to nurture new industries, such as apparel and Western-style baked goods, among other things, to ameliorate the drop in employment.

In Osaka, a large-scale reclamation project had to be converted to a housing development, though the reclamation had started for manufacturing

Figure 7.2   Kansai region

industries soon after the commencement of high economic growth. Osaka City Hall had to change the project to the establishment of a new jurisdiction with a planned population of 40,000, instead of creating an industrial area. The cause for this significant policy change was that land demand for manufacturing was overestimated at the planning stage. The Osaka prefectural government, furthermore, had decided to reclaim other land for an industrial complex. The shipbuilding, petrochemical, and steel industries were in place after completing the complex in the early 1960s. These were, unfortunately, medium-scale factories with small production, because the enterprises involved did not plan to invest heavily due to already existing factories in other regions.

By the time the land reclamations were completed by the public sector, industries in metropolitan areas no longer needed the sites because of technology innovation and changed demand. The private sector did not always follow the public sector's intention. Industrial restructurings in the private sector came faster than the public sector's development projects.

The waterfront in Kansai became a main target area for development policy by the central government after the 1980s. There were as many as 2000 hectares of unused land that had been used for heavy industry including power plants and gas facilities. The reason the waterfront was regarded as a target for redevelopment was clearly that the areas were mostly owned by large enterprises, which had strong influence on both local and central government. Lawmakers passed the Osaka Bay–Area Development Act in 1992, creating a mandate for the central government to redevelop the deteriorated seashore owned by major enterprises. The phrase "World City" was included in one article in the law because business communities and local governments were willing to establish a global city in the Kansai region. Osaka is now ranked, unfortunately, as a minor city in the world urban network (Taylor 2002). Major projects in the area included Kansai International Airport, which opened in 1994, and Universal Studios Japan (USJ), which was opened on land rented from a conglomerate representing Kansai. USJ, opened in 2001, became the most attractive theme park in western Japan after Tokyo Disney Resort.

Only a few projects were realized, including USJ and the Covered Athletic Dome, even though government and business had planned to expand leisure industries and dwelling units in waterfront areas. Unused lands were left for a long time, and redevelopment projects were not completed until recently. Major transnational companies that originated in OMA, however, have returned to invest in production of liquid crystal products and batteries, changing their business strategies after 20 years of international business operations.

Manufacturing industries in suburban areas

Before World War II, there were already numbers of white-collar commuters and students who traveled daily to Osaka city so that commuter trains were already being operated by private enterprises. A metropolitan area was formed on a smaller scale in the 1930s. In the high economic growth periods, nevertheless, it expanded largely with the population inflow to the central cities, and their rehousing in suburban areas followed industrial relocations. Both manufacturing relocations and housing developments have caused metropolitan restructuring. These two types of growing land use were planned to be geographically apart because factories in this period created noise and heavy traffic. The public sector desired to establish industrial parks and housing geographically apart in the outer suburbs, whereas the two land uses were closely located in the inner suburbs and near central districts (Figure 7.3). In inner suburbs, urban functions, factories, small stores, and consumer services were densely placed, often creating urban sprawl. Land use planning was not successful in this area, and sprawl was extensive in the inner suburbs. About 20,000 small and medium-sized factories had formed in the industrial districts neighboring Osaka city, which was said to be the largest industrial agglomeration in the world. Housing estates increased with a mixed pattern of small private projects and large-scale planned ones in the hilly areas between Osaka and the city of Kyoto (Uesugi 2009). Locational density of urban functions differs between inner and outer suburbs. The difference between the two types of suburbs has caused different locational patterns of retail and personal service industries.

Large manufacturing enterprises started to relocate their factories to the countryside in order to obtain more affordable land and labor as the regional policy was introduced in the 1970s. Within OMA, industrial districts for consumer goods also developed rapidly in the high economic growth period and started declining continuously after that period.

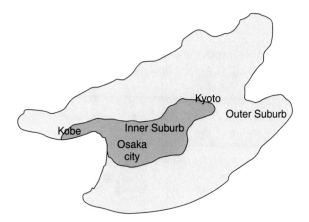

Figure 7.3   Concept of Osaka Metropolitan Area (OMA)
Source: Author

Strict competition for urban land use had forced a continuous decline in local industries, which were composed of small and medium-sized enterprises. Manufacturing and housing competed to obtain land for their growth. Major factories could move into the countryside because of regional policies, whereas small and medium-sized enterprises and the agglomerated districts failed because they could neither relocate easily nor survive in the competitive urban environment.

One of the major characteristics in Kansai manufacturing is the multitude of small and medium-sized enterprises. These firms had difficulties moving out from industrial districts; nonetheless they managed to run their business where they originated. For example, there was a district of consumer blanket makers in southern OMA. The industry grew rapidly in the 1960s, producing about 90 percent of the total production in Japan. The industries, however, continued to decline steadily in the 1970s and onward. Now, the district has almost disappeared with increasing imports of cheaper goods largely from China. There were numerous districts for similar consumer goods which followed identical decay patterns in Kansai. The real estate of former blanket factories was converted to housing units for urban dwellers. There were increasing job opportunities for service industries in the metropolitan area as well, even as the factory workers were urged to discover new jobs.

The outer suburbs provided good places for new industrial location with low population density in agricultural and hilly areas. One typical place among these, the southern part of Shiga prefecture, became a suitable site for industrial locations with road-widening projects and highway construction along major transportation corridors between the two metropolises of Osaka and Nagoya. Textile industries, at first, began to locate here in the 1960s, whereas in the 1970s, the range of machinery industries increased and played a crucial role in economic growth. Many branch plants of large enterprises, for example in electrical and metal fabrication, were located in the area and contributed to development. The industrial structure of Shiga changed such that the share of large factories dominated. There were fewer small and medium-sized factories in comparison to other prefectures. Electrical industries making home appliances employed large numbers of employees per factory. Considering employment, enterprises with headquarters in Osaka and Tokyo employed workers largely in Shiga factories. In other words, branch plants of large enterprises employed larger numbers of total workers, whereas a local industry had only a small number of employees.

The regional labor market was restructured by industrialization and suburbanization in OMA. Manufacturing employment changed greatly within OMA because of the challenging fluctuations of the economy from the high economic growth period, through the bubble economy, and into the continuing recession in the 1990s. During the bubble economy, manufacturing employment expanded in suburban areas including Shiga, although it had already started to decrease in central cities of the metropolitan area. Large plants in outer suburbs maintained their employment levels by changing production systems to manage diverse products and small-quantity production instead of mass production as in the 1970s. In the 1990s, however, employment substantially decreased with the hollowing out of factories and increasing overseas businesses of large enterprises. Temporary employment and foreign workers including Japanese Brazilians increased in this region as well as Tokyo and Nagoya. The number of Japanese South Americans in Shiga in 2007 was 17,000, up from only 1000 in 1990. As a result of the labor shortage in the 2000's, the Japanese government relaxed its immigration policy. The regional labor market in OMA has been changing its character.

Kansai manufacturing companies started to relocate their factories to other Asian countries beginning in the middle of the 1980s as the yen appreciated as a stage in the advancement of the countryside within Japan. These shifts had critical impacts upon existing industrial districts made up of small and medium-sized industries in OMA. Major enterprises had, in addition, a trend for moving their headquarters to Tokyo in order to expand their business activities. This tendency was clearest in the finance and commerce industries in Osaka, whereas enterprises in Kyoto, mainly manufacturing industries, did not show such behavior. The behaviors in the two cities vary and attracted study of the causes of the difference between the two cities. Many businesses in Kyoto are part of the electronics industry and have rather short corporate histories with a start-up character, despite having a large number of employees and transnational operations. Kyoto has the nature of an industrial city, even as the traditional industries have been in critical decline since the 1990s.

Service industries in the central cities

A local condition of interest in the Kansai region is that the three central cities are set geographically apart each other. After World War II, Osaka and Kobe needed to redevelop on a large scale because of widespread destruction in those cities, and therefore land readjustment projects were implemented based on war-damage reconstruction. Kobe had unique strategies fully utilizing its power as an ordinance-designated city. The city planned to reclaim land by transporting soil and sand from the hilly areas and also to develop the excavated sites to correspond with the city's rapid population increase in the 1970s. The former small town of Kobe had become a large metropolis with unique development strategies growing out of the Meiji Era.

Osaka intended not only to redevelop three existing city centers but also to create two new subcenters, which were planned to be located on the east and west sides of the city. City Hall was planning to create a new east-west development axis to absorb economic power concentrated in the Central Business District because the three existing city centers were aligned north-south.

The issues of urban growth in Kyoto, on the other hand, differed from those of the other two cities because it was not much damaged during the war. Kyoto was an inland city, unlike the other two, and the locational difference brought different growth patterns for manufacturing industries other than heavy industries. Policy issues for urban development were different in all three cities. Osaka had a rather small jurisdiction in spite of its 2.5 million population, whereas Kyoto and Kobe had large jurisdictions including agricultural areas.

A common issue regarding developed areas in these cities was realized with economic growth, namely inner-city deterioration since the 1960s. Quite different policies were pursued for the same inner-city problems, because the situations and distribution of these areas were clearly different among the three cities. A comprehensive policy was formalized and carried out in Kobe, which had suffered a serious problem along its coastline.

In retail, activity generally increases and decreases in accordance with changes of population in market areas. This relationship might be observed, at a large scale, as a competition between metropolitan centers and suburban retail districts. Retail needed to catch up with rapid population increases in the inner suburbs in the 1960s. Suburban consumers had, on the other hand, obtained greater freedom within OMA because of developed public transportation and highways. OMA has two dominant regional consumption markets: central markets consisting of major shopping districts in central cities and outer suburban markets boasting new multipurpose shopping centers (supermarket, retail, restaurants, and entertainment) and revitalized suburban city centers. The suburban market grew impressively in accordance with population growth during the 1970s, 1980s, and 1990s. The central markets, however, did not decrease severely because these centers had been strongly connected to suburban consumers by public transportation and highways. Shopping streets in residential areas were heavily impacted in central cities. Rigorous competition between the central and suburban markets has continued in OMA.

In the latter half of the 1990s, population trends fundamentally changed in OMA because of population increases in central cities following the Tokyo metropolitan area. This was referred to as "gentrification", which had emerged in Western cities in the 1970s. High-rise condominiums started to develop in central cities because of declining land prices largely due to the economic downturn. Suburbanization had finally ended in major metropolitan areas. Looking at families who moved into these newly constructed high-rise residential units, a majority came from within the same central cities whereas few families returned from the suburbs. Families who prefer urban circumstances have begun to reside again in high-rise dwelling units in central cities rather than detached houses in suburban areas.

The wholesale and financial industries in Kansai have continued to establish head offices and transfer the functions to Tokyo. This corporate behavior can be thought of as a necessary situation for the region. It is rational that a corporation, having arrived at a certain level, would intend to expand its business in Tokyo, the hub of the nation. Enterprises in Kansai were also expanding their business to other regions within Japan, utilizing resources accumulated within the region.

At the same time, new industries in information processing and other areas were growing in Tokyo, where the headquarters of large enterprises were concentrated. As for information processing, the industry did not grow in Kansai on a large scale in spite of policy assistance. A number of branch offices in this industry have located in Osaka adding small-scale companies based in Kansai with most of the headquarters located in Tokyo. This pattern of increasing branch offices has been reflected by a local condition of Kansai for service industries.

Research parks in the hilly inland

Suburban research parks should be reviewed in comparison with the waterfront area. Central and local governments started to establish a type of new town in the 1980s, in which it was planned to introduce a variety of national and private research institutions. These were called "science cities" or "research parks", to be located mainly in the outer suburbs (see Figure 7.3) and adjoining areas. Science cities were of different types – namely, those supported by the national government such as Kansai Science City in the southern part of Kyoto prefecture, and those established by prefectural governments. These were, in total, large-scale suburban developments that have not been completed even today because of the collapse of the bubble economy at the end of the 1980s. Many smaller science cities were planned by prefectural governments and national industrial policy in the period of the bubble economy.

Bass (1998) clearly stated that Japan has a complicated system among central and local governments for exploiting science cities. All prefectural governments in Kansai had planned to establish science cities pushed by the central government. The Kinki Research Complex Plan (KRC Plan) was started to establish science cities based on a national study for developing the R&D capacity of Kansai. Central government had anticipated that the capacity would be expanded in Kansai Science City where a national project was underway. Local governments and business communities, however, had responded to central government that Kansai would increase the capacity in many science cities in a dispersed spatial pattern of smaller operations in conjunction with the regional development plan for prefectures. Kansai answered with its prefecture-based plan that was quite different from

Tsukuba Research Park in Tokyo, the largest and most successful science city in Japan. As a result, it was envisaged that more than 30 percent of Japanese science cities would be located in Kansai.

Japanese industrial structure shifted increasingly to R&D functions for manufacturing in the 1980s. This shift has been a fundamental transformation concerning the relationship between manufacturing and housing estate projects in metropolitan suburbs. Increasing research capacity can easily be placed with housing in urban environments. Science city projects were therefore realized based on a changing industrial structure in Japan. This type of urban expansion accurately reflected the technological innovations of manufacturing as well as other corporate behavior.

The KRC Plan was incorporated in the fourth national development plan, started in 1987, which saw sharp debates in The National Diet on regional policy between Kanto and other regions. The draft plan had an ambition for recreating Tokyo as a world economic center just like New York or London. Kansai and other regions bitterly opposed the draft plan, which would have injected huge national funds only into Kanto and Tokyo. The plan was changed, then, due to the severe opposition by other prefectures including those of Kansai.

The KRC Plan had covered the Kansai region including some neighboring regions and positioned Kansai Science City with a central research function accompanied by a number of smaller ones. Smaller cities were planned to be integrated by high-speed information networks and highway systems. The KRC Plan included as many as 37 science cities. The second-largest city was a technopolis development established in 1985 in Hyogo prefecture that was recognized as one of 26 national research parks across Japan. Hyogo prefecture had planned as many as ten science cities. The prefectural government intended to raise R&D capacity via the KRC Plan because the largest Kansai science city was situated in a remote site within the prefecture. The prefecture had an urban development plan in which the population was targeted as 25,000 in the technopolis. A large-scale synchrotron radiation facility was placed in the city as a main research center, one of the largest experimental facilities in the world. The resident population, however, did not increase in the city in spite of its population plan. The resident population remained only 1700 in 2008, including all residents of detached houses, condominiums, rented homes for researchers, and university dormitories. The population did not increase because the site was in a remote, hilly place, inconvenient for commuting to workplaces in urban areas. It had insufficient living conditions without retail stores and other essential services as well.

Only a few institutions located in the science cities, even though numerous such cities were created in OMA. Infrastructure works for the cities, requiring leveling of hilly areas, took a long time. Large enterprises did not realize their plans to invest in new research institutes due to the prevailing sluggish economy of the 1990s. A discrepancy between slow public works and the private sector's quick decision making based on economic conditions had resulted in the same situation as in the waterfront developments. The Kansai Economic Federation (KEF) did not intend to get deeply involved after the plan was established in the national and prefectural plans, though KEF had been keen for the KRC plan itself. Business communities have tended to respond quickly to economic trends in general. Central and local governments' large urban redevelopment works find it difficult to respond to changes in a volatile economy.

Kansai enjoys the second-largest industrial agglomeration in Japan and has a good share of R&D function as well. The total number of R&D institutions, including public and private, reached half that of the Kanto region, 2200, by the early 2000s. These two regions, Kanto and Kansai, dominate in terms of research institutions in Japan, with more than 70 percent of the total. Although national R&D institutions are generally located in Kanto, the capital region, there exist many private institutions established by large enterprises in Kansai. This function could be created in existing buildings or sites instead of in newly prepared science cities in remote hilly areas. Research operations need not necessarily be situated in a newly developed city and can be set even in an existing facility within the enterprise. Major enterprises thus did not build their research institutions as prefectural governments and KEF had anticipated. The plan for Kansai's science cities failed, including Kansai Science City, although its population is increasing with housing projects as a bedroom suburb. The character of the city has become greatly different from the same type of national research park in Tsukuba in Tokyo.

Kansai's local situation and system of prefectures

Industrial structure outside OMA

Another local condition of Kansai should be considered by investigating small urban centers positioned in intermediate and mountainous areas outside OMA. For example, a city located in the northern part of Hyogo prefecture was famous for a local bag-making industry during the high economic growth period. The industry, however, has since declined with increasing imported cheap commodities from Asian nations since the 1980s. Growing borderless economic activities had crucial repercussions even in a small manufacturing center in a mountainous area in Kansai.

But, there is another type of local industry in the western part of Hyogo prefecture outside OMA. Nishiwaki has a reputation for a cotton textiles industry for a long time. The industry still has a competitive edge and economic power, even though it is gradually declining. The number of factories and persons engaged have been decreasing continuously in the city. However, it has not arrived at a drastic decrease, different from local industries in the metropolitan area.

Local industries and branch factories contributed to maintaining job opportunities in small cities in peripheral Kansai. These locations were promoted by a range of factors, including improving industrial infrastructure and supportive policies from prefectures and cities. Adding to these, a local condition of a metropolis's adjacent areas is a relative advantage in introducing new technologies and services. The huge market of metropolitan areas provides an essential condition for surviving local industries. Geographical proximity to a metropolis, moreover, has demonstrated a relative advantage when trying to attract a new factory. It became difficult, however, for the local cities to continue their growth by attracting branch plants when overseas expansions of Kansai enterprises accelerated in the 1990s. Industries for economic growth had to be changed from manufacturing to other industries in many regions after the appreciation of the Japanese yen. Accordingly, sightseeing and tourism-related businesses have become the most important industry in that economic environment.

One district, Northern Hyogo, can be observed as a case study for increasing tourism. In the 1990s, the number of tourists visiting a former castle town there reached one million yearly. It is often said that one million tourists in a year is necessary for a tourist destination to obtain an established position in Japan. Job opportunities continued to increase in the district, even though the tourists started to decrease after a powerful earthquake struck Kobe city in 1995. Promotion policies by City Hall had encouraged the opening of a large resort hotel in 1993, utilizing a former factory site. City Hall gave a series of benefits to the hotel owner, who had been born near the district. The district became a convenient sightseeing destination for people living in OMA and created job opportunities based on the incoming tourists. A characteristic of this district was that many of the tourists were older travelers who stayed only a short time on the way to other attractive destinations with hot springs.

Peripheral areas in Kansai include places in a metropolitan area's vicinity, but not within the metropolitan area. Geographical proximity brings business opportunities in manufacturing industries and a range of service industries as well as tourism.

Visitors to Kansai deserve attention because there are a huge number of business and sightseeing visitors from other regions in Japan as well as from foreign nations. If we need not stick to conventional industrial classifications, it will be possible to develop a new view of industry that unifies both recreational and business visitors. Both types of visitors commonly stay in hotels, use public transportation, and visit restaurants for meals. The behavioral patterns of both are unexpectedly similar, though their respective destinations are different: sightseeing spots and business opportunities. To promote this industry, it is appropriate to reorganize the current industrial groupings which are clearly divided by type such as transport, hotel, and others. New York, London, and Singapore can be observed as useful examples for supporting this group of industries. Kansai has plenty of historical resources to contribute to developing this industry.

There should also be a focus on improving quality of life in cities, to satisfy residents and visitors to Kansai, different from the industry-centered view that was firmly in place after World War II. Central government has been regarding cities as a place where a range of industries are developing for economic growth. Additionally, Japanese citizens desired economic growth until the end of the 1980s. It is now necessary to view Japanese cities from the demand side instead of the supply side. In European nations during the welfare state period, there was a primary policy goal of improving urban dwellers' labor and housing. Cities were certainly a place of industrial growth; nonetheless, it was clear that cities had to provide upgraded living standards for the everyday life of the citizenry. The social and economic roles of cities vis-à-vis the nation seem to differ between Japan and the Western nations even today.

The bubble economy came to a halt at the end of the 1980s; subsequently it has come to the point that cities can be considered from the demand side of residents and visitors. A typical example of the societal change can be identified in that citizens have become aware of preserving and improving the urban landscapes in which they live. Cities started to enact ordinances for preserving the landscape, and finally, the central government enacted a law on landscapes in 2005 following this change within society.

Debates on the province system

Introducing a province system will have a crucial influence on Japanese regional economies over the long term. The regional economies have been influenced by globalization of economic activities and an increasingly aged population. A new governance system of regions will contribute to creating new regional markets. Both business communities and central government have been interested for different reasons, whereas citizens have broadly ignored the issue. Local business communities, above all, have grave concerns because a new system would be intimately related to their business activities because of unavoidable restructuring of existing regulations.

Local business communities in Kansai and Kyushu have been insisting on introducing the system for a long time. KEF started championing it as early as the 1950s. Central government meanwhile promoted amalgamating cities and towns to prepare for high economic growth. In accordance with their policy, KEF started to propose a new governance system to obtain more freedom for business activities across prefectural borders. KEF submitted its first proposal in 1955 and has continued submitting it with changes in purpose and content. The government has considered the province system through the Local Government System Research Council as well. The council submitted a report on an ideal approach to creating a province system in 2006. A province system, however, has not been finalized yet for introduction, because a more fundamental discussion is needed concerning role sharing between local and central government. The new governance system has also been discussed with consideration of administrative and fiscal reforms due to the severe financial constraints of central and local governments.

A discussion on decentralization of power under the current prefecture system has progressed in Kansai due to the business community's initiatives. The Kansai large area mechanism's current system was established in 2007. It consists of prefectures, ordinance-designated cities, KEF, and others. This mechanism has established the Kansai wide wide-area union by the end of fiscal year 2010. The union is an organization based on the present prefecture system and will be a special public entity excluding Nara prefecture. Nara opposes the union, claiming that it would be an ineffective governance system. It became possible to create this organization after revising local autonomy laws. Wide-area union was pursued at first among prefectures in the Tohoku region with legislative amendments in the 1990s. It was not, however, realized. Governors of prefectures and others will be in charge of operating the wide-area union. The union plans to handle area-wide clerical work on disaster prevention, tourism, medical treatment, licensing, and qualifying examinations in the first stage of its establishment.

It is said that regional economies will never be revitalized, even if wide-area union were introduced. It could be true that the effects of the new administrative system might not be noticeable to the regional economies if observed soon after inauguration. The example of Third Italy, however, shows that regional economies have been revitalized because provinces practiced their own effective industrial policies. The Kansai region can learn the experiences of Third Italy's urban policies coordinated by industrial policy, although population size and industrial structure for the two regions are greatly different. Creation of a province system was accomplished in Italy in the 1970s and in France in the 1980s. The reasons for introducing province systems seem to be alike in these two nations. Central government aimed for more efficient and reduced governance, and local governments, on the other hand, desired to obtain more self-reliant governance systems.

A questionnaire survey of governors of Japanese prefectures shows that the majority of them are for introducing a new province system. Local governments are willing to obtain more self-determination as well. There remain, however, a lot of issues in creating and managing a province system by amalgamating present prefectures. Both central and local governments are influenced by lobbying groups of business communities currently active in Japan. The Japan Business Federation in Tokyo has robust influence on the central government, and KEF has influence on both central and local government.

Large enterprises that make up KEF share the feature that they cannot easily relocate their facilities to other regions. These include an electric power company, a major gas supplier, and private railway companies. These enterprises are establishing a series of subsidiary companies aside from electricity and gas and are increasing the variety of service businesses as well. Their new businesses include telecommunication, building maintenance, and house repair, among other activities. As a consequence, there is a bigger influence on the regional economies, though individually these services are not so remarkable.

Private railway companies play a crucial role in regional development in Japan. A certain corporation, for example, founded not only its railway system but also a terminal department store in Osaka city in the 1920s. It established a women's operetta troupe near another terminal in its railway system and even developed housing along the railway lines. This was then a unique business model for a private railway company in a densely populated society, largely different from Western nations. Railway companies moved forward to engage urban development projects in Kansai, and these facts influenced urban developments in other regions. Osaka's urban structure had changed drastically in the pre-war period because of the private railway companies. There was no fundamental restructuring in Kyoto due to its conservative atmosphere as a former national capital. Osaka city, however, developed rapidly as it helped construct a modernized nation-state facing the Western nations in the pre-war period.

During the high economic growth period, some smaller cities were described as *company towns* where a large manufacturing company and its subcontractor firms dominated the economy. The expression *regional monopoly* was also used in explaining the situation wherein local enterprises' management of traffic systems had crucial influence on urban areas. In larger metropolitan areas, however, a variety of enterprises located within the area due to rapid economic growth. There was no situation in which only a small number of large enterprises demonstrated a crucial influence on the entire metropolitan area at that time. Although railway companies had been opening affiliated retail stores and department stores along the railway lines, this was unremarkable in a fluid society in which there was rapid economic growth. Nonetheless influences by some large enterprises seem to be clearer in metropolitan areas at present, unlike in the above-mentioned former period.

When we consider a province system, it would be better to create a system that involves a mixture of social organizations in the governance system, not only of business communities but also of relevant organizations representing labor and consumers. The society has to identify entities to be involved in decision-making processes for governing the decentralized province. Only if small and medium-sized enterprises and the urban dwellers are properly involved in the system can proper development policy be realized – instead of the current system in which large enterprises have decisive power for creating policy in the region.

In setting up a province system, the amalgamation of current jurisdictions into provinces becomes a critical issue. The best regional definition cannot be formulated because regional definitions vary even among ministries of the central government. KEF asked a prefecture in Shikoku to join the Kansai region in order to define Osaka Bay as an inland sea. This geographical division does not appear appropriate for the regional economies of Japan.

There seems to be an issue regarding the size of OMA within the Kansai region. OMA should be broken up into smaller areas for purposes of distributing and balancing administrative power. Currently, OMA dominates the region with regard to economic activities and population. It might not be appropriate to deliver administrative power to a large metropolitan area that was decided by the central government only for statistical convenience.

Conclusion

This chapter has discussed one of the major Japanese regions, Kansai, based on the locality debates among UK geographers since the 1980s. In this work, regional economies were observed in the context of two contradicting concepts – namely, necessary relationships between regions and local conditions in a region while evaluating a region's role in its national economy. The Kansai region has three central cities, Osaka, Kyoto, and Kobe, and has a large metropolitan area in comparison to other major regions in Japan.

The locations of three central cities can be identified as a major local feature in the metropolitan area. The dispersed location of three central cities created a distinctive value for the regional economy, avoiding over-concentration in one major city such as in the Tokyo metropolitan area. The locational pattern of central cities has contributed to dispersed population growth within the metropolitan area.

Peripheral areas within Kansai have maintained economic activities utilizing geographical proximity to the metropolitan area. A variety of local industries have developed in conjunction with the market forces provided by the metropolitan area. Tourism has also developed, providing convenient tourist destinations for urban dwellers.

Osaka Metropolitan Area experienced heavy industrial relocation for more than 20 years since the 1950s. Major companies in the region increasingly moved their headquarters to Tokyo or their factories to rural Japan in order to obtain larger domestic markets. Regional economies of Kansai have continued to deteriorate since the 1970s. Reorganization of the metropolitan area's industrial structure has been rapid, and hence the regional labor market has changed drastically. Population regrowth in central cities began in the 1990s after suburbanization had terminated. Regional consumption markets in the metropolitan area have been changing throughout the post-war period, even today. Regional markets are being reorganized still, at a high velocity.

There is a possibility that tourism will grow in the region, if business and sightseeing visitors can be integrated as behavioral entities, because historical resources are abundantly present. Kansai has the most mature society in Japan. Additionally there are growing services, though considerable industrial production of material and intermediate goods remains.

Amid this background, local business communities and local governments are preparing to introduce a decentralized province system, as was introduced in Italy and France. Local major enterprises of electricity, gas, and transport have harnessed their public relations strength in favor of establishing a system to obtain more freedom for their business activities. If a province system is implemented, it would result in major transformations within regional economies. To implement the system, KEF initiated the establishment of the Kansai large area mechanism in 2007. The mechanism includes a plan to establish a new organization, a wide-area union, which is a special entity based on the current prefecture system.

References

*In Japanese with English abstract

AJAEG (2005) Special Issue: Changing Agglomeration of the Japanese Manufacturing Industry. *Annals of the Japan Association of Economic Geographers* 51(5): 439–511.

Bass, S. (1998) Japanese research parks: National policy and local development. *Regional Studies* 32(5): 391–403.

Hino, M. (1995) The agglomeration of branch offices and their recent changes in major Japanese cities.* *Annals of the Japan Association of Economic Geographers* 41(3): 192–207.

Ikuta, M. (1991) Retail location development and its impact upon the consumer spatial behavior in the Japanese urban system. *Asian Geographer* 10(1): 79–88.

Ikuta, M. (1998) Restructuring of urban system in Japan, South Korea, and Malaysia. In Matsubara, H. (ed.), *A Comparative Study on the Urban Systems in Asian Countries: Systems of Cities in Japan, Korea and Malaysia*, 251–74. Fukuoka: Asian-Pacific Center.

Ikuta, M. (2008) *Kansaiken no Chiikisyugi to Toshisaihen: Chiikihatten no Keizai Chirigaku* (Regionalism and urban restructuring in Kansai, Japan: An economic geography for regional development). Kyoto: Minerva Shobo, In Japanese.

Johnston, R.J. (1991) *A Question of Place: Exploring the Practice of Human Geography.* Oxford, Cambridge: Blackwell.

Kato, K. (2003) On the "theory" of economic geography: Reconsideration.* *Annals of the Japan Association of Economic Geographers* 49(5): 35–50.

Keating, M. (1998) *The New Regionalism in Western Europe: Territorial Restructuring and Political Change*. Cheltenham, Northampton: Edward Elgar Publishing, p.73,115.

Massey, D. (1984) *Spatial Divisions of Labour: Social Structure and the Geography of Production*. London: Macmillan.

Suda, M. (1993) The location of branch offices of manufacturing industries in Japan.* *Annals of the Japan Association of Economic Geographers* 39(3): 439–511.

Taylor, P.J. (2002) *World City Network: A Global Urban Analysis*. New York, Abingdon: Routledge.

Uesugi, M. (2009) Cellular automata analysis of urban sprawl in the Northeastern Osaka from the 1960s to 1970s. *Geographical Review of Japan, Series A* 82(6): 618–29.

Young, H.W., and G.C.S. Lin (2003) Theorizing economic geographies of Asia. *Economic Geography* 79(2): 115.

8
Trading Area and Locational Decision of Foreign Affiliates in Osaka Prefecture

Sawako Maruyama

Introduction

Background of analysis

Since the 1990s, the Japanese government has recognized the significance of inward foreign direct investment (FDI) and eased regulations in order to promote it. The government reviews the system and conditions for accepting FDI at both national and local levels. Governments expect that foreign affiliates will affect local economies through job creation, capital inflow, and the improvement of productivity through the transfer of management resources, among other things. The expectation for inward FDI has been rather high in local governments in recent years.

The purpose of foreign affiliates varies from case to case, and there are several types of affiliates. For example, sales affiliates are one major type, especially in developed countries. Another major type is a production affiliate with a plant, and their purpose, among others, is to produce in the neighborhood of their market. There are other purposes which may vary between developed countries and developing countries. In many cases, production in developing countries tends to aim for low-cost labor, whereas production in developed countries tends to take advantage of resources such as technology or highly skilled labor. Other than these types, there are R&D affiliates, finance affiliates or regional headquarters, and so on. In many cases, there is a possibility to create new trade flow. *World Investment Report 2006* mentions the following feature as an impact on a host economy.

> ... since the affiliates are constituent elements of the TNCs involved, they are parts of the TNCs' respective value chains, both within the host country and internationally. They establish backward (with suppliers) and forward linkages (with distributors and sales organizations), which can stimulate production in supplier and distributor firms and organizations

Table 8.1 Location of foreign affiliates by prefecture, 2004

	All industries	Manufacturing	Non-Manufacturing		All industries	Manufacturing	Non-Manufacturing
Tokyo	1,564	373	1,191	Hiroshima	6	4	2
Kanagawa	224	90	134	Ishikawa	5	3	2
Osaka	147	43	104	Yamagata	4	4	–
Hyogo	61	27	34	Okinawa	4	–	4
Aichi	35	14	21	Hokkaido	3	3	3
Chiba	34	12	22	Fukui	3	3	–
Saitama	25	13	12	Nara	3	2	1
Shizuoka	16	13	3	Iwate	2	1	1
Ibaragi	11	7	4	Miyagi	2	2	–
Fukuoka	11	4	7	Gumma	2	1	1
Mie	9	5	4	Toyama	2	1	1
Shiga	8	7	1	Shimane	2	1	1
Kyoto	8	6	2	Aomori	1	1	–
Niigata	7	5	2	Fukushima	1	–	1
Nagano	7	6	1	Tottori	1	1	–
Gifu	7	2	5	Yamaguchi	1	1	1
Tochigi	6	6	–	Nagasaki	1	–	1
Yamanashi	6	2	4	Kumamoto	1	–	1

Source: METI Survey of Trends in Business Activities of Foreign Affiliates, 2005 (39th)

in the host country and constitute a channel for the transfer of technology. (UNCTAD 2006, 183)[1]

For local governments, the implementation of effective measures for promoting the localization of foreign affiliates is an important issue, and they focus on location-promoting measures to support the establishment of new companies. However, in most cases, foreign affiliates choose either the Tokyo or Kanto metropolitan area for their head office in Japan. Table 8.1 shows that the location of foreign affiliates is heavily concentrated in the metropolitan area around Tokyo. By prefecture, Tokyo has 1564 affiliates, which corresponds to 70 percent of the total. In Kanagawa, the prefecture adjacent to Tokyo, there are 224 affiliates. These two prefectures therefore cover 80 percent of the total. In western Japan, Osaka – which is a metropolitan center of the Kansai region – has 147 affiliates, and Hyogo – which boasts an international environment in the city of Kobe – has 61 affiliates. From this result, it is obvious that the locations of foreign affiliates are unequally distributed. It is not easy for local governments to attract foreign investment, because in most cases the attention of foreign companies shifts toward Tokyo[2].

Osaka prefecture has an exceptionally high percentage of the allocation of foreign affiliates in spite of its location in the Kansai region, a metropolitan center of western Japan. What makes foreign affiliates choose to operate in Osaka? Although there are several studies on foreign affiliates in Japan, the factors explaining the decision regarding where, or in which region within Japan, they should base their activities are not clear. In this case, which points should we look at as factors affecting locational decision? One possible aspect is the relationship with trade partners. It seems to be natural for foreign affiliates to be located close to their trade partners; they can do business efficiently with good communications and low transport costs. This suggests that the foreign affiliates which have stronger connections with Osaka companies tend to have a base in Osaka. That is to say, the concern is to consider the relationship between trade activities and the location of foreign affiliates. Therefore, this chapter examines the trade relations and locational background of foreign affiliates using a questionnaire provided to foreign affiliates in Osaka prefecture. It aims to reveal the background of location of foreign affiliates focusing on their trade relations. Few attempts have been made at investigating the trade activity of foreign affiliates in Japan, and focus must cover both trade behavior and locational decision.

The content of this chapter is as follows: the remainder of this section surveys previous studies. The next section introduces briefly the methodology and the overview of the collected data. Then the data from the questionnaire is analyzed. After that, two case reviews of foreign affiliates in Osaka are provided and some issues are discussed. The final section offers concluding remarks and policy implication.

Literature

Rapid growth of FDI inflow around the world since the 1980s has raised issues concerning multinational corporations (MNCs). In the field of international trade, a large number of studies have been made both theoretically and empirically. In theoretical literature, the "OLI framework" was developed by Dunning (1977). Recent development has been made by Markusen (2002) in the "knowledge-capital" approach as the general-equilibrium models of trade. Meanwhile, the effect and the determinants of FDI have mostly been investigated in empirical literature. The effects, or the determinants of FDI, generally differ by industry or by host/home country, and there are a considerable number of empirical studies. Therefore, only analyses on inward FDI in Japan are introduced here.

Foreign affiliates in Japan have been studied focusing on the exclusive nature of the Japanese market – for example, the difficulty of conducting takeovers (Weinstein 1997), or the understatement in the statistics (Feenstra 1999). In recent years, several empirical studies have used micro-based data on foreign affiliates to investigate their productivity. Paprzycki and Fukao (2008) conducted a comprehensive study on foreign affiliates in Japan: it includes political and historical analyses in Japan, besides empirical investigations of total factor productivity. The most salient characteristic of their analysis is that they examine the determinants on total factor productivities using a firm-level database. One of the interesting results is that foreign firms in Japan show better performance than their domestically owned counterparts. Some others analyze the profitability in a similar way – for example, Fukao and Murakami (2003), Yoshida and Kimura (2006), and Kimura and Kiyota (2007). They compare the productivity and the profitability of the foreign affiliates in Japan with those of Japanese domestic companies. They show that the introduction of foreign capital would improve profitability and productivity or that it would make the performance of the foreign affiliates higher than that of domestic companies. Yoshida and Kimura (2006) explain the background as the increase of profit-earning opportunities and reduction of costs by trading in global markets, although the relationship between profitability ratio and international trade are not examined. In other studies, Asaba (2005) analyzes the shift of performance before and after the introduction of foreign capital, using the data for companies through cross-border M&A. His result shows that the introduction of foreign capital improved the profitability of companies acquired.

These analyses have generated interesting findings; however, little attention has been given to the following two issues concerning the purpose of this chapter. One issue is that there is a small amount of empirical analysis investigating trade behavior of foreign affiliates in Japan[3]. Yamawaki (2004b) is one of the few examples which directly examine procurement of foreign manufacturing affiliates. In this analysis, the determinants of the import share of total procurement and the existence of distribution subsidiaries are investigated using probit estimation. His result from regression analysis shows that the import share is high among the MNCs which locate labor-intensive production stages for intermediate goods outside Japan. In another analysis, Yamawaki (2004a) tests the relationship between the probability of exit of foreign affiliates and two variables concerning trade behavior: export share and import procurement share. Estimation results show that the higher the share of export/import is, the lower the probability of exit is. This supports the hypothesis that the foreign affiliate that has access to the parent's global sourcing advantage and exporting opportunities is more likely to survive in Japan. These studies have revealed the trade activities of foreign affiliates as a part of global value chains to some extent; however, linkages with local companies remain unclear.

The second issue is that they do not pay attention to where foreign affiliates are situated. There are few studies analyzing this point; one reason is that most foreign affiliates are located or concentrated in the Kanto metropolitan area. There are enough samples for statistical analysis except in the metropolitan areas of Kanto, Kansai, and Tokai. In addition, the governmental statistics such as *Survey of Trends in Business Activities of Foreign Affiliates* by the Ministry of Economy, Trade and Industry (METI), or other surveys by the government, do not offer regional aggregation. This makes it difficult to analyze regional characteristics of the activities of foreign affiliates, and thereby most studies mention only regional distribution or tend to deal with case studies of specific firms in the region. Such a lack of analysis underlies a difficulty for local governments in making policies attracting foreign affiliates.

The Kansai metropolitan area, which has a certain amount of foreign affiliates, is analyzed nonetheless in only a small number of studies. The Osaka Prefectural Institute of Advanced Industry Development (2008) examines firm-level databases of foreign affiliates in Osaka prefecture, the center of the Kansai region. They find some characteristics of Osaka: there is a higher share of small-sized and Asian-based affiliates compared to affiliates in Kanto, and there are numerous foreign affiliates in industries with an agglomeration of local companies. Their results show that almost half of the foreign affiliates mainly procure intermediate goods through local backward linkages in Japan as well as Osaka. Furthermore, from the estimation results it is concluded that there is no obvious difference in profitability by region in which foreign affiliates are located. This means that locating in Osaka/Kansai area does not create any disadvantages for the activity of foreign affiliates. Schlunze (2008) further analyzes, concentrating on the R&D activities. Using an original survey, the process of the locational decision making, the formation of R&D organizations, and their integration in the regional innovation system are analyzed. He investigates the locational features by prefecture and by industry, and the characteristics of R&D

organization. One of his main findings is that the accessibility and the land/lease/rent price are the most important issues for deciding the location for R&D divisions. Additionally, the presence of customers and clients, the market size, and the proximity to the firm's factory are other important factors for their location. Yoshida and Kimura (2006) also investigate the regional trend of foreign affiliates. They compare the import and export ratio among three metropolitan areas of Kanto, Kansai, and Tokai. They find a different relationship of import and export ratio between Tokai and the other two regions, although the cause is not obvious.

Methodology

Framework of the questionnaire

This chapter analyzes the trade relations of foreign affiliates using original data collected through a questionnaire survey. The questionnaire used for this work aimed to investigate the business activities of foreign affiliates. It includes questions about the attributes of affiliates, trade conditions, networks with companies inside and outside Osaka, reasons for the locating decision, and evaluation and information sources. In the next section gleaned data are analyzed concerning the following three questions:

- Which area is where most of your suppliers/customers are located?
- How large a share in trade do Osaka companies hold for all your suppliers/customers?
- What made you to decide to locate in Osaka?

The first two questions are to grasp the degree of connection between foreign affiliates in Osaka and Osaka companies. In the third question, we introduce two phases about connection. One is the connection with the existing trade partners before starting an operation; the other is with future trade partners. The choices for these questions are discrete and qualitative; therefore the descriptive analysis are conducted.

The questionnaire was a mail-in survey conducted among foreign affiliates having headquarters in Osaka prefecture with more than a 20 percent share of foreign capital. The questionnaire was sent in March 2006 to be answered as of December 31, 2005, using the Statistics Bureau list "Establishment and Enterprise Census 2001"[4]. It includes sectors such as manufacturing, wholesale and retail, construction, information-communication, transportation, finance, and services. The number of valid deliveries was 194, and the number of valid responses obtained was 44 (response rate 22.7 percent). While the number of responses is not enough to analyze statistically or with cross-tabulation, the results from the questionnaire do reveal valuable information.

Overview of the data

Before starting the main analysis, we will provide a brief overview of the responses. The features of the affiliates responding to the questionnaire were clear enough to allow classification according to sector, country of origin, company size in employees, and year of establishment. This gives a concrete image of a typical response – small-sized wholesalers and retailers.

Sector and the country of origin

Of 44 affiliates, 25 (56.8 percent) belong to wholesalers and retailers (Table 8.2(a))[5]. Affiliates established for the sake of direct sales in the Japanese market are classified in wholesalers. Therefore, some of them have manufacturing parent companies. Another 13 affiliates (29.5 percent) are manufacturing companies. The other 6 affiliates (13.6 percent) belong to other non-manufacturing, which includes construction, ICT, transport, and services.

Concerning the country of origin, European-based affiliates dominate, with 40.9 percent. Following this are Asian-based affiliates with 36.3 percent, and US-based affiliates with 22.7 percent. When we regard European-based and US-based affiliates as one group, or "Western-based", it accounts for two-thirds. One difference between Western-based and Asian-based affiliates is that the former include a lot of manufacturing companies, especially among US-based firms. In contrast, most of the Asian-based affiliates are wholesalers or retailers.

Number of employees

Regarding company size, almost half of the affiliates (43.2 percent) are small companies with fewer than ten employees (Table 8.2(b)). 70 percent of total affiliates have less than 50 employees – that means most of the foreign affiliates belong to small and medium-sized companies. One reason for this fact is that more than half belong to wholesalers/retailers which do not always need a lot of workers as, for example, factories do. As we see above, most Asian-based affiliates belong to the wholesaler/retailer sector. That results in another difference between the two groups concerning the number of employees. Almost all Asian-based affiliates are small in size. In contrast, Western-based affiliates are found in various size ranges.

Year of establishment

As for year of establishment, differences among sectors are not significant as is the size of companies (Table 8.2(c)). Rather, the difference between Asian-based and Western-based is obvious: Western-based affiliates tend to be older and long-operating, while Asian-based affiliates tend to be new and established since 1985. This is not surprising, because the economic development and growth of many Asian countries began in the 1980s.

Table 8.2 Number of affiliates and composition

(a) By sector and country of origin

		Asian-based			Western-based			Total
		China	NIEs	Other Asia		US	Europe	
Total	16 (36.3)	6 (13.6)	8 (18.2)	2 (4.5)	28 (63.6)	10 (22.7)	18 (40.9)	44 (100.0)
Manufacturing	1 (7.7)	–	1 (7.7)	–	12 (92.3)	7 (53.8)	5 (38.5)	13 (100.0)
Wholesaler, Retailer	14 (56.0)	6 (24.0)	7 (28.0)	1 (4.0)	11 (44.0)	1 (4.0)	10 (40.0)	25 (100.0)
Other Non-manufacturing	1 (16.7)	–	–	1 (16.7)	5 (83.3)	2 (33.3)	3 (50.0)	6 (100.0)

(b) By number of employees

		0–9	10–19	20–49	50–99	100–299	300+	UnKnown	Total
By sector	Total	19 (43.2)	6 (13.6)	6 (13.6)	6 (13.6)	4 (9.1)	1 (2.3)	2 (4.5)	44 (100.0)
By sector	Manufacturing	3 (23.1)	1 (7.7)	1 (7.7)	4 (30.8)	2 (15.4)	1 (7.7)	1 (7.7)	13 (100.0)
By sector	Wholesaler, Retailer	14 (56.0)	5 (20.0)	5 (20.0)	1 (4.0)	–	–	–	25 (100.0)
By sector	Other Non-manufacturing	2 (33.3)	–	–	1 (16.7)	2 (33.3)	–	1 (16.7)	6 (100.0)
By region	Asian-based	13 (81.3)	2 (12.5)	–	–	–	–	1 (6.3)	16
By region	Western-based	6 (21.4)	4 (14.3)	6 (21.4)	6 (21.4)	4 (14.3)	1 (3.6)	1 (3.6)	28 (100.0)

(c) By year of establishment

		Before 1979	1980–4	1985–9	1990–4	1995–9	After 2000	Total
By sector	Total	12 (27.3)	2 (4.5)	8 (18.2)	4 (9.1)	12 (27.3)	6 (13.6)	44 (100.0)
By sector	Manufacturing	6 (46.2)	1 (7.7)	1 (7.7)	–	3 (23.1)	2 (15.4)	13 (100.0)
By sector	Wholesaler, Retailer	4 (16.0)	1 (4.0)	6 (24.0)	3 (12.0)	8 (32.0)	3 (12.0)	25 (100.0)
By sector	Other Non-manufacturing	2 (33.3)	–	1 (16.7)	1 (16.7)	1 (16.7)	1 (16.7)	6 (100.0)
By region	Asian-based	–	–	5 (31.3)	2 (12.5)	5 (31.3)	4 (25.0)	16 (100.0)
By region	Western-based	12 (42.9)	2 (7.1)	3 (10.7)	2 (7.1)	7 (25.0)	2 (7.1)	28 (100.0)

Questionnaire data analysis

Trading area

First, the trade network of foreign affiliates for both procurement and sales is analyzed. The questionnaire asked the following two questions: the areas where most suppliers/customers are located (multiple answers up to 2 options), and the share of Osaka companies in all suppliers/customers. The former question is intended to discover the degree of network with each area, and the areas are divided into "Inside Osaka", "Kansai Area", "Western Japan", "Other Japan", "Overseas (Asia)", and "Overseas (excluding Asia)". The latter is about network with Osaka, asking the share of Osaka companies with the following options: "less than 10 percent", "From 10 to 30 percent", "From 30 to 50 percent", and "More than 50 percent". These questions were set for each of procurement and sales.

Analysis starts with the result of the first question regarding procurement, "where the foreign affiliates have their procurement partners". In most cases they purchase from overseas and sell in the domestic market (Table 8.3). 68.8 percent of Asian-based affiliates have suppliers "Overseas (Asia)", while 72.0 percent of Western-based (including European- and US-based) affiliates have them "Overseas (excluding Asia)". This shows a close relationship between parent companies or group companies. Following those overseas areas, most foreign affiliates have their suppliers in "Other Japan", which includes eastern and central Japan and accounts for 31.7 percent of the total. Foreign affiliates which answered "Inside Osaka" account for only 22.0 percent. From these results, it can be said that there is a weak backward linkage between foreign affiliates in Osaka or with Osaka companies.

Next, we take a look at the second question, the share of trade partners of foreign affiliates that Osaka companies make up among all suppliers. The share described in the choices is calculated as the ratio of the number of suppliers in Osaka to the number of all suppliers. "Less than 10 percent" is the most commonly chosen answer and accounts for 68.3 percent (Table 8.4).

Table 8.3 Areas in which most suppliers are located (multiple answers up to two options)

	Total		Asian-based		Western-based	
Inside Osaka	9	(22.0)	3	(18.8)	6	(24.0)
Kansai Area	7	(17.1)	2	(12.5)	5	(20.0)
Western Japan	4	(9.8)	2	(12.5)	2	(8.0)
Other Japan	13	(31.7)	4	(25.0)	9	(36.0)
Overseas (Asia)	17	(41.5)	11	(68.8)	6	(24.0)
Overseas (excluding Asia)	20	(48.8)	2	(12.5)	18	(72.0)
Total	**41**	**(100.0)**	**16**	**(100.0)**	**25**	**(100.0)**

Table 8.4   Share of Osaka companies among all suppliers

	Total		Asian-based		Western-based	
Less than 10%	28	(68.3)	12	(75.0)	16	(64.0)
From 10 to 30%	5	(12.2)	1	(6.3)	4	(16.0)
From 30 to 50%	2	(4.9)	2	(12.5)	–	
More than 50%	6	(14.6)	1	(6.3)	5	(20.0)
Total	**41**	**(100.0)**	**16**	**(100.0)**	**25**	**(100.0)**

Table 8.5   Areas in which most customers are located (multiple answers up to two options)

	Total		Asian-based		Western-based	
Inside Osaka	19	(45.2)	9	(56.3)	10	(38.5)
Kansai Area	9	(21.4)	5	(31.3)	4	(15.4)
Western Japan	8	(19.0)	1	(6.3)	7	(26.9)
Other Japan	30	(71.4)	8	(50.0)	22	(84.6)
Overseas (Asia)	7	(16.7)	5	(31.3)	2	(7.7)
Overseas (excluding Asia)	3	(7.1)	1	(6.3)	2	(7.7)
Total	42	(100.0)	16	(100.0)	26	(100.0)

This means that two-thirds of foreign affiliates have most of their suppliers outside Osaka. Another fact arising from the data is that 20.0 percent of Western-based affiliates have more than half of their suppliers in Osaka. This situation is observed only among Western-based affiliates, although more than half of the affiliates in this group appear to have a weak linkage with Osaka companies.

How about the responses regarding the partners in sales? Table 8.5 shows the areas in which most customers are located from the first question asking about sales. It is obvious that "Other Japan" is the most frequent answer with 71.4 percent, indicating the existence of customers mainly outside of Osaka as with the location of suppliers. The second most common answer is "Inside Osaka" with 45.2 percent, and it is followed by "Kansai Area" with 21.4 percent. There are more affiliates which have trade partners in Osaka. We can say that foreign affiliates have stronger forward linkages with Osaka companies than backward linkages. In contrast to procurement, "Overseas" is less often chosen as a destination of sales. However, in the case of Asian-based affiliates the percentage of "Overseas (Asia)" is rather high compared to Western-based affiliates.

Table 8.6   Share of Osaka companies among all customers

	Total		Asian-based		Western-based	
Less than 10%	16	(39.0)	5	(31.3)	11	(44.0)
From 10 to 30%	15	(36.6)	5	(31.3)	10	(40.0)
From 30 to 50%	3	(7.3)	1	(6.3)	2	(8.0)
More than 50%	7	(17.1)	5	(31.3)	2	(8.0)
Total	41	(100.0)	16	(100.0)	25	(100.0)

Regarding the percentage of trade partners in Osaka among all customers considered in the second question, the share is not very high. The trade partners of foreign affiliates are predominately companies outside Osaka. The answer "Less than 10 percent" regarding partners in Osaka accounts for 39.0 percent, and next "From 10 to 30 percent" accounts for 36.6 percent (Table 8.6). We can thus determine that there are more foreign affiliates with customers in Osaka compared to suppliers, but the response of "More than 50 percent" is not very different between procurement and sales – 14.6 percent and 17.1 percent, respectively. This tendency is stronger among Western-based affiliates.

From these results, the following features of the trade area of foreign affiliates in Osaka are revealed. Firstly, based on the number of trade partners, most of the affiliates have suppliers overseas, while customers in Japan are outside Osaka. The share of Osaka companies is low in both procurement and sales. Secondly, these features show the trade pattern of foreign affiliates in Japan: they import products or intermediate goods from overseas and sell them, or value-added manufactured goods, throughout Japan. That means that foreign affiliates in Osaka have weak backward and forward linkages with Osaka companies. By comparison, regarding sales, Asian-based affiliates seem to have a closer relationship with Osaka companies.

Reasons for locational decisions

The analysis of the trading area shows that trade partners of foreign affiliates in Osaka are not limited to local companies in Osaka or the Kansai region, but are spread across a wide area beyond. In spite of those weak linkages with local companies, what made foreign affiliates decide to locate in Osaka? We further asked foreign affiliates about their reasons for deciding their location in Osaka in the questionnaire. As options we offered the following ten reasons:

[1] Existence of partner(s) in capital or technical alliances
[2] Accessibility to existing business partners in Japan
[3] Agglomeration of potential companies as business or alliance partners

[4] Access to existing business partners overseas
[5] Existence of companies which had the same country of origin
[6] Easy acquisition of human resources
[7] Cheaper cost of having an office
[8] Good infrastructure
[9] Easy to get support for business in need
[10] Attractive policies by local government

Options [1] to [5] focus on the relationship with partners. The affiliates which chose [1], [2], and [4] suggest emphasis on a relationship with existing partners before entering into the Japanese market. Table 8.7 shows the responses to that question with multiple answers.

The highest response for all affiliates is "[2] Accessibility to existing business partners in Japan", with 57.1 percent. This implies positive evaluation of the transportation network of Osaka: Kansai International Airport, high-speed Shinkansen railway lines, and expressways. The high number of responses indicates that these affiliates decided their location in relation to business partners before entering into the Japanese market. "[1] Existence of partner(s) in capital or technical alliances" is the second-highest response, with 31.0 percent. In contrast, "[3] Agglomeration of potential companies as business or alliance partners", which includes future trade partners after entering the Japanese market, is low, with a response of 16.7 percent.

"[7] Cheaper cost of having an office" is the third-highest reason to choose Osaka, with 23.8 percent. In fact, office rent and wages are lower in Osaka in comparison to Tokyo, in addition to the convenience in business circumstances such as infrastructure and logistics. Local governments tend to think that these points appeal to foreign affiliates; however, the observer must note that the low cost for the office is merely in third position, not the top. It is interesting that "[10] Attractive policies by local government" gets the lowest response among all options. One possible reason is that most foreign affiliates came into Japan before the deregulation of inward FDI. Additionally, it is likely that local governments had not taken measures to support foreign affiliates. Later inquiry targeting only recently established affiliates might see changes in the perception of local government's role.

From these results, it appears that foreign affiliates emphasize *what they already had* rather than *what they could have in the future*. The foreign companies need strong reasons to allocate affiliates, and the existence of partners appears to be enough. Thus it appears that a local business partner for foreign companies is necessary before they establish affiliates in Osaka.

There is again differentiation of responses between Asian-based and Western-based affiliates. Analyzing with regard to country of origin, there is a difference between the responses of Asian-based affiliates and Western-based affiliates. "[1] Existence of partner(s) in capital or technical alliance" has a high response of 42.3 percent among Western-based affiliates, whereas

Table 8.7 Reasons for locating in Osaka (multiple answers)

	Total		By country of origin				By affiliate size			
---	---	---	Asian-based		Western-based		Less than 10 employees		More than 10 employees	
[1] Existence of partner(s) in capital or technical alliance	13	(31.0)	2	(12.5)	11	(42.3)	6	(31.6)	7	(33.3)
[2] Accessibility to the existing business partners in Japan	24	(57.1)	9	(56.3)	15	(57.7)	10	(52.6)	13	(61.9)
[3] Agglomeration of potential companies as business or alliance partners	7	(16.7)	4	(25.0)	3	(11.5)	3	(15.8)	4	(19.0)
[4] Accessibility to the existing business partners overseas	6	(14.3)	3	(18.8)	3	(11.5)	3	(15.8)	3	(14.3)
[5] Existence of companies which had the same country of origin	3	(7.1)	2	(12.5)	1	(3.8)	2	(10.5)	1	(4.8)
[6] Easy acquisition of human resources	7	(16.7)	1	(6.3)	6	(23.1)	1	(5.3)	5	(23.8)
[7] Cheaper cost of having an office	10	(23.8)	4	(25.0)	6	(23.1)	7	(36.8)	3	(14.3)
[8] Good infrastructure	6	(14.3)	1	(6.3)	5	(19.2)	2	(10.5)	4	(19.0)
[9] Easy to get support for business in need	7	(16.7)	3	(18.8)	4	(15.4)	2	(10.5)	4	(19.0)
[10] Attractive policies by local government	2	(4.8)	1	(6.3)	1	(3.8)	1	(5.3)	1	(4.8)
[11] Others	10	(23.8)	5	(31.3)	5	(19.2)	5	(26.3)	4	(19.0)
Total	42	(100.0)	16	(100.0)	26	(100.0)	19	(100.0)	21	(100.0)

it is only 12.5 percent for Asian-based affiliates. Thus, it seems that Western-based affiliates place more emphasis on existing relationships. "[6] Easy acquisition of human resources" and "[8] Good infrastructure" are other items valued only by Western-based affiliates (23.1 percent and 19.2 percent, respectively). They require comprehensive conditions for local operation. In contrast, Asian-based affiliates consider other issues to be important. For example, "[3] Agglomeration of potential companies as business or alliance partners" is valued among 25.0 percent of Asian-based affiliates, and this is rather high compared to Western-based affiliates.

Comparing small affiliates (with fewer than ten employees) and large affiliates (with more than ten employees), there is little difference apparent. We can mention that "[6] Easy acquisition of human resources" is high only among large affiliates (23.8 percent), while "[7] Cheaper cost of having an office" is high only among small affiliates (36.8 percent).

From the results of analysis, it is revealed that foreign affiliates emphasize existing partners rather than future partners. In the next section, the case studies reveal the background of this characteristic.

Case studies

In this section, case studies of two foreign affiliates are made. These cases are based on interview surveys with the directors conducted in March 2006. The main purpose of these surveys is to investigate more concrete reasons for the choice to locate in Osaka. There are some existing case studies of foreign affiliates in Japan; however, most of them are of large companies such as P&G. In contrast, this study focuses on small companies which are typical of foreign affiliates in Osaka.

Case study: Firm A, the Asian-based affiliate

Firm A is a foreign affiliate established with 100 percent capital by a Taiwanese manufacturer of pneumatic equipment. The firm started operation in 2003 in Osaka in order to import and sell products made by the parent company in Taiwan. Sales utilizing its global network is one of the company's strengths. The company first decided to go into the Japanese market to supply the Japanese parent companies of user companies in China.

The reasons the parent company decided to establish this office in Osaka are summarized in the following advantages. Firstly, Osaka has geographical advantages including high accessibility. Osaka lies almost in the center of Japan, and so from there it is easy to get around. The firm has to cultivate new customers not only inside but also outside of the Kansai region. For the small firm with only four staff members, convenience of travel from Osaka to the rest of Japan helps its operating activities. Secondly, it can transport containers directly from ports to the office location. Osaka has both seaports and an airport, and the expressway network makes it easy to transport from ports by road. This is another geographical advantage.

Thirdly, management appreciates the fact that Osaka is traditionally a commercial center and an area of shop-floor production – which is called "mono-zukuri" in Japanese. For customers in other countries, prices have priority of purchasing, while Japanese customers require quality and timely delivery, as well as other issues in addition to price. Osaka companies especially face tough requirements within Japan, therefore Firm A management thinks that doing business there enables them to develop their skills in operating activities and services.

Case study: Firm B, the European-based affiliate

Firm B, with fewer than ten employees, was established as a Japanese sales affiliate of a global manufacturer which has its origin in Denmark. The group companies develop and sell printing machines, parts, and accessories. The market for printing machines is dominated by German and Japanese manufacturers, and their products are assembled as components in printing machines of those manufacturers. Therefore, their customers are mainly manufacturers of printing machines.

Before establishing the office in Japan, the company already had customers in Japan, who imported and bought directly from Denmark or other overseas affiliates. As the amount of trade increased, the company decided to start operations in Japan to provide better services in the field. It provides products as well as after-sales services to both printing machine manufacturers and end-users.

Management chose Osaka as the location of their office for the following reasons: accessibility to overseas using Kansai International Airport, low maintenance costs of the office and livability. Concerning the first point, their office is a base not only for the Japanese market but also for the Asia-Pacific area centering on East Asia. They sell and provide services in this area from Japan; customers in Taiwan, Korea, and China, for example, contact the Japanese office when they want to import their products. Furthermore, technical staff from Japan join engineers sent from the group to points throughout this area. The existence of Osaka International Airport is essential for their function as the control office of the Asia-Pacific area.

Concluding remarks and policy implication

This chapter analyzed the relationship between foreign affiliates and their trade partners, using the results of the questionnaire. The main findings are summarized as follows.

Analyzing the trading area on the procurement side, most affiliates have connected deeply with overseas companies. At the same time, foreign affiliates which have strong connections with Osaka companies are small in number. Additionally, the share of suppliers in Osaka is very small for most companies. These two facts show the weak backward linkages with Osaka companies. It might be difficult to change this structure if we consider the industrial feature of foreign affiliates in Osaka. There are numerous whole-sale traders which seem to have been established as sales affiliates for the products of parent or group companies. On the sales side, the majority of foreign affiliates have their customers in other parts of Japan. Most affiliates regard other parts of Japan as more important areas, and the biggest reason is that this definition of "other" includes Eastern Japan and therefore Tokyo. Unlike the procurement side, "Inside Osaka" holds the second-highest response, which is relatively low for suppliers. Concerning only Asian-based affiliates, "Inside Osaka" is the top response. Still, the share of customers in Osaka is small according to the results of the second question. These results show that forward linkages with Osaka companies are at a low level, although they are stronger compared to the procurement. As a whole, it is clear that foreign affiliates in Osaka have weak linkages – both backward and forward – with Osaka companies.

Although foreign affiliates in Osaka have a rather weak connection with Osaka companies currently, they had strong relationships when they started their operations. They decided to locate their offices in Osaka consider-ing the existence of and accessibility to their business partners. It is worth pointing out that they emphasize their existing business partners, rather than potential partners in future. In other respects, Osaka is valued for its cheaper cost, easy acquisition of human resources, and business support. This is an interesting result; it would appear that foreign affiliates value Osaka as an alternative metropolitan area to the Tokyo or Kanto area. Cost is cheaper in comparison to Tokyo, and Osaka remains suitably convenient.

The case studies of two foreign affiliates illustrate these features. In the case studies based on the interview survey, both affiliates are typical of for-eign affiliates in Osaka. They are small in number of employees and were established in order to sell products in the Japanese market. It is interest-ing that these two have something in common and consistent with the findings of the previous section. One point is that they had business with Japanese companies to some extent before starting operations in Japan. This fact turned their attention to Osaka as one of their choices. Another point is that they value the quality access from/to overseas. As they are parts of a global value chain, they have to consider transport costs both domestically and globally. They think Osaka fulfills those conditions.

These findings show the possibilities for local governments to promote location of foreign affiliates in their region. First, foreign affiliates choose to locate in the region if they have a strong business relationship with local companies. One effective way to build a relationship before coming to the region is to support local companies expanding their business overseas. They will find business partners there, and some of those partners may become parent companies of foreign affiliates. They may be interested in the techniques of local companies in the region and the Japanese market. Above all, it is a great opportunity to let them know the name and the characteristics of the region. In the case of Japan, it is not rare that foreign businesses know only the capital city, Tokyo.

Second, for the promotion of inward investment to the region, it would be efficient to target the specific industry in which the region already has an industrial agglomeration. In such an industry, there would be potential trade partners and opportunities to access other sources of technologies for foreign affiliates. Needless to say, local governments have to carefully examine the industrial structure of the region for determining a suitable target industry.

Third, local government should prepare measures to support foreign affiliates after they start business in the region. Weak backward linkages between foreign affiliates and local companies are issues here. Most local governments provide support only for starting operation in the region, and the measures for supporting foreign affiliates are rather new. Local governments can, for example, enhance follow-up support of affiliates in the region; additionally they should provide information of related industries or companies and at the same time get some feedback. They also should note that it is not always affiliates themselves who determine the route of procurement – in some cases, the parent company plays an important role. Supporting foreign affiliates is not only for those needing to acquire new trade partners; indeed, it can create opportunities for local companies to join the value chains of foreign affiliates and their parent companies. In a related move, Japan External Trade Organization (JETRO) has already started a matching service between foreign companies and local small and medium-sized companies.

To carry out these measures, two perspectives are essential for local governments. One is a "long-term" perspective. It often takes time to get results as well as to design the regional industry that is desired. Another is a "global" perspective. Local governments should know the strength and weakness of the region's industries in the globalized economy and actively transmit information appropriate for overseas. Obviously, it is necessary to share these two perspectives with local companies.

Notes

This chapter is based on the data collected under the project "Business operation of Asian-based companies in Osaka and effect on local companies and regional economy" at Osaka Prefectural Institute for Advanced Industry Development. Part of this work has already been presented in Osaka Prefectural Institute for Advanced Industry Development (2006b), available only in Japanese.

1. For the details of backward and forward linkage, see also UNCTAD (2001).
2. Note that Tokyo is the location of head offices in Japan; in other prefectures there are mainly subsidiaries, local offices and plants of these affiliates.

3. This issue is investigated empirically in several works on Japanese outward FDI. They found that the local sales and the local procurement contribute to the profitability of affiliates; see Sazanami and Kawai (1998), Brimble and Urata (2006), Ito and Fukao (2006).
4. The details and the results of the questionnaire appear also in Osaka Prefectural Institute for Advanced Industry Development (2006a), available only in Japanese.
5. Number in parentheses in the table is the share of the total.

References

Asaba, S. (2005) Do foreign shareholders change Japanese firms? (in Japanese). *Hitotsubashi Business Review* 53(2): 46–59.

Brimble, P., and S. Urata (2006) Behavior of Japanese, Western, and Asian MNCs in Thailand: Lessons for Japanese MNCs. JCER Discussion Paper no. 105. Japan Center for Economic Research.

Dunning, J.H. (1977) Trade, location of economic activity and the MNE: A search for an eclectic approach. In B. Ohlin, P.-O. Hesselborn, and P.M. Wijkman (eds), *The International Allocation of Economic Activity*. London: MacMillan.

Feenstra, R.C. (1999) Facts and fallacies about foreign direct investment. In M. Feldstein (ed.), *International Capital Flows*. Chicago: University of Chicago Press.

Fukao, K., and Y. Murakami (2003) Do foreign firms bring greater total factor productivity to Japan? Hi-Stat Discussion Paper Series no. 4, Hitotsubashi University. http://hdl.handle.net/10086/14074 [Accessed February 10, 2010].

Ito, K., and K. Fukao (2006) Determinants of the profitability of Japanese manufacturing affiliates in China and other regions: Does localization of procurement, sales, and management matter? RIETI Discussion Paper Series, 06-E-037, Research Institute of Economy, Trade and Industry.

Kimura, F., and K. Kiyota (2007) Foreign-owned versus domestically-owned firms: Economic performance in Japan. *Review of Development Economics* 11(1): 31–48.

Markusen, J. (2002) *Multinational Firms and the Theory of International Trade*. Cambridge, MA: MIT Press.

Osaka Prefectural Institute for Advanced Industry Development (2006a) *Osaka keizai no gurobaruka no jittai* (Survey on the actual condition of globalization in Osaka economy). (Only in Japanese)

Osaka Prefectural Institute for Advanced Industry Development (2006b) *White Paper on the Economy and Labor 2006*. Osaka Prefecture . (Only in Japanese)

Osaka Prefectural Institute for Advanced Industry Development (2008) *Gaishi-kei kigyou no katsudou to tiiki keizai (Business Activities of Foreign Affiliates and Regional Economy)*. (Only in Japanese)

Paprzycki, R., and K. Fukao (2008) *Foreign Direct Investment in Japan: Multinationals' Role in Growth and Globalization*. New York: Cambridge University Press.

Sazanami, Y., and H. Kawai (1998) Business activities of Japanese firms in Europe, Asia, and North America (in Japanese). *Mita Journal of Economics* 91(2).

Schlunze, R.D. (2008) Location and role of foreign firms in regional innovation systems in Japan. *Ritsumeikan International Affairs* 6: 1–25.

UNCTAD (2001) *World Investment Report 2001, Promoting Linkages*. New York and Geneva: United Nations.

UNCTAD (2006) *World Investment Report 2006, FDI from Developing and Transition Economies: Implications for Development*. New York and Geneva: United Nations.

Weinstein, D. E. (1997) Foreign direct investment and *keiretsu*: Rethinking U.S. and Japanese policy. In R.C. Feenstra (ed.), *The Effects of U.S. Trade Protection and Promotion Policies*, 81–116. Chicago: University of Chicago Press.

Yamawaki, H. (2004a) Who survives in Japan? An empirical analysis of European and U.S. multinational firms in Japanese manufacturing industries. *Journal of Industry, Competition and Trade* 4(2): 135–53.

Yamawaki, H. (2004b) The determinants of geographic configuration of value chain activities: Foreign multinational enterprises in Japanese manufacturing. *International Economics and Economic Policy* 1(2–3): 195–213.

Yoshida, K., and F. Kimura (2006) *Gaishikei Kigyou to Kokunai Kigyou no Chiiki-betsu Zaimu Bunseki* (Regional and financial analysis on foreign affiliates and domestic companies) (in Japanese). Graduate School of Economics, Nagoya City University and Development Bank of Japan, Tokai Branch *Tokai Chihou ni Okeru Tainichi Chokusetsu Toushi (Inward Foreign Direct Investment in Tokai Area)*, pp. 31–40.

Part III

Spaces of International Management

9
How Does US Educational Experience Shape the Everyday Work Environment of Japanese Legal Professionals?

Tim Reiffenstein

Introduction: whither economic geographies of Japan?

Several years ago, Henry Yeung (2007) wrote an editorial that challenged economic geographers to remake their discipline through research on East Asia. In comparison to the 'theoretical saturation' of Anglo-American and European perspectives that have long dominated the agenda in economic geography, Yeung presented East Asia as an overlooked emerging region, both in terms of empirical studies and in its potential for theoretical advancement. He notably illustrated his argument by observing the relative absence of scholarship on Japan by economic geographers over the last 30 years, a period characterized by Japan's remarkable arc from ascendant economic superpower to stagnant giant. In the few years since Yeung's editorial was published, it is apparent that East Asia is very much moving towards mainstream disciplinary significance. The same cannot be said of Japan, which if anything has dropped further from view.

Indeed, as its economy has soured and its place in the world shifted, the image of Japan held by non-Japanese economic geographers remains static, dominated by a focus on manufacturing. From an international management geography perspective, perhaps the two most interesting and dynamic research avenues – the hybridization of the Toyota model (Florida and Kenney 1991, Abo 1995, Majek and Hayter 2008), and the flying geese model of Japanese foreign direct investment (Edgington and Hayter 2004, Hobday 1995, Reiffenstein and Nguyen, 2011) – reinforce the emphasis on both manufacturing and outward-oriented investment. The domestic economy, on the other hand, remains largely out of view. A lacuna is similarly evident in our understanding of the Japanese service industries. These gaps are highly problematic since they tend to leave place-based models of Japan

155

such as Tokyo's function in the global-city system comparatively under-detailed (Sassen 2001, Beaverstock et al. 1999a). Both New York and London have featured prominently and deservedly as empirical foci for research on professional services and other higher-order functions that are assumed rather than examined when it comes to Tokyo, the world's largest and most innovative city (Florida 2008).

The growing volume of research on legal internationalization has yielded important theoretical insights for economic and management geography on key topics such as tacit knowledge, communities of practice, professionalization and face-to-face interaction (Beaverstock et al. 1999b, Warf 2001, Casper 2001, Teubner 2001, Beaverstock 2004, Morgan and Quack 2005, Faulconbridge 2008, Jones 2007, Flood and Sosa 2008). As a professional service, law is often recognized as a key enabler of international economic activity, with international lawyers and the firms they work for being touted as the 'shock troops' of capitalism. Perhaps the key question guiding this research is how do law firms and the professionals they employee adapt to the various national contexts where the firm locates? We know that the internationalization of law firms produces a range of organizational and individual adaptations. Silver et al.'s (2009) recent comprehensive study found evidence suggesting *glocalization* – the simultaneous diffusion of a firm's home-country institutional signature and its enculturation to the host-country setting – as the dominant response to market forces. It is important to recognize, however, that the bulk of work in this field has privileged an ideal typical 'global law firm' that is very much an Anglo-American species operating within a largely English-speaking realm. This focus also reflects market forces as global law firms based in these two countries dominate the industry. In contrast, the implication of internationalization for the Japanese case, for which there exists a growing body of literature, has yet to be examined by geographers or business scholars.

Empirically, Japan serves as a useful context to investigate the variegated nature of glocalization in law. The last 20 years have witnessed a gradual deregulation of the Japanese legal environment, a process that has produced, as it is often described, the 'Americanization' of the sector. We know something of how both international and domestic law firms are responding to this situation, and also how the new breed of Japanese law schools are reshaping professional legal training in response to market forces. Simultaneously we are aware of significant numbers of Japanese attorneys who undertake graduate legal training at US universities (Silver 2006). Yet we do not know how this training is incorporated into their professional practice back in Japan, how this experience contributes to the glocalized international firm, and how it more broadly shapes the diffusion of US influence in Japan.

The present chapter endeavors to make some headway in addressing these gaps. It builds on recent studies that explore the link between professional education and practice (Waters 2009, Faulconbridge and Hall 2009) by examining the implications of international legal education and training for Japanese legal professionals once they return home. This process is conceptualized in reference to Thrift's (2002) idea of cultural circuits of capital that describes the diffusion of 'best practice' management knowledge and discourse through networks of professionals via education, consulting, and the popular business literature (cf. Gertler 2001). Applied to the empirical study, this framing allows us to make sense of (1) the search and selection strategies guiding Japanese attorneys who seek to train in the United States, the world's premier market for legal services and legal education; (2) their experience while at American law schools; and (3) the utility of this training for the sojourner when they return to work in Japan. Evidence from interviews with Japanese lawyers is presented to advance the argument that the circulation of international legal knowledge into Japan by Japanese is encultured by geographical difference and the hybridization of experience in ways that, perhaps counter-intuitively, work against the grain of incipient Americanization of the Japanese legal system. In particular, the chapter demonstrates how regulatory norms that govern, respectively, the depth of legal knowledge Japanese typically acquire in the United States and the division of labor within the Japanese legal service sphere limit the degree to which the actors within the cultural circuit can fully utilize their internationally acquired knowledge. Instead of glocalization, it appears we confront a situation of structured bifurcation, with Japanese and non-Japanese performing complementary but less than fully integrated functions. The implication of these findings for management geographies are twofold as they suggest, first of all, that Japan serves as a special but significant case for theory building. Second, they point to specific challenges for managing internationally trained legal talent in the Japanese case that may speak to more general problems that occur in managing beyond Anglo-American-European regulatory and linguistic contexts.

The chapter is organized as follows. The next section summarizes the progress of deregulation and internationalization in the Japanese legal sector by emphasizing the recent evolution in the provision of legal services. The third section addresses the implications of internationalization for legal training in reference to both the Americanization of Japanese law schools and the pathway whereby Japanese seek training abroad. The fourth part of the chapter presents the results of interviews with Japanese legal professionals in which they connect their international educational experience with their everyday work in Japan. The final section then situates these educational sojourns in the context of the broader cultural circuit.

Legal internationalization and Japan

National legal systems have evolved along distinctive path-dependent trajectories characteristic of their respective varieties of capitalism/national business systems/national innovation system (Hall and Soskice 2001, Whitley 1999, Reiffenstein 2009). Regulatory differences, variations in training regimes, professionally sanctioned codes of practice, and diverse cultural attitudes that shape, for example, remuneration and promotion schemes all pose challenges for the management of transnational legal services.

The institutional bases of the Japanese legal sector have long reflected the selective adoption and adaptation of international legal influences. Thus in the Meiji period (1868–1912), the initial modern configuration of the Japanese legal system derived its inspiration from Germany. Through a conscious process of scanning and selection that conforms to Westney's (1987) interpretation of the 'rational shopper thesis', the architects of modern Japan established a course for the nation's legal system that in many ways still bears the original signature of the Continental civil law model (Takayanagi 1963, Foote 2008).

In the aftermath of the Second World War, the Americans introduced various aspects of US law. However, since the Americans relied so heavily on key players in the Japanese business, bureaucratic and government communities to adapt and implement the reforms, the reorientation was only partial (Oppler 1976). Following the US-Japanese trade disputes of the mid-1980s, Japan conceded in 1987 to allow foreign lawyers to practice law in Japan, albeit in a severely limited capacity as advisers about the laws of their own country (Ramseyer 1986). It was therefore not until well into the 'lost decade' that followed the bursting of Japan's asset bubble in 1990 that endogenous pressure advocated for a fundamental change to the Japanese legal system along broadly American lines. This recent period of deepening legal Americanization can be viewed in several ways – for example, in terms of the introduction of certain common law procedures in the judicial process (e.g. the lay judge jury system). Of particular relevance to the topic of this chapter, and more generally in relation to the theme of management geography, the most notable shifts concern deregulation and internationalization of the corporate legal sphere (Foote 2008).

Foreign lawyers, international law firms and shifts in the Japanese legal sphere

The role of foreign lawyers (*gaiben*) in Japan is still extremely limited. Indeed, there are currently no non-Japanese licensed as *Bengoshi* (attorneys at law). However, following the 1987 introduction of the Special Measures Law Concerning the Handling of Legal Business by Foreign Lawyers Law (Gaikoku Bengoshi Ho), foreign attorneys won the right to practice law in Japan, but not Japanese law. Their professional sphere was therefore that of a regulated enclave that by necessity was purely outward in orientation. In the following year 47 *gaibens* practiced in Japan, while the total population never exceeded 85 until 1998. At present there are still only 325 *gaibens* licensed in Japan (Nichibenren 2010). While the limited operational scope of *gaiben* has remained consistent, the structure of the legal environment in which they operate and the players operating within this sphere have undergone several significant shifts (Sibbit 2002).

The initial response to the 1987 Foreign Lawyers Law was that a number of large US law firms entered the Japanese market – with 31 US law firms having established branch offices by 1991 (Abel 1994). Yet once they gained this footing and took their bearings, dissatisfaction set in. This is because one of the key restrictions of the law is that it prohibited foreign firms from employing or creating partnerships with Japanese *bengoshi* to assist with cross-border transactions. At the same time, Japanese law firms could hire *gaiben* to complete the foreign side of any deal, a situation that left international law firms at a significant disadvantage. Further agitation from the American Bar Association and US trade representatives produced a second wave of reform in 1994 that allowed for the formation of joint ventures between foreign and Japanese law firms. Yet this concession still came with its own limits, as joint venture firms were not allowed to appear before Japanese courts or administrative organs or give advice solely on Japanese matters. In other words there always had to be an international dimension to their work. The most recent watershed moment in this progression came in 2005 with a revision that allowed for full integration between foreign and Japanese law firms. Notably, however, the demarcation between the occupational scope of *gaiben*, who are still prohibited from practicing Japanese law, and *bengoshi* is still sacrosanct, and any interpretation of Americanization within Japanese law needs to keep this in mind.

In this integrated yet functionally bifurcated environment, the actual strategic behavior of international law firms is instructive. Jones Day, for example, which bills itself as 'one firm worldwide', entered Japan in 1989. In 2002, it initiated a joint venture with Showa Law Office, an arrangement that has since been fully integrated. Aronson (2007: 67–68) quotes John Roebuck, the former senior partner of the Tokyo branch, on the firm's evolution:

> When [we] were permitted to add domestic capability, [we] did so as rapidly as we could ... with the addition of domestic capability, the *gaiben* can now work in collaboration with their Japanese *bengoshi* colleagues. And even though the outbound work is still present and the *gaiben* continue to work on it, now *gaiben* can also work on other things such as inbound work on behalf of foreign clients in collaboration with their Japanese colleagues.

Jones Day Tokyo currently has a staff of 56 lawyers, eight of whom are *gaiben*. Given this figure, it is apparent that much of the work of this office is performed by its Japanese *bengoshi*. The nature of this work, though, as the quotation above suggests, is often of a cross-border nature and demands a management approach that favors glocalization. Thus we know that particular firms have changed as they adapt following their entry to, and in response to regulatory changes in, Japan. More broadly, what are the implications of international firms' entry for the domestic Japanese market?

The introduction of international competition and deregulation has prompted a phase of evolution in the broader sector for legal service provision in Japan. Until the mid-1990s, the structure of Japanese legal service provision was fairly static. Large Japanese law offices focused exclusively on cross-border work and indeed were called 'shogai jimusho' (international firms). There was little demand for domestic legal and regulatory questions because Japanese firms generally preferred consulting bureaucrats. For a long time, Japanese law firms were quite small and lagged the rapid expansion of Anglo-American firms that traced closely the financial 'big bangs' in those markets during the 1980s (Sibbitt 2002). Recently, though, there has been a trend toward much larger law firm sizes in Japan that has been accompanied by a spate of mergers. As Japanese firms in the sector have expanded, their growth has been fuelled principally by a considerable uptake of domestic business that was formerly the domain of bureaucrats. Meanwhile these new mega-firms compete on their international side with the services offered by the Japanese attorneys working for international law offices. In response to this competition, there has been something of a cultural shift in the management of Japanese firms to catch up with the practices employed by the foreign firms (Aronson 2007).

To summarize, then, we have reached a situation in which foreign law firms are expanding primarily by hiring Japanese attorneys. Japanese law firms, meanwhile, are seeking to add Japanese talent that will allow them to retain their original emphasis and advantage in cross-border transactions. Both international firms and the international departments of Japanese law firms therefore have broadly similar training demands for the attorneys they hire. To address these concerns it is necessary to compare domestic and international routes for professional education in order to understand the premium commanded by those with international and especially US training.

Calls for reform and the advent of the new Japanese law school

In 2001, Japan's Justice Reform Council (JRC 2001) published a scathing critique of the nation's existing standard of legal education and mode of professional accreditation. The JRC pointed to two major structural flaws. The first was that Japan was vastly under-lawyered, with only 17,000 practicing *bengoshi* (attorneys at law) for a population of 127 million. The genesis of this problem lay in the exceedingly low pass rate of 2–3 percent for the Japanese bar exam. The second problem, they argued, was that Japan's system of legal training lacked a practical basis in preparing legal graduates for the sorts of work performed by legal professionals. As a classic expression of the civil law tradition, undergraduate 'faculties of law' (*hōgakubu*) emphasized a generalist curriculum based around the various facets of the legal code. As Maxeiner and Yamanaka (2004) note, the similarities to the German legal training regime of the nineteenth century remain 'substantial'.

One key feature of the prior Japanese model was the concentration of power amongst the elite 'top five' law faculties, who over the last 50 years accounted for 75 percent of all students who passed the bar exam. Traditionally these venerable institutions, such as the University of Tokyo, were better known for producing the nation's bureaucratic elite rather than lawyers (Omura et al. 2005). Yet there was growing evidence that the top graduates were eschewing the trajectory of a bureaucratic career and were instead seeking work as attorneys in private practice, a career path for which their education left them poorly prepared (Milhaupt and West 2003). Given this disconnect between the curricula of law faculties, the content of the bar exam, and realities of professional practice, a parallel system of legal training cram schools (*juku*) had emerged to handle the topics that appeared on the bar exam; a trend that further highlights the similarities amongst nations rooted in the civil law tradition (Steiner 2007).

To stem the ossification of this environment, and in response to post-bubble societal discourse to make Japan more internationally competitive (see e.g. Yamamura 1997), the JRC advocated for the adoption of an explicitly American model for legal education and lawyer training. The terminology is important since they called for the introduction of 'law schools' to replace the existing 'faculties of law'. The new schools, they argued, were to be 'professional schools providing education especially for training of the legal profession' (JRC 2001). Since 2004 more than 60 graduate law schools have been established at Japanese public and private universities. Depending on whether students studied law as a first degree (in *hōgakubu*), students under the new model will take between two and four years of classes. Since the first cohorts from the revised system have just entered the profession, the jury is very much out on whether the reforms have been effective. Yet at this early stage a number of significant areas for adjustment are evident.

An oft-cited critique is that the law schools are producing too many graduates, even with a more relaxed bar exam, for them to be effectively absorbed by the existing system (Jones 2008). Indeed Aronson (2007: 21) quotes the senior Japanese partner at the Tokyo branch of an international law firm as stating that "because of the expanded number of graduates the overall quality of new graduates is unfortunately somewhat lower than before. So we need to spend much more time educating and training new lawyers to become good business lawyers." At the schools themselves, there have also been numerous pedagogical challenges including decisions on curricula and teaching methods. For example, how will Japanese students and faculty unaccustomed to, respectively, class participation and eliciting student input, respond to the more open classroom? Still further, while there have been some adjustments in the rankings of Japanese law schools in the performance of their grads on the bar exam, several of the schools that have improved have done so by adopting a cram school–like focus that gives too much emphasis to exam preparation and not enough emphasis to broader professional training. All things considered, and in the absence of studies that evaluate the evidence of effectiveness of these still embryonic reforms, it is fair to say the system for legal training in Japan is in considerable flux. Importantly, though, given the demand for talent that is attuned to the requirements of Japan's increasingly international legal sector, it is evident that many law firms (both domestic and international) are not waiting for the 'new law schools' to provide this specialized training. Instead, they appear disposed to seeking new staff with international credentials or ensuring that their existing staff acquire international experience.

The internationalization of American law schools

Faulconbridge and Hall (2009) draw on Nigel Thrift's concept of cultural circuits to illustrate how professional training shapes the discursive environment of legal practice. Besides imparting the information content of professional education, law schools socialize their students to carry into their careers cognitive and embodied practices that reproduce, respectively, the national and in many cases a particular school's brand of problem-solving, and the exclusionary culture of the profession. Yet they move one stage further than Thrift in calling for research that investigates the key tension between

> the ways in which such activities are often offered and regulated at a national level while individuals are entering fundamentally transnational professional service firms and have transnational careers. (Faulconbridge and Hall 2009: 173)

Faulconbridge and Hall investigate this problem in the context of Anglo-American jurisdictions and firms, leaving open the question of how these processes work in respect to Asian, and specifically non-Anglophone, examples. In the discussion that follows, the US context remains as the legal education provider; however, the nationality of the Japanese consumer is introduced as a contingent variable. The point that I want to explore is how US training reinforces exclusionary tendencies in the profession amongst lawyers of different national backgrounds.

Silver's (2006) excellent data-rich study provides a good overview of the overall constitution of the US market for international legal training. She shows how American law schools have successfully tapped into the deep market to provide professional training to an international clientele. Over 100 US law schools now offer graduate-level LLM programs, a one-year degree that in many cases is designed exclusively for foreign law students. These programs have been risk-free, income-generating ventures for many of the schools involved. This is because the law schools are able to offer places to foreign applicants in a way that does not affect their performance in the objective, widely acknowledged and competitive rankings offered by publications such as *US News and World Report*. The schools' reputations benefit further since they can brand themselves as 'international'. While the US schools have clearly benefitted, the implications for their foreign students are much less understood.

Silver provides some insight into the benefits and challenges of this experience for foreign students. For example, students benefit by gaining a familiarity with the content of US law. They also profit from the opportunity to improve their English communication skills in authentic, real-time settings. In her analysis it appears as though these intangible skills are overshadowed by more tangible signifiers of their experience. These include how the fulfillment of the course requirements for the one-year degree make them eligible to sit the bar exam in a few select jurisdictions, most notably New York. The accreditation of a US law degree and especially one from a blue-chip school, and New York bar registration, thus prove vital in structuring the cultural circuit along distinctly organizational and geographical lines. The principal drawback is that the curricular and extra-curricular experience does not adequately provide the opportunity for international, and particularly non-Anglophone, students to interact with and cultivate social networks with American students. So we have some idea of the motivations and selection strategies that stream international students into US LLM programs. On the other hand, the way that these experiences and accreditations shape the graduates' later work, particularly when they return to their home country to practice, is poorly understood.

Case study: Japanese attorneys and US law schools

As part of a larger project on internationalization and Japanese law, I conducted a series of ten interviews with US-educated Japanese attorneys in June 2009. Six of these paths are presented for comparison (Table 9.1). There is some variability in pathways the subjects took before, during and after their US sojourn. We can distinguish, for instance, between attorneys who studied law as undergraduates and those who studied science, between attorneys who have passed the Japan bar and those who have not, and whether the attorney works for a Japanese firm (*shogai jimusho*) or an international one. Some clear commonalities are also evident. Most notably, almost all of the respondents' US education costs were covered by employers. Also, despite attending a variety of US schools, they all sat the New York state bar exam. To

Table 9.1 Case study examples: Japanese subjects with US law school experience

Case	A	B	C	D	E	F
First degree (Place)	Law (Japan)	BSc, MSc (US)	BSc, MSc, LLB(Japan)	Law (Japan)	Law (Japan)	Law (Japan)
Japan Bar (Bengoshi)	Yes	No	No	Yes	Yes	Yes
Gap between graduation and Bar exam success	2 years	N/A -worked as patent translator in US law firm	N/A – worked as company researcher, patent attorney	4 years	5 years	1 year
Work in Japan prior to US sojourn	5 years	N/A	9 years	4 years	4 years	3 years
Japanese employer covers US training costs	Yes	N/A	Yes	Yes	Yes	Yes
US law degree	NYU (LLM)	Syracuse (JD)	George Washington (LLM)	NYU (LLM)	Northwestern (LLM)	Duke (LLM)
US Bar Admission	NY	NY, D.C.	NY	NY	NY	NY
US work experience	1 year	5 years at Washington office	No	No	One year internship	One year internship
Japan work experience	Shogai Bengoshi Firm	Intnl. Firm: 7 years, 2 as managing partner	Japanese Patent Law Office	Intnl. Firm	Intnl. Firm	Intnl. Firm (intern at Washington office)

make sense of these crude figures, drawn from an admittedly small sample, the results I present below are intended to be illustrative rather than exhaustive. They are organized according to the following three themes: (1) the search and selection strategies guiding Japanese attorneys who seek to train in the United States, the world's premier market for legal services and legal education; (2) their experience while at American law schools; and (3) the utility of this training for the sojourner when they return to work in Japan.

Search and selection

Amongst the various respondents, the most common pathway to training in the United States was initiated in early to mid-career and followed university, passage of the Japanese bar exam and work for either a Japanese *shogai jimusho* or an international firm. The motivation then is primarily to improve one's international skills in the face of evolving home-market demands, coupled with a personal desire for an overseas experience. In many cases, this decision was made with the knowledge that their firm would pay their sojourn expenses. Where things get interesting is in the search and selection strategies. All the respondents consulted publications that reproduced American rankings and seemed to be aware that this was the standard practice. For example,

> I checked a ranking of schools and asked more senior lawyers who studied abroad for advice. I think the Japanese tend to apply to the same schools. (D)
> [the main searching tool was] the magazine. There were many American magazines, and they often featured top 100 law schools at that time. I bought and read those magazines. They provided thorough information on what school had good reputation in what area of practice. (C)

From there, the respondents then applied to a range of schools and selected the highest-ranked school that accepted their application. Some attorneys chose schools based on particular practice specializations, yet these cases still conformed to the overall pattern.

> I wanted to go to a university famous for intellectual property, but I did not pass the exams. So then I went to Northwestern just because I passed their entrance exam. (E)
> I think I submitted 10 applications. Actually I failed for some schools and I got accepted by some schools and among those schools that accepted me, NYU seemed to be a good school. (A)

The search process also took into account US regulatory geographies, with many students looking beyond the degree to the bar exam.

I've heard NY bar exam is the easiest to take for foreigners. Other states often demand you to take JD for three years at a law school. I wanted to take only Master degree. And … even if you take a bar test in a small state, nobody knows this state in Japan. (D)

Respondents thus clearly took into consideration how the optics of any choice would be regarded back in Japan. These perspectives (viewed, obviously from hindsight) hint towards the way that their American training is incorporated in their career once they return home. First, though, it is important to understand the exact nature of their experience.

Experience

Once abroad, the experiences of the Japanese sojourners also suggested a degree of commonality. Several stressed the brevity of their 'one year' programs, which lasted on average about nine months, or two semesters. As a condition for acceptance in some LLM programs, it was necessary for some to take an intensive pre-degree course in US law fundamentals.

I studied an introduction to U.S. law at a summer course at UC Davis for four weeks. It covered concepts so rapidly. For example, a teacher took only three hours to explain contract or tort law. It covered many subjects, but in a superficial way. (D)

There is thus a lot to convey and absorb in a short period of time, so it is critical that we understand the nature of course delivery and how this was received.

The content and pedagogical style of US law schools go hand in hand. Reflecting the deductive institutional signature of American-style common law, the interactive case study method stood out as a distinctive component of their experience. Softer institutional distinctions from Japan, such as academic culture and attitude, also came across.

They used the so-called Socratic Method where teachers question students and students answer to get to the point … The basic way of studying is also different in the US from in Japan. In the US, the textbook consists of actual cases or extracts from cases, but in Japan we study law through basically the interpretation of statutes and legislation. (A)

In Japan, teachers speak and students listen. But in the U.S, teachers ask students and they reply. I think it is more "active" whereas I would call Japanese classes "passive." (D)

First of all, I remember the case study method. To understand each case, I had to read many books in English. Of course it was difficult. In the U.S. I had to study hard, but not in Japan … I rarely attended at a class at (Japanese) university when I was a student. (E)

I got the impression that law school students there were really studious ... Especially students in JD program. I heard there that if you got good marks they could get into a good lawyer's office. Although this doesn't apply to all the schools in Japan, it's common that as long as you graduate from a famous school other things do not really matter. In the United States, on the other hand, you need good marks even if you are in a good school. (C)

To make sense of this more vigorous learning environment and its curriculum, the respondents often drew upon their experience of Japanese law school as a comparative basis for understanding. Perhaps the biggest difficulty they encountered, then, was in adapting to the delivery of content in English by native English speakers. One respondent who had had the benefit of English-language instruction of US law topics at a Japanese university still found this difference in preparation telling.

At my Japanese university we had to learn the U.S. law in English. However, both teachers and students were Japanese, not native English speakers. (D)

Common limitations in oral/aural English were reported by most of the respondents, once again by referring to these weaknesses as a being particularly Japanese in nature.

As you know, the Japanese are often good at reading and writing even though they are hopeless at speaking and listening... In fact the general rules for Japanese and other foreign students are that they can get by with their reading and writing skills... For example we would be tested in oral exams, but the presentation was made in writing, so it wasn't so much of a challenge for those of us who were not good at speaking or listening. (E)

Ultimately, language limitations proved a deciding factor in steering the career decision following US training. One respondent observed that the LLM had limited utility for those foreign students who actually wanted to work permanently in the United States. While it provided students with a foundation in US law, it was inadequate for training students in the sorts of communication skills necessary for working in America.

Our industry is basically an industry of language, preparing documents and arguing in the court. It's not like a doctor or scientific job. For that perspective, I thought I would have a more interesting career back in Japan. (A)

Legacy of US sojourn

What is the ultimate benefit of US legal training for Japanese lawyers when they return home? It appears as though the benefits fall into two categories. The first legacy is that the tangible outcomes of their sojourn (degrees, New York bar license) help to enhance their relations with their clients. For instance, for Japanese clients these accreditations signal a particular standard of knowledge and skill.

> It can be a sales point to enhance your ability. For example, Japanese companies' administrators who have studied abroad often have the New York bar (even though they are not lawyers). So, if you do not have it after studying abroad, it might not be seen favourably. (D)

Thrift's concept of the cultural circuit is useful here in explaining the cosmopolitan values and expectations within the Japanese business community and its legal interface. Essentially, the New York bar license stands for a degree of familiarity with American business law; it can thus be read by those in the know as a basic standard of quality assurance for Japanese business relations with the United States. The extremely narrow and idiosyncratic nature of this designation is not really taken into consideration, and in practice it appears as though New York is allowed to represent the broader United States in an unproblematic manner. The one respondent with the more advanced JD designation was working as managing partner of an international firm's Tokyo office. Yet rather than use his credentials to actually practice US law, he spent most of his time as a rainmaker, trying to drum up business from Japanese clients in need of representation in the United States.

> Within the law firm I do a lot of marketing and customer service, at least relative to the other attorneys...I also became a liaison for the case that attorneys in our US offices are working on. When they have some problems with Jap clients or firms they will ask me to contact them to resolve any issues. (B)

Respondents further reflected on how their law school experience, as codified through an LLM designation, could be used to enhance relations with US clients and connections.

> When I meet American lawyers, I can say I have studied at NYU for one year. NYU is ranked as the 6th best school now, I think. That makes them trust me. (D)

Beyond the credential factor, the second main benefit of the US sojourn is that in certain situations, the knowledge and skills acquired abroad enable specific utilities in working with clients. Thus, as one respondent commented:

> At my [international] firm, the clients are often from the U.S. Since I know both the American legal system and Japanese legal system, I can explain their differences, and it is much easier for clients to understand. (E)

We learned earlier how when studying abroad, the attorneys framed their experience through an explicitly comparative lens. As the above quotation reveals, lawyers are able to highlight this comparative aspect in helping their clients understand cross-border files. The respondents all declared the experience helped them improve their English communication skills.

> ...the skill to talk (in English) on the phone, this is I think one of things I gained through studying and staying in the US for two years. I used to be uncomfortable talking on the phone. Talking to someone face to face was okay, but talking on the phone was a different story. I did not know how to deal with it. But sometimes making a phone call is necessary. I used to hate calling up a foreign attorney even when I had to, but now it is not a problem. (C)

More broadly, through their American experience the respondents accumulated profession-specific cultural capital that is highly prized as the Japanese legal sector anticipates Americanization. The following is a recollection by one attorney of his motives for pursuing a US education.

> Japanese government and courts are very likely to follow the American style...so from that point what I was learning will be very useful knowledge when I come back to Japan. That was what was in my mind. (D)

As the above quotation reminds us, the pursuit of US education by Japanese attorneys benefits a range of actors along the cultural circuit.

Discussion: the cultural circuit of US legal education

The sojourn of Japanese attorneys to US law schools affects four main sets of actors in the cultural circuit: US law schools, the student, the student's employer and the Japanese legal system (Table 9.2). Put another way, the sojourn activates three main linkages in the cultural circuit: between individuals and law schools, between individuals and employers and between firms and the broader legal sphere.

Table 9.2 How does the education of Japanese students benefit US law schools, individuals, firms and the Japanese legal sector (drawbacks/challenges in parentheses)?

School	Individual	Firm	Japanese Legal Sector
• Short-term revenue (less likely than US students to become future donors) • International image benefits domestic recruiting • (Variability in schools' preparation/ eligibility for state-specific bar exam)	Hard Skills • Learn fundamentals of US law • Acquires branded Degree • Accreditation before state bar Soft Skills • US deductive pedagogical style (case study) • Language development, especially English real-time communication skills Other: • US degrees and internships are often financed by law firm back in Japan • (rarely fosters social networks with American students)	*Shogai Bengoshi* Firms • US accreditation provides quality assurance to maintain Japanese clients, inbound files • US enculturation International Law Firms • Accesses Japanese talent • US accreditation provides quality assurance to win Japanese clients • US enculturation matches glocalization objectives; facilitates understanding between *gaiben* and *bengoshi* • (Japanese law still regulates functional distinction between *gaiben* and *bengoshi*)	• Internationalization • US influence makes sector more competitive • Complements training regimen at Japanese law schools • (Makes lingering flaws of Japanese law schools/policy more apparent) • Broadens, accelerates US-Japanese cultural circuit: either Japanese legal practices shift closer to US, or reinforces *wakon yosai* variety of capitalism

Japanese student ←→ US law school: LLM as juku

In some respects, the US LLM programs function almost as *juku* (cram schools), providing a service that implicitly is oriented to facilitate *not* the practice of law in the United States, but rather passing the New York bar exam.

A lingering drawback of the LLM programs is that they are poorly construed to enable grads to work in the US legal market (Silver and Freed 2006). LLM programs operate alongside of JD programs in many of the US schools, yet they remain functionally distinct from them, and this is ultimately reflected in the career horizons available to each stream. Moreover, the Japanese students (clientele) appear to be aware of this. In this sense, the cultural circuit already begins in a kind of an enclave, and this environment casts a shadow downstream.

US trained attorney ←→ law firm in Japan

After a work commitment that spans on average about four to five years, Japanese employers invest in their talent by selectively dispatching them overseas. This experience provides these attorneys with the hard and soft cultural capital to work on a growing volume of cross-border files between Japan and the United States. Yet, crucially, their work takes place within a new regulatory enclave that is still off-limits to *gaiben*, who still complement but do not substitute for *bengoshi* (Ramseyer 1986). International law firms attempt to obviate this distinction by concentrating teams of *bengoshi* and *gaiben* under one roof. Meanwhile the *shogai jimusho* seek to retain their traditional advantage for cross-border business by cultivating or hiring *bengoshi* with US training. Yet fundamentally the geographical structure of the *shogai jimusho* is distinctive, in that they cannot draw upon an international branch network and this tends to sharpen the demand for English fluency amongst their US-trained staff. Cautiously, for much more fieldwork needs to be done to verify this, my impression was of more confident English skills amongst Japanese attorneys who did *not* work alongside native English-speakers (*gaiben*). These two approaches to glocalization are responses to the broader institutional dynamics in their professional environment.

Firms ←→ Japanese legal sphere

International business and especially financial deregulation have prompted Japanese regulatory change, and this has altered the country's legal interface with the rest of the world, in particular in regard to the United States. Both variants of firm structure that operate in this environment on the surface appear to strengthen the purported 'Americanization' of legal practice and professionalism that is emerging in Japan. Yet on closer inspection, this is still very much a hybrid variety. History suggests that exogenous influences on the Japanese legal sector could also be read as contributing to a *wakon-yosei* (Western method, Japanese spirit) attitude in adapting US influence to the distinctive cultural and regulatory context of Japan. Key evidence for this is that the growth of the Japanese legal sector that has accompanied its increased internationalization is still driven by the uptake of primarily Japanese graduates. As long as the cohort who trains in the United States learns in an enclave-like setting, and as long as his or her scope of practice is preferentially regulated at home, the glocalization that is taking place in both *shogai jimusho* and international firms will still be a Japanese translation rather than a duplication of the US model. As Gertler (2001: 21) noted some time ago, "the prospects for strong convergence are limited at best, and will remain so as long as national institutional frameworks retain their distinctive character."

Conclusion: implications for management geography

This chapter has argued that although the internationalization of Japanese law has implied the adoption and adaptation of US legal method and style, these elements have persistently been adapted *from* an American system and *into* a Japanese setting that both retain distinctive regulatory and institutional foundations. The case study evidence suggests that Japanese attorneys who study at US law schools intensively absorb both the content and method of US legal practice. At the same time, their experience before and after their sojourn is still constrained by professional and regulatory convention. The communication skills they acquire during the sojourn enhance their fluency in international law, yet only so far. This is because the present cultural division of labor privileges specific functions for Japanese and international attorneys that tend to reinforce existing communicative strengths and weaknesses for each group.

Thus far the implications of these findings for management geography have been largely implicit. Now I offer several concluding remarks that might guide future research in the new sub-discipline. The first observation is that Japan represents a fascinating yet overlooked context for theoretical development. This is especially the case when we consider questions of hybridization and glocalization in international business. While the outward-oriented implications of these trends have been explored, the question of internationalization within Japan remains poorly understood. Yet as this chapter's findings suggest, certain themes stand out for greater scrutiny. Most importantly, though Japan's communicative position in respect to the Anglophone business world has been addressed by political economists and management scholars (e.g. Johnson 1980, Holden and Von Kortzfleisch 2002), geographers have failed to appreciate this linguistic distinctiveness, how it shapes the Japanese variety of capitalism, and how it is handled within firms.

On this last point, we can see that the growing literature on the globalization of law needs to better address the specific management challenges posed by non-Anglophone jurisdictions. Especially given the very pronounced linguistic basis of the profession, we need to develop better models that capture how various firm configurations around the world overcome language barriers. Yet unless our empirical palette includes studies of non-Anglophone places, language will remain off our radar screen. This study has suggested that mid-career overseas training in the United States gives Japanese participants some faculty for legal translation. International firms in particular could perhaps do more to encourage their Japanese staff to further develop their real-time English language skills. Yet this is unlikely to happen as long as the profession is regulated in a culturally bifurcated manner.

References

Abel, R. (1994). The future of the legal profession: Transnational law practice. *Case Western Reserve Law Review* 44, 737–60.

Abo, T. (1996). The Japanese production system: The process of adaptation to national settings. In R. Boyer and D. Drache (eds), *States Against Markets: The Limits to Globalization*, 136–54. London: Routledge.

Aronson, B. (2007). The brave new world of lawyers in Japan: Proceedings of a panel discussion on the growth of corporate law firms and the role of lawyers in Japan. *Columbia Journal of Asian Law* 21, 45–70.

Beaverstock, J. (2004). Managing across borders: Knowledge management and expatriation in professional legal service firms. *Journal of Economic Geography* 4, 157–79.

Beaverstock, J., Taylor, P., and Smith, R. (1999a). A roster of world cities. *Cities* 16(6), 445–58.

Beaverstock, J., Smith, R., and Taylor, P. (1999b). The long arm of the law: London's law firms in a globalising world economy. *Environment and Planning A* 13, 1857–76.

Casper, S. (2001). The legal framework for corporate governance: The influence of contract law on company strategies in Germany and the United States. In P. Hall and D. Soskice (eds), *Varieties of Capitalism: The Institutional Foundations of Comparative Advantage*, 387–416. Oxford: Oxford University Press.

Chan, K-W. (2005). Foreign law firms: Implications for professional legal education in Japan. *Journal of Japanese Law* 10, 55–80.

Edgington, D., and Hayter, R. (2000). Foreign direct investment and the flying geese model: Japanese electronics firms in Asia-Pacific. *Environment and Planning A* 32(2), 281–304.

Faulconbridge, J. (2008). Negotiating cultures of work in transnational law firms. *Journal of Economic Geography* 8, 497–517.

Faulconbridge, J., and Muzio, D. (2007). Reinserting the professional into the study of globalizing professional service firms: The case of law. *Global Networks* 7, 249–70.

Faulconbridge, J., and Hall, S. (2009). Educating professionals and professional education in a geographic context. *Geography Compass* 3, 171–89.

Flood, J., and Sosa, F. (2008). Lawyers, law firms and stabilization of transnational business. *Northwestern Journal of International Law and Business* 28, 489–525.

Florida, R. (2008). *Who's Your City? How the Creative Economy Is Making Where to Live the Most Important Decision of Your Life*. New York: Random House.

Florida, R., and Kenney, M. (1991). Organization vs. culture: Japanese automobile transplants in the US. *Industrial Relations Journal* 22, 181–96.

Foote, D. (2008). *Law in Japan: A Turning Point.* Seattle: University of Washington Press.

Gertler, M. (2001). Best practice? Geography learning and the institutional limits to strong convergence. *Journal of Economic Geography* 1, 5–26.

Hall, P.A., and Soskice, D. (eds). (2001). *Varieties of Capitalism: The Institutional Foundations of Comparative Advantage.* Oxford: Oxford University Press.

Henderson, W. (2007). The globalization of the legal profession. *Indiana Journal of Global Legal Studies* 14(1), 1–3.

Hobday, M. (1995). *Innovation in East Asia: The Challenge to Japan.* Cheltenham, UK: Edward Elgar.

Holden, N., and Von Kortzfleisch, H. (2004). Why cross-cultural knowledge transfer is a form of translation in more ways than you think. *Knowledge and Process Management* 11, 127–36.

Johnson, C. (1980). Omote (Explicit) and Ura (Implicit): Translating Japanese political terms. *Journal of Japanese Studies* 6(1), 89–115.

Jones, A. (2007). More than 'managing across borders?' The complex role of face-to-face interaction in globalizing law firms. *Journal of Economic Geography* 7, 223–46.

Jones, C. (2008). Law schools come under friendly fire. *Japan Times*, January 29.

Justice Reform Council (2001). Recommendations of the Justice System Reform Council – For a Justice System to Support Japan in the 21st Century. http://kantei.go.jp/foreign/judiciary/2001/0612report.html [last accessed 12 February 2010].

Omura, M., Osanai, S., and Smith, M. (2005). Japan's new legal education system: Towards international legal education? *Journal of Japanese Law* 10, 39–54.

Oppler, A. (1976). *Legal Reforms in Occupied Japan: A Participant Looks Back.* Princeton, NJ: Princeton University Press.

Majek, T., and Hayter, R. (2008). Hybrid branch plants: Japanese lean production in Poland's automobile industry. *Economic Geography* 84, 333–58.

Maxeiner, J., and Yamanaka, K. (2004). The new Japanese law schools: Putting the professional into legal education. *Pacific Rim Law and Policy Journal* 13, 303–28.

Milhaupt, C., and West, M. (2003). Law's dominion and the market for legal elites in Japan. *Law and Policy in International Business* 34, 451–98.

Morgan, G., and Quack, S. (2005). Institutional legacies and firm dynamics: The growth and internationalization of UK and German law firms. *Organization Studies* 26, 1765–85.

Nichibenren (2010). Outline of the Japan Federation of Bar Associations, http://www.nichibenren.or.jp/en/about/index.html, accessed 23 February 2010.

Ramseyer, M. (1986). Lawyers, foreign lawyers and lawyer substitutes: The market for regulation in Japan. *Harvard International Law Review* 27, 499–520.

Reiffenstein, T. (2009). Specialization, centralization and the distribution of patent intermediaries in the United States and Japan. *Regional Studies* 43(4), 571–88.

Reiffenstein, T., and Nguyen, H. (2011). The international developmental state: The Japanese intellectual property system in Vietnam. *Geoforum* 42(4), 462–72.

Sassen, S. (2001). *The Global City: New York, London, Tokyo.* Princeton, NJ: Princeton University Press.

Sibbitt, E. (2002). The new world of corporate lawyering in Japan. *Chicago Journal of International Law* 3, 503–11.

Silver, C. (2006). Internationalizing U.S. legal education: A report on the education of transnational lawyers. *International and Comparative Law Journal* 14, 143–75.

Silver, C., and Freed, M. (2006). Translating the US LLM experience: The need for a comprehensive examination. *Northwestern University Law Review Colloquy* 101, 23–30.

Silver, C., Phelan, N., and Rabinowitz, M. (2009). Between diffusion and distinctiveness in globalization: US law firms go glocal. *Georgetown Journal of Legal Ethics* 22(4), 1431–72.

Steiner, M. (2007). Cram schooled. *Wisconsin International Law Journal* 24, 377–95.

Takayanagi, K. (1963). A century of innovation: The development of Japanese law 1868–1961. In A.T. von Mehren (ed.), *Law in Japan: The Legal Order in a Changing Society*. Cambridge, MA: Harvard University Press.

Teubner, G. (2001). Legal irritants: How unifying law ends up in new divergences. In P. Hall and D. Soskice (eds), *Varieties of Capitalism: The Institutional Foundations of Comparative Advantage*, 416–41. Oxford: Oxford University Press.

Thrift, N. (2002). Think and act like revolutionists: Episodes from the global triumph of management discourse. *Critical Quarterly* 44, 19–26.

Warf, B. (2001). The global dimensions to US legal services. *Professional Geographer* 53, 398–406.

Waters, J. (2009). In pursuit of scarcity: Transnational students, 'employability', and the MBA. *Environment and Planning A* 41, 1865–81.

Westney, D. (1987). *Imitation and Innovation: The Transfer of Western Organizational Patterns to Meiji Japan*. Cambridge, MA: Harvard University Press.

Whitely, R. (1999). *Divergent Capitalisms: The Social Structuring and Change of Business Systems*. New York: Oxford University Press.

Yamamura, K. (1997). The Japanese political economy after the 'Bubble': Plus ça Change? *Journal of Japanese Studies* 23, 291–331.

Yeung, H.W-C. (2007). Editorial – Remaking Economic Geography: Insights from East Asia. *Economic Geography* 83, 339–48.

10
Global Operations of Japanese MNEs' Hybrid Factories: Management Geography Framework

Tetsuo Abo

Introduction

In this work, we try to illuminate and analyze the global overall situation of the different types of "hybrid factories" of Japanese firms, the mixture between Japanese and local management and production systems, in the major regions of the world, using our management geography approach. We, the Japanese Multinational Enterprise Study Group (JMNESG), have developed the concept of hybrid factory and undertaken large-scale field studies since the early 1980s in North and South America, East and South Asia, and Western and Central – Eastern Europe. This research focuses on five main issues. First, we give a brief explanation on the theoretical framework of our management geography approach. We suggest that various business/management models based on socio-cultural differences are closely connected to those of geographical locations along with historical contexts, and such differences are one of the essential factors determining the comparative or competitive advantage of industries or nations. Second, we look at typologies of different patterns of the "hybrid factory" (mixture of parent factory and local factory) by region. Third, we discuss the dynamic directions of various locational patterns of hybrid factories from one region to another. We examine whether there is divergence or convergence. Fourth, we analyze the strategic implication of different patterns of hybrid factories for the global management of Japanese or foreign firms in terms of performance such as efficiency, quality, and profitability. Lastly, we give our concluding remarks regarding what type of Japanese hybrid factory is appropriate for a specific local condition of management environment and market.

The ideal Japanese model may not be always the most desirable for overseas production and sales. High quality and relatively high cost do not necessarily make a product competitive in the markets of developing or newly developed economies such as China, India, and Africa. In the developing economies "appropriate" levels of quality and price can be stronger in occupying larger share in the "volume zone" of the markets. The critical question is how various types of Japanese hybrid factories can facilitate the knowledge and practical steps to attain the adaptation process requisite to such a mission. In reality it has not been easy for Japanese firms to change their basic management style in comparison to Korean, Chinese, or even Indian firms.

Theoretical research framework

We first explain the preliminary concept of "management geography."

Exploratory concept of management geography

Figure 10.1 shows a conceptual overview of relationship among each concept that compose the main elements of management geography.

There is a tier structure composed of several concepts ordered from bottom to top according to their chain of dependence. Location is at the bottom as a basic determinant of the chain that has strong influences on socio-cultural framework in many ways such as differences in topography, natural resources, and constitutions of people. Socio-cultural frameworks come next as a crucial determinant of various business models by influencing mainly the nature and attributes of organizations. Then, various types of hybrid factories are at the top as the products of the influences of the business models in different locations. In terms of academic discipline the locational and socio-cultural factors are treated respectively in geography and management theory, and to some extent economics. We propose that "management geography" must treat together both locational and socio-cultural factors and integrate them into a more synthesized (comprehensive) analytical framework. We emphasize that geographical elements in terms of locational differences as well as historical background are one of the most essential factors that affects socio-cultural context in a nation or region. Geographical difference would be on the horizontal axis, while historical

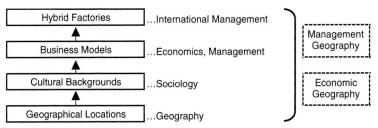

Figure 10.1 Conceptual figure of management geography

factor constitutes the vertical axis. In ordinary social sciences historical differences and changes are usually the main factors determining the differences in social and economic situations.

Why do we need to focus on geographical distinctions? Locational factors
include size (space and distance), layout (seaside, inland, island, mountain
side, plateau, basin, plain, river, and so on), weather, natural resources, and
human ethnicities. These factors play important roles in creating various
differences and diversity of socio-cultural frameworks, and then, of the fundamental systems and organizations of societies that have significant effects
on differentiating the types of business models: hunting vs. agricultural
society, individualism vs. groupism, short term vs. long term orientation,
competition vs. cooperation orientation, top-down vs. worksite orientation,
differentiation vs. equality orientation, and so on.

The above depiction can be illustrated using the Japanese case, which is
opposed to the American case. In Japan, we find very homogeneous and
inward-looking people who are products of the locational and historical
environment – small islands, the Far East (a periphery far away from the
Western centers, and monsoon weather), larger amounts of mountainous
slopes and basins, poor reserves of natural resources, a limited number of
ethnicities, about three hundred years of self-imposed exclusion due to the
closed-country policy preceding the modern era. There exists a unique set
of social institutions and systems which are quite historical thus giving rise
to distinct socio-economic attributes; group-oriented ways of communicating and behaving among familial people in a small world, worksite-oriented
cooperative ways of working, and all-member-involvement-style cooperation and competition within a firm or between firms. At the center of the
above socio-cultural and economic behavior lies the historical cooperative
style of working in the irrigation systems in rice-agriculture-led farming,
which is more or less common in the monsoon region in Southeast Asia.

Socio-cultural distance and organizational theory

There is a need to clarify whether a socio-cultural framework can really
exert important effect on the business model. Traditionally there has been
strong rejection of incorporating cultural elements into social sciences. The
discussions around "global standardization", which have diffused especially
along with the "IT revolution" from the United States into the rest of the
world since the 1980s, stress the significance of socio-cultural approach that
stresses the difference in performance of business models or management
systems from one society to another. Although the standardization model
has been powerful in the globalization era, there are certain limitations for
such a direction. The limitation is indicated not just by the recent IT recession and declining American economy, but also by the existence of different

styles of market competition which are determined by distinct organizations and systems of firms, governments, and other institutions in various societies. Therefore, one must study the relation between socio-cultural approach and organizational approach with respect to business model or management system.

Organization theory, presented by Coase (1937) and Williamson (1975), is an approach to comprehensively qualify an application of market fundamentalist theory. According to organization theory, an internal transaction within a firm can save costs compared with external market transaction costs between firms. This makes clear the necessary precondition for micro-level corporate management to exist. But it does not clarify the qualitative differences between the corporate organization systems that stem from the socio-cultural backgrounds of these organizations. In that sense, organization theory is included in the global standardization approach but cannot adequately explain the reasons for such variations among forms of organizational administration, corporate governance, management system, and so on, from one country to another. Therefore, to incorporate the distinct ways of organizational and managerial functions of firms in different locations into business and management models, organization theory needs to be complemented by culture-oriented management theories, which take into account knowledge and methodology of geography. This is the foundation of our preliminary concept of management geography.

Three types of markets, organizations, and business models in three major regions

Table 10.1 summarizes relations of markets, organizations, and business models in the United States, Japan, and Europe.The key characteristics of markets and organizations by region are divided into three categories: market fundamentalism in the United States (UK) and cooperative organization-orientation in Japan (Asia) and regulative organization-orientation in Europe.

In the United States, there is a huge inland space with large variation of topography and plentiful natural resources and large variety of different ethnicities and kinds of people mostly based on modern immigrations from the various regions in the world, and the historical colonial past. Therefore, external market was the best institution to connect different types of people and far distant locations and to distribute various materials and resources to the appropriate places. Here, the necessary management resources are mostly procured as "ready-made" products. In Japan, as mentioned earlier, cooperative organization-orientation, in the form of internal market transactions within firms (e.g. long-term employment and training system) or even between firms ("semi-internal market" such as *keiretsu* or sub-contracting

Table 10.1   Three Types of market, organization and business model in three major regions

	USA (UK)	Japan (East Asia)	Continental Europe
principal characteristics	market fundamentalism	cooperative organization-orientation	regulative organization-orientation
nature of market	external market	internal market-orientation in firms	internal market-orientation in community
nature of organization	rule and law-based administration	group-based administration	social regulation-based administration
corporate governance	owners' control	employees' control	owner-employees' joint control
management system	rigid demarcation, individual-based division of labor	flexible demarcation, worksite-oriented all members involvement	regulation-based demarcation, specialist-led division of labor

relationships) is distinguished in the functions of market mechanism. Here, the necessary management resources are mostly prepared as "made-to-order" products. In (mainly Continental) Europe, many medium-sized countries in a large inland territory have common rivers, mountains, cultural traditions, and histories. Here regulative organization-orientation exerts influence on the communities more strongly than in Japan not only in the form of laws but also in social customs. Long-term-orientation is partly based on Stone Age culture and wide bundled division of labor is derived from a historically relatively limited variety of style of living in terms of kinds of foods, houses, and clothing.

An important difference regarding organization-orientations between Japan and Europe lies in the "cooperative" or "regulative" attributes. One of the most popular regulative institutions in Europe is the national or local level qualification system of promotion and payment ladder in firms. This can be regarded as a microscopic form of large bundled division of labor. With distinctive systems, such as "Tarif" in Germany and "Cadre" in France, it is difficult for the Japanese transplants to apply the Japanese-style company-level qualification systems which are more flexible in implementing individual-based evaluation and reward methods using wider job rotations and OJT practices (Abo, 2001b). Business models, corporate governances, and management systems also vary according to the differences in the nature of markets and organizations in the three regions. As depicted in Table 10.1, the system of corporate governance is owners' control in the United States (though a historical change from "managerialism"), employee control in Japan, and owner-employee joint control in Europe.

International comparison of hybrid factories

Based on the above understanding of the relationship between management styles and their geographical backgrounds, we have developed an analytical framework, the "application-adaptation (hybrid) evaluation model," and the key concept of "hybrid factory" for our research.

"Application-adaptation (hybrid) evaluation model" and "five-point grading system" as the analytical framework for our research

This survey seeks to investigate the management and production systems of major Japanese manufacturers with comparative advantages such as automakers and electric machinery makers, compare the situation of mother factories in Japan with those of subsidiaries' factories abroad, and then, measure and evaluate the degree of overseas transfer of Japanese systems by utilizing the "application-adaptation (hybrid) evaluation model" and the "five-point grading system." For this purpose, an ideal model for the composition of Japanese management and production systems (see Table 10.2) has been developed based on the results of our surveys on Japanese parent factories. The introduction and transplanting of each factor item constituting the Japanese system into an overseas factory is referred to as "application," whereas any modification made to an original factor in accordance with the local management environment is called "adaptation." The "five-point grading system" is designed to quantitatively show the results of the application-adaptation evaluation. For instance, if an overseas factory

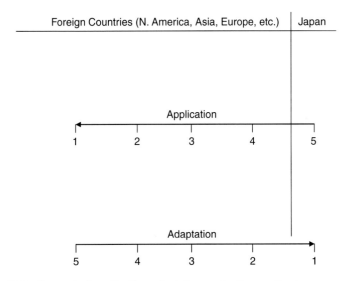

Figure 10.2 Concept of application-adaptation evaluation method

Table 10.2 Application ratio of the Japanese production system at overseas Japanese plants

	N.A. (01)	N.A. (89)	UK (97)	C.W.E. (98)	W.E.	K/T (92)	S.A. (93)	China (02)	E.A.	C.E.E. (03)
I. Work Organization and Administration	3.2	2.9	3.4	3.0	3.1	3.7	3.3	3.5	3.5	3.3
1. Job classification	4.1	3.7	4.4	3.2	3.6	4.9	4.5	4.4	4.7	4.1
2. Multi-functional skills	3.0	2.6	3.3	2.8	3.0	2.9	2.6	3.0	2.7	2.8
3. Education and training	3.7	2.9	3.5	3.1	3.2	3.4	3.3	3.5	3.3	3.4
4. Wage system	2.3	2.4	2.8	2.8	2.8	3.9	3.1	3.4	3.5	2.9
5. Promotion	2.9	3.1	3.4	3.1	3.2	3.7	3.1	3.4	3.4	3.3
6. Supervisor	3.2	2.9	3.4	3.1	3.2	3.4	2.9	3.3	3.2	3.1
II. Production Control	3.4	3.3	3.5	3.1	3.3	3.5	3.4	3.3	3.4	3.3
7. Equipment	3.9	4.3	3.9	3.4	3.6	3.5	4.0	3.8	3.7	3.9
8. Maintenance	3.1	2.6	3	2.8	2.9	3.3	3.0	3.1	3.2	2.8
9. Quality control	3.4	3.4	3.6	3.1	3.3	3.6	3.2	3.2	3.4	3.1
10. Process management	3.5	3.0	3.6	3.2	3.3	3.5	3.2	3.3	3.4	3.3
III. Procurement	2.6	3.0	2.5	2.8	2.7	3.2	3.2	3.0	3.2	2.7
11. Local content	1.8	2.7	1.9	2.8	2.4	2.9	3.1	3.0	3.0	2.6
12. Suppliers	2.9	3.9	2.7	2.9	2.8	3.5	3.8	3.3	3.7	2.8
13. Methods	3.1	2.5	2.9	2.8	2.8	3.2	2.8	2.8	3.0	2.7
IV. Team Sense	3.3	3.2	3.3	2.7	2.9	3.4	3.2	3.0	3.3	2.9
14. Small group	2.6	2.5	2.7	2.5	2.6	3.2	2.9	2.6	3.0	2.2
15. Information sharing	3.6	3.6	3.6	2.8	3.1	3.5	3.3	3.1	3.4	3.2
16. Sense of unity	3.7	3.5	3.7	2.8	3.1	3.6	3.3	3.4	3.5	3.2

V. Labor Relations	3.7	3.6	3.6	3.2	3.3	3.4	3.1	3.1	3.2	3.4
17. Hiring policy	3.6	3.4	3.3	3.1	3.2	3	3.1	2.9	3.0	3.2
18. Long-term employment	3.5	3.4	3.4	3.2	3.3	3.3	3.0	3.0	3.2	3.0
19. Harmonious labor relations	4.2	4.4	4.2	3.5	3.8	4.0	3.3	3.7	3.6	3.8
20. Grievance	3.7	3.3	3	3.1	3.0	3.2	3.1	3.0	3.1	3.4
VI. Parent-Subsidiary Relations	2.8	3.6	2.8	3.0	2.9	2.3	2.9	2.7	2.6	2.9
21. Ratio of Japanese	2.1	3.7	2.4	2.6	2.6	1.5	1.6	1.8	1.5	1.9
22. Delegation of power	3.1	3.6	3.0	3.2	3.1	2.7	3.2	3.0	2.9	3.1
23. Position of local managers	3.1	3.6	3.0	3.1	3.1	2.7	3.8	3.2	3.3	3.6
Average of All Items	3.2	3.3	3.3	3.0	3.1	3.3	3.2	3.2	3.3	3.1

1) From the database of JMNESG (research year)
2) N.A.: North America, UK: the United Kingdom, C.W.E.: Continental West Europe, W.E.: Western Europe, K/T: Korea/Taiwan, S.E.A.: South East Asia, E.A.: East Asia, C.E.E: Central and Eastern Europe

is found to have implemented a certain factor of the Japanese system 100 percent, an application ratio score of "5" (meaning zero modification, and consequently, the adaptation ratio score of "1") will be given to that factory, while an application score of "1" (meaning 100 percent modification into the local system, and consequently, an adaptation score of "5") will be given if no transfer of Japanese factors has been made (See Figure 10.2). Any scores referred to hereinafter represent application scores unless otherwise specified.

Table 10.2 summarizes the major portion of the evaluation results. By analyzing data listed in this table, it is possible to examine the degree to which various factors defining the Japanese management system have been transplanted in Japanese factories overseas and to compare the situations by region or country (and by industry, though this not shown in this chapter), or between different points of time. This "six-group, 23-item evaluation" is an orthodox, performance-oriented approach focusing on efficiency and quality which examines – from the viewpoint of Japanese parent companies and their factories in Japan – to what extent their competitive advantage has been transplanted into subsidiaries' factories overseas. On the other hand, the "four-perspective evaluation system," though not used so much here, was developed as a means to analyze situations from the viewpoint of each host community, thus shedding light on the substance and nature of technology transfer.

We then take up an analysis of five specific countries and regions, each of which will be discussed later. Of these, however, China and Central and Eastern Europe are not included because their evaluation scores are still preliminary because the surveys were conducted less than two years ago.

Characteristics of Japanese management and production systems: international transfer models approach

First, we briefly explain how the Japanese model described above should be understood. The characteristics of the Japanese management and production systems (Abo, 1995; Itagaki, 1997) lie, first and foremost, in the way of defining authority and responsibility broadly and loosely. This would allow substantial versatility for each worker of a factory to divide and/or combine job tasks with other workers, consequently enabling the factory to turn out a wide range of products in small lots and respond to the changing needs of the market quickly and flexibly. Again, in order for workers to demonstrate a certain degree of competency for making judgment so that they can cope with any changes in the condition of their workplace (*genba shugi*, or shop floor–oriented system), each one of them must be equipped with adequate and broad knowledge and skills in accordance with his or her assigned position at the workplace (Koike, 1988). This compelled companies to nurture employees through in-house on-the-job training based on the premise of "lifetime employment," which led to the establishment of a "person-centered" job performance evaluation system (as compared to American-style "job task–centered" wage system). The introduction of such person-centered system – a kind of ability-based grade system that combines a merit-rating system and a seniority system – has enabled the formation and utilization of human resources in a "made-to-order" or "homemade" manner, hence, the formation of an internal labor market system. The system is suitable for the type of sectors and businesses in which relatively homogeneous and inward-looking people get together to carry out certain tasks while balancing competition and cooperation. In addition, the practice thrives where product differentiation and meticulous quality control, even in an environment of mass production, hold the key to success and therefore many of those at the workplace are required to have substantial ability to make judgment and willingness to improve their personal work skills. To borrow terms used in a taxonomy of technologies that has been recently presented by Fujimoto et al. (2001), this particular Japanese system is also suitable for industries with "integral-type" production system – for instance, the automobile industry, in which the designing and manufacturing of a product requires the fine-tuned *suriawase* (tight coordination) of technologies by each member involved in the process ranging from the designing of molds to the final stage of assembling and inspections. This system is distinguished from the "modular-type" production system such as "Dell production system" for computers that has been receiving much attention in conjunction with the IT revolution – which is to assemble ready-made parts and materials procured from outside market on an as-needed basis and in a cost-oriented manner.

What requires pointing out here is the relationship between the reversal in economic fortunes in the 1990s and the change in the status of the Japanese management system. Although it is necessary to pay due attention to the recent moves made by some leading Japanese companies (primarily major electric and electronics machinery assembly companies whose business performance temporarily deteriorated) to overhaul the lifetime employment system and/or the age-based remuneration system and to carry out a large-scale restructuring, we do believe that these Japanese systems still remain sufficiently valid as a prototype of the Japanese model so far as the sectors of industry and the nature of technology are adequately defined. This is to say that while building such an ideal type of management representing each stage of the times, we also need to measure the distance from the ideal type of management as a methodological means to evaluate the current state of affairs.

Six-group, 23-item evaluation

With regard to the details given in Table 10.2, we would like to go directly into the evaluation of results while skipping explanation for each item or group

(Abo, 1994; Itagaki, 1997). The average score of the 23 items of seven countries and regions falls in the range between 3.0 and 3.3. This means that some sort of "hybrid management" system – in which a little more than half the elements are of Japanese attributes, with the remaining elements reflective of local characteristics – is being implemented in Japanese factories operating in each of these regions. Alternatively, by focusing on the fact that the average scores for all the regions – including North America, where Japanese factories have been operating for more than a decade, along with relatively new destinations such as China and Central and Eastern Europe – remain within this range, we can assume that, as far as average scores are concerned, there is little likelihood for overseas Japanese factories to get substantially closer to the level of their parent factories in Japan. In a sense, these evaluation results may provide a concrete clue to determine the limit of generalization with regard to the internationalization of Japanese production systems. However, average scores themselves are no more meaningful than what has been discussed above. For instance, higher scores for equipment, local content (rate of locally procured materials and parts), and JPN ratio (ratio of Japanese expatriates to total employees) indicate a greater likelihood of achieving production efficiency that is comparable to that of mother factories in Japan. At the same time, however, this can be interpreted negatively because, as discussed later,

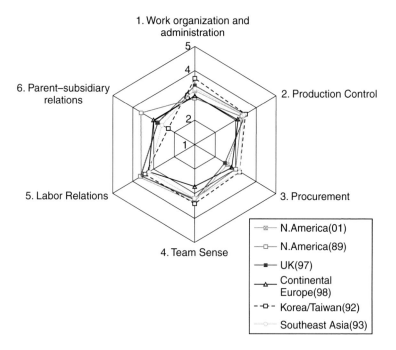

Figure 10.3   Comparison of Japanese hybrid plants in the six world regions

such a situation – characterized by high scores for both "Material-Result" and "Human-Result" (i.e. heavy reliance on the transfer of ready-made materials and personnel from Japan) – is undesirable from the viewpoint of adaptation to local environment. What is more important from the standpoint of "management geography approach" is the semantic content of various differences, which we will discuss in the following section.

A six region–based comparison across the world is presented with regard to such analysis. First, we will take up five countries and regions – North America (1989 and 2001), UK, Central Western Europe, Korea/Taiwan, and South Asia. Later, we will take up China and Central Eastern Europe. Figure 10.3 provides a succinct picture of regional differences in the situations of hybrid factories focusing on the six aspects of their characteristics. The major points of argument derived from this are as follows.

Different patterns: Conspicuous regional differences in scores for the six groups of characteristics and various hexagonal shapes are observed among the following groups of countries and regions.

North America (89) and Continental Europe versus South Korea, Taiwan, and Britain

What is noteworthy here is a sharp contrast between these two groups of regions and countries with factory patterns for North America (89) and Continental Europe being almost mirror opposites of those for South Korea, Taiwan, and Britain. Specifically, North America (89) and Continental Europe have relatively low scores for G-I Organization/Administration, which forms the "core personnel-related portion" of the Japanese system, and high scores for G-VI Parent/Subsidiary, whereas South Korea, Taiwan and Britain post high scores for G-I and low scores for G-VI. That is, the degree of transfer of G-I remains rather modest in North America (89) and Continental Europe despite the considerable involvement of Japanese parent companies as indicated by the high ratios of Japanese expatriates to total employees. On the other hand, hybrid factories in South Korea, Taiwan, and Britain have been achieving the higher degree of G-I transfer despite having relatively little involvement from Japanese parent companies.

Of these contrasting results, differences between North America (89) / Continental Europe and South Korea / Taiwan are attributable to differences between the United States and Europe versus East Asia. Given the distance between the two sides in terms of historical and social backgrounds, this is quite a convenient result for the cultural approach. But the big question remains as to how to explain the case of Britain, which shows the same tendency, though less conspicuously, as South Korea and Taiwan. The Anglo-Saxon background may be what differentiates Britain from Continental Europe. In that case, however, Britain should have shared similar characteristics with North America, which also has an Anglo-Saxon background.

For now, let's point out that British industry, after nearly a hundred years of decline, was coming to a turning point thanks partly to the drastic social reform implemented by former Prime Minister Margaret Thatcher, and that both Wales and Scotland, where many Japanese companies have set up factories, have social characteristics similar to those of Japan.

Meanwhile, Southeast Asia (Thailand, Malaysia, and Singapore) and North America (01) fall in between the above two groups. The positioning of Southeast Asia is to some extent imaginable given the background of this region, which, while historically influenced by Europe, has a sizable population of overseas Chinese. Yet the case of North America (01) came as a bit of surprise because the result of the 2000–01 survey shows that the situation of this region has changed substantially since 1989 when we conducted the previous survey there, and that the hexagon for North America (01) has become similar to that of Britain. As we are still trying to determine the meaning of this, we shall steer clear of going into further analysis here.

South Korea, Taiwan, Southeast Asia, and North America (89) versus Britain and North America (01)

Differences can be found with regard to G-III Parts Procurement for which South Korea, Taiwan, Southeast Asia, and North America (89) mark conspicuously high application scores while Britain and North America (01) have low scores and Continental Europe comes in between. Things are somewhat complex for G-III because the meaning of scores can vary based on attribution to different items within the group. Generally speaking, however, the high scores for Southeast Asia are reflective of the fact that the region does not have a sufficiently developed domestic parts industry and therefore Japanese factories need to rely on parts imported from Japan and/or those procured from Japanese-affiliated suppliers operating in the region. In contrast, the presence of a well-established domestic parts and components industry and the implementation of strict local content requirement (particularly in the 1990s, when the survey was conducted) are deemed to have contributed to these high scores for Europe. Here again, the 2000–1 survey on North America has found a sharp drop in the application score (sharp increase in the adaptation score) as compared to the results in the previous survey. This is attributable to the expansion and deepening of local production, particularly in the automobile sector, and the subsequent reinforcement of supply bases for procuring the relevant parts and material.

Common patterns

A group for which all the regions have scores close to each other

Regardless of region and time, scores for G-II Production Control are, almost without exception, close to each other. This is because production control represents the "core portion of Material" of the Japanese production system, a key condition that is required and has a direct impact on the strength of the system. Indeed, this group is composed of the kind of items which companies would place great emphasis on. As shown in Table 10.2, much of the production equipment is either made in Japan or made by local affiliates of Japanese equipment makers with some adjustments so that they fit the needs of each user company, thus resulting in almost equally high scores across the board. Also, Japanese expatriates are substantially involved, either directly or indirectly, in both quality control and operation management to realize conditions that are as close as possible to (though not perfectly the same as in the Japanese system at home) and to ensure that no problems arise. With respect to maintenance, a considerable gap is observed between North America (89) and Continental Europe, which is attributable to the difference in the education and training systems of the two regions. However, the score for this item in North America (01) has come to a level comparable to that of Britain. It is noteworthy that such a significant change is observed after more than ten years since Japanese factories began to operate in the region, because this indicates the possibility that a certain degree of change can be made to the existing regional patterns.

Continental Europe versus the others

For G-IV Team Sense, Continental Europe has a conspicuously high score while scores for all the other regions are at or around 3.3. To be sure, a closer look at the detailed breakdown of results based on the 23-item classification in Table 10.2 shows that scores for small group activities are concentrated at the lowest level ranging between 2.5 to 2.7 except for South Korea, Taiwan, and Southeast Asia. Indeed, all the regions but Continental Europe posted high scores for the other two items – information sharing and the sense of unity – and this resulted in the above-mentioned outcome for G-IV. In Continental Europe, there still exists the traditional idea of dichotomy in the division of social classes, which translates into the division between labor and management. Under such labor-management relations, there would be a limit to the introduction of personnel policies or the formation of human relationships based on the principle of unanimous participation and cooperation. On the other hand, it seems quite natural that many aspects of the Japanese system such as a company cafeteria, parking lots, and company parties for all employees are welcomed in many regions, as long as these aspects do not require the "self-sacrifice" of time and labor on the part of employees under some sort of "peer pressure" as is the case with small group activities.

Inter-industry comparison in six groups

As discussed earlier in relation to Porter's arguments, the competitive advantage of industry differs by country and/or by region. Therefore, a certain industry whose comparative advantage lies in attributes of the Japanese system has different "compatibility" with different regions to which the system is transferred, which is more or less reflected in the patterns of hybrid factories. In a brief or casual observation, we can notice a sort of "affinity" between an industry and a region. While in North America, overall application scores for the automobile assembly far exceed those for electric and electronics assembly, in Southeast Asia the relation becomes quite reversed (see Abo, 2007).

Comparison of strategic typologies

It is a common-sense management theory that apart from the regional and inter-industry differences discussed above, individual companies' independent decisions –different management strategies – result in differences in the patterns of hybrid factories. However, instead of focusing on some individual cases, here, we would like to point out that even such strategic decisions made by individual companies are governed by macroeconomic market conditions and can be captured as a general trend that is common to specific region and/or industry.

Summary and some practical implications

Up to this point, we have summarized the results of our research and surveys, which have been conducted across the world in the past 20 years, presenting them in the form of international comparison along the lines of our research theme concerning the international transferability of the Japanese management and production systems. Specifically, I have clarified the geographic distribution of Japanese hybrid management and factories across the world and sorted out their respective features either as generalities or peculiarities observed in various patterns of international transfer of these systems. What has become apparent is that each business management system has a certain degree of organizational cultural traits that are unique to the country or region in which the system has been developed, and that it is inevitable for the Japanese system, in which such traits are particularly strong, to be substantially transformed or modified in accordance with the management environment in the country or region to which it is transferred.

From the standpoint of practical application in corporate management, a company cannot sufficiently secure its competitive advantage simply by transferring only the easily applicable "general" aspects of the management and production systems. Rather, the success or failure of its local management hinges largely on how various factors constituting the peculiar aspects of the Japanese management and production systems can be modified and transplanted into local operations in a way to effectively retain the merits of the systems. Therefore, no progress can be made by mere highlighting differences, peculiarities, or the difficulty of transplanting the systems. What is of utmost importance is how to overcome the difficulty in practice. I do hope that the findings of our research on hybrid factories will provide some suggestions and guidance to help companies overcome such difficulty.

Theoretically, there is no ruling out the possibility that we find, through our analysis and evaluation of various hybrid factories, cases that exhibit an interesting blend of different management systems or those in which hybridization has been proactively pursued. Therefore, we could discuss, based on the above-described results of our study, about the possibility of a "desirable hybrid model" or a "practical hybrid model" in the international transfer of the Japanese system, looking into the situation of hybrid factories in several different patterns of hybridization. Yet, here, due to the space limitation, we exercise restrain to simply describe the details of such parts (see Abo, 2007, pp. 25 onward for more detail). It is therefore tenable to summarize our findings and present as a tentative theory on the selection of a "desirable" or "practical" model for hybrid factories in the international transfer of the Japanese management and production systems.

First, a model which is created simply by extracting common patterns is just a systematic generalization and does not have much substance. This may have a certain degree of usability as a ready-made method under situations in which some sort of management decision must be made with limited resources and in a limited time frame, for instance, when Japanese companies need to quickly make a series of decisions concerning their overseas operations. However, based on what is perceived to be appropriate evaluation and judgment from the viewpoint of our hybrid management model theory, a combination of the second model, which incorporates factors peculiar to each region and type of industry, and the third one – the "flexible general model" that is dependent on the trend of global convergence, would be the most plausible direction to take. Based on this premise, final decisions by each company would be made as a strategic choice with an eye on market conditions (scale, diversity, etc.) and cost factors (local factors and conditions).

Concluding remarks

Our concluding remarks are premised on providing an answer to the question of what are critical issues regarding divergence or convergence while considering the Japanese hybrid factories from the perspective of management geography? Based on our findings on "hybrid factories" above, as the concluding remarks here, I will illuminate the results by taking up two distinctive directions, either toward divergence or convergence. The direction of the movement is found to depend on two major factors – local management environment and corporate strategy – which in turn are primarily affected by market conditions such as production costs and scale of sales.

Divergence and convergence of Japanese hybrid factories worldwide

The degree toward divergence is principally determined by differences in the managerial environment, a factor that influences "adaptation." The differences are twofold: the degree of difference from the original Japanese system, and the number of variation patterns. The first type of difference depends on the socio-cultural distance from Japan. For example, Japanese plants in the United States and, to a certain extent, Continental Western European countries, may require far greater adjustments than their counterparts in the East Asian region. The second type of differences relates to the scope of Japanese subsidiaries' expansion overseas, since the managerial environment differs to some extent in each country or region. The broader the geographical scope, the greater the number of variation patterns.

Convergence can be observed as a process in which a system becomes closer to what we call the "East Asian pattern." This pattern, compared to the conventional "American" or "Fordist" system, and the traditional craftsman system of Continental Europe, places heavy emphasis on human-related elements by maintaining flexible and group-oriented organizational structures and administration systems, process-oriented engineering techniques in production control, and long term-oriented relations between end-product producers and associated parts and components suppliers. This system, which is similar to but not identical with the original Japanese-style system seen in Japan, may be a possible global model that retains some of the essential core elements of the competitive advantages of the Japanese management and production system.

We therefore in summary point out two possible and interesting trends: increasing divergence on one hand and deepening convergence on the other. Hence, an ever greater variety of "hybrid factories" are emerging as Japanese manufacturers expand their geographical scope of operations with economic globalization, and move into emerging markets such as China, India, and Central and Eastern Europe. At the same time, however, it is likely that there will be a notable trend toward convergence or a reduction in differences in the application-adaptation patterns of "hybrid factories." Hereafter, we will try to elucidate these trends and their strategic implications for the Japanese and world manufacturing companies, using the data, analysis, and discussions in the preceding sections.

Diverging patterns

We can see various diverging patterns for the surveyed hybrid factories by region and by industry. From the perspective of management geography, region-related diverging patterns are more interesting and should be given more attention.

Region-based divergence

While the total average scores are incredibly close from one region to another as shown above in Figure 10.4, a great variety of differences in the 23 element items of Japanese production system is shown by region and by items. However, we shall not delve into such details so we will describe the more principal diversity in the Japanese hybrid factories worldwide using six groups.

As was shown in Table 10.2, principal regional differences can be seen in scores for the six groups, between the three major regions, North America (89 and 01), Western Europe and East Asia (92–93, 02, China included), and in Figure 10.5, so different shapes of the hexagons are observed.

In Figure 10.6, looking at three European regions (the UK, Continental West Europe, and Central and Eastern Europe), some differences in the shapes of the hexagons are seen in the new European community.

Converging patterns

Time-based convergence

The most noteworthy change in terms of the convergence of hybrid patterns at Japanese overseas plants is observed between North America (89) and

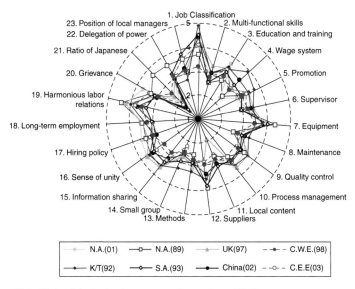

Figure 10.4   Hybrid factories in seven major regions, 23 items

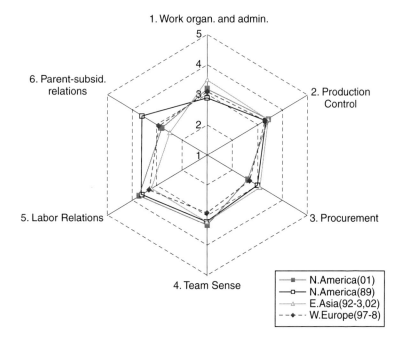

Figure 10.5 Hybrid factories in three major regions, six groups

North America (01) – (See Figure 10.1 and earlier arguments). This is a large-scale convergence of the six-group hexagon for North America (01) from an extreme North American type (89) to a similar pattern to Western Europe, or an intermediate between North America (89) and East Asia, or in other words, toward an "East Asian pattern."

The "East Asian pattern" can be seen as a desirable one for Japanese hybrid factories in the sense that, above all, the higher human-core portion of Japanese production systems, as shown by the higher application score for GI, is realized with much lower involvement by the Japanese parent company (higher participation of local management people), represented by the low score of GVI, although the level of local procurement of materials is also low as represented by a high score in GIII (mentioned above). The "East Asian pattern" in the shape of the hexagon for the UK is very suggestive. For one thing, there is yet no research evidence showing a historical change from a more typical European type to the present one in the long run, as was observed in a short period of just ten years or so in North America.

Region-based convergence

So far, as clarified above, while there are many divergent shapes in the six-group hexagons by region and industry for Japanese hybrid factories

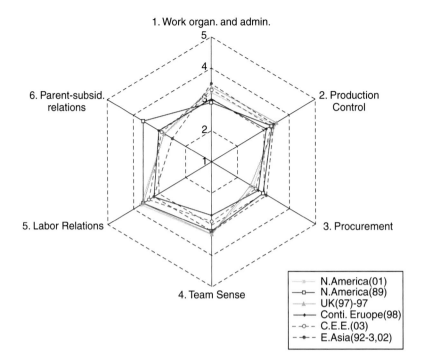

Figure 10.6 Hybrid factories in N.A., UK, C.W.E., C.E.E., and E.A., six groups

worldwide, some especially important cases of convergence, such as North America (01), can be observed. As a whole, early in the twenty-first century the shapes of almost all the hexagons observed, except for that of Continental Western Europe (also N. America (89)), seem to be converging toward the "East Asian pattern" (See Figure 10.6).

Is there a trend toward an "East Asian pattern"?

As mentioned above, the "East Asian pattern" of Japanese hybrid factories can be seen as the most desirable one among many, so this direction of the convergence should be welcomed by Japanese companies. However, to what extent is this true in practice? There are likely two main reasons for the trend toward the "East Asian pattern." First, needless to say, the "affinity" for Japanese systems may be critical in East Asian countries, where the socio-cultural background is familiar to Japan's. Yet, this is not the case in the UK, where historical and political changes in the social structure may have created a kind of "affinity" or compatibility with Japanese systems.

Second, the strategic responses by Japanese companies to local market and business conditions are thought sometimes to be decisive. This is typically the case for North America (01), or more precisely, of Japanese automobile manufacturers in the US and Canada, though they had to make great additional investments to compensate for the application gap originating from socio-geographical differences.

The implication of global divergence and convergence of the Japanese hybrid factories: From the perspective of management geography approach

Now, what we can see as one of the focal points of global management model in the early twenty-first century would be a kind of tug of war between two directions – divergence and convergence – regarding international competitiveness of Japanese hybrid factory. Diverging trends seem to be progressing when the space for the business activities of Japanese or Asian firms is remarkably expanding in terms of not only its depth in developed regions such as the US and Europe but also in its spread to developing regions such as Brazil, Russia, India, and China (the BRIC countries). On the other hand, converging trends can also clearly be seen when those companies have accumulated lots of the techniques and know-how for foreign management during their experiences abroad for more than three decades since the 1980s and the strategic efforts by Japanese firms and globalization sentiment worldwide have impacted the direction toward the spread of some popular types or methods of Japanese production systems such as Toyota production system (TPS) or "lean production system," *kaizen*, QCC, *kanban*, JIT, *keiretsu*, and so on.

Thus, we can ask the question: which direction is more powerful or more important? This is not a simple or easy question because the currently typical Japanese-style production system is not necessarily the best model for the global market, especially in the markets of rapidly expanding newly industrialized countries (NICs) such as China (Abo, 2011), India, and even Africa. The pertinent point to emphasize is, in short, whether the Japanese-type high-quality and relatively high-cost products can take some sizable share in "volume zone" of rapidly growing markets such as those in the BRIC countries. In reality, the typical Japan-led manufacturing products such as electronics home appliances, motorcycles, and even automobiles have been losing dominant competitive edges in comparison to Korean, Taiwanese, and Chinese firms, in the markets of the BRIC countries and the other developing regions such as ASEAN and Africa according to information from JMNESG research in 2009.

Therefore, what are the major issues facing the Japanese management and production systems? One of the main problems for Japanese companies would be a kind of "mismatching" of demand side and supply side between markets and producers. Namely, the demand levels in Chinese or Indian markets, for example, are to supplied products of "appropriate quality and far lower price," compared with the Japanese type ("excessively") "high quality and relatively high price" which can occupy only a minimum share of 5% or so in the market for high-class performance and added-value products.

Hence, if Japanese companies want to resolve this kind of "mismatching," they would have to be more flexible in choosing their market segments. In other words, they should have different criteria regarding the level of quality and price from market to market – that is, products of lower quality and price for lower-income customers and vice versa. In theoretical speculation we can suppose such a rational way of thinking, but actually it would be difficult to implement. Difficulty is specifically closely connected to brand image strategy and brands are integrally tied to quality matters as the key element of competitive advantages for most Japanese manufacturing companies. Actually many Japanese companies have tried various ways of coping with such problems, Honda Motorcycle in China, for example (Abo, 2011). Toyota, however, might be one of the typical examples of such efforts. It is recently well known that Toyota has had serious problems with quality defects such as accelerator pedals as well as in business performance. It can be pointed out that one of the reasons for these problems would have come from the results that Toyota may have tried to match different criteria to its markets by way of introducing a little lower level of quality of parts in the US market where customers have more price-orientation than quality though it is much busier in its sales and production activities, or training of human resources, compared with those in Japan (according to the JMNESG's research observations carried out in 2000–1, see Kawamura, 2010). Recently the numbers of recalled products have increased for Honda as well. Nevertheless, Toyota, or at least TPS itself, will somehow be able to survive as one of the world's leading manufacturing techniques for a long time. Supporting this assertion, Mr. Oberhelman, the CEO-elect of the world's leading construction machine maker, Caterpillar Inc., commented, right after Toyota's quality problem was reported, that they would continue to use the main part of TPS (*The Nikkei Shinbun*, February 13, 2010).

In conclusion, then, we can say that the "East Asian pattern" is recommendable in the sense that it can function practically in a foreign environment as an international or global model for Japanese hybrid factories. It can smooth the global expansion of the Japanese model, including its introduction by foreign manufacturers. This global spread of the "East Asian pattern" can be regarded as a process of overcoming or weakening the difference in managerial environments stemming from geographical-cultural variety, company strategies, or globalization of markets. In other words, it is a process of convergence, and also to a certain extent, the product of divergence in the Japanese production system reflected in the East Asian–type hybrid factories.

References

Abegglen, J.C. (1957), *The Japanese Factory,* MIT Press

Abo, T. (1989), "The Emergence of Japanese Multinational Enterprise and the Theory of Foreign Direct Investment", in Shibagaki, K., Trevor, M., and Abo, T., eds., *Japanese and European Management,* Tokyo University Press

Abo, T. ed. (1994), *Hybrid Factory: The Japanese Production System in the United States.* NY: Oxford University Press

Abo, T. (2000), "Spontaneous Integration in Japan and East Asia", in Clark, G.L., et al., eds., *The Oxford Handbook of Economic Geography,* Oxford University Press

Abo, T. (2003), "Japanese Hybrid Factories in Germany: Survival in a Different Environment", Park, S-J., and Horn, S., *Asia and Europe in the New Global System,* Palgrave-Macmillan

Abo, T. (2004), "An Integrated Theory of Management Geography: Japanese Hybrid Factories in the Three Major Regions," in Gupta, V. ed., *Transformative Organizations,* Response Books

Abo, T. (2007), *Japanese Hybrid Factories: A Comparison of Global Production Strategies,* Palgrave Macmillan

Abo, T. (2011), "The competition strategies of Japanese manufacturing firms in China, 1990s-2000s: Their positioning problems in the competitive advantages through transfer of the Japanese production systems", in Abo, T., ed., *Competing Chinese and Foreign Firms in Swelling Chinese Economy: Competition Strategies for Japanese, Western and Asian Firms,* LIT Verlag

Adler, P.S. (1993), "The Learning Bureaucracy: New United Motors Manufacturing, Inc.," in Staw, B.M., and L.L. Cummings, eds, *Research in Organizational Behavior,* JAI Press

Boyer, R., E. Charron, U. Jurgens, and S. Tolliday, eds. (1998), *Between Imitation and Innovation: The Transfer and Hybridization of Productive Models in the International Automobile Industry,* Oxford University Press

Clark, Kim B., and Takahiro Fujimoto (1991), *Product Development Performance,* Harvard Business School

Coase, R.H. (1937), "The Nature of Firm," *Economica,* N.S.1937, 4

Dore, R.P. (1973), *British Factory – Japanese Factory,* University of California Press

Fujimoto, T. (1999), *The Evolution of a Manufacturing System at Toyota,* Oxford University Press

Fujimoto, T., Takeishi, A., and Aoshima, Y. (2001), *Bijinesu Ahkitekucha(Business Architecture),* Yuhikaku

Hall, E.T. (1976), *Beyond Culture,* Anchor Books

Itagaki, H., ed., (1997), *The Japanese Production System: Hybrid Factories in East Asia,* Macmillan

Kawamura, T., ed. (2010), *Hybrid Factories in the United States: The Japanese-Style Management and Production System under the Global Economy,* Oxford University Press

Kenney, M., and R. Florida (1994), *Beyond Mass Production,* Oxford UP

Koike, K. (1988), *Understanding industrial relations in modern Japan,* Macmillan

Kumon, H. and Abo, T. (2004), *The Hybrid Factory in Europe: The Japanese Management and Production System Transferred,* Palgrave Macmillan

Liker, J.K., Fruin, W.M., and Adler, P. eds. (1999), *Remade in America: Transplanting and Transforming Japanese Management Systems*, NY: Oxford University Press

Oliver, N., and Wilkinson, B. (1988), *The Japanization of British Industry*. Oxford: Blackwell

Porter, M. (1990), *The Competitive Advantage of Nations*, New York: Free Press

Williamson, O.E. (1975), *Market and Hierarchies*, New York: Free Press

Womack, J.P., Jones, D.T., and Roos, D. (1990), *The Machine that Changed the World*, Rowson Associates, Macmillan

11
Spaces of Japanese Management: Toward a Dynamic Hybridization Theory

Katsuo Yamazaki

Introduction

How does time affect Japanese management in foreign countries? In order to resolve this question, the same research was conducted in 1989 and again in 2000 in the United States at companies in the same industries. In addition, the same longitudinal research at the same companies in Brazil and Argentina was compared in 2001 and 2006.

The research was based on the hybrid theory, which Japanese Multinational Enterprise Study Group (JMNESG) established and published in 1992, (Abo, 1992) in Japanese and in 1994 (Abo et al., 1994) in English. Furthermore, an idea of the theory is extended to its management geography approach. I suggest that management models based on socio-cultural differences are closely connected to those of geographical locations along with historical contexts, and such differences are among the essential factors that determine a comparative or competitive advantage of an industry or nation (Porter, 1990).

Business and management environments are characterized by constant change, activity, or progress, so that Japanese management styles in foreign countries must be more adaptable to the environment or may take more applicable change to be consistent in high quality. Abo et al. (1994) explored the potential for the effective transfer of Japanese management and production systems. These systems have been credited for much of the competitive superiority that Japanese manufacturing firms have achieved in the midst of cultural environments that differ considerably from their own (Porter, 2000). Their examination of local plants reveals a dynamic interplay between two opposing forces or tendencies: (1) application of the Japanese system and (2) adaptation to local conditions. This forms the basis of what they identified as the "hybrid theory" (Itagaki, 1997). The data consists of 23 items regarding management styles which are evaluated from 1 to 5 with statistical analysis of the resulting scores. The research was conducted based on the hybrid theory.

The Japanese-American automotive components industry in the United States

In the process of globalization, a global corporation develops strategic allies and sourcing partners. The automobile assembly industry is no exception and faces fiercer international competition than many other industries. A transnational alliance such as Renault-Nissan's alliance between France and Japan is a typical phenomenon in this industry. As the automobile industry moves globally to survive cutthroat competition, related industries, such as automotive components suppliers, undoubtedly must also cope with globalization.

In Japan, 511 automotive component-manufacturing companies, or nearly all auto-related parts companies except those producing batteries, belong to the Japan Auto Parts Industries Association (JAPIA). According to the 2000 JAPIA annual report, their combined sales totaled $124 billion in 1998. The companies had approximately 250 subsidiaries in North America engaged in strong competition. According to JAPIA's 1999 survey, their sales averaged $125 million per company in 1997 compared with $115 million in 1996. Sixty-three percent of the products were sold to Japanese transplants such as Honda of America MFG (HAM), Toyota Motor Manufacturing (TMM), and Auto Alliance International (AAI), while 25 percent were for the "Big Three" – that is, GM, Ford, and Daimler-Chrysler (JAPIA, 1999, 2000).

In 1989, Abo et al. (1994) carried out research on Japanese-American companies, including some Japanese automotive components companies in the United States. Their objective was to establish an analytical model that could be generalized to all Japanese companies in the United States. For this purpose they visited and surveyed approximately ten automotive components companies out of the 138 that existed in the United States before the North American Free Trade Agreement (NAFTA), which took effect in January 1994. Since then, some manufacturers of labor-intensive products have relocated plants from the United States and Canada to Mexico to compete more successfully in the largest auto market in the world at that time.

The history of JAPIA members manufacturing in North America shows, with some exceptions, that most of the Japanese companies that pioneered production in North America were subsidiaries of Japanese auto manufacturers. These transplants preferred to deal with the North American subsidiaries of the same suppliers that their parent companies dealt with in Japan. One of the main reasons for this preference was their desire to manufacture automobiles with the same high quality as their parent companies in Japan (Yamazaki, 2003).

In 1982, HAM was the forerunner among Japanese auto-manufacturing transplants manufacturing passenger cars. Their suppliers, who had established business connections with Honda in Japan, established project teams to set up their own plants in the United States, especially in Ohio and neighboring states. Other Japanese automakers soon followed suit, establishing their own plants and similarly relying upon cooperative relations with their own suppliers.

In other words, the strong business rapport between manufacturers and their suppliers, which was characteristic of the business environment in Japan, was also applied to the business environment surrounding transplants in North America. This type of strategic industrial sourcing remains typical in the automotive industry and consists of vertically integrated systems from manufacturer to supplier (Nishiguchi, 1994).

Once the headquarters of each JAPIA member determined its strategy for manufacturing industrial goods in North America, they had to decide on the kind of management style to implement at their subsidiaries. At the same time the transplant customers requested that the JAPIA subsidiaries should supply the same high-quality products that are available in Japan and at prices that are competitive in the North American market (Cole, 1999).

In order to respond to this request, the next essential question was how to transfer the techniques and know-how from the mother plants in Japan to the subsidiaries in North America. In order to achieve a competitive price, the subsidiaries needed to use, to some extent, local materials that were cheaper than materials imported from Japan. There also needed to be a transfer of substantial management and information management resources.

In such cases, the issue was how smoothly these companies would be able to transfer their technologies or management styles to other countries. If companies were successful in these transfers by employing certain methods or management styles, then these styles might be relevant to their corporate strategies. The auto assembly manufacturers in North America stood amid altered surroundings in 1989 from those in 2000, as did the automotive components manufacturers in those same years. The two different research efforts on management style in 1989 and 2000 were industry-wide as well as at the individual company level.

The methodology, research questions, and results in 1989 and 2000

To be sure, those 11 years had a profound impact on the Japanese economy, management styles, and strategies. Thus, it is important to take a closer look at the automotive components industry and to clarify how the Japanese automotive components companies in North America adapted to American management systems to achieve continuous improvement through this time period. This further research on Japanese automotive components companies in North America analyzes the characteristics of this industry through the hybrid theory (Yamazaki, 2003).

Because this study was a follow-up to and based on the Abo et al. (1994) work regarding hybrid theory, it addressed the following overall research questions:

Q1: *Compared with the 1989 survey, did the results of the 2000 survey indicate that time affected the degree to which companies leaned toward application of the Japanese system?*

The outcome is shown in the hybrid evaluation in terms of a six-group and 23-item classification in Table 11.1.

A five-point evaluation of 23 items is used to provide a quantitative measure of the relationship between application and adaptation. The criteria for evaluation are shown in Table 11.2. On the basis of observations at the target plants, a score of 5 is awarded to an item that reveals the maximum

Table 11.1 Comparison between the surveys in 1989 and 2000

	5-Point Evaluation		Points Correlation	Standard Deviation	
	survey year		Between the two survey years	survey year	
	1989	2000		1989	2000
I. Work Organization and Administration	3.1	3.3	0.62	0.64	1.17
1. Job classification	4.2	3.7		0.79	1.19
2. Job rotation	2.7	3.4		0.67	1.22
3. Development and training	2.9	3.5		0.57	0.79
4. Wage system	2.6	2.4		0.50	1.21
5. Promotion	3.3	3.4		0.82	1.32
6. First-line supervisors	3.0	3.4		0.47	1.31
II. Production Control	3.6	3.2	0.88	0.50	1.24
7. Production equipment	4.8	3.6		0.42	1.31
8. Maintenance	2.8	2.5		0.79	1.06
9. Quality control	3.9	3.4		0.31	1.26
10. Operations management	3.0	3.1		0.47	1.34
III. Procurement	3.0	2.6	0.11	0.80	1.19
11. Local content	2.7	1.8		1.05	1.07

continued

Table 11.1   Continued

	5-Point Evaluation		Points Correlation	Standard Deviation	
	survey year		Between the two survey years	survey year	
	1989	2000		1989	2000
12. Suppliers	3.7	2.8		0.67	1.36
13. Procurement method	2.6	3.3		0.68	1.13
IV. Group Consciousness	3.8	3.6	1.00	0.75	1.21
14. Small group activities	2.9	2.7		0.79	1.62
15. Information sharing	4.1	3.9		0.78	0.99
16. Sense of unity	4.4	4.1		0.68	1.01
V. Labor Relations	4.1	3.6	0.76	0.44	1.07
17. Hiring policy	3.8	2.9		0.63	0.91
18. Job security	3.8	3.0		0.79	1.10
19. Labor unions	5.0	4.3		0.00	1.00
20. Grievance procedures	3.9	4.0		0.35	1.26
VI. Parent–Subsidiary Relations	4.2	2.7	0.82	0.70	1.05
21. Ratio of Japanese expatriates	4.6	3.6		0.96	1.39
22. Delegation of authority	4.0	1.7		0.67	0.61
23. Managerial position of Americans	4.0	2.8		0.47	1.15
Average of all items	3.6	3.2		0.62	1.16

degree of application of the Japanese system and a score of 1 is applied to an item that is considered closest to the American system. Items that are found to be situated between these two extremes are scored accordingly. Local plants of Japanese automotive components companies in North America find themselves in a dynamic interplay between two forces or tendencies: application of Japanese systems and adaptation to local conditions. Because of this dichotomy, the question arises of how elements of Japanese management and production systems are applied at local plants, as well as how specific measures and practices are sustained in those elements (Fujimoto et al.,

Table 11.2 Criteria for application-adaptation (hybrid) (23-item, six-group) evaluation

Group	Item	Score	Criteria
I. Work Organization and Administration	1. Job classification (JC)	5	Number of JCs is 1 or 2.
		4	Number of JCs is 3 to 5.
		3	Number of JCs is 6 to 10.
		2	Number of JCs is 11 to 50.
		1	Number of JCs is 50 or more.
	2. Job rotation (JR)	5	JR is carefully planned and frequently conducted within and beyond work teams. Its clear aim is training of multi-skilled workers (e.g. training table kept by team leaders and supervisors).
		4	JR is planned and frequently conducted within but not beyond work teams.
		3	JR is frequently conducted within work teams.
		2	Rigid job assignment system is moderated to some extent (job reassignment when product mix is changed; frequent product mix change, etc.).
		1	JR is nonexistent; job assignment is rigid.
	3. Education and training	5	1) On-the-job training (OJT) is the main system for training multi-skilled workers, together with long-term systematic training. 2) There is a training system for team leaders and maintenance personnel through OJT and systematic training; sending trainees to Japan and bringing trainers from Japan with special training programs and facilities.
		4	1) Workers are trained through OJT, and special preparations and arrangements are made to accommodate this. 2) Training of supervisors (team leaders) and maintenance personnel in Japan; special training programs and facilities (e.g. a training center).
		3	1) OJT is emphasized; team leaders have some responsibility for training workers; team leaders have assistants for task training. 2) Some training program for team leaders or maintenance personnel exists inside or outside the company.

continued

Table 11.2 Continued

Group	Item	Score	Criteria
		2	1) OJT is not emphasized; some arrangements exist for outside training (e.g. reimbursement for school fees). 2) Outside education and training is recognized as a job qualification.
		1	1) OJT is not emphasized. 2) No special inside training program for team leaders or maintenance personnel.
	4. Wage system	5	"Person-centered" wage determination main criterion is length of service (*Nenko*); personal evaluation (PE) conducted by supervisors, closed to workers.
		4	Wages determined mainly by length of service, and partly by objective PE that includes worker input and requires worker approval.
		3	Simplified JC system is introduced; PE system determines wages.
		2	Simplified JC determines wages; PE system does not determine wages.
		1	Rigid and detailed JC system determines wages.
	5. Promotion	5	1) Worker promotion based on length of service (*Nenkoh*) and PE, which is conducted by direct supervisors. 2) Internal promotions to supervisor with recommendations by direct supervisor.
		4	1) Based to some extent on length of service (*Nenkoh*). 2) Internal promotions to supervisor with recommendations by direct supervisor.
		3	1) Based on PE and specific qualification; seniority does not play a strong role; job posting. 2) Supervisors internally promoted through job postings; corporate skills significant; seniority rule is not rigid.
		2	Based on seniority and PE and conduct and utilize job posting.
		1	1) Based on seniority and utilize job posting. 2) A high percentage of supervision recruited from outside the company.

Table 11.2 Continued

Group	Item	Score	Criteria
	6. First-line supervisors (or team leaders)	5	Internally promoted and function as team leaders and have technical control of production process including industrial engineering (IE) functions.
		4	Some as above (5 points) but to a lesser degree.
		3	Most supervisors internally promoted; weak team management and weak process control functions (e.g. no active role in job rotation or multi-skill training; may have assistants for IE).
		2	Some supervisors internally promoted; role is mainly labor management and discipline.
		1	Internal promotion is not a rule; role is exclusively labor management and discipline.

2001). In this sense the question lies in an international transfer model for the Japanese management and production systems. Therefore, the survey scores of 5 to 1 are called the application scores. Table 11.2 indicates how to give 23 items scores from 1 to 5 (Yamazaki et al., 2009).

II. Production Control

7. Equipment

5: 76%–100% of equipment imported from Japan.
4: 51%–75% of equipment imported from Japan.
3: 26%–50% of equipment imported from Japan.
2: 1%–25% of equipment imported from Japan.
1: 0% of equipment imported from Japan.

8. Maintenance

5: Shop-floor are internally trained and promoted to maintenance personnel (including inexperienced workers hired separately from ordinary workers); preventive maintenance is emphasized, shop-floor workers have some maintenance roles.
4: Same as above (5 points) but including some experienced workers hired separately from outside; preventive maintenance and shop-floor workers' roles in maintenance are not stressed.

3: Experienced workers hired separately but receive additional internal training before being promoted to maintenance personnel; shop-floor workers do not have any commitment to maintenance.

2: Same as above (3 points) but experienced workers are sometimes hired directly as maintenance personnel.

1: Maintenance personnel employed mainly from outside and maintenance by engineers is emphasized.

9. Quality control (QC)

5: Emphasis on QC conducted by workers during the actual process.

4: QC conducted by workers during the process but there are insufficient accommodations for this (e.g. workers have no line-stop authority; QC or zero defects (ZD) circles are not very active).

3: QC conducted by specialists during each process; QC and quality checks by specialists from an independent QC section also emphasized (high proportion of such checks).

2: QC relies on checks by specialists from an independent QC section; relatively close checks are conducted during each process (number of QC specialists is relatively low).

1: Quality checks by QC specialists on completed products (post-process and outgoing inspections) are emphasized.

10. Operations management

5: Flexible setup and special arrangements to cope with line failures or defects (e.g. coordination and cooperation among first-line supervisor and team leaders, preventive maintenance, machine fail-safe devices (Pokayoke), production control signal board (Andon), standard procedures and work manuals brought in from Japan and modified and improved to accommodate local conditions (line balance adjustments, etc.); high product mix, frequent product changes; reduction of die-change time is achieved to the same extent as in Japan.

4: Setup is less flexible than above (5 points), work manuals and maintenance know-how obtained from Japan; local job improvement (*kaizen*) is achieved to a much lesser extent; lot size is relatively small; die-change time approximate, though slightly less than that in Japan.

3: Moderate product mix (relatively large lot size with some batch production, etc.); standard procedures and work manuals brought in from Japan but with only slight modifications to accommodate local conditions.

2: No specific provisions for coping with line fails or defects; operations control is engineering-oriented; local IE specialists establish and modify standard procedures.

1: Operations control is highly engineering-oriented (engineering section has dominant role in machinery operation and maintenance); production based on large lot methods.

III.   Procurement

11.   Local content

5: 20% or less
4: (21%–40%
3: 41%–60%
2: 61%–80%
1: more than 80%

12.   Suppliers

5: Material and parts mainly procured from Japan.
4: Procured from sister plants or Japanese suppliers located overseas (United States, Canada, southeast Asia, Mexico).
3: High proportion of procurement from Japanese suppliers in the United States and Canada.
2: Procurement from Japanese suppliers in the United States and Canada, but the proportion of U.S. suppliers is high.
1: Most procurement from US suppliers.

13.   Procurement method

5: Japanese subcontracting system exists with local suppliers.
4: To some extent the Japanese subcontracting system exists with local suppliers; technological assistance and long-term contracts are applied to US suppliers.
3: Some arrangements are made to reduce parts inventory as much as possible; technological assistance is attempted with US suppliers.
2: Local suppliers are held to strict observance of delivery times.
1: Mainly spot trading with US suppliers; parts inventories are relatively high in order to cope with delayed delivery.

IV.   Group Consciousness

14.   Small group activities

5: All workers participate voluntarily and play significant roles.
4: More than 50% of workers participate.
3: 20% to 50% of workers participate.
2: Less than 20% of workers participate, or only in special "model" cases; some emphasis is placed on meetings and suggestions for quality and productivity.
1: No small group activities.

15.   Information sharing

5: Company-wide information sharing and communications actively practiced (e.g. meetings for all employees, president meets all employees in small groups, vigorous small group activities, open-style offices).

4: Various provisions for information sharing exist but to a lesser degree than above (5 points).

3: Attempts are made at information sharing at each level in the company through meetings and other means.

2: Meetings are held before work begins.

1: No special provisions for information sharing.

16.   Sense of unity

5: Various devices and practices such as company uniforms for all employees, open parking, social events, and morning ceremonies.

4: Many of the above devices and practices are implemented but to a lesser extent (e.g. uniforms are not compulsory).

3: Only some of the above are practiced.

2: Only some social events are held.

1: There are no special practices.

V   Labor Relations

17.   Hiring policy

5: Applicants are carefully, meticulously screened; plant site selected where there is a homogeneous work force.

4: Applicants are selected with care; plant site selected where there is a homogeneous work force.

3: Plant site selected where there is a homogeneous work force; if plant site is traditional industrial area, applicants are selected with care.

2: Special hiring considerations only if plant is located in a traditionally industrial area.

1: No special selection for hiring; plant is located in a traditionally industrial area.

18.   Job security

5: Explicit (written) no-layoff policy that seeks to avoid layoffs as much as possible; provisions for long-term employment.

4: Layoffs are avoided as much as possible, but this policy is not explicit and there have been no layoffs; provisions for long-term employment.

3: Layoffs are avoided as much as possible but have occurred on rare occasions.

2: Layoffs are avoided as much as possible but have occurred many times.

1: Layoffs are prone to occur if at all likely.

19.   Labor unions

5: There is no union, and labor relations are peaceful.

4: There is no union, but there are some problems in labor relations (e.g. attempts at organizing a union), or there is a union but relations are very cooperative.

3: There is a union and a cooperative tendency with the union (e.g. management-labor consulting system exists); or there is no union but there have been organization drives.

2: Union exists but it has relatively low membership; there have been strikes but otherwise the union is not very active.

1: Union is 100 percent organized and there have been strikes.

20. Grievance procedures

5: There is no union, and grievances are resolved mainly on shop floor and through managerial channels.

4: There is no union, and personnel department intervenes in the process of resolving grievance; or there is a union and grievances are resolved mainly on shop floor.

3: There is a union, and official grievance procedures are formalized, but emphasis is on shop floor and through managerial channels.

2: There is a union and official grievance procedures; grievances tend to be resolved on shop floor.

1: There is a union and official grievance procedures; there are many grievances; grievance procedures include external arbitration.

VI. Parent-Subsidiary Relations

21. Ratio of Japanese expatriates

For plants with 500 employees or more (with less than 500 employees, add 1% to the following ratios):

5: 4% or more

4: less than 4% but more than 3%

3: less than 3% but more than 2%

2: less than 2% but more than 1%

1: less than 1%

22. Delegation of authority

5: Parent in Japan makes plans and decisions.

4: Subsidiary submits suggested plans and parent decides.

3: Subsidiary submits plans and parent evaluates and gives or withholds approval.

2: Subsidiary makes plans for approval by parent.

1: Subsidiary makes and approves its own plans.

23. Managerial position of Americans

5: Most important senior management positions, including president, are held by Japanese.

4: President is Japanese, and many important positions are held by Japanese.

3: Japanese and Americans share management positions and important positions roughly equally.

2: President is American, and majority of important positions are held by Americans.

1: President is American, and all important positions are held by Americans.

A greater standard deviation indicates that a greater variety of management styles are in use among the automotive component companies over this period. The 11 years between the two occasions on which the two surveys were conducted had an effect on the ability of differing management styles to cope with adverse circumstances in the automobile assembly industry. According to the t-test for sample means and standard deviations, companies adapted their management styles and results-oriented processes over time.

Figure 11.1 based on Table 11.1 shows how differently the management styles of 23 items changed in 1989 and 2000. The most radical change was in delegation of authority (Item 22) while, contrarily, there was almost no change in promotion, operations management, and grievance procedures. Item 22 is closely related to Item 21, ratio of Japanese expatriates, and Item 23, managerial position of Americans. Generally, the headquarters of Japanese automotive components companies, as their subsidiaries in foreign companies grow rapidly, would prefer to allow subsidiaries to be free because

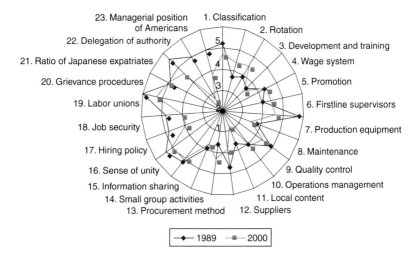

Figure 11.1   23 items change of score, 1989 and 2000

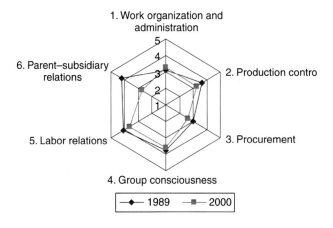

Figure 11.2 Six-group scores in 1989 and 2000

of intra-firm trust and the high cost of maintaining Japanese expatriates. Figure 11.2 and 11.3 depict more clearly changes in Group VI items.

Promotion is a key factor in Group I, work organization and administration, and is related to other items in Group I. The most typical Japanese management styles are characterized by the items in Group I. Neither operations management nor grievance procedures appear to be rigid items in management and might change later.

Figure 11.2 is based on the survey data. Only Group I tended to be slightly in 2000 than in 1989. Other groups acquired less application scores in average, especially Group VI, parent-subsidiary relations. This phenomenon in industry is often encountered in Japanese global management. However, the automotive component companies in the United States Company X and Company Y had results that stood out from other companies.

Q2: Did time affect the four-perspective evaluation in internationalization and transfer of a Japanese management model?

The four-perspective evaluation focuses on the results and methods application of human and material elements. The human-methods quadrant consists of items related to the manner in which the workforce operates and to its organization and administration. The material-methods quadrant comprises all methods related to quality control, maintenance, and procurement. The two result quadrants of human and material consist of all the human and material elements that are introduced directly from Japan (Abo et al., 1994).

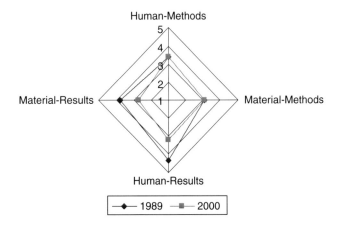

Figure 11.3   Four-perspective evaluation in 1989 and 2000

The evaluation in Figure 11.3 depicts the direct application of human and material results of the Japanese system on the horizontal axis and application of human and material methods on the vertical axis. The methods refer to the transfer of intangible techniques and know-how necessary for organization building and personnel administration. The results refer to the transfer of tangible or ready-made hardware such as machines, parts, or even Japanese staff, which may not leave any local trace at all when repatriated.

The quadrants of human-methods and of material-methods evidenced no differences between the two surveys. The Japanese automotive components companies in the United States maintained very continuous and "usual" production methods at least till 2000. This implies strongly that the Japanese production system was emphasized by management items relating to human-methods and material-methods.

Comparison of management at US companies X and Y in 1989 and 2000

Company X manufactures brakes for four-wheeled autos with 475 employees under a Japanese president. It is 100 percent Japanese-owned, and about 15 Japanese expatriates worked in engineering, manufacturing, and sales. Its products are supplied promptly based on orders from not only Japanese automobile assemblers but also American ones. The company is classified as independent in terms of *Keiretsu* (Griffin and Pustay, 1998). It was established in the state of Kentucky.

Company Y manufactures seats for four-wheeled autos with about 670 people under a Japanese president. Its capital is 100 percent Japanese-owned,

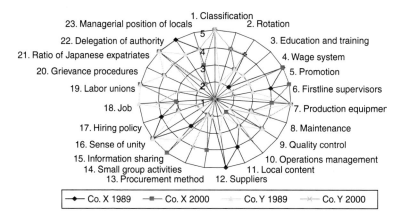

Figure 11.4 Twenty-Three-item scores at companies X and Y in 1989 and 2000

and about 20 Japanese expatriates worked in engineering, manufacturing, and sales. Its products are sold to one specified Japanese-American joint-venture auto assembler and its American company. Company Y has a firm *keiretsu* connection with one Japanese auto assembler. It is located in Michigan state.

Figure 11.4 indicates that the two companies are totally different from each other in management style although they belong to the same industry in the United States and are owned 100 percent by their parent companies. Furthermore, both are led by Japanese presidents. The research asks companies to make a choice scoring from 1 to 5 points each. As Figure 11.4 is somewhat complicated, it is impossible to say the companies had lower scores in 2000 compared with 1989 on average. It is implicative that differences among customers and locations may affect management styles (Cole, 1999).

Figure 11.5 shows management styles' comparison between 1989 and 2000. At Company X six management groups other than group consciousness had lower scores, although at Company Y all groups had lower scores. Group I, work organization and administration, did not change drastically at the two companies between 1989 and 2000. Other groups changed appreciably. It implies that the core of Japanese management style is found in the Group I items (Fujimoto, 2001).

Concerning the human-methods quadrant in Figure 11.6, three dots other than Company Y in 2000 are concentrated in 4. The material-methods is similar to the human-methods data with three dots concentrated, though on different values. The former might be explained by the previous note about Group I, that it includes the core of Japanese management style. The

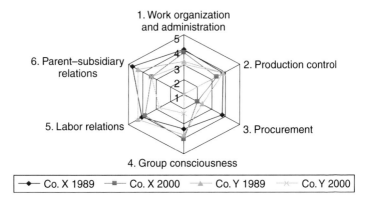

Figure 11.5 Six-group scores at companies X and Y in 1989 and 2000

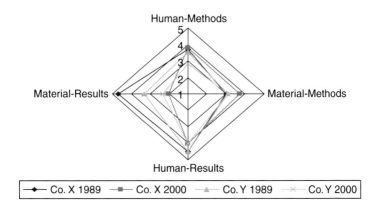

Figure 11.6 Four-perspective evaluation at companies X and Y in 1989 and 2000

latter is an anomalous case as it may result from actions Company X took upon learning from experience.

Three Latin American companies cases

Company A is a 100 percent Japanese enterprise located in Manaus, Brazil, which surrounds an industrial free zone and started manufacturing motorcycles in 1976. The production volume has been increasing every year since 1994, and the company produced more than one million two-wheeled vehicles in 2005. There were 6100 employees including 23 Japanese expatriates in 2005. JMNESG visited the location twice, in 2001 and 2006.

Company B is also a 100 percent Japanese corporation collocated with Company A. Company B was established in 1994 and started production

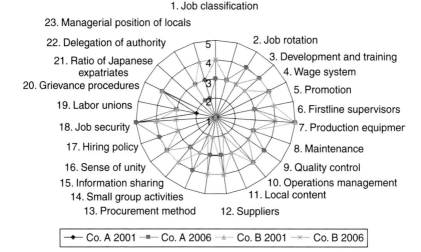

Figure 11.7 Twenty-Three-item scores of two Brazilian companies in 2001 and 2006

in 1997. Its products were delivered directly to motorcycle manufacturers in Manaus and to a bus manufacturer in São Paulo, Brazil. About 80 people including three Japanese expatriates worked there in 2005.

Three radar graphs of 23 items are used for analysis (Yamazaki et al., 2009).

Figure 11.7 shows that most items have the same application scores in 2001 and 2006 at both companies. The data suggest that the five-year time difference may not affect management styles decisively in Manaus, Brazil. Manufacturing in a free trade zone may impact management easier than in a regular industrial area. Further study is required.

Figure 11.8 shows that Company A's labor relations changed and received more application scores, while parent-subsidiary relations got less, and other groups remained unchanged. Company B results indicate that all groups except work organization and administration changed slightly in both directions. Only procurement group received more application scores, and others less.

Figure 11.9 shows that the human-results quadrant in 2006 at Company A is slightly different from that in 2001, whereas the other three quadrants are the same. Except for the material-methods quadrant, in Company B the other quadrants got lower scores in 2006 compared to 2001.

Company C is located in Cordoba, Argentina, and manufactures automotive components for four-wheeled vehicles. It delivered products to Japanese and European automotive assemblers in Argentina. Furthermore, it was established in 1996 and solely owned by its parent company. A single Japanese expatriate, the president, and 160 employees worked there. Its management was unique in that one Italian engineer directed factory operations with all Argentine managers and workers.

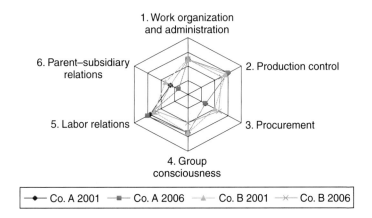

Figure 11.8   Six-group scores of two Brazilian companies in 2001 and 2006

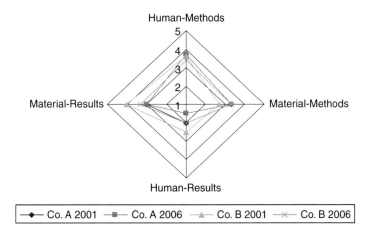

Figure 11.9   Four-perspective evaluations of two Brazilian companies in 2001 and 2006

There are few Japanese manufacturing companies in Argentina. Supposing that Company C represents Argentina, and to compare Company C with the average scores of the two Brazilian companies, see Figure 11.10.

The material-methods quadrants have the same increasing score trend in both countries in 2001 and 2006. Although other quadrants result in different scores, similar diamond figures for both countries result. Specifically, the human-methods quadrant shifts from 3.9 to 3.6 in Brazil, and from 3.4 to 3.6 in Argentina, the human-results quadrant moves from 2.3 to 1.8 in Brazil

Figure 11.10 Four-perspective evaluations of Brazil and Argentina companies in 2001 and 2006

while remaining 1.5 in both years in Argentina, and the material-results quadrant goes from 3.5 to 3.2 in Brazil and from 3.3 to 3.7 in Argentina. Neither positive nor negative directions of scores changed in Brazil and Argentina.

Conclusion

The Japanese automotive components' industry in the United States in 1989 and 2000, and two companies in Brazil and one in Argentina in 2001 and 2006, were analyzed in order to shed light on how time affects Japanese management in foreign countries. As time progressed, management items with lower scores became competitive. Eleven years affected the material-results and human-results quadrants profoundly. The companies had enough time for localization of material and human resources in the North American case. In Latin America, five years did not impact management significantly, and no Latin American model was found. Through these analyses, it is clear that the core of Japanese management systems lies among the human-methods quadrant items (Yamazaki, 2007).

It would be important to clarify, through more focused research, how the Japanese automotive components' companies in North America have adapted to American management systems to achieve continuous improvement after 2001. Follow-up research might be extended to the field of strategy, rather than only looking at its relationship to strategy. Strategy discussion generally includes the profit of the company (Itagaki, 2002). Most of the subsidiaries in North and Latin America do not publicize their financial data. Therefore, future research that can overcome such difficulties would be most effective and strategic.

References

Abo, T. (1992). Transferring Japanese Type of Production System to U.S.A. ('Nihonteki Seisanshisutemu no Taibei Iten' in Japanese), Institute of Social Science, The University of Tokyo, *Modern Japanese Society: Volume 7*. Tokyo: University of Tokyo Press.

Abo, T., ed. (1994). *Hybrid Factory: The Japanese Production System in the United States*. New York: Oxford University Press.

Cole, R. (1999). *Managing Quality Fads: How American Business Learned to Play the Quality Game*. New York: Oxford University Press.

Fujimoto, T., Takeishi, A., and Aoshima, Y., eds. (2001). Bijinesu Akitekucha: Seihin, Soshiki, Purosesu no Senryaku-teki Sekkei (Business Architecture: Strategic Design of Products, Organizations, and Processes), Tokyo: Yuhikaku. (In Japanese).

Griffin, R., and Pustay, M. (1998). *International Business*. Addison Wesley Longman, Inc.

Itagaki, H. (1997). *The Japanese Production System: Hybrid Factories in East Asia*, London: Macmillan.

Itagaki, H. (2002). Japanese multinational enterprises: Paradox of high efficiency and low profitability. *Asian Business and Management* 1(1): 101–24.

Japan Auto Parts Industries Association (1999). Annual Report for Foreign Activities ('Kaigai jigyo chosa' 1998), JAPIA (in Japanese).

Japan Auto Parts Industries Association (2000). Annual Report for Foreign Activities ('Kaigai jigyo chosa' 1999), JAPIA (in Japanese).

Nishiguchi, T., (1994). *Strategic Industrial Sourcing*. New York: Oxford University Press.

Porter, Michael E. (1990). *The Competitive Advantage of Nations*. New York: Free Press.

Porter, Michael E. (2000). Locations, clusters, and company strategy, in *The Oxford Handbook of Economic Geography*, edited by Clark, G., Feldman, M., and Gertler, M. Oxford University Press.

Yamazaki, K. (2003). *The Management Style of Japanese Automotive Components Companies in North America*. Proquest Company, Michigan, USA.

Yamazaki, K. (2007). *Golden Rules in Japanese Overseas Management*, ('Kaigai Keiei No Tessoku' in Japanese). Tokyo: Kodansha.

Yamazaki, K., et al. (2009). *Japanese Management Style in Latin America*, ('Ratenamerika niokeru nihonkigyo no keiei' in Japanese), Tokyo: Chuokeizaisha.

12

Survival Strategies of a Local Industry and the Characteristics of Its Overseas Operations: A Case Study of the Glove-Related Industry in Eastern Kagawa, Japan

Atsushi Taira

I. Introduction

Purpose of the study

This study aims to explain the survival strategy of a local industry located outside the major metropolitan regions of Japan and characteristics of overseas operations of this industry from a geographical perspective through a case study of the glove-related industry in eastern Kagawa on Shikoku, the smallest of Japan's major islands. Since the 1980s, globalization of the Japanese economy has rapidly progressed; large firms in the manufacturing industry, such as textile, petrochemical, steel, automotive, and electronics firms, led the trend, followed by small and medium-sized firms. These firms began foreign operations in order to cope with rising personnel costs and to expand their offshore markets. Most firms are headquartered in Tokyo or Osaka; there are, however, not a few small and medium-sized firms headquartered outside the major metropolitan areas which have a significant share in sales in Japan and also are conducting active foreign operations.

On the other hand, an increasing number of localities are struggling to attract business to help combat population shrinkage. Many local governments have been eager to arrange industrial space with high-level infrastructure to attract firms, but actual success stories are few. However, if there exist good small and medium-sized firms, as described above, it would be possible to establish a new industrial cluster based on those firms.

This study focuses on "glocal strategies" of small and medium-sized firms consisting of a local industrial complex in Japan. As recent discussion about globalization and localization has it, local, regional and global matters are closely related to each other (Cox, 1997; Morisawa and Ueda, 2000). Today, firms are asked to cope with demands from a variety of geographical areas with different scales and to adapt to those diversified regions. It is fair to say that the term "glocal" was born for answering the demand of such an era. However, as Taira (2005a) said, the discussion on glocal matters seems to be rather abstract, and there is still a paucity of empirical studies which explain the glocal phenomena in the real world. Further, empirical studies so far are likely to focus on the operations of large firms. As a result, we have just a small number of studies, such as Itakura (2005), on glocal strategies of small and medium-sized firms. Clusters of small and medium-sized firms have played an important role in many regional economies, and their continued presence is necessary for the sustainable development of those regions.

The hypothesis of this study is as follows. So far, it is said that when manufacturing firms expand their business outside their original country, they are likely to divide their operations into two groups: domestic and foreign (Vernon, 1966). In fact, while manufacturing firms relocate manufacturing operations for standardized products overseas (especially into developing countries) for cheap labor, they are likely to keep manufacturing operations for unstandardized or value-added products, and R&D functions, in the host country. Yet currently, we are witnessing the emergence of rapidly growing economies represented by China and India. It is easy to assume that the rather simple strategies described above may not go well. The main questions of this study are what kind of strategies the firms in the study area are taking, and how the home region and overseas regions are interconnected. Recently, it is reported that in Japan some manufacturing firms are returning a portion of overseas operations (Asahi Shimbun, 2005). But this move is seen mostly among large firms such as Matsushita (Panasonic). It is not clear whether small and medium-sized firms are following the same trend or not.

Methodology

First, the domestic position of the glove-related industry in eastern Kagawa will be examined through the analysis of relevant statistics and materials. At the same time, the patterns of historical development of the industry will be explained based on published and unpublished documents of *Nihon Tebukuro Kogyo Kumiai* (the Japan Glove-Related Companies' Association) and those of the local chamber of commerce, and materials published by firms in the region. Simultaneously, characteristics of inter-firm relations in the industrial complex will be explored through interviews to the representative persons of the association of the glove-related industry, and published and unpublished materials related to the industry. Also, the relationships of the industrial complex with the outside regions both domestic and overseas will be examined. Then, case studies of representative international firms of the industry will be conducted to describe characteristics of their domestic and international management, and their future strategy to survive in the competitive market in relation to the importance of sharing and developing "implicit knowledge" in the region. In the analysis of overseas operations of the glove-related industry in eastern Kagawa, China will be investigated as a country attracting numerous firms. Additionally in China, the Shanghai Metropolitan Area, which houses many glove-related firms from eastern Kagawa, was selected as a field research area. The fieldwork was conducted in eastern Kagawa from March to August 2008 and in China in December 2008.

The next section will overview the discussion on activities of multinational corporations (MNCs) and spatial characteristics of industrial agglomeration and will try to bridge them. The following section will explain the historical development and the current status of the local industry in eastern Kagawa, and Section III will explain the characteristics of foreign operations of the industry, putting emphasis on the operations in China. Section IV will explore the local-global strategies of the glove-related industry and firms and the implication of the region of eastern Kagawa as a home base of the industry.

II. Industrial agglomeration and operations of multinational corporations

Since the 1980s, we have witnessed increasing interest in industrial agglomeration and rigorous debates on topics such as the spatial configuration, embedded and shared implicit knowledge in locale places, learning region as the center of knowledge creation and innovation, not only in economics but also in geography and sociology (Piore and Sabel, 1984; Scott, 1988; Porter, 1990; Krugman, 1991; Florida, 1995; Takeuchi, 1994; Seki, 1997; Watanabe, 1997). Among them, currently, "innovative milieu" (environment of technological innovation) is attracting researchers' attention (Yamamoto, 2005). Here, "milieu" refers to the whole entity of regional relations which includes production system, economic and social actors, and particular culture which procure collective learning processes (Matsubara, 2006). According to Malmberg (1966), profits of agglomeration are not simply economic but sensitive, social, cultural and institutional. But these discussions seem to remain abstract, and we need more empirical studies on these subjects. Yamamoto (2005) claims that geographical accessibility plays a key role in the discussion of agglomeration but that existence of region or locale is itself of importance for understanding these phenomena.

On the other hand, along with expanding of overseas operations of firms, there is a growing number of geographical studies on MNCs.[1] So far, a variety of characteristics of MNCs have been examined; the main themes are the structures of MNCs (Hymer, 1960), processes of multinationalization of firms (Vernon, 1966), intra-firm trade (Helleiner, 1981), characteristics of operations of multinational firms through eclectic approach (Dunning, 1979) and strategic arrangement of MNCs in the world to gain competitive advantage (Porter, 1986). Currently, the importance of synergy and knowledge economy is also discussed (see e.g. Dunning 2000a, 2000b). The meaning of locality is also attracting researchers' attention in the studies of MNCs (e.g. Coe and Lee, 2006). Most recently, roles of "culture" in the interrelations between the host society and foreign firms have been debated (Depner and Bathelt, 2005). Even MNCs have some attributes originating from their country of origin. Thus, as Tacconelli and Wrigley (2009) have demonstrated, when operating overseas, coordination of the culture of the host country and that of the home country will be of importance for MNCs.

From a geographical point of view, since there are differences of spatial patterns of affiliations of MNCs at the national scale and at the local scale, studies at the various scales are of importance, although not enough of the latter have been conducted (Taira, 2005b). During the past decade, I have conducted research on spatial characteristics and strategies of Japanese-affiliated corporations at local scales: metropolitan and local regions in the United States, France and South Korea (Taira, 2001, 2002, 2004, 2005a).

Industrial agglomeration in a country and internationalization of firms' operations (multinationalization of firms) are deeply interconnected. However, both phenomena are likely to be discussed separately, and so far there is a paucity of studies which analyze relations of the two phenomena from a geographical point of view in earnest. Also, most of the previous studies on operations of multinational firms have dealt with rather large firms. On the other hand, studies analyzing internationalization of small and medium-sized firms are scarce except for a few examples such as Itakura (2005). This is one reason this study focuses on survival strategies and characteristics of internationalization of a leading local industrial complex in Japan.

III. Characteristics of the region of eastern Kagawa as a glove-related industrial space and its transformation

Current situations of the local industrial complex

Glove-related firms are agglomerated in the city of Higashikagawa, in eastern Kagawa: Figure 12.1 shows the location of the city of Higashikagawa, and Figure 12.2 overviews the region of eastern Kagawa. The glove-making industry dates back to the Meiji Era (1868–1912), celebrating its centenary in 1988. After the Meiji Era, the glove-making industry expanded. There are rather undesirable characteristics of physical geography in the region, but the region had and has a local milieu and culture which have produced talented entrepreneurs as represented by Shunrei Hutago and Tatsukichi Tanetsugu, founders of the glove-making industry. It is possible to say that

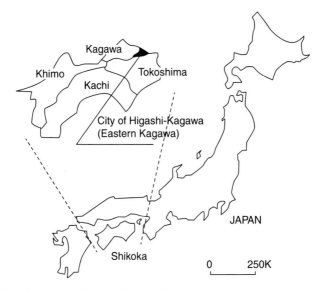

Figure 12.1   Location of Eastern Kagawa in Japan

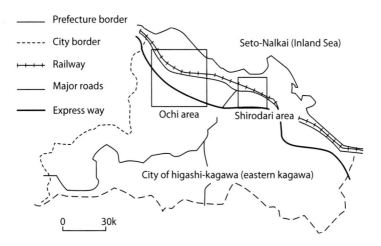

Figure 12.2   Detailed map of Eastern Kagawa (Higashi-Kagawa)

the region of eastern Kagawa is an "industrial district" to which Pyke and Sengenberger (1990) have referred. Glove-related firms in this region have been competing with each other to increase their share of the domestic market, yet at the same time, there are cooperative projects for the growth of the region known as the "town of gloves."

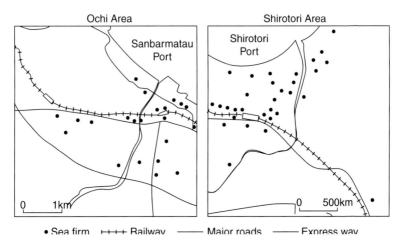

Figure 12.3   Agglomeration of glove-related firms in Eastern Kagawa
Source: Nihon Tebukuro Kogyo Kumiai

The glove-related industry in eastern Kagawa still holds 90 percent of the production share in Japan, reaching 43 billion yen, and is a leading local industry of which Kagawa prefecture is proud (Shikoku Bureau of Economy, Trade and Industry, 2009). The number of firms is around 120, mostly small and medium-sized; the number of employees in the region is about 1700, and 71 percent of the total firms have fewer than 21 employees onsite. The glove-related industry has grown to become the leading production center of glove-related items in the country, through supplying products not only to the domestic market but also to overseas ones. In the 1970s, however, exporting became less profitable due to severe international competition. As a result, the glove-related industry changed its strategy to be more domestic oriented, and at the same time, it started overseas operations aggressively, at an early point compared to other industries in Japan. For the domestic market, the glove-related industry in eastern Kagawa has been making not only gloves for winter use but also gloves for sports and leisure such as golf, baseball, skiing, and motorbiking; fashion gloves; and protective and medical gloves. The main customers have been department stores, specialty stores, and discount stores around the country. For a long time, for professional brokers in Japan, the region of eastern Kagawa has played an important role as a center for purchasing products. Recently, direct sales through the Internet and at shops owned by the glove-related firms have begun. Small firms have been expanding production of made-to-order items, using their advanced skills. This strategy has attracted the attention of related fields in other regions as a survival strategy of a local industry.

At the same time, the industry in eastern Kagawa has tried to diversify its products with new items in addition to gloves. Various indoor goods have been produced in the process of making knit gloves. Also, a variety of leather sacks and leather clothes have been made using glove-related knowledge and technology. Currently, this local industry is struggling to transform itself into a center of making general everyday items based on advanced technology of glove-making. In the region, the mode of production varies by firm: some firms make various products along with gloves, and others concentrate solely on making gloves, especially those of high quality. It should be noted that this industrial complex has a rare character found in few other regions in the country.

As said before, the majority of glove-related firms are located in the eastern part of Kagawa prefecture, especially concentrated in the city of Higashikagawa (population 34,979 in 2010) with two agglomerations in the Ochi and Shirotori areas. In the Ochi area, over 20 firms are located around the Sanbonmatsu railway station, and in the Shirotori area, over 30 firms are located around the Shirotori station (Figure 12.3). Currently, on-site, firms in these areas mainly produce sample items, goods of high quality in small numbers, and goods to be shipped at short notice due to high production costs. Ninety-seven percent of raw and intermediate materials for making leather gloves on-site come from overseas and 5 percent are domestic. Among overseas-purchased materials, 90 percent come from Asia, 5 percent from Europe, and the remaining 5 percent from other areas. Meanwhile 70 percent of raw and intermediate materials for making knit gloves come from overseas and 30 percent are domestic. All overseas materials come from Asian countries.

Sales in the glove-related industry in eastern Kagawa experienced ups and downs after the 1950s (Figure 12.4). Domestic sales surpassed sales in export in the late 1960s. Sales in export peaked in the early 1970s (7.58 billion yen in 1971) and began diminishing thereafter. On the other hand, domestic sales grew steadily, reaching 65 billion yen in 1991. But after that the growth stopped and began shrinking to 38.7 billion yen in 2005 – that is, 60 percent of the 1991 peak. The total sales also peaked in 1991 with 65.2 billion yen and then experienced the same downward transition. Thus, it is a big challenge for the industry to stop the sales reduction and to turn it upward.

The number of members of the Japan Glove-Related Companies' Association has also shown the same trend (Figure 12.5). Although that number peaked at about 250 by 1970, it shrank to about 100 in 2005. This could be an indicator that the industry is shrinking as a whole, but it is also possible to think that competitive firms have survived a restructuring phase of the industry. In fact, as detailed later, some firms are expanding their foreign production, especially in China. Thus, a careful investigation is needed to grasp the whole performance of the industry.

Currently, for the glove-related industry in eastern Kagawa, glove sales reach about 70 percent of the total in domestic sales (Table 12.1). Among

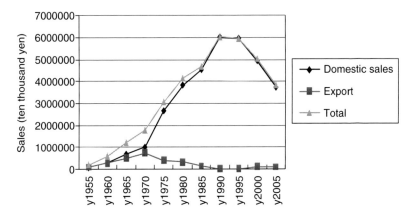

Figure 12.4 Domestic and export sales of the glove-related industry in eastern Kagawa

Source: Nihon Tebukuro Kogyo Kumiai

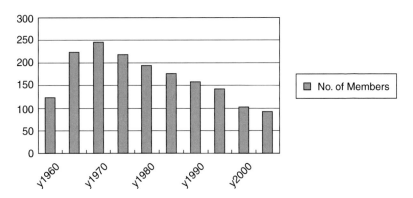

Figure 12.5 Transition of the number of members of Nihon Tebukuro Kogyo Kumiai (The Japan Glove-related Companies' Association)

Source: Nihon Tebukuro Kogyo Kumiai

them, the sales of fashion-related items hold two-thirds of the total (18.2 billion yen in 2006) and the rest is sport-related items (8.4 billion yen in 2006). At the same time, the fact that the total sales' share of 30 percent comes from new (non-glove-related) items (12.1 billion yen in 2006) shows that those items are gaining an important position in the industry.

On the other hand, in terms of export sales, new items hold 90 percent of the total, overwhelming glove-related goods (Table 12.2). Almost all of these export items are sent to North America, especially to the United States. In 2006, among export from Japan, sales of glove-related items were

Table 12.1   The contents of the current domestic sales of the glove-related industry in eastern Kagawa

	2005	2006
Gloves for fashion-use	1,700,150 (46%)	1,817,567 (47%)
Gloves for sports	818,597 (22%)	838,934 (22%)
New items	1,211,315 (32%)	1,209,498 (31%)
Total (ten thousand yen)	3,730,062	3,865,999

Source: Nihon Tebukuro Kogyo Kumiai

Table 12.2   The contents of the current sales for export of the glove-related industry in eastern Kagawa

	2005	2006
Gloves	2,070 (2%)	6,511 (5%)
New items	106,592 (98%)	119,354 (95%)
Total (Ten thousand yen)	108,662	125,865

Source: Nihon Tebukuro Kogyo Kumiai

65 million yen, while those of non-glove-related goods reached 1.2 billion yen. This means that in export, new products play the role which glove-related items played before. Now, most glove-related items for overseas are exported directly from affiliated operations in foreign countries, especially in China, as detailed later.

Factors for maintaining the leading position in the country

There are three factors through which the glove-related industry in eastern Kagawa has maintained its leading position in Japan. First, the area has a pool of highly skilled workers who have a professional spirit and can create an innovative environment. Secondly, there is a regional mechanism which maintains the innovative environment created by those skilled workers. Thirdly, there exists a learning region embedded geographically and a cooperative relationship among glove-related firms which aims to establish a local brand to overcome the subcontractor status of department stores and large retailers. Those three factors are interrelated and play a critical role for creating the "local milieu."

An officer of the Japan Glove-Related Companies' Association (interviewed in November 2008) said that the share of direct sales has been increasing gradually to about 10 percent of the total. Direct sales are projected to continue to grow through expansion of product offerings. A representative company in the region has started its direct sales through opening its own retail shop in downtown Tokyo. Attracted by this move, synergy effects are expected to grow among firms.

At present, a critical challenge lies in evaluating influences of the financial crisis, which started in the United States in autumn 2008. As of February 2010, there are few indicators in Japan which signal recovery of its economy. It is expected that for now, times will continue to be difficult for the Japanese economy and society in general. The glove-related firms in eastern Kagawa will have to cope with fluctuation of demands both inside and outside the country.[2]

IV. Characteristics of overseas operations

Overview

The glove-related industry in eastern Kagawa, as described before, began active foreign operations in the 1970s. A factor for this move was the difficulty of gathering workers in labor-intensive manufacturing sectors, including the glove-related industry, in the context of strong economic growth in Japan. At first, the mode of foreign operation was mainly joint ventures for making goods with local partners in the host countries. Wholly owned subsidiaries were established there soon after. The first foreign operations began in neighboring South Korea and Taiwan. And later, with soaring personnel costs that resulted from the economic growth there, the manufacturing operations shifted to other Asian countries such as China, Indonesia and Sri Lanka. Among them, China plays a leading role not only as a manufacturing place but also now as a distribution center including checking and handling, and more recently as an R&D location. Currently, the glove-related industry in eastern Kagawa is positively establishing its subsidiaries in the market region: stocking and sales offices have begun operations in North America (the United States) and Europe (Switzerland and Italy). As a whole, a global network made by a local industry complex in Japan is emerging.

In 2009, in the glove-related industry in eastern Kagawa, the sales share of overseas production reached 80 to 85 percent of the total. Table 12.3 shows the overseas operations for production in 2006. At that time, 74 firms had foreign operations for production: 22 of them (30%) were directly engaged in production, and the rest had contracts with local partners for production. The overseas operations expanded into nine countries, especially into East and Southeast Asian countries. China dominated the number with a share of 61 percent (45 operations).

Table 12.3 Foreign operations for production of the glove-related industry in eastern Kagawa (2006)

Country (Region)	No. of foreign operations	No. of direct operations	No. of consignment operations
China	45	16	29
Korea	8	1	7
Indonesia	6	1	5
Taiwan	5	1	4
Philippines	4	1	3
Vietnam	3	1	2
Sri Lanka	1	1	0
Hong Kong	1	0	1
Pakistan	1	0	1
Total	74	22	52

Source: Nihon Tebukuro Kogyo Kumiai

Operations in Asia

As mentioned before, firstly South Korea and Taiwan were targeted for foreign operations for the glove-related industry in eastern Kagawa. South Korea has a similar climate to Japan and thus similar glove use in its cold winter. A number of companies began producing gloves there: Masan, a free export area in the south region, was a favored location. Soon after, with high economic growth of South Korea following Japan, personnel cost jumped accordingly. The glove-related firms operating in South Korea from eastern Kagawa were required to consider alternative places for production in order to cut costs. As a result, some companies decided to close their operations in South Korea; the closure of plants brought severe protests from local workers and cost a lot of money and time for the relevant firms.

It was China, which started its new open economic policy in 1978, that attracted Kagawa's subsequent foreign direct investment. In China, the Greater Shanghai region, composed of the city of Shanghai and parts of Jiangsu, Zhejiang, and Anhui provinces became a center for direct investment for the reasons that there were personal relationships between the Chinese group visiting Kagawa and the local people in Kagawa, that there were direct flights between Shanghai and Osaka, and that Shanghai was a leading metropolis of China. Another center for direct investment was in the north, consisting of Beijing, Tianjin and Shandon province. The factors for choosing this region were again the existence of direct flights from Osaka and the major ports of the country, and the fact that it was a metropolis with a large labor pool. Although these regions were advanced regions in the country, the fact was that infrastructure was not adequate for the business of foreign-affiliated firms. Also, Chinese workers' way of thinking was different due to their socialist system. Therefore, in the early stage, it was quite difficult for glove-related eastern-Kagawa firms to make profits. But later, throughout the 1990s, strongly assisted by the central government, China achieved very rapid progress, becoming the so-called factory of the world. Particularly, the Greater Shanghai region saw remarkable growth as the center of the Chinese economy (Depner and Bathelt, 2005). In the first decade of the twenty-first century, many foreign-affiliated firms were established in Kunshan, Suzhou, Wuxi and Hangzhou, all located in the suburbs of Shanghai. With newly established domestic firms, this suburban region has become a representative space of agglomeration of the manufacturing firms in Greater Shanghai. The metropolitan regions of Beijing, Tianjin and Dalian have also attracted an increasing number of Japanese- and Korean-affiliated firms (Seki, 1999, 2007).

With economic growth, personal incomes soared also in China. This has been especially the case in Shanghai. As a result, newly located foreign-affiliated firms in the Greater Shanghai region were required to take measures to cope with the rise of production cost due to personnel and material costs. One measure has been stricter cost management through localization of business and an empowerment of firms themselves through maintaining an advanced technology standard for manufacturing and the constant innovation of business patterns. Another measure has been relocation. A possibility is to (re)locate plants and offices to inland China and/or to other countries, where operations cost less. The former is still tentative because the infrastructure connecting coastal and inland regions, such as highways and high-speed railroads, is not very good and this shortcoming offsets the benefits from low labor costs in inland regions. The latter has been partially realized through investing in countries in Southeast and South Asia. Currently, glove-related firms in eastern Kagawa have operations in Indonesia, Vietnam, the Philippines and Sri Lanka. Scattering operations to some extent would be a critical strategy to avoid problems stemming from operating in a single country.

Operations in Europe and America

A unique characteristic of overseas operations of the glove-related industry in eastern Kagawa among similar local industries is that it established not only manufacturing plants in Asia but also sales offices in America and Europe in the 1980s, as an early Japanese investor in those regions. At first, overseas sales were slow due to rather low publicity. As a result of hard work, the number of buyers and clients has increased.

Currently, in North America, there is one glove-related company from eastern Kagawa which has sales offices (subsidiary companies) in the state of New York as well as in Canada, and transactions with local buyers in those countries are active. As outdoor activities including winter sports are popular in the United States and Canada, glove-related firms in eastern Kagawa are making efforts to sell sport- and leisure-related gloves there.

In Europe, two glove-related firms of eastern Kagawa have stocking and sales offices (subsidiaries) in Switzerland and Italy, respectively. Also there is one company in eastern Kagawa which is making high-quality leather goods as an original equipment manufacturer (OEM), based on contracts with prestigious European firms. Their sales representatives are located in ten countries in Europe including Italy, Germany, France, the UK, and Spain. Europe is a leading place of manufacture for leather-related goods, and European people are fond of sports including winter ones. Thus it is critical to continue market research through those overseas offices.

Additionally, for securing good raw materials, the companies have looked worldwide. Ethiopia, Indonesia, India and Pakistan are attractive to glove-related firms in eastern Kagawa as countries supplying leather-related raw materials. It is expected that glove-related firms in eastern Kagawa will continue to make efforts to secure good raw materials and explore new markets at the global scale.

V. Survival strategies at the glocal scale and agenda of the local industry

Relationships among firms, including colocation and face-to-face contacts, are of importance for clusters (Depner and Bathelt 2005). But leading glove-related firms in eastern Kagawa do not have very much contact with each other. A top manager of a leading company (interviewed in June 2008) says that spatial proximity of the industry is not as important as before because each leading company has its own production networks inside and outside the regional cluster. At the same time, however, the place name of "eastern Kagawa" still matters as a representative "brand" in Japan. Leading firms use this regional "brand" to attach extra value to their products. It can be formulated that clustering matters more in vertical relations of firms than horizontal relations in the case that leading firms have some sort of independent management capabilities including those for operating overseas. In other words, leading firms in eastern Kagawa are the main actors to build networks and expand them, enrolling other actors inside and outside the cluster.

Thus the point of the survival strategies of the glove-related industry in eastern Kagawa is the existence of the brand power of Higashikagawa (eastern Kagawa) as the place of the "glove" and the mechanism of maintaining it. There, it is critical to balance maintaining the "place with the brand" with high quality and management flexibility of corporations. As described before, a milieu which brings about entrepreneurs has been in place here for a long time, and this milieu has been helping the maintenance and the development of the space as a learning region. Firms in the area as a whole help create the industrial complex regarding competitive cooperation. The association of the glove-related industry plays the role of facilitator and mediator, leading the industry at one time or backing it up at another time.

Currently, the agenda the glove-related industry is tackling with the cooperation of the association of the industry is as follows: first, and critically, maintain a skilled labor force. In 2008 the industry began a program for developing a skilled and professional labor force through a qualification test drawing on the German "Meister" system. It was initially introduced for sales professionals and is to be introduced for production technicians soon. Meanwhile, the aging of skilled laborers is progressing; the average age is around 55. Hungary, where the representatives of the industry in eastern Kagawa visited recently, has a national institution for teaching youngsters to become professionals. An officer of the association of the industry said in an April 2008 interview that it is expected that the Japanese government will establish the same kind of institution as a state measure.

Another critical item on the agenda is creating the original "brand" of the industry. The glove-related industry in eastern Kagawa has long been dependent on specialized wholesalers for selling its products. Currently, however, the firms are trying to establish their original brand and increase profits through expanding the networks for direct sales. For example, the industry started the brand called "Globe Design" in 2003 as a regional brand of leather-related general merchandise using its leading leather-processing technology. Additionally the industry obtained the Japanese Industrial Standard (JIS) in 2008. The City of Higashikagawa and the Higashikagawa Chamber of Commerce have established the "Japan Brand" mainly consisting of leather-related items and are supporting the "Globe Design" goods. Most recently in July 2009, the Japan Glove-Related Companies' Association opened an outlet shop in the shopping area in downtown Sanbonmatsu in eastern Kagawa in collaboration with about 20 local firms as an initiative for increasing direct sales.

In order to grow the original brand, relentless improvement of quality of glove-related items and diversification of goods through adapted glove-making technology are important. As mentioned above, the industry has been producing not only gloves for winter use but also a variety of other sorts of gloves, corresponding to the increasing interests in sports and leisure and in health. Other than gloves, the industry has also been producing many items made of leather-related materials. As a whole, the glove-related industry in eastern Kagawa has been making efforts to become a general center for everyday items. It seems to be the creation of an expanding "regional brand" based on the reputation of the "glove town."

Currently, however, about 80 percent of the industry's products are produced in foreign countries, and overseas affiliates have begun to play a role in R&D. Thus, at present, the meaning of "local industrial complex" has become unclear. For multinational firms, what kind of functions should the headquarters in the local industrial complex execute? First, there is a central function as the node of global-local networks and second, there is, after all, the function of product development of the highest-quality goods to maintain the local brand. Attracting and developing human resources with expertise about each process, from planning and development, to production (at least making prototypes and trial items), to sales, is necessary.

The agenda of foreign operations includes selling products in emerging economies – especially in China, which has the largest population in the world. Currently, the population of the Chinese middle class is growing not only in the coastal regions but also inland. Since the northern and western regions in China have cold winters, these regions are expected to be a good market for glove-related products. Also, the function of planning and development is key for the business. It becomes increasingly important to develop and make products near the market to respond correctly to market trends and local tastes. Competition in product development between the headquarters in eastern Kagawa and foreign affiliates may give rise to synergy effects in the firm. Another agenda item is to expand the business in new markets in other emerging economies. Russia and neighboring countries could be target markets. Russia, especially, has enjoyed rapid growth recently. Although Russia is affected by the global recession, its cold winter and the growth of a rich population in such a vast country may contribute to a market for glove-related items. Third, new types of gloves, mentioned above, can also be sold in emerging economies if the geographical characteristics of these regions and the tastes and preferences of the people there are carefully researched. In any case, it would be critical for the glove-related industry in eastern Kagawa to continuously build active and flexible glocal strategies.

VI. Conclusions

This study's goal was to explain the survival strategies of a local industry located outside the major metropolitan areas of Japan and the characteristics of its overseas operations through a case study of the glove-related industry in eastern Kagawa.

The glove-related industry in eastern Kagawa still commands about 90 percent of the domestic market and is a leading local industry in Kagawa prefecture. The number of the firms engaged in glove-making is about 120, and most of them are small or medium-sized companies. This industry has developed not only by selling products in Japan but also by exporting to foreign countries. Eventually export became less profitable due to severe international competition, and the industry shifted its target more to the domestic market. Also, some firms actively began to establish production sites in foreign countries. In the meantime, a variety of gloves, such as those for sports, fashion, and protection from UV radiation, were made and shipped to market. The major clients for the industry have been department stores, specialty stores, and volume sales stores. The industry has produced a variety of items in addition to gloves in order to diversify its products. Various items have been produced based on glove-making knowledge and technology including bags, clothes and related items. Currently, this industry complex aims to transform itself into a general industrial complex of everyday items. The mode of production and the structure of firms of the industry in eastern Kagawa are novel compared with other local industrial complexes in Japan: some are producing a variety of products along with gloves, and others are concentrating on making gloves.

The glove-related industry in eastern Kagawa has actively expanded its operations in foreign countries since the 1970s, early in comparison to other Japanese industries. A factor in this development was a labor shortage in labor-intensive industries including this industry due to Japan's rapid economic growth at that time. Firstly, the mode of foreign operation was mainly production partnership with the local firms in the host countries. Soon thereafter, direct investment through affiliated companies began. The glove-related industry in eastern Kagawa went to neighboring South Korea and Taiwan first. Later, due to the rise of personnel costs along with the economic growth in these regions, this industry located and relocated foreign production operations to China, Indonesia and Sri Lanka. Now, China plays a role not only in production but also in checking and handling and R&D, even if only in part. Overall, global expansion of operations of the glove-related industry in eastern Kagawa is active: purchasing and sales offices have been established in Europe and North America. As a result, the industry is realizing global-local networks of operation.

There are three factors whereby the glove-related industry in eastern Kagawa is leading the market in Japan: first, there is a pool of skilled workers who can create an innovative environment and professional spirit; second, related to the first, there is a mechanism which maintains the innovative environment as a learning region which is geographically embedded; and third, there is an alliance of competitive cooperation among firms in the industry complex, which helps to create a "local brand" through the efforts of individual firms developing their individual original brands. For the glove-related industry in eastern Kagawa to continue to survive in the competitive world, it will be critical to keep making active and flexible glocal strategies as before. Tradition and flexibility are the key points which other industries in Japan can learn from this case.

Acknowledgements

I would like to thank many persons in the glove-related industry in eastern Kagawa for their kind cooperation in this study. My appreciation also goes to the Japan Society for the Promotion of Science (Grant-in-aid for scientific research no. 19520679) for their financial support.

Notes

1. See Taira (2005b) for details.
2. An officer of the Japanese Glove-Related Companies' Association said that the demands from customer companies and department stores are diminishing. The local office of NHK (a semi-public TV and radio station in Japan) in Shikoku reported on February 27, 2009, that a president of a glove-related firm himself was visiting recycling firms with trial gloves to get new customers to cope with the abrupt decrease in demand for workers' gloves from an important customer company making automobile parts.

References

Asahi Shimbun (2005): Kokunai kaiki: Koyo wazuka (Returning to Japan with creating a small number of employment). *Asahi Shimbun*, Aug. 25.

Coe, N.M., and Lee, Y.-S. (2006): The strategic localization of transnational retailers: The case of Samsung-Tesco in South Korea. *Economic Geography*, 82(1), 61–88.

Cox, K.R. (ed.) (1997): *Spaces of globalization: Reasserting the power of the local.* Guilford Press, New York.

Depner, H., and Bathelt, H. (2005): Exporting the German model: The establishment of a new automobile industry cluster in Shanghai. *Economic Geography*, 81, 53–81.

Dunning, J.H. (1980): Towards an eclectic theory of international production: Some empirical tests. *Journal of International Business Studies*, 11 (summer/spring), 9–31.

Dunning, J.H. (2000a): Globalization and theory of MNE activity. In Hood, N. and Young, S. (eds), *The globalization of multinational enterprise activity and economic development*, 21–52. Macmillan, London.

Dunning, H.H. (2000b): *Regions, globalization, and the knowledge-based economy.* Oxford University Press, Oxford.

Florida, R. (1995): Toward the learning region. *Futures*, 27, 527–36.

Helleiner, G.K. (1981): *Intra-firm trade and the developing countries.* Macmillan, London.

Hymer, S. (1960): *The international operations of national firms: A study of direct foreign investment.* MIT Press, Cambridge, MA.

Itakura, H. ed. (2005): *Keisu Bukku Chihohatsu Kigyono Chosen: Shikoku Shusshin Kigyo no Gurobaru Senryaku* (A case book about the challenges of firms located in the local area: Global strategies of the firms in Shikoku). Zeimu Keiri Kyokai, Tokyo.

Krugman, P. (1991): *Geography and trade.* Leuven Univ. Press, Leuven.

Malmberg, A. (1996): Industrial geography: Agglomeration and local milieu. *Progress in Human Geography*, 20, 392–403.

Matsubara, H. (2006): *Keizai Chirigaku* (Economic geography). Univ. of Tokyo Press, Tokyo.

Morisawa, K. ,and Ueda, H. eds. (2000): *Gurobarizeishon to rokaraizeishon* (Globalization and localization). Univ. of Tokyo Press, Tokyo.

Piore, M., and Sabel, C.F. (1984): *The second industrial divide: Possibilities for prosperity.* Basic Books, New York.

Porter, M. (1990): The *competitive advantage of nations.* Free Press, New York.

Pyke, F., and Sengenberger, W. (1990): Introduction. In Pyke, F., Becattini, G., and Sengenberger, W. (eds), *Industrial districts and inner-firm cooperation in Italy*, 1–9. International Institute for Labor Studies, Geneva.

Scott, A.J. (1988): *New industrial spaces.* Pion, London.

Seki, H. (1997): *Kuudoka wo Koete: Gijutsu to Chiiki no Saikochiku* (Going beyond hollowing situation). Nihon Keizai Shinbunsha, Tokyo.

Seki, M. (1999): *Ajia Shinjidai no Nihon Kigyo* (Japanese corporations in the new Asian Era). Chuo Koron Shinsha, Tokyo.

Seki, M. (ed.) (2007): *Meido in Chaina: Chuken, Chusho Kigyo no Chugoku Shinshutsu* (Direct investment of Japanese small and medium-sized corporations in China). Shin Hyoron, Tokyo.

Shikoku Bureau of Economy, Trade and Industry (2009): *Shikoku Keizai Gaikan* (Outline of economy in Shikoku), Shikoku Keizai Sangyokyoku, Takamatsu.

Tacconelli, W., and Wrigley, N. (2009): Organizational challenges and strategic responses of retail TNCs in post-WTO-entry China. *Economic Geography*, 85, 49–73.

Taira, A. (2001): The spatial characteristics and strategies of Japanese-affiliated companies in the Seoul Metropolitan Area. *Annals of the Japan Association of Economic Geographers*, 47, 196–214.

Taira, A. (2002): Spatial characteristics and strategies of Japanese-affiliated companies in the Midwest of the United States: Localization or specialization? *Geographical Review of Japan*, 75, 730–49.

Taira, A. (2004): Locational characteristics of multinationals and the local socio-economy in the Alsace Region, France. *Memoirs of the Faculty of Education, Kagawa University, Part I.* 122, 15–28.

Taira, A. (2005a): A critical review of geographic studies of multinational corporations. *Geographical Review of Japan*, 78, 28–47.

Taira, A. (2005b): *Spatial dynamics and strategies of Japanese-affiliated companies: A geographical study at the sub-national scale in the United States, Korea and France.* Kokon Shoin, Tokyo.

Takeuchi, A. (1996): *Kogyo Chiiki no Hendo* (Transformation of industrial space). Taimeido, Tokyo.

Vernon, R. (1966): International investment and international trade in the product cycle. *Quarterly Journal of Economics*, 80, 190–207.

Watanabe, Y. (1997): *Nihon Kikai Kogyo no Shakaiteki Bungyo Kozou: Kaiso Kozo, Sangyo Shuseki karano Shitauekesei* Haaku (Social division of labor of the Japanese machinery industry: Analysis of subcontract from the point of class structure and industrial agglomeration). Yuhikaku, Tokyo.

Yamamoto, K. (2005): *Sangyo Shuseki no Keizai Chirigaku* (Economic geography of industrial agglomeration). Hosei Daigaku Shuppankai, Tokyo.

13
International Production Allocation Strategies of Japanese Animation Studios

Kenta Yamamoto

Introduction

The observation that economic competition between regions is intensifying through economic globalization has become a well-worn cliché. Many scholars have debated this phenomenon as it became pronounced on a global scale during the last century. The study of multinational companies (MNCs) and industrial agglomeration are representative examples. The goal of either argument is discerning the spatial structure operating under the globalizing economy. However, their respective approaches are different: the one attempts to reveal globalization as a spatial expansion of business activities from the viewpoint of business administration; the other tries to position globalization as a structural change in local space from the viewpoint of economic geography.

Study of multinational companies

The pioneers of study in this field are Vernon (1966) and Helleiner (1973). In their studies, they both demonstrate a division of labor relations in regions that have opened to the global economy. Because many industrialized countries made the transition to an international division of labor after having achieved an advanced level of development, the consumption and development of products are now the primary production roles in those countries. Consequently, developing countries have come to serve as production bases for advanced countries.

Hymer pointed out in his theory of multinational enterprise (1976), incorporating the location theory of Chandler and Redlich (1961), that hierarchical structures are now being utilized in international cities because of allocation strategies by multinational enterprises (MNEs). This thesis, which is related to internal structure changes in MNEs, has developed into advanced and accurate theories such as the internalization theory presented by Buckley and Casson (1976) or the theory of firm-specific advantages by Rugman (1981). These theses have been integrated into Dunning's eclectic theory (1980). The analyses have particularly addressed the organizational institutionalization and restructuring of manufacturing enterprises that have become multinationals. Scholars have debated this system in relation to the flow and the accumulation of capital among advanced countries, or between advanced countries and developing countries.

As a consequence of this global change in economic structure from the late 1970s to the early 1980s, the perspective on the world economy changed from a hierarchy on the national level to a network structure at a local level. Under the local network structure, actors are not always related vertically. In other words, the networks among enterprises using this model are usually horizontal. Amin and Thrift (1992) suggest this shift as "a move from an international economy to global economy" (p. 574). They advocate the importance of not only internalization and vertical integration as an inter-enterprise division of labor in MNCs, but also external economy and inter-enterprise division of labor for support of business activities such as new subcontracting structures, joint businesses, strategic alliances, and network organizations. Porter (1986) characterizes allocation of business activities by MNCs as a matter of "geographic scope" (p. 22). The competitive strategy of MNCs on an international scale is an extension of that used on a national scale. He defines the world as a single large region and points out the importance of companies building "value chains" by allocating "value activities" efficiently among world markets.

As another example, Bartlett and Ghoshal (1989) present a transnational theory of global companies. They classify companies as "international", "global", "multinational", and "transnational" according to their administrative organization. Transnational companies are the most competitive––their administrative organization necessitates global-scale efficiency, environmental adaptation (and flexibility), promotion, and correspondence for innovation. To achieve such requirements, transnational companies enforce not only integration but also cooperation among departments. Doz (2001) further developed Bartlett's concept and propounded meta-national concepts. The companies that are meta-national achieve competitive advantages through networks that enable companies to access specialized knowledge worldwide.

According to scholars who accept the world- (or global-) city theory, such as Friedmann (1986) and Sassen (1991), this global structural change of economic activities is defined as the "emerging paradigm" (Friedmann, 1995, p. 26). In other words, under this new paradigm, the world economy is restructured particularly in and around "world cities" that offer various large external economies comprising the production services and financial support activities of MNCs.

Study of the industrial agglomeration

Of course, geographic scholars have addressed this phenomenon. Markusen (1996) and Saxenian (1994, 2006), in particular, attracted attention among agglomeration theorists during the mid-1990s. Markusen (1996) shows four models of interregional networks: (1) Marshallian industrial districts, (2) hub-and-spoke districts, (3) satellite platform districts, and (4) state-anchored districts. On that basis, he claims "Improving cooperative relations and building networks that reach outside of the region might prove more productive for some localities than concentrating on indigenous firms" (Markusen, 1996, p. 310). These regions become new economic centers under a division of labor structure by attracting large MNCs from beyond their regions. He defines "some localities" as hub-and-spoke districts and satellite platform districts. Busan and Singapore are prime examples of hub-and-spoke districts that have developed as transnational hub cities. Bombay (Mumbai) is the best example of a satellite platform district, which has grown as a direct result of businesses derived primarily from the IT industry in the United States.

Saxenian (2006) devotes particular attention to high-tech regions in developing countries such as Taiwan and Israel, which have already established their status as centers of global IT, and China and India, which have become new centers. Silicon Valley's open atmosphere, Saxenian (1994) contends, is promulgated in these budding regions by entrepreneurs, designated as "Argonauts", who received their education in technology and management know-how when they worked in Silicon Valley. Furthermore, these regions, which are led by the Argonauts, maintain connections with Silicon Valley. Regarding networks in Silicon Valley and these other regions, Saxenian emphasizes "the advantages of combining the specialized and complementary capabilities of producers located in distant regions" and that "[it] is the region, with its cluster of specialized producers and capabilities, and the networks that span these regions more than the individual firm that increasingly defines the contours of global production" (Saxenian, 2006, pp. 330–1).

Consequently, recent studies of agglomeration theory are underscoring the importance of networks that have been built among actors in global economies by corporations and individuals.

Purpose and methodology of this study

The focus in this study on MNCs concerns their shift from internal spatial structures to local spatial networks built out of MNCs. On the other hand, the focus in relation to industrial agglomeration emphasizes the significance of individual networks over global space. These arguments are connected to each other, and the border between them is becoming more and more fuzzy.

As we look forward to global cities, the function of cultural creation is attracting attention as a new field of economic activity in the global economy (Pratt, 1997; Scott, 2000; Power, 2002; Kong and O'Connor, 2009). However, there are few studies that analyze how the firms or studios serving this creative function build spatial relationships under an international division of labor, and we instead find only studies about "runaway production problems" in the American motion picture industry (Miller and Leger, 2001; Elmer and Gasher, 2005; Scott and Pope, 2007).

In accordance with this recent trend in research, the purpose of this study is to examine the spatial structure of the international division of labor in the animation industry, one of the culturally important industries in Japan, through a comparison of each production allocation strategy used by three studios having different backgrounds, while incorporating recent studies about MNCs and industrial agglomeration.

First, an outline of the animation industry in eastern Asia, especially Japan, South Korea, and China, is provided by some statistical data, wherein the results from the author's studies on the actual conditions of the international division of labor in the industry are shown. Second, to clarify the international division of labor formed between Japan and other countries, interviews of the directors or managers of the studios were conducted in 2008 and 2009, and three studios were chosen for the case study because of their allocation strategies. The interviewers asked the directors or managers about corporate history, the careers of top executives, the development of the division of labor, the work or the products exchanged between studios, and the criteria for selecting subcontractors. The interviews reveal not only the determinants for each studio's allocation strategies, but also the characteristics of the executives' careers, and this is essential because their careers influence the studios' selection of strategies. Finally, the international spatial structure of the industry is exhibited as the integrated conclusion of these studies.

Structure of the animation industry in East Asia

In this chapter, the production processes, the division of labor, and the market structure of the animation industry in eastern Asia are described.

Production processes

Production processes in the Japanese animation industry comprise the following three classifications, which are usually managed as tasks in their respective production departments:

1) Pre-production: projecting, script, character design, storyboard, layout
2) Production: key picture, animation picture, coloring, background
3) Post-production: sound effects, SFX, editing

The direction department manages these processes. Animation studios enable production by dividing these processes among cooperative studios. Although digitalized animation has become popular throughout the world, labor-intensive production processes are still the norm in the departments of key pictures, animation pictures, and coloring in Japanese animation. Animators draw pictures on paper with pencil, and a painter colors the animation pictures scanned into a computer. In all, 3000–4000 pictures are necessary for a 25-minute-long animated sequence.

Yamamoto (2007) explained the transaction characteristics and labor market that inform the structure of the Japanese animation industry. Japanese animation studios are classifiable into two types according to their role in the industry. They include primary contractors, which act as comprehensive producers; they also include professional subcontractors engaging in specific processes. Primary contractors receive work orders from their clients and produce animation images using their own labor and the labor of cooperative studios. Professional subcontractors continue some processes begun by other studios and then deliver partially finished products to those studios.

International division of labor

An international division of labor has already developed in the industry, just as it has in the American movie industry. Table 13.1 shows distribution regions for subcontractors in the industry; specifically, the table shows that South Korea and China are major subcontracting countries for the industry. Major jobs ordered by Japanese studios from companies in South Korea include not only animation pictures and coloring, but also key pictures. Furthermore, Table 13.2 details the major reasons that Japanese studios order from South Korea, including "shortage of own labor" (9, 60.0%), "complementing processes" (7, 46.7%), and "short lead time" (5, 33.3%). Japanese studios transact with Korean studios for their complementary skills, as well as their fast turnaround. However, the major processes that Japanese companies order from Chinese firms are limited to animation pictures and coloring. Japanese studios emphasize a "shortage of own labor" (6, 85.7%), "cheap labor" (5, 71.4%), and "short lead time" (4, 57.1%) regarding transactions with Chinese studios. In this case, their strategy is to obtain cheap labor to complement their own available labor. These results suggest that Japanese studios apparently emphasize quality rather than cost when they contract work out to Korean studios, while they emphasize cost rather than quality when they order work from Chinese studios.

Short lead time is essential to the Japanese animation industry under an international division of labor with South Korea and China. The short lead time is sustained using transportation systems. The use of the transportation industry is specialized for animation products traded between Japan, South Korea, and China. Additionally, there is a cooperative transportation

Table 13.1   Subcontracted animation processes by region

| Process | South Korea | | China | | | | Indonesia | | U.S.A. | |
	Seoul	-	Shanghai	Wuxi	Changzhou	-	DPS	BDO	L.A.	-
Production										1
Key Picture	5	2			1					3
Animation Picture	5	4	2	2	1	2				2
Coloring	4	4	2	2	1	2				1
Background	5						1	1		2
Edit									1	
-		2								
Order(s)	11	4	2	2	1	2	1	1	1	3

DPS = Denpasar, BDO = Bandung, L.A. = Los Angeles, - = unknown
Source: Yamamoto (2009).

Table 13.2   Japanese studios' emphases when they contract work out to Korean and Chinese studios

Items	South Korea (%)		China (%)	
Complementing processes	7	(46.7)	2	(28.6)
Shortage of own labor	9	(60.0)	6	(85.7)
Short lead time	5	(33.3)	4	(57.1)
Trust in quality of products	3	(20.0)	1	(14.3)
Associated studio	0	(0.0)	1	(14.3)
Cheap labor	3	(20.0)	5	(71.4)
Conventional transaction	5	(33.3)	0	(0.0)
Transaction with the high ground	0	(0.0)	1	(14.3)
Number of respondents	15	(100.0)	7	(100.0)

Source: Yamamoto (2009).

organization operated by several animation production studios. The transport schedule accommodates the studios' needs by running every day between the countries involved. The actual transactions take place through the cooperative management of transport. First, materials such as key pictures and layouts are brought into the duty studio in Japan. A staff member in the duty studio brings these materials to South Korea or China by flying on a passenger plane on an "outbound flight". A second staff member from the duty studio of subcontractors in China and/or South Korea receives products at the airport and carries them to the studios. Subcontracting studios joining this cooperative transportation system receive packages and send them to the doorstep of the duty studio. Korean and Chinese studios send back partially finished products to the client by "backload flight" as needed. Japanese staff members stay at subcontracting studios and bring back packages collected from Chinese or Korean cooperative studios to studios in Japan. Therefore, rapid business with foreign subcontractors is supported by this cooperative transportation system.

Market scale and structure

Figure 13.1 shows changes in the number of Japanese animated features playing in the Japanese market from 1961 to 2008. In all, 197 new productions were broadcast on TV in 2008. According to the "Digital Content White Paper 2006", annual sales from the Japanese animation industry in 2005 were 2122.4 million USD, of which 91.8% was from the domestic market.

It is also important to analyze trends in the Korean and Chinese animation industry, which sustain labor in the Japanese animation industry. According to Table 13.3, overseas transactions account for 106.6 million USD: they make up 52.2% of annual sales in the Korean animation industry.

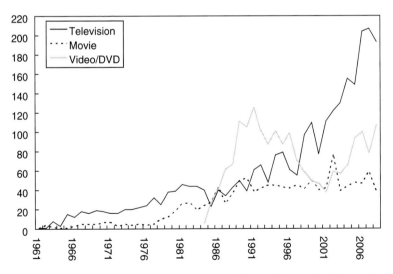

Figure 13.1 Number of newly produced animated features by market/format, Japan, 1961–2008

Source: "1997 Animage Pocket Data Notes", "Animage" (237, 249, 261, 273, 285, 297, 309, 321, 333, 345, 357, 369).

Subcontracting from overseas firms accounts for 84.8 million USD and the greatest share (41.5%), whereas "Original products / Copyright" is the largest (26.0%) sector in the domestic market, accounting for 48% of annual sales. Major clients are Japan (34.0%) and the United States (24.0%). The Korean animation industry has a final consumer market, but this market is not sufficiently large to sustain the industry; subcontracts from foreign companies are needed to sustain the industry.

In the case of China, according to the State Administration of Radio Film and Television, Development and Revolution Research Center (SARFT-DRRC) (2006), domestic production of Chinese animation is 43,000 minutes per year; the production of subcontracts for foreign studios accounts for 30,000 minutes per year. In this context, SARFT-DRRC (2006) states that the Chinese industry "remains in the early stages of development" and mostly provides "manual laborers" subcontracting jobs for the strong animation industries in Japan, South Korea, and the United States. As Qin (2006) points out, Japanese products accounted for 10 of the top 15 animation programs in annual broadcasting time in China in 2004.

As demonstrated above, both the demand and the supply of Japanese animated features are greater than those of features produced exclusively by industries in other East Asian countries, and so the Japanese products

Table 13.3   Annual sales and import/export values in the Korean animation industry*

Department	Total		Domestic		Foreign		Export	Import
	span Sales amount (USD thousands, %)						Import and export values (USD thousands)	
Original products/ Copyright	70,119	(34.3)	53,083	(26.0)	17,008	(8.3)	8173	5228
Subcontracting	99,353	(48.6)	14,495	(7.1)	84,850	(41.5)	74,504	0
Re-subcontracting	1300	(0.6)	968	(0.5)	332	(0.2)	348	0
Post-production	789	(0.4)	798	(0.4)	0	(0.0)	0	0
Distribution Service	32,483	(15.9)	27,999	(13.7)	4469	(2.2)	276	0
Marketing/ Advertisements	–	–	–	–	–	–	0	91
Others	1050	(0.1)	303	(0.1)	0	(0.0)	0	0
Total	204,305	(100.0)	97,647	(47.8)	106,658	(52.2)	83,301	5319

*Based on questionnaire surveys of 163 animation production companies by Korea Creative Content Agency

Source: Korea Creative Content Agency (2004).

are exported to neighboring countries. Ultimately, the prolific production schedule for Japanese products is sustained only through a division of labor between Japan and neighboring countries.

Case studies

As described in the preceding chapter, the division of labor relations, not only among internal studios but also in Korean and Chinese studios, is well developed in the Japanese animation industry. Production allocation strategies for the international division of labor differ based on the nature of the studios' management. The three studios in this study have different allocation strategies and are analyzed to clarify the status of the international division of labor and the determinants of each allocation strategy.

Studio A

Studio A was established by Taiwanese entrepreneurs in 1996 as a trading firm, but the studio became a professional subcontractor for animation pictures and coloring processing in 2004. Before establishing Studio A in 1996, the manager had previously run a Japanese-language school in Tokyo. He had no direct connections with the Japanese animation industry at that time. However, he later helped a Taiwanese animator establish his own studio. Through this experience, he was able to join Shanghai-based networks that acted as foreign subcontractors in the animation industry. When Studio A started animation-production services in 2004, the Shanghai-based network helped him subcontract animation pictures and coloring processes begun in Wuxi, an industrial suburb of Shanghai, and form business associations with those studios.

He is the only staff member at Studio A; no production department exists in the studio. Studio A takes orders from Japanese animation studios and orders the work from an associated studio in Wuxi. The transportation method for Studio A's partially finished products is the cooperative transportation system described in the preceding chapter.

The associated studio in Wuxi was derived from another studio in Wuxi through Studio A's funding. The studio is strictly prohibited from taking orders from other studios when contracting with Studio A. Consequently, the associated studio is a de facto subsidiary based on its background origin, capital flow, and the operational power between Studio A and the Wuxi studio.

The manager of Studio A, who received an MBA from a Japanese university, is intimately acquainted with the rigors of business administration. Although he had never previously worked in the animation industry and had no skills related to animation production, he entered the industry because he felt that the industry had a future. Language is not a barrier for him because he is a native Chinese. He also has strong ties with the

Shanghai region, an important region for the international division of labor with the Japanese animation industry, based on the experience of trading firms and a Taiwanese animation studio in Shanghai. There, he started an animation service that specifically addressed animation pictures and coloring, for which the Chinese industry has cost advantages. To avoid expensive investment and management risks in Japan, he orders all of his Japanese studio work from Chinese cooperative studios.

This is the structure of the international division of labor under Studio A's network: it is a simple division of labor between Japan and China as a client and producer, respectively. Studio A was able to choose this structure because the manager had strong business administration skills and close ties to Chinese studios.

Studio B

Studio B was established in 1986 by an assistant director of a Japanese animation firm. In its infancy, the studio was a subcontractor for foreign animation studios centering on the US market. In the 1990s, Japanese studios became Studio B's major clients, and the studio became a primary contractor after 2000.

Studio B subcontracted labor-intensive processes to Korean studios in order to reduce production costs through networks the manager had built up during his earlier career as an assistant director. In contrast to the case of Studio A with its Wuxi subsidiary, the transactions of the Korean production studio are not limited to those with Studio B. Korean studios are allowed to have transactions with Japanese studios other than Studio B. Studio B has changed business partners several times. The reasons include poor relations among managers, financial trouble, and competing transactions among rival studios in Japan.

Studio B established a subsidiary in Wuxi that specializes in processing animation pictures and coloring processes because the manager understood the animation boom in the 1990s as an opportunity for business expansion and tried to take orders for animation pictures or coloring from other studios. This subsidiary studio takes orders only from Studio B. After the Wuxi studio was established, relations between Studio B and the Korean studios changed. Studio B ordered animation pictures and coloring from the Wuxi studio and ordered key pictures, layout, and quality checking of pictures from the Korean studios.

Studio B's example reveals the change in relations between Studio B and foreign studios. Early on, the Studio B manager had been dealing with Korean studios, using knowledge of networks gained in his experience in the industry. Later, the studio began transacting with Chinese studios in order to enable business expansion. Studio B chooses partners depending on the jobs it needs, but no transactions exist between its Chinese or Korean subcontractors. The production allocation strategy of Studio B is that of developmental forms of bilateral trade under competition between South Korea and China.

Studio B has flexibly changed its production allocation along with its development. Primary contractors such as Studio B must manage various processes and produce a series of animation productions. They often require not only high management capability but also stable production volume. Subsequently, Studio B established a subsidiary studio to handle labor-intensive processes with cheap labor in the Shanghai region. On the other hand, Korean studios had accumulated refined skills through transactions with Japanese studios. As a result, Studio B was able to subcontract some processes that necessitated high skills such as storyboard and layout, processes linked directly to the market's tastes and the sensibilities of creators.

Studio C

Studio C was created in 2002 when a Korean assistant director established a semi-independent branch of a larger Japanese studio. The Japanese studio was a professional subcontractor for animation pictures and coloring processes. The manager of the parent studio encouraged the manager of Studio C, who worked at another studio, to establish his own business. The new studio received animation pictures and coloring jobs subcontracted from the parent studio in its early stages. The studio received orders in Japan and performed production in Wuxi, China. The studio started to take orders from other studios in 2003. The capital ties between the parent studio and Studio C dissolved because the parent studio sold off Studio C in 2005.

Studio C established a subsidiary studio in Seoul in 2006, thereby changing the transactional relations between Studio C and subcontractors from Japan and China to include South Korea as well. Studio C takes orders in Japan and then orders work from the Korean studio, in turn. The Korean studio then subcontracts the work to a Chinese studio. Money flows between the Japanese studio and the Korean studio. Material, such as key pictures and animation pictures drawn on paper, flow between Japan and China. There is money flow typified by employment costs and upkeep costs between South Korea and China. Studio C can have costs in China kept to a minimum by these transactional flows.

Studio C must choose this strategy because of currency restrictions by the Chinese government. Under bilateral trade between Japan and China, the group could not share the profits of the Chinese subsidiary. On the other hand, under tripartite trade made possible by the addition of South Korea, the group can share the profits between Japan and South Korea because money transfers are not limited between Japan and South Korea. Transaction relations among Studio C's group studios differ from competitive relations between Korea and China, as seen in the case of Studio B. The production allocation strategy of Studio C is based on the accommodative division of labor relations among the three regions. The element enabling

Studio C to change its transactional relation from simple bilateral trade to tripartite trade is that the manager is from South Korea, a participating location in the trade. It is easy for that manager to exploit advantages from using Korean networks.

Discussion

Table 13.4 outlines the activities of Studio A, Studio B, and Studio C and the origin and experience of each manager. In these three cases, the studios' production allocation strategies are dependent on factors such as the nationality of the manager, the role of the studio in the industry, the transactional history between regions, and the accumulation of specialized skills in each region. For example, Korean or Chinese managers have built strong networks based on ties in their respective home countries, as in the cases of studios A and C. These studios can enact a division of labor through a local subsidiary with relative ease. The head of Studio A can be categorized as a "hybrid manager" as defined by Schlunze and Plattner (2007). And the network Studio C has built is definable as one of the variations of the network built by the Argonauts (Saxenian, 2008). For cases in which the manager is Japanese, it has been difficult to establish a subsidiary in a foreign country. Such companies typically transact with foreign studios through the network that managers constructed when they were employed at a parent studio. In this case, subcontractors have no capital ties with prime contractors and transactional relations between them are flexible. In fact, a Korean studio that Studio B had initially dealt with had been working with other Japanese studios simultaneously.

The transactional history among Japanese studios and the subcontracted regions is also an important determinant for studios' international allocation. The transactional history between the Japanese and Korean animation industries is longer than that between the Japanese and Chinese industries.

Table 13.4 Outline of activities of Studio A, Studio B, and Studio C and origin and experience of each manager

	Manager		Studio	
	Origin	Last job	Service type	Transaction partner(s)
Studio A	Taiwan	Language School Manager	Professional subcontractor	China
Studio B	Japan	Animation Assistant Director	Primary contractor	South Korea, China
Studio C	South Korea	Animation Assistant Director	Professional subcontractor	South Korea, China

The Korean industry has been improving specific skills as a competitive advantage against China, which has an advantage in labor-intensive jobs because of cheap labor costs. Studio B, as a prime contractor in the industry, can reduce production costs by outsourcing upper processes, such as key pictures and layouts, to Korean studios and lower processes, such as animation pictures and coloring, to Chinese subsidiary studios.

Conclusion

The determinants of each strategy were examined through an analysis of the three studios' production allocation strategies. In this section, the findings of this chapter will be summarized and the unique structure created by the international division of labor in the animation industry will be examined.

Japanese animated features are produced by Japanese studios under an international division of labor among eastern Asian regions, mainly centering on Seoul in South Korea and Shanghai in China. This labor structure has been developed for the purpose of reducing production costs. Labor-intensive processes, such as animation pictures and coloring, are subcontracted to Korean and Chinese studios. However, this sharing of roles differs depending on the production allocation strategies of studios.

Figure 13.2 presents the spatial structure of the international division of labor in the industry. The division of labor relations among Japan, South Korea, and China appears on the surface to be cooperative. However, not all relations are always cooperative according to allocation strategies by actual economic actors. In this chapter, various spatial structures were revealed. Studio A transacts with a Shanghai subcontractor in a one-on-one relationship using the network operated by its Chinese manager. The Tokyo studio dominates the Shanghai studio through capital control. Orders, materials, and money move between these two regions. This is an example of a simple transactional structure. By comparison, Studio B transacts with both the Seoul and Shanghai regions using networks the manager built based on his career in the industry. Skill and price competition between Seoul and Shanghai are severe, so the Tokyo studio chooses studios in Shanghai or Seoul appropriate to their quality or price requirements. Studio C gives studios in each city specialized roles in their division of labor structure. Orders and money flow between Tokyo and Seoul, and materials flow between Tokyo and Shanghai. Because the studios' capital is controlled by Studio C, the flexibility of transactions with other studios is very low. Studio C offers subcontracted studios sufficient stable work, and the division of labor relationships between the three cities is realized cooperatively. The spatial structure of the Japanese animation industry in eastern Asia has emerged as an overall structure of multilayered relationships under networks built by various managers, such as Argonauts, hybrids, and Japanese actors.

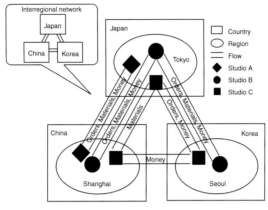

Figure 13.2 Spatial structure of international division of labor in the Japanese animation industry

Acknowledgment

The author gratefully acknowledges Mr. Shinnosuke Iijima and Mr. Derek Lattimer for their helpful suggestions. This investigation was funded by a Grant-in-Aid for JSPS Research Fellowships for Young Scientists (No. 20–3145).

References

(* in Japanese, ** in Japanese with English abstract, *** in Chinese)
Amin, A., and Thrift, N. (1992). Neo-Marshallian nodes in global networks. *International Journal of Urban and Regional Research*, 16, 571–87.
Bartlett, C.A., and Ghoshal, S. (1989). *Managing across Borders: The Transnational Solution*. Harvard Business School Press, Boston.
Buckley, P.J., and Casson, M. (1976). *The Future of the Multinational Enterprise*. Macmillan Publishers, London.
Chandler Jr., A., and Redlich, F. (1961) Recent developments in American business administration and their conceptualization. *Business History Review*, 35, 1–27.
Doz, Y., Santos, J., and Williamson, P. (2001). *From Global to Metanational: How Companies Win in the Knowledge Economy*. Harvard Business School Press, Boston.
Dunning, J.H. (1980). Towards an eclectic theory of international production: Some empirical tests. *Journal of International Business Studies*, 11, 9–31.
Elmer, G., and Gasher, M. (2005). *Contracting Out Hollywood: Runaway Productions and Foreign Location Shooting*. Rowman & Littlefield, Oxford.
Friedmann, J. (1986). The world city hypothesis. *Development and Change*, 17, 69–84.
———. (1995). Where we stand: A decade of world city research. In Knox, P.L.K., and Taylor, P.J. (eds), *World Cities in a World-System*. Cambridge University Press, Cambridge.

Helleiner, G.K. (1973). Manufactured exports from less-developed countries and multinational firms. *Economic Journal*, 83, 21–47.

Hymer, S. (1960). *The International Operations of National Firms and Other Essays: A Study of Direct Foreign Investment*. Massachusetts Institute of Technology Press, Cambridge, MA.

Kong, L., and O'Connor, J. (2009). *Creative Economies, Creative Cities: Asian-European Perspectives*. Springer, New York.

Markusen, A. (1996). Sticky places in slippery space: A typology of industrial districts. *Economic Geography*, 72, 293–313.

Miller, T., and Leger, M.C. (2001). Runaway production, runaway consumption, runaway citizenship: The new international division of cultural labor. *Emergences: Journal for the Study of Media & Composite Cultures*, 11, 89–115.

Porter, E.P. (1986). *Competition in Global Industries*. Harvard Business School Press, Cambridge, MA.

Power, D. (2002). "Cultural Industries" in Sweden: An assessment of their place in the Swedish economy. *Economic Geography*, 78, 103–27.

Pratt, A. (1997). The cultural industries production system: A case study of employment change in Britain, 1984–91. *Environment and Planning A*, 29, 1953–74.

Qin, X. (2006). *Zhongguo donghuapian de chanye jingjixue yanjiu* (Economic study of the Chinese animation industry)***. China Market Press, Beijing.

Rugman, A.M. (1981). *Inside the Multinationals: The Economics of Internal Markets*. Columbia University Press, New York.

Sassen, S. (1991). *The Global City: New York, London, Tokyo*. Princeton University Press, Princeton, NJ.

Saxenian, A. (1994). *Regional Advantage: Culture and Competition in Silicon Valley and Route 128*. Harvard University Press, Cambridge, MA.

———. (2006). *The New Argonauts*. Harvard University Press, Cambridge, MA.

Schlunze, R.D., and Plattner, M. (2007). Evaluating international managers' practices and locational preferences in the global city – An analytical framework. *Ritsumeikan Business Review*, 46(1), 63–89.

Scott, A.J. (2000). *The Cultural Economy of Cities: Essays on the Geography of Image-Producing Industries*. Sage, London.

Scott, A.J., and Pope, N.E. (2007). Hollywood, Vancouver, and the world: Employment relocation and the emergence of satellite production centers in the motion-picture industry. *Environment and Planning A*, 39, 1364–81.

State Administration of Radio Film and Television Development and Revolution Research Center (2006). *2006 Report on Development of China's Radio, Film and Television***. Social Sciences Academic Press, Beijing.

Yamamoto, K. (2007). Agglomeration mechanism of the animation industry in Tokyo: Focus on business-to-business transactions and the labor market. *Geographical Review of Japan*, 80, 442–58**.

———. (2009). *Tokyo, souru, shanhai niokeru animeshon sangyono shuseki mekanizumu nikansuru chirigakuteki kenkyu* (Geographical Study of the Agglomeration Mechanism of the Animation Industry in Tokyo, Seoul and Shanghai). Doctoral thesis of Tohoku University**.

Vernon, R. (1966). International investment and international trade in the product cycle. *Quarterly Journal of Economics*, 80, 190–207.

Zhongguo donghua nianjian bianjibu (2006). *Zhongguo Donghua Nianjian 2006 (China Animation Yearbook 2006)****. Zhonguo guangbo dianshi chubanshe, Beijing.

14
Adjusting to a Distant Space: Cultural Adjustment and Interculturally Fluent Support

William W. Baber

Purpose

Foreign managers may experience difficulties, even crises, in their adjustment to a host culture. Nonetheless, many survive, and some become comfortable and successful in their new environment. The purpose of this chapter is to consider the presence and types of cultural informants as well as their roles in acculturation and adjustment to a host culture by foreign expatriate managers, specifically in Japan. The role of the cultural informant will be studied through interviews with business managers. This subject has remained little addressed despite the large amount of literature on cross-cultural management, including cross-cultural mentoring.

In order to explore how managers learn about the business environment in their host country, this chapter will briefly review the concepts of culture shock, culture, cultural adjustment, expatriate managers, cross-cultural comparison, mentors, and cultural informants. Data is drawn from the experience of foreign managers in Japan based on face-to-face as well as email interviews.

Background and literature review

Sojourners in a host country may follow the ups and downs described in Culture Shock Theory (CST). CST as originally explained by Oberg (1960) holds that an individual who spends significant time in a new culture will pass through certain distinct phases of experience before possibly reaching a satisfactory state of synthesis in the new culture. These stages are usually referred to as honeymoon, crisis, recovery (or negotiation), and adjustment (Oberg, 1960) or simply as high and low points (University of Minnesota, 2009). Recently, culture shock has come to be seen as a process of managing change (Ward et al., 2001). Figure 14.1 goes to greater depth than

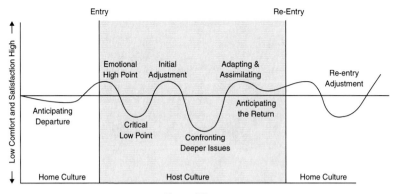

Figure 14.1   Culture shock curve
Source: University of Minnesota

many renderings of the culture shock curve because it shows the experience of some individuals in repeating crisis and adjustment. In Figure 14.1, the phase referred to as Adapting and Assimilating corresponds to Oberg's 1960 conceptualization of adjustment.

Adjustment refers to the last stage of the time abroad, the one in which the sojourner has become able to synthesize the experiences and interpret the cultural differences without overly simplistic judgments such as "good" or "bad" (Ward et al., 2001). These processes of culture shock apply broadly to all sojourners, as well as to workers and managers (Oberg, 1960; Ward et al., 2001).

Success and adjustment

In this writing, the term "expatriate manager" refers only to managers dispatched from a foreign headquarters, usually for a limited term. On the other hand, the term "foreign manager" refers to managers who are from foreign locations but who were not dispatched from headquarters. They may reside in the host country for reasons other than work for the current employer.

In the ideal situation, expatriate or foreign managers mature into individuals whose adjustment to the host culture is well synthesized with their previous cultural experiences. Moore (2009) showed that this synthesis predicts assignment success, which is defined as completion of assignment. Regarding language learning, combination of the home culture's social and linguistic reality with that of the target culture results in a third culture, a metaphorical place in which the learner synthesizes a new understanding (Kramsch, 1994). Successful adjustment coupled with strategic business vision allows the creation of a new cultural space in which new synergies are generated for personal and work life (Schlunze and Plattner, 2007). Schlunze and Plattner term the foreign manager who has undergone this transformation a *hybrid manager*. The term "hybrid manager" refers to a foreign manager working in a host country who has deep understanding of the home and host countries and who is well adjusted to the host culture and socially embedded in it (Schlunze and Plattner, 2007).

Time and experience appear to play a vital role in the development of these managers. Indeed, some hybrid managers begin as classic expatriates but elect to remain in the host culture, eventually gaining the in-depth knowledge and network that distinguishes the hybrid manager from other expatriate managers (Schlunze and Plattner, 2007; Plattner, 2008).

Social embeddedness as defined by Schlunze and Plattner (2007) builds on Granovetter's (1985) concept of economic embeddedness and appears to play a role in expatriate success and failure. Tung (in Mead, 2005) reported in her 1987 work that the top two reasons for early repatriation of expatriate managers were difficulties in adjustment by the manager's spouse and difficulties in adjustment by the manager. In their 1986 work on culture shock, Furnham and Bochner support the notion that interpersonal relationships that include supportive connections are important. They go on to suggest that a binational support group might be most helpful, though they provide no investigation into the question. Moore (2009), however, demonstrates that bicultural attainment predicts sociocultural adaptation, which subsequently predicts assignment success. Thus, the inputs to successful social embeddedness and adaption support the success of expatriates.

Here it is informative to consider the meaning of culture. Many definitions of "culture" are offered in anthropology, ethnography, psychology, and elsewhere; this piece concerns itself with the notion of culture as a web of meanings created by humans, the *culture2* described by Hunt (2007). This definition includes the learned behaviors and interpretations that groups of people mutually understand in ordinary life (Petersen, 2004), as well as the ideas, beliefs, and norms generally common to a group and which guide their behavior (Goodenough, 1973). These definitions fit well with Oberg's (1960, p. 179) description of culture: "the sure, familiar, largely automatic way of getting what you want from your environment." By extension, understanding culture in a way that is compatible with the people around is generally desirable for the foreign manager who seeks to get predictable and desirable results from his new surroundings. Because different cultures interpret events and develop solutions in different ways (Trompenaars and Hampden-Turner, 1998), it is clearly sensible for sojourners to learn the local culture and its many interpretations and solutions of the environment around them in order to meet their goals and needs.

While there are significant and often clear differences among cultures, as well as unclear differences, it is not obvious how to compare cultures. Two systematizing approaches have generated interest by employing dimensions to show relative importance of opposing cultural variables. Both restrict their analyses to culture at the national level. Neither approach purports to describe or predict the actions of individuals. The first, developed by Hofstede based on analysis of IBM employees, takes five dimensions into account. The second, jointly developed by Trompenaars and Hampden-Turner, employs seven dimensions to describe and compare cultures.

The dimensions proposed by Hofstede as well as those of Trompenaars and Hampden-Turner, however, must be considered cautiously. To consider these dimensions to apply to all individuals in a cultural group would be to fall into the trap of stereotyping, as the authors themselves warn. Nonetheless, as Baskerville (2005) summarized regarding Hofstede, comparison and study at a national level does not account well for ethnic heterogeneity: there are too few dimensions to allow deep insight. Furthermore, the possible impact of IBM on Hofstede's data has not been well addressed Baskerville (2005). The same problematic issue regarding nations as a starting point for cultural comparison applies to the work of Tromepanars and Hampden-Turner. Additionally, Szkudlarek (2005), among other commentators on Tromepanars and Hampden-Turner, rejects the description of all the world's cultures in terms of a few cultural dimensions as gross oversimplification.

With the dimensions of Hofstede as well as Trompenaars and Hampden-Turner, and their criticisms, in mind, as well as with other social factors, Japan in particular offers a difficult environment for foreign managers, especially for those from Western countries, according to academic and business observers (Peltokorpi, 2008). Though often overlooked by academia, Japan offers multiple regions as well as minorities, and class differences. It is within such a complex milieu that the support of a knowledgeable informant becomes increasingly valuable, even indispensable, to the foreign manager interested in succeeding in his or her surroundings.

The cultural informant compared to the mentor

The cultural informant is not to be confused with a workplace mentor. Accordingly, let us define the cultural informant and explain how this role differs from that of the more familiar figure of the mentor. According to the *Shorter Oxford English Dictionary* (2005) *mentor* means "an experienced and trusted advisor or guide; a teacher, a tutor." In the business world, the word "mentor" suggests a person who will support the career advancement of the person in his or her care, the mentee (Kram, 1988). Kram specifically notes two types of mentoring functions: career and psychosocial. Kram's psychosocial functions include modeling, but this modeling does not include the in-depth cultural knowledge which cultural informants may be able to provide but which is not expected of mentors. Crosby (1999) reviews 18 studies on mentoring which focus repeatedly on career goals, hierarchical relationships, and other points common to mentoring. Of those reviewed by Crosby, only one overtly includes the notion of coaching with a strong psychosocial content. The mentor, nonetheless, is not a business coach as defined by Leonard and Swap (2005) – a person committed to transferring in-depth business knowledge through intensive interaction.

Lack of research on informants and adjustment

While recent research has examined the impact of cultural distance, language proficiency, expatriate type, and personality traits such as emotional stability and cultural empathy (Peltokorpi, 2008), there remains little research on the input by individuals such as cultural informants to the adjustment process.

Ward et al. (2001) summarize research that has shown positive effects of on-site mentoring regarding improved expatriate adjustment to the target culture while pointing out that this kind of mentoring occurs on an ad hoc basis. Feldman and Bolino (1999) found expatriates were able to gain advantages from mentoring regarding socialization as well as global business issues. Unfortunately, discussion about the cultural fluency of the mentor who helps with social adjustment remains absent. While mentors can play a role in the issue of socialization and adjustment, there is no research on or discussion of the deeper involvement found with the cultural informant. Precisely this gap invites investigation to build understanding of the adjustment process.

Considering the nature of the cultural informant, the *Shorter Oxford Dictionary* defines *informant* as "a person from whom a linguist, anthropologist, etc. obtains information about language, dialect, or culture." This definition, though in common use in the fields mentioned and many more, mischaracterizes the cultural informant as merely a bearer of information. From the researcher's point of view, a cultural informant is a person who provides a researcher with insight into a culture, subculture, organization, or other group of people. Put rather more carefully by Coan and Allen (2007), "the cultural-informant approach utilizes individuals who are, for one reason or another, sensitive observers in a specific cultural setting."

Although Mead (2005) describes the tasks of the mentor in the host culture as including living adjustment to local culture, this support does not cross deeply into the territory of the cultural informant. In the work at hand, the cultural informant is defined by the standards laid out in Table 14.1 and is not to be confused with the mentor, despite some overlap.

Whereas the mentor is primarily concerned with career and workplace issues, the cultural informant navigates deeper into the tangle of interactions and understandings that differentiate cultures from each other. Examples

Table 14.1 Comparison of cultural informant and mentor

Cultural Informant	Mentor
Is socially embedded in the target culture, or even in both cultures	May be on-site or in home country
Is partially or very proficient in target language and culture	Is established in his or her field, but not necessarily socially embedded
Advises in situational incidents in business and many other areas	Is technically proficient in his or her field
	Is a guide into management
Advises on social cues	Offers work-related network access
Provides ad hoc advice	Offers some behavioral guidance
Is accessible, even giving instant feedback	Advises in situational incidents related to business and management
May be only one of several cultural informants of the adjusting manager	Shares a trusting relationship with the mentee
Need not be related to the adjusting manager's work world	Is usually the mentee's only mentor
	May support specific career goals with mentee
Need not be established in work or society	May contribute to cultural socialization
Need not be technically proficient	Because of high status, may offer only low or moderate accessibility, but is committed
Need not have a deep personal relationship with the adjusting manager	

Sources: Feldman and Bolino, 1999; Schlunze, 2007; and Gudykunst and Nishida, 1994

Sources: Kram, 1998; Feldman and Bolino, 1999; Kay and Hinds 2007; Leonard and Swap 2005; Mead, 2005; Ward et al., 2001; Zachary, 2000

of the depth and difficulty of these differences are laid out by Gudykunst and Nishida (1994) in such cases as nonverbal communication, turn-taking in conversation, managing expectations, uncertainty reduction, direct and indirect address, and many other areas.

A new figure emerges

This writing differentiates further between the cultural informant, who offers culturally sensitive observation, and the *interculturally fluent inform-ant*, who is knowledgeable in both the host culture and the foreign man-ager's home culture. An informant with any lower level of ability may not only be of limited help, but may confuse and mislead the incoming foreign manager unintentionally. By way of example, a well-qualified intercultur-ally fluent informant supporting a manager from the UK working in Japan will be familiar with business-related pop culture such as the TV show *The Office* as well as with Japanese business manga such as "Kachou Kosaku

Shima." Where the cultural informant is not well versed in both cultures, the informant will not be able to relate complex situations such as minority status, treatment of aggrieved employees, or threats from organized crime to analogous issues in the other culture.

These requirements are far higher than definitions previously offered for the cultural informant. Thus it is time to leave behind the cultural inform-ant and introduce the interculturally fluent informant. This individual does have the background to support the foreign manager's transition from unknowing newcomer to knowledgeable culturally fluent manager, and even beyond that to hybrid manager. With the key issue of advanced cultural competence in mind, the characteristics of an interculturally fluent informant will be introduced with the interview findings of this research.

The role of the interculturally fluent informant in learning and motivation

Schematics and frameworks such as those of the expatriate experience (Thomas, 1998) and the acculturation process (Ward et al., 2001; Moore, 2009) have no place for nor mention of a role such as a mentor or cultural informant. Similarly, while human resources literature offers exemplary content on cultural preparation (Briscoe and Schuler, 1995), it does not spe-cifically identify the need for interaction with individuals who can guide and negotiate on an intercultural basis. Because of this lack, it is to learning and language acquisition that we must turn to find hints about how a cul-tural informant has impact.

In participant modeling therapy, timely expert feedback helps the recipi-ent develop corrective experiences that result in change (Bandura, 1977). Similarly, the cultural informant who can provide fast, even immediate responses, can be a key actuator of learning for the foreign manager seek-ing to improve in knowledge and comprehension of the target culture. Sojourners can build their self-efficacy and motivation through modeling the behavior (Bandura) of the members of the host culture, especially with knowledgeable feedback and input from the cultural informant. The cul-tural informant can support the foreign manager's learning in cultural flu-ency, business issues, language, and other areas.

The cultural informant is not a language teacher, yet because language and culture are so entwined, cultural informants will unavoidably teach some language skills whether systematically or incidentally (Gudykunst and Nishida, 1994). Further, as Kramsch (1991) suggests, biculturalism should be as much a focus as bilingualism for the learner. As the foreign manager is guided by the cultural informant into the culture, language skills must not fail to keep up to avoid limiting further development. Indeed, language and culture are inseparable for the learner: Attinasi and Friedrich (1995) refer to *linguaculture*, a single universe of language and cultural experience. Kramsch (1991, 1996) supports the notion that culture should be inherently taught along with the target language, as it creates the context in which the need to exchange information and opinions arises.

The combination of language and culture training may contribute to the adjustment process of the foreign expatriate. Thomas (1998, p. 263) uses a graphic, "Conceptual Framework of the Expatriate Experience," showing four sequential categories of process. The third of these is "outcomes of overseas assignments," within which are three varieties: individual, organizational, and adjustment. This last one refers to adjustment in general living, work, and interactions. It may be in this area that the cultural informant has appreciable impact on the life and experience of the foreign expatriate manager.

In his 2008 work, Thomas adds to the notion of cultural fluency with his discussion of biculturals. These are individuals who "have a dual pattern of identification...with different cultures" (p. 256). Thomas asks whether the process of culture switching by biculturals can help understand how global managers choose their actions. Moore (2009) clearly links bicultural ability with assignment success. This study seeks to better understand intercultural informants–those people who are highly capable in two or more cultures–and their relationship with both foreign managers and hybrid managers.

Despite the large number of details to be learned, the information transferred by the informant must not be limited to discrete bits of information, as if a long-term training course were in process. The interculturally fluent informant is a key transmitter of unspoken, common understanding that is necessary for real comprehension of a culture and its members. This kind of knowledge is known as tacit knowledge (Polyani, 1967) and must be gained over time through deep interaction with knowledgeable individuals. Successful transfer of tacit knowledge will allow the learner to eventually react as a native would to situations that are new to him or her. Another author (Devos, in Thomas, 2008) refers to the subconscious and non-volitional learning that accompanies familiarization with a new culture. For example, the manager who has gained sufficient tacit knowledge will be able to select appropriate gifts for business clients without seeking advice from others.

Hypotheses

The above discussion on the state of research regarding foreign managers and how they interact with the host environment leads to the formulation of two hypotheses:

1. Cultural informants are in place in the lives of foreign managers.
2. Cultural informants all largely meet the descriptive criteria presented in Table 14.1.

These hypotheses will be discussed in the section on findings below.

Methodology

The participants were informed that their data would remain private and would not be stored with personal names or company names. Email exchanges were stripped of personal data before they were saved to computer, while the original emails were deleted. Notes and recordings were kept without names. All individuals agreed to participate voluntarily with no reimbursement. Managers were selected based on their availability and accessibility. Manager B was dropped from the study, as this individual was Japanese with experience in North America rather than a foreign manager in Japan.

The interviews abstracted here were based only on email for Managers C and E. Manager A allowed previously recorded conversation from a workshop to be considered. The interviews with Managers D, F, and G occurred face to face and were recorded with the permission of the interviewee.

What the cultural informant means to the manager – interview abstracts

Abstracts from spoken and written interviews with hybrid managers are included here. Although the focus is on hybrid managers, this is not to suggest that the expatriate manager, or indeed any sojourner, cannot benefit from an interculturally fluent informant.

The interviews conducted to generate insights into the role of the cultural informant consisted of four initial questions, which can be found in the appendix to this chapter.

Interview abstracts

Manager A: Australian, male, head of human resources of Kansai branch of an international hotel

Manager A notes his wife of some years as the most important input to learning about working life in Japan. His wife is Chinese but has lived in Japan for some time and is very fluent in Japanese culture and work life. Both have lived and worked mainly in Japan, but with employment histories elsewhere in Asia. Manager A notes that he developed unique synergies based on Japanese and Australian working culture. This manager also noted that the benefit of working in a typically Japanese environment during his first years in Japan as well as intentionally developing and maintaining various networks of social and work-related contacts.

Key Informant A: This individual is non-Japanese but was experienced in Japan at the time she first met Manager A; relationship is spouse and coworker.

Manager C: American, male, consultant and educator

Manager C notes his Japanese spouse, who lived and worked some years in the United States, as serving as a cultural informant and role model regarding business as well as day-to-day life. An additional business associate has provided ongoing in-depth guidance in points from office behavior to business socializing. This cultural informant, a Japanese individual, lived and worked in the New York financial industry for several years and is broadly fluent in the working culture of that area and industry.

Key Informant C: This individual is a Japanese businessperson with moderately high intercultural and language fluency and is highly embedded in local and international business networks.

Manager D: German, male, full-time employee of Japanese-German joint venture, IT specialist

Manager D notes his boss, the head of the joint venture, as being highly fluent in both Manager D's home culture and Japanese culture. This interculturally fluent informant is Manager D's primary source of information about Japan, though his Japanese spouse and day-to-day work life also provide insight into Japan. Manager D's superior has specifically charged him to find ways to create a "third way" which will adapt German and Japanese business styles to each other.

Key Informant D: This individual appears to be an interculturally fluent informant of the same home culture as Manager D and has high management experience in the host country (Japan) with active connections to associations and institutions outside of the employing company.

Manager E: Canadian, male, CEO and entrepreneur

Manager E notes his spouse/business partner as the key figure in his adjustment to Japanese work life, though she has no experience with the work life and work culture of Canada or the English-speaking world. While Manager E's first years in Japan were informed by another Canadian with more experience, the greatest adjustment occurred as he developed his business in the context of Osaka's Japanese business environment. Now he finds himself providing guidance to other foreigners, particularly regarding the Japanese work ethic. This manager is integrated into business networks such as the Canadian Chamber of Commerce and other Japanese-foreign networks.

Key Informant E: This individual is a spouse and business partner, Japanese, with low or no intercultural fluency particularly regarding the work world outside of Japan.

Manager F: Swedish, male, CEO

Manager F notes a non-Japanese friend with high experience in Japan, as well as some Japanese individuals, as key figures in his adjustment to Japanese work and life. His level of contact with the non-Japanese individual was never high enough to provide instant input, however. Manager F is married to a non-Japanese and thus does not get instant feedback about Japan from this source either. Manager F indicates that working in Japanese business situations as the sole foreigner was the most important factor in his deep acculturation.

Key Informant F: This individual is highly familiar with Japan and the home country; however, this individual does not qualify as an interculturally fluent informant because of low accessibility.

Manager G: British, male, CEO of Japan affiliate of UK aerospace enterprise

Manager G notes a longtime friend, confidant, and business colleague as the key figure in his adjustment to Japanese work and daily life. This informant is highly bicultural, with long-term experience including education and work in both Japan and Manager G's home culture. Manager G's relationship with this informant extends many years, and contact has been frequent. This manager makes use of personal and professional networks, but these were not as important in his adjustment as the interculturally fluent informant mentioned above.

Key Informant G: This individual appears to be an interculturally fluent informant of the same home culture as Manager G.

Interview findings

Hypothesis 1: the cultural informant is in place in the lives of foreign managers.

Accepted: Despite the small scope of this study, all managers had multiple cultural informants whose knowledge they could draw on in work or daily life.

Hypothesis 2: cultural informants all largely meet the descriptive criteria presented in Table 14.1.

Rejected: It became clear during the interviews that some managers availed themselves of informants of special ability. These informants differentiated themselves from usual cultural informants through
3. their quality; and
4. their ability to interpret the host culture to the foreign manager.

The following list of characteristics of these individuals, *interculturally fluent informants,* comprises conclusions drawn from the interviews in this study and echoes points found in Thomas (1998, 2008), Schlunze (2007), Schlunze and Plattner (2007), Plattner (2008), and Moore (2009).

- Highly fluent in home and host languages
- Highly fluent in home and host work cultures
- Highly fluent in home and host life cultures

- Aware of subtle variations among groups and regions in home and host cultures
- Able to communicate, due to shared experience, accurate conceptualizations and explanations of the host culture to the foreign manager
- Embedded in social networks of home and host cultures – for example, professional associations, alumni networks, and social organizations
- Readily available and in frequent contact

Lastly, perhaps due to the close nature of the support, the foreign manager is unlikely to have more than one informant of this sort.

Thus, there appear to be at least two types of informants that significantly contribute to the experience and knowledge of the interviewees. Specifically, the interviews touch on points that match the characteristics of cultural informants (Table 14.1, above) and the interculturally fluent informant. For both types, the relationship with a key informant tends to be long-term and involve frequent contact. Additionally, both kinds of informant are readily accessible and in frequent contact with the manager. The fundamental difference between the two types lies in the interculturally fluent informant's high fluency in the host and home work cultures as well as life cultures. Generally, this type of informant appears to be uncommon, perhaps due to their unusually high level of cultural fluency, and only two of the interviewees had this sort of informant. The two interculturally fluent informants identified in this study are senior figures with long experience and deep cultural awareness.

Additional findings

Additional findings are that:

- All the interviewees had some kind of cultural informant
- Most interviewees had more than one informant providing important frequent input
- All cultural informants were clearly embedded in Japanese life, work, or both
- Interviewees A, C, and E mentioned their own involvement in social and business networks
- Interviewees A, C, D, and E mentioned spouses as cultural informants (Generally spouses provided valuable input, but in most cases they could contribute little work experience that would bridge the cultures.)
- Interviewees A, D, and E mentioned time spent in day-to-day Japanese business environments as important to their adjustment.

With the above ideas in mind, the cultural informant can be seen as part of the foreign manager's support schema in Figure 14.2.

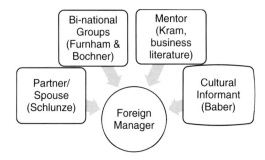

Figure 14.2 Personal support schema of a foreign manager

Next steps

Future research will concern itself with the mechanisms by which cultural informants support foreign managers' adjustment and the development of hybrid managers. Additional research may consider where in the culture shock curve or conceptual framework of the expatriate experience the cultural informant appears to be most effective. Further characterization remains to be done regarding the numbers and types of cultural informants that foreign managers may have and the nature of their interaction. Additionally, benefits foreign managers may receive from cultural informants such as acceleration of adjustment and quality of adjustment invite further investigation. These points warrant further investigation in the context of adjustment and the development of the hybrid manager.

Appendix: Interview of hybrid managers regarding cultural informant

The following four questions provided the basis for communication and follow-up questions.

1. Have you had a particular person(s) who helped you adjust to and understand the culture and life of Japan?
2. If so, were they a native of the new culture?
3. If so, what was your relationship to that person:

   friend   spouse   girl/boyfriend
   coworker   boss   other_____

4. Any further comment about how they helped:....

References

Attinasi, J., and Friedrich, P. (1995). Dialogic breakthrough: Catalysis and synthesis in life-changing dialogue. In B. Mannheim and D. Tedlock (eds), *The dialogic emergence of culture*, 33–53. Champaign: University of Illinois Press.

Bandura, A. (1977). *Social learning theory.* Englewood Cliffs, NJ: Prentice-Hall.

Baskerville-Morely, R.F. (2005). A research note: The unfinished business of culture. *Accounting, Organizations and Society* 30, 389–91.

Brisco, D.R., and Schuler, R.S. (1995). *International human resource management,* 2nd edition. New York: Routledge.

Coan, J., and Allen, J. (2007). *Handbook of emotion elicitation and assessment.* New York: Oxford University Press.

Crosby, F. (1999). The developing literature on developmental relationships. In A. Murrell, F. Crosby, and R. Ely (eds), *Mentoring dilemmas: Developmental relationships within multicultural organizations.* Mahwah, NJ: Erlbaum.

Feldman, D.C., and Bolino, M.C. (1999). The impact of on-site mentoring on expatriate socialization: A structural equation modeling approach. *International Journal of Human Resource Management* 10 (1), 54–71.

Furnham, A., and Bochner, S. (1986). *Culture shock: Psychological reactions to unfamiliar environments.* New York: Methuen.

Goodenough, W. (1973). *Culture, language, and society.* Reading, MA: Addison-Wesley.

Granovetter, M. (1985). Economic action and social structure: The problem of embeddedness. *American Journal of Sociology* 91 (3), 481–510.

Gullahorn, J.T., and Gullahorn, J.E. (1963). An extension of the U-Curve Hypothesis. *Journal of Social Issues* 19 (3), 33–47.

Gudykunst, W., and Nishida, T. (1994). *Bridging Japanese/North American differences.* Thousand Oaks: Sage Publications.

Hofstede, G. (1986). Cultural differences in teaching and learning. *International Journal of Intercultural Relations* 10, 301–20.

Hofstede, G. (2001). *Culture's consequences: Comparing values, behaviors, institutions, and organizations across nations.* Thousand Oaks: Sage Publications.

Hofstede, G., and Hofstede, J.H. (2005). *Cultures and organizations: Software of the mind.* New York: McGraw-Hill.

Hunt, R.C. (2007). *Beyond relativism: Rethinking comparability in cultural anthropology.* Lanham, MD: AltaMira Press.

ITIM International (2009). Retrieved February 25, 2009, from: www.geert-hofstede.com.

Kay, D., and Hinds, R. (2007). *A practical guide to mentoring: Play an active and worthwhile part in the development of others, and improve your own skills in the process,* 3rd edition. Oxford: How to books.

Kram, K. (1988). *Mentoring at work: Developmental relationships in organizational life.* Lanham, MD: University Press of America.

Kramsch, C. (1991). 'Culture in language learning: A view from the U.S.' *Foreign language research in cross-cultural perspective.* (Eds. K. De Bot, C. Kramsch, & R. Ginsberg). Amsterdam: John Benjamins BV.

Kramsch, C. (1996). *Context and culture in language teaching,* 3rd edition. Oxford: Oxford University Press.

Leonard, D., and Swap, W. (2005). *Deep smarts.* Boston: Harvard Business School Press.

Mead, R. (2005). *International management: Cross-cultural dimensions,* 3rd edition. Malden, MA: Blackwell Publishing.

Moore, T.M. (2009). The sojourner's truth: Exploring bicultural identity as a predictor of assignment success in American expatriates. Unpublished manuscript. North Carolina State University.

Oberg, K. (1960). Culture shock: Adjustment to new cultural environments. *Practical Anthropology* 7, 177–82.

Peltokorpi, V. (2008). Cross-cultural adjustment of expatriates in Japan. *The International Journal of Human Resource Management* 19 (9), 1588–1606.

Petersen, B. (2004). *Cultural intelligence: A guide to working with people from other cultures*. Boston: Intercultural Press.

Plattner, M. (2008). Mobile eliten im 21. jahrhundert. *JapanMarkt* 17 (12), 30–2.

Polanyi, M. (1967). *The tacit dimension*. London: Routledge and Kegan Paul Ltd.

Schlunze, R.D., and Plattner, M. (2007). Evaluating international managers' practices and locational preferences in the global city – An analytical framework. *Ritsumeikan Business Review* (ritsumeikan keiei gaku) 46 (3), 63–90.

Schlunze, R.D. (2007). Spurring the Kansai economy – Embedding foreign corporations. *Ritsumeikan International Affairs* (ritsumeikan kokusai chiiki kenkyu), 5 (6), p. 17–42.

Szkudlarek, B. (2005). Book Review: Building cross-cultural competence: How to create wealth from conflicting values. *Management Learning* 36, 518–23.

Thomas, D.C. (1998). The expatriate experience. In J.L.C. Cheng and R.B. Petersen (eds), *Advances in international comparative management*, vol. 12. Stamford and London: JAI Press.

Thomas, D.C. (2008). *Cross-cultural management*, 2nd edition. Thousand Oaks: Sage Publications.

Trompenaars, F., and Hampden-Turner, C. (1998). *Riding the waves of culture: Understanding diversity in global business*. New York: McGraw-Hill.

University of Minnesota (2009). Learning Abroad Center. Retrieved February 12, 2009, from http://www.umabroad.umn.edu/parents/preDepartureCrossCultural.html.

Ward, C., Bochner, S., and Furnham, A. (2001). *The psychology of culture shock*. Hove: Routledge.

Zachary, L. (2000). *The mentor's guide*. Hoboken, NJ: John Wiley & Sons.

Part IV
A New Perspective

15

New Geographies of Global Managerial Practice: The Case of Business Services

Andrew Jones

1. Introduction

In recent decades, economic globalization has radically transformed the ways in which firms in all sectors organize themselves and operate in the global economy (Dunning 1993; Morgan et al. 2001; Dicken 2007). Since the 1980s in particular there has been a recognition within a range of social science disciplines – notably management and business studies, economic geography and organizational sociology – that firms have been subject to a wide set of transformations linked to the intertwined transnationalization, amongst other influences, of their organizational form, operations, working practices and markets (cf. Ashkensas et al. 1995; Bartlett & Ghoshal 2002; Galbraith 2000). Whilst earlier understandings of internationalization of firms thus focused on rather narrower concepts of the multinationalization through the setting up of productive facilities in multiple countries or the acquisition of existing national champions (Cohen et al. 1979; Held et al. 1999; Morgan 2001), the nature of the transnationalization of corporate activity has shifted in new and complex ways in the last 15 years that social scientists have struggled to keep up with (Jones 2009). This has resulted in widespread debate about the respective validity of (often) competing concepts of multinational, transnational or global corporations (Doremus et al. 1998; Dicken 2003; Jones 2005) and a growing recognition of the empirical and theoretical difficulty in effectively understanding the complexity of corporate forms and activities in the contemporary global economy. Existing theories of the multinationalization of firms have thus been increasingly challenged by complex forms of 'corporate globalization' as, for example, firms restructure towards global organizational forms or implement sophisticated global production networks (Davidson & De la Torre 1989; Berggren 1996; Nohria & Ghoshal 1997; Coe et al. 2004; Dicken 2007).

However, across the social sciences – and in economic geography in particular – a small but growing 'socioeconomic' literature has begun to respond to the complexity of corporate globalization processes by examining the significance of social relations, intra- and inter-firm social networks and sociocultural practices in global economic activity (Thrift 1997; 2000; Taylor 2000; Yeung 2002; Jones 2005; Grabher & Ibert 2006). One of the key arguments emerging from this literature is that corporate globalization is producing both new kinds of global managers (Faulconbridge & Muzio 2009a) and new geographies of global managerial practice (De la Torre et al. 2000; Yeung 2005b; Palmer & O'Kane 2007; Faulconbridge & Muzio 2009b). This represents the entry point for this chapter. Its key proposition is that the emergence of both 'global managers' and 'global managerial practices' corresponds to a crucial transformation in contemporary global economy which much of the management literature has been relatively slow to engage with. Drawing on a small but growing 'management geography' literature (Gertler 2003; Yeung 2005b; Jones 2005; Gluckler 2005; Hall 2008; Comunian 2009; Faulconbridge & Muzio 2009a), it argues for an empirical and theoretical approach towards corporate globalization that seeks to understand the transnationalization of firms as a process that goes beyond the establishment of global production or office networks, or the transnational mobility of employees. Rather, it argues that corporate globalization is leading to a sea change in how firms are managed at the global scale. This equates to a whole range of complex logistical, intercultural and technological transformations that blur boundaries among firms, national economic spaces and markets. Central to these transformations are the activities of global managerial professionals who represent the key actors in the propagation of new forms of 'corporate globality' (cf. Jones 2005) that increasingly constitute firms as integrated globalized organizations rather than conglomerations of national, regional or local components. These global managers are thus increasingly at the forefront of principal wealth-generating activities undertaken by firms in the contemporary global economy.

These arguments have a series of further implications for social scientific thinking about transnationalization of firms. The chapter contends that in order to effectively conceptualize the nature of contemporary transnationalization of firms, a management geography approach – by foregrounding new geographies of global managerial practice – provides scope to generate a better understanding of how firms become successful and competitive at the transnational scale than existing approaches currently provide. It does so by engaging with the complex set of managerial practices that enable ever larger and geographically dispersed transnational firms to operate effectively. In this respect, the chapter therefore proposes a framework that seeks to conceptualize global managerial practices around four dimensions: power and control, client business acquisition and retention, knowledge management and innovation, and organizational culture and coherence. In particular, it examines how the practices around corporate control and organizational culture / coherence are bound into new and dynamic corporate geographies that present significant challenges for existing place-focused concepts of global corporate operation. The chapter illustrates the utility of such an approach in presenting research into transnational business-service firms in a number of different industries.

The rest of the chapter develops these arguments in a series of stages. The next section provides a critical overview of the key transformations associated with corporate globalization that provide the context for the emergence of new forms of managerial practice in the contemporary global economy. The key contention is that contemporary economic globalization has produced a new form of global management in the world's largest transnational firms and that this presents a series of new and unresolved challenges for corporate operation. The third section then moves on to use a 'management geography' approach to develop a framework for better theorizing the nature of global managerial practice in contemporary transnational firms. The utility of this approach is elaborated upon in the fourth section, which considers the significance of global managerial practices around corporate control and culture in the transnationalization of business-service firms over the last 20 years. To do so, it draws on more than a decade of research into the globalization of a range of business-service industries including investment banking, management consultancy, legal services, accountancy and advertising. Finally, the chapter ends by drawing together a series of concluding arguments relating to how future research into corporate globalization can benefit from a management geography perspective that foregrounds global managerial practices as a key factor in the development of global economic activity.

2. Corporate globalization: the context of developing global managerial practices

Debates about the internationalization or transnationalization of firms go back to the 1960s and earlier (Cohen et al. 1979; Bartlett & Ghoshal 1998; Held et al. 1999; Dicken 2007). However, over the last two decades the ongoing development of an increasingly interconnected global economy has produced a series of more specific arguments in the social sciences about how large firms are becoming more globalized (Morgan et al. 2001; Dicken 2007). Earlier theoretical propositions about growth in number and size of firms with multinational operations (multinational corporations, or MNCs) have been superseded by a debate about the degree to which firms have become fully transnationalized or even 'truly global' corporations (Doremus et al. 1998; Dicken 2003; Jones 2005). Disagreements about how 'corporate globality' might be defined notwithstanding (Morrison et al. 1991; Mourdoukoutas 1999; Preston & Young 2002), management theorists, economic geographers and other social scientists have become increasingly interested in processes of *organizational globalization* that have been occurring in large firms in all sectors of the economy (Bartlett & Ghoshal 1998; Galbraith 2000; Jones 2005; 2009). In this respect, a growing literature has thus consolidated the argument that economic globalization at the corporate level is producing radical changes in the nature of the world's largest firms (Dicken 2007; Yeung 2009). Also clear from studies of firms in many different industries is that organizational globalization in these firms – what can be termed *corporate globalization* – is neither a uniform nor unproblematic process and that strategies and approaches for achieving a degree of corporate globality vary enormously among firms within and across industries (Jones 2003; Palmer & O'Kane 2007; Faulconbridge & Muzio 2009a). Furthermore, and central to the arguments of this chapter, the emergence (or otherwise) of corporate globality (and the degree to which it is successful) is heavily dependent on the key role of senior managers and a range of globalized working practices (Kipping 1999; Gluckler & Armbruster 2003; Gluckler 2005; Jones 2007; 2008; Faulconbridge 2008; Hall 2006; 2008). Before I consider these practices in depth, it is necessary to examine at least two interrelated dimensions of wider corporate globalization that form the context in which global managerial practices have developed in recent decades.

The construction of globalized firms

Corporate globalization is most obviously manifest in the emergence of organizations that resemble 'global firms' in the contemporary world economy. In broad terms, there remains no consensus in the social sciences on what corresponds to a 'multinational' as opposed to either a 'transnational' or 'global corporation' (Bagchi Sen & Sen 1997; Doremus et al. 1998; Dicken 2003). Such a linear 'scaling up' corresponded to a territorially based notion of national firms 'internationalizing' and then operating increasingly across and between national economies rather than operating multiple discrete productive facilities in more and more countries (Jones 2005). As Dicken (2007) emphasizes, the development of many actual large firms does not well fit any sequential series of ideal-type models. Not all firms fit all (or in fact any) of the criteria around territorially conceived ideas of a transition from 'national' to 'transnational' operations, and the possible criteria by which corporate globality can be assessed extends beyond those issues (Jones 2005; 2007).

However, several elements of firm-level globalization are important in forming the context for the transformation of managerial practices. First, and perhaps most significant, is ongoing organizational restructuring towards 'corporate globality'. This involves the formation of business organizations that operate as a coherent single unit across the globe, rather than being divided up geographically into subunits – generally on a national or regional basis. This kind of divisional restructuring is also often accompanied by a concomitant reorganization of financial structures within these firms (Ashkensas et al. 1995; Roberts 1998; Jones 2003). These forms of restructuring are increasingly being used as a definitional basis for the concept of the 'global corporation' within a growing body of management literature (e.g. Wortzel & Wortzel 1997; Carrel et al. 2000) and writings amongst organizational sociologists (e.g. Davidson & De la Torre 1989; Mourdoukoutas 1999). Organizational restructuring achieves greater globality by uncoupling (as much as possible) functional aspects of firms' form to geographical units (Ashkensas et al. 1995; Galbraith 2000). For example, this represents a dismantling of multiple back-office divisions in every country or region in which a transnational corporation (TNC) operates and the centralization of such functions at specific 'global' locations serving a firm on the planetary scale. In that sense, 'organizational globalization' is about the reconstruction of internal divisions and departments that focus on the global operational scale rather than being delimited (and often replicated) in multiple countries (Pauly & Reich 1997; De la Torre et al. 2000; Morgan et al. 2001).

A second aspect to firm-level globalization is the way in which firms in all sectors are increasingly reorganizing themselves so they can be better integrated into globalized markets. Whilst firms have long been involved in international markets through trade and foreign direct investment in overseas productive operations (Held et al. 1999; Dicken 2007), in recent decades the growth in size and extent of the operations of transnational firms has deepened and become significantly more complex. For example, in manufacturing TNCs the evolution of increasingly complex global production networks, the development of the 'global factory', global subcontracting and outsourcing (Malmberg 2003; Coe et al. 2004; Dicken 2007) are all bound into strategies for entering new national markets, improving competitiveness against global competitors and creating more efficient global-scale production systems. Similarly, firms in service industries are equally competing increasingly in a global marketplace and reconfiguring their operations to enable them to do so (Lewis 1999; Bryson et al. 2045; Gluckler 2005; Pain 2008).

Clearly, in reality there is both enormous diversity among firms and industries in the nature of corporate structures and market integration, as well as substantial constraints as to how far internal restructuring can be carried (Bartlett & Ghoshal 1998; Preston & Young 2002) – for example, different countries will still require specific 'national-level' differences on regulatory or legal grounds. Nevertheless, what is also clear is that to implement and subsequently maintain both organizational transformation and orientation to globalized markets requires a radical transformation in the working practices of managers in these firms. Where managers previously held responsibility for geographically defined organizational divisions, managerial roles now cover functional components of firms that often cover multiple national economic spaces. The running and operation of new glo-balized firms thus has led to the reconfiguration of manager responsibilities and consequently the kinds of practices their roles require them to under-take (Gertler 2004; Depner & Bathelt 2005; Jones 2007; Faulconbridge 2008; Faulconbridge & Muzio 2009b).

New forms of globalized work

Bound into the transformation of the internal organizational architecture of firms as they globalize, corporate globalization is also producing new kinds of work in the global economy. The proposition here is that work itself is becoming globalized as a form of practice – what I term 'global work' (cf. Jones 2008) – and that this represents a new and important transformation linked to the wider globalization of economy and society. In relation to the development of global managerial practices, five major transformations in the nature of work are significant. Firstly, there are the transformations to the associations that constitute work as a set of social practices in the con-temporary world. Work at the scale of the individual is becoming bound into distantiated sets of relationships (Giddens 1990; Tomlinson 1999; Beck 2002) that are breaking down the conventional and existing conceptions of jobs, firms and labour markets. Work is becoming spatially and temporally reconstituted as a consequence of various globalization processes, which means there is a need to reconsider how it is theorized as an activity. In essence, this means developing a theoretical understanding of how work is a multiply distantiated form of social practice that is shaped by and also shapes distant entities. Work is generally understood as being undertaken by an individual (the worker) in a specific place (the workplace). Instead, in the contemporary global economy the agency to affect change by workers (the activity of work) is increasingly constituted through a network of rela-tionships that 'perforate' scales (Amin 2002) and also how the place/space in which work occurs as an activity (increasingly) exceeds a given physical location. Physical places of work are thus only one space – and, for many forms of work, an increasingly less significant one – in which work is being 'done' in the contemporary world. Work is occurring in, for example, social, technological and informational spaces that have a very different form to physical workplaces. Nowhere is this more evident than in the organiza-tional spaces of globalizing firms (Yeung 1998; Jones 2008; 2009).

Second, and following on, is the scalar transformation in the embodied practices which people undertake when they 'do' work. Workplaces need to be reconceptualized as existing across multiple spatialities, and many forms of work are also involving growing physical mobility of the workers them-selves. In many industrial sectors, a growing proportion of the labour force is undertaking new forms of work mobility including substantial increases in work-related travel and long-term working away from their home local-ity. International business managers travelling for transnational firms are the most obvious example, but in fact they represent only a small proportion of workers who are undertaking new forms of mobility associated with globalization across a diverse range of sectors[1]. Global work is also producing shifts in work-related personal movements on a daily basis in terms of commuting, home-working and travel to/from new spaces for work activities (Dale & Burrell 2008; Millar & Salt 2008; Faulconbridge & Beaverstock 2008; Beaverstock et al. 2010).

Third, the experience of doing work is changing. In other words, not only does work exceed physical workplaces and workers are more mobile, but what workers are *doing* is also changing and represents a different form of spatialized experience as a consequence of globalization. Globalization is not only an 'external' factor that produces economic pressures on firms to change their activities in response to global markets, competition, global supply chains and so forth (Sadler 1997; Coe et al. 2004; Dicken 2007) but is bound up in the way in which working practices have also been transformed by the globalization of economic activity. What a worker *does* on a day-to-day basis, for example, is being shaped by a variety of influences that increasingly span the global scale. Shift times, managerial relationships and organizational crises in distant places all impact on the minutiae and everyday details of working experience in ways that have not been the subject of theoretical attention (Elger & Smith 2005).

Fourth, the nature of the power relations within which both workers as social actors and also jobs as abstract organizational tasks are entangled is being transformed by globalization. Increasing proportions of workers in both the developed and the developing world are employed by TNCs whose management and ownership is organized at the global scale (Dicken 2007). This is producing new and complex sets of power relations in the corporate workplace. Workers in many industrial sectors are no longer accountable to managers in the same geographical locations as they are (Harvey et al. 2000; Morgan 2001; Jones 2002). Furthermore, even where lines of control are still apparently similar to the existing conception of their occurrence in relatively discrete forms within workplaces, power and control over workers is now increasingly bound into multiscalar and complex inter- and intra-organizational sets of relations. The increasingly complex geography of corporate ownership has also contributed to a transformation of power relationships between the worker and the employer. More and more workers are thus bound into sets of power relations that cannot simply be theorized within a specific location.

Fifth, the nature of work*places* themselves is being transformed. Whilst people obviously always undertake work in a given physical place at a certain time, the nature of their work needs to be understood as existing across a variety of spaces and through an actor network which includes non-human elements. Workplaces can no longer be adequately defined as discrete physical spaces (factories, offices), and in many globalizing industries the actual physical space in which work is undertaken has become increasingly insignificant in terms of affecting the outcome of working practices (cf. Debrah & Smith 2002; Taylor & Bain 2005). A globalization of work therefore has entailed enrolment of multiple contexts in the constitution of working practices themselves. These include virtual, organizational and social spaces that shape the outcomes produced by work practices (cf. Dale & Burrell 2008).

3. Conceptualizing the geographies of managerial practice

The processes of corporate globalization discussed so far have an enormous range of implications for different industries, firms and workers in the global economy, but the focus of this chapter is on an issue that has received only very limited attention to date: how corporate globalization is transforming managerial practices within firms. This specific concern draws on an identifiable shift in the interests of many economic geographers towards a concern with the concept of an economic practice itself. Economic geographical thinking about practices concerned with itself is diverse; the concept of economic practices has emerged as a central thread in the subdiscipline and in particular in work that falls within the management geography category (Yeung 2002; Ettlinger 2003; Jones 2005; Hall 2008; Comunian 2008; Faulconbridge & Muzzio 2009b). Economic geographers have utilized a broad definition of economic practices corresponding to 'stabilized, routinized, or improvised social actions that constitute and reproduce economic space' (Jones & Murphy 2010; 2011). The focus is on the practices through and within which economic actors and industrial communities embed knowledge, organize production activities and interpret and derive meaning from the world (ibid). Furthermore, of particular concern for economic geographers has been the way in which corporate globalization develops a complex set of needs and constraints around physical co-presence for corporate employees, and how the need for face-to-face interaction is balanced by other, technologically mediated economic practices in the globalizing world economy (Gertler 2003; 2004; Storper & Venables 2004; Jones 2007). A small management geography literature has thus begun to apply this perspective to managerial practices (Ettlinger 2003; Gluckler 2005; Grabher & Ibert 2006; Hall 2008; Faulconbridge & Muzio 2009b) in a way quite different to the dominant approach deployed within management studies that tends to theorize management of firms with meso-level concepts (for example, management processes and structures) that operate within the existing (but relatively simplistic) territorially based models of form and internationalization of firms (cf. Jones 2003; Dicken & Malmberg 2001; Dicken 2007). The key argument therefore is that developing a management geography approach develops a distinctly geographical theoretical understanding of how the key economic practices of managers within large transnational firms are central to ongoing processes of corporate globalization and also the success or otherwise of transnationalizing firms in all sectors of the global economy. By shifting the empirical and theoretical emphasis onto individual and collective practices by managers within and between firms, the aim is to develop more effective conceptualization of what leads to corporate growth, competitiveness and innovation in the contemporary globalized era.

I will shortly turn to examine in some depth the utility of such an approach in understanding the recent and radical changes occurring in transnational business-service firms, but before I do this, I want to outline, using a management geography perspective, a theoretical framework for thinking about the nature of global managerial practices. In this respect, I suggest that at least four different dimensions of these practices need to be conceptualized in order to capture the nature and role of managers in large transnational firms in the contemporary global economy. The significance of each of these generic dimensions of managerial practice will of course vary among firms and sectors, but the wider contention is that these attributes of practice are amongst the most significant in shaping corporate globalization as a wider phenomenon.

The first and perhaps most obvious dimension of global managerial practice concerns power and control within transnational firms. The increasing transnationalization of corporate forms requires considerable work on the part of key senior managers within firms in order for operations scattered across many physical locations at the planetary scale to be coordinated effectively. Furthermore, as transnational firms have become much larger than firms in any previous period (and indeed organizations more generally), the challenges and complexities faced by senior management in these firms are novel. Corporate globality creates a series of limitations on the capacity of senior managers to wield control over corporate activities for a range of reasons: the friction of distance, lack of co-presence with employees under management or cultural differences in subsidiary firms in multiple countries. Conceptualizing the specific nature of how control is orchestrated, how managerial power is wielded and the spatiality of the social interactions that surround these activities thus requires an understanding of the multiple practices undertaken by managers and how these are organized and coordinated at the global scale.

Second, global managerial practices are for many transnational firms central in the processes by which they both acquire and retain business as well as enter new markets. Obviously the degree to which different forms of managerial practice are important in the way firms sell their products varies enormously by industry, but what is important as firms transnationalize their businesses is the nature of practices bound up in interpersonal and social networks at the global scale that lead to firms 'doing' business. For a Chinese manufacturing firm, for example, this may be about the practices senior managers are involved with amongst actors in supply chains, distributions networks and intermediary operations in Europe or North America. In contrast, for a North American business-service firm the nature of interpersonal relations and practices senior managers engage in with key individuals in client firms is crucial (Jones 2003; 2008; Faulconbridge 2006). Yet in both cases, corporate globalization means that senior managers are embroiled in a range of practices that constitute the key activities for the firm to undertake business.

The third dimension to global managerial practices surrounds knowledge and innovation within and between firms. As the global economy has become more informational- and wealth-generation-bound in innovation and creativity (Brown & Duguid 1991; Wenger 1998; Nonaka & Teece 2001), senior managers are increasingly involved in a range of activities that affect the capacity of transnational firms to manage knowledge and foster innovation at the global scale (Coe & Bunnell 2003; Gertler 2003; Faulconbridge 2006). Whilst clearly, and as will be discussed shortly, knowledge- and innovation-related managerial practices are at the heart of many business-service firms, such practices are also important in firms in all sectors. Understanding how managerial practices may lead to more or less effective forms of knowledge management and innovative outcomes in increasingly transnational firms is thus a potentially powerful explanatory tool in better theorizing corporate operation and development.

Finally, a fourth dimension to global managerial practices concerns those practices linked to the development of global corporate culture and organizational coherence. The transnationalization of firms requires an increasing level of both infrastructure and working practice by employees to maintain organizational coherence at the global scale (cf. Morgan 2001), with the development of a common corporate culture shaping employee behaviour seen as an important aspect of maintaining coherence. Senior managers are involved in a range of practices that seek to foster certain elements of global corporate culture and produce greater organizational coherence as a consequence. The degree to which these practices are successful potentially represents an important contributor ultimately to the degree to which achieved corporate globality is achieved and thus to whether firms manage to successfully transnationalize their operations. Again, the specific nature of managerial practices enrolled in the development and maintenance of corporate coherence varies among firms and the nature of industries, but in generic terms it represents an increasingly key function of managers in transnational firms.

4. Global managerial practices in business services

Having outlined a fourfold framework for thinking about the significance of global managerial practices in the contemporary transnationalizing firms, I now want to elaborate on its utility by presenting an overview of research into the nature and significance of emerging global managerial practices in a key sector of the contemporary economy: business services. Over the last couple of decades, research has indicated that in common with other industries, business-service industries have become increasingly globalized. In general terms, since the late 1980s firms in investment banking, management consultancy, insurance, legal services, advertising and accountancy have begun to move out of nationally based markets and operations to transnational ones (Enderwick 1989; Aharoni 1993; Daniels 1993; Lewis 1999). This process has been a progressive and uneven one, varying among both different business-service industries and national economies (Bryson et al. 2004; Jones 2007; Pain 2008). However, the major drivers behind this shift are at least threefold.

First, as TNCs have developed in all industry sectors, business activity has escaped the limits of national economies and moved into new markets at the global scale (Dicken 2007). TNCs represent the major clients (i.e. the market) for business services that have followed their market and transnationalized their activity (Bryson et al. 2004). In this respect, business-service firms have had to respond to the needs of their clients for global-scale services (Majkgard & Sharma 1998; Nachum 1999; Strom & Mattson 2005; 2006). Second, within many business-service sectors such as investment banking, the globalization of markets has also been accompanied by the development of larger transnational service firms and a concomitant greater degree of corporate globality (Jones 2003; Faulconbridge & Muzio 2009a). Organic growth and acquisition of overseas firms has produced a growing number of business-service firms that are themselves transnational. These service TNCs are at the forefront of the production, distribution and consumption of services in the global economy (Bryson et al. 2004). Clearly this is entwined with the globalization of markets for these services in complex ways (Roberts 1998; Warf 2001; Miozzo & Miles 2002). Third, many business-service firms are embedded in economic globalization as key actors who have developed informational products the purpose of which is to facilitate the globalization of markets and firms in other sectors (Roberts 2006). This driver varies by industry, but certainly investment banking and management consultancy are heavily involved in providing advisory services to client firms on how to transnationalize their operations and do business in markets at the global scale. An important component of much professional business-service advice in a range of subsectors is thus concerned with helping other firms develop, for example, effective *corporate globality* (in spheres such as operations, Information Communication Technology (ICT), human resources and information management) as they transnationalize which is essential for them to compete effectively at the global scale (cf. Jones 2005).

Given the context of wider corporate globalization in business-service industries, I now draw on a body of research data collected over the last decade that considers how two specific dimensions to globalizing managerial practices have emerged in new geographical configurations. Using the framework outlined in the first part of this chapter, I do this by presenting elements of three different research projects undertaken between 1999 and 2009 that provided insight into the evolving nature of global managerial practice in investment banking, management and strategy consultancy, legal services, advertising, architecture, accountancy and information technology consultancy. The first of these projects (1999–2002) examined transnational working practices in the investment banking and management / strategy consultancy industries for firms located in leading global cities (London, New York and Tokyo). As well as secondary data sources from firms, it comprised in-depth interviews with over 80 senior managers in banks and consultancy firms. The second project examined the same issues in legal services firms based in London (2003–6) involving interviews (around 35) with senior partners and human resources directors in UK and European firms. The third body of data draws on projects that has examined the transnational business-service industry amongst small and large firms in lower-tier city regions in the UK economy (for example, Manchester, Birmingham and Belfast), using both secondary data and in-depth interviews with senior managers conducted primarily in two periods: 2001–3 and 2007–9.

Clearly, significant differences in managerial practices exist among firms in these industries, and the nature of industry and corporate globalization has evolved over the decade during which these projects were undertaken, but my proposition is that a series of common dimensions to these practices are evident.

Global practices of control in transnational services firms

When I joined [name of bank], it was only a couple of thousand people in a dozen countries – that was eight years ago. Now we have over eight thousand in something like 75 locations across 40 different countries.
                    (Director, Human Resources, UK investment bank, London)

The research I have undertaken over the last decade suggests that the kind of corporate globalization described in the extract above is producing a dramatic reconfiguration of the way in which managerial power is exercised, implemented and distributed in business services. Global managers are increasingly bound into a series of practices centred on tackling the (increasingly) difficult challenge in running transnational business-service firms. I want to make three arguments based on research into a number of industries.

The first is that the practices of strategic and managerial power in these transnational service firms are enacted by a global network of stakeholder managers, rather than being simple acts undertaken by a small number of specific senior managers in a head office. Practices of strategic control are spread through many business-service firms in a way which does not always necessitate the 'centre' being heavily involved in individual business decisions. Senior managers located in head offices do, of course, have enormous potential power, but this power is normally diffused through the transnational management hierarchy. For example, in investment banks and management consultancy firms, 'global corporate strategy' was set by (beneath Board level) 'global management committees' (cf. Jones 2002):

> *Every year, a budget is put together, which is reviewed by the Management Committee…but at a strategic level, that management committee will talk about various decisions, but in the business management perspective it is decentralised down to the front-line products and the geographies.*
>
> (Managing Director, Equities and New Issues, German investment bank, London)

> *We have a group of partners in each of the major sectors of the business who meet regularly to talk about where that part of the business is going…and how successful this has been…erm…and they feed ideas back to other partners who are courting new business. So our general strategy is informed by these meetings between the people close to the business…*
>
> (Senior Partner, US consultancy firm, New York)

In this sense, financial power is negotiated and wielded by senior management from a centralized perspective. Yet, as one director of capital markets explains below, the market context of investment banking is such that there is no written strategy for the company. Global corporate strategy is a negotiated and fluid phenomenon that emerges from across a transnational network of managers at different levels in the corporate hierarchy:

> *So global strategy is all very well, but it's really the guys with their ears to the ground who know what you should be doing. Certainly in a global firm, I can't know how the Japanese market is going medium term – or not more than partially, any case. I'd need so-and-so who sits in Tokyo…and he can certainly change strategy, yes. So it's a two-way thing to some extent…*
>
> (Director, Capital Markets, Swiss investment bank, London)

> *Individual partners and even MCs [management consultants] who are dealing with clients, who are providing the service…they have a lot of autonomy to follow a certain line of argument or take certain decisions…Making sure that process doesn't get out of sync with what the rest of the company is doing – that's the trick.*
>
> (Senior Partner, US management & strategy consultancy, Boston)

The agency's strategy is something that comes from a discussion with New York and elsewhere ... so, yes, it is not dictated from here ... you need a close sense of what is going on in other markets to make those kind of [strategic] decisions ...
(Partner, UK advertising agency, London)

The managerial practices that constitute strategic power in these firms are, therefore, not simply located in head offices or specific places, but rather demonstrate a complex geographic form through a network of managerial actors. One managing director explained it in this way:

Essentially individual centres act very much on their own initiative. We encourage quite a high degree of autonomy in the different centres, encouraging local management to use their local skills optimally. And that's proved very successful ... it requires a good degree of understanding and co-operation between the global management team. In fact, philosophically I think the company is quite keen not to create rigid lines of responsibility amongst that team ...
(Managing Director, Global Head of Money Markets, US investment bank, London / Paris)

Senior managers, who are often based in head offices, are the people who make a decision, but there is thus a considerable involvement in the practices of corporate control by junior managers who are engaged in business activity. In that sense, contrary to the image of centralized power practiced in transnational head offices, strategic power is diffused through a series of management practices undertaken by a range of managers across a firm's global operation.

Second, where senior managers do exercise 'centralized' power in transnational business-service firms, it tends to be at the global scale. They may not directly intervene in the day-to-day running of businesses by line managers in a given country or region, but their interventive power becomes apparent at the level of transnational corporate strategy:

Our world-wide managing director ... may get involved to arbitrate or because he sees something in any particular country which that particular country cannot see because he has the overview. There was a situation last month like that ... So he was able to add value, to bring global perspective and as a result, we have put additional resources onto that.
(Managing Partner, US management consultancy firm, Chicago)

No, no one makes a major decision over the phone. Obviously ... senior partners meet regularly as you might expect, and when that refers to what we are doing overseas, then that means travelling to meet the local partner ... in reality though there has to be a degree of trust, these guys [local partners] necessarily have a fair amount of autonomy.

(Senior Partner, law firm, London)

The key element of 'central' power practices is the role of 'transnational over-view'. This senior manager has power in terms of dictating what 'the wider picture' is beyond a given national context, and he is also the mediator who resolves conflicts that arise lower down in the managerial hierarchy.

Third, the consequence of these networked and diffuse managerial con-trols in business-service firms is that managerial practice in many business-service sectors is increasingly bound to different forms of mobility and ICT practices. Senior managers, rather than wielding power from a global city–based head office, spend an (often substantial) amount of time travelling (cf. Jones 2010). The practice of managerial control, whilst supported by information technologies, relies heavily on direct social contact between managers at different levels:

That's really what being a senior guy is all about. I spend most of my time on business trips. On a plane somewhere to have a meeting of regional heads, or meeting the man in Sydney who's running a project we're doing at the moment in Australia. Or my counterpart in Los Angeles. You see…well, there's no IT system in the world that will change that. IT – email, video-conferencing, tel-econferencing whatever – only helps you keep up to date. A lot of decisions are never made over the phone…
(Divisional Manager, Japanese investment bank, New York)

Even in a relatively small firm like this, there is no way with our global opera-tions that David [Divisional Head] can take direct responsibility for what the New York or Hong Kong office is doing. We are small in North America and so you have to rely on them, but globalization [of the firm]…it does also mean a lot of travel. Chatting on Skype is fine, but you have to go out there to really know what's going on, to get a feel for how they are doing…
(Senior Partner, UK advertising agency, London)

Whilst the use of ICT is bound to the practices of control, key decisions rely on senior managers flying out to branch office locations several times a year or more. Command and control, therefore, in these business-service industries at least, is by its nature a negotiated, complex and diffuse process that arises through a network of (admittedly differently empowered) scat-tered social actors. Where service-sector products are knowledge-based in this way, senior managers operating from head office locations are better understood as heading a network of people who have different inputs and a share of influence in the decision-making process.

Global corporate coherence and culture

The second example of how managerial practices are being transformed as a consequence of ongoing corporate globalization in business services concerned the role that management practice plays in fostering organi-zational coherence in a globalized firm and generating a common global corporate culture. The two forms of global managerial practice are of course intertwined as cultural issues represent one dimension to the relations and connectivities that hold firms together as their operations become more extensive in different locations around the globe. I want again to make three arguments in this respect.

First, in many business-service industries, senior managers are engaging in a range of practices that aim in one way or another to engender a common sense of corporate culture amongst employees scattered across the globe. Corporate globalization in a divisional or ownership sense does not mean that business-service firms become integrated transnational organizations. In business services, where the service product is informational and heavily reliant on employee behaviour, values and practices, this is a key challenge for managers. In seeking 'to break free from the multinational corporate model, one of the most difficult but important barriers is 'getting all of the people in the company to think and act as one' [Senior Partner, US consultancy firm, New York]. This process is especially important as corporate globalization in many business-service industries often occurs through merger-based acquisitions of foreign competitors, thus it is a challenging task:

> *There are certainly some big tasks for us. I know from past experience that mergers are not always happy marriages, and it opens up a whole number of issues about culture. Other companies do things differently, people have different values, they behave in different ways. Getting these two companies to blend together is not going to be easy, we know that. But it has to be the long-term goal.*
> (Executive Director, Corporate Finance, Anglo-German investment bank, London)

Second, for transnational business-service firms it is clear that these global managerial practices surrounding corporate culture are not just aimed at achieving a desirable goal, but are in fact essential if firms are to compete effectively in an increasingly globalized market for business services. Managers are thus increasingly involved in a range of global managerial practices whose focus is, in essence, on quality control in relation to the knowledge products that business-service firms provide to clients. Managers in legal-service firms, for example, are engaged in a variety of practices that seek to retain the high degree of behavioural consistency needed for these firms to enter new markets. For a legal-service or architecture firm the only practicable way to achieve this is for senior managers to physically base themselves in a new centre, enabling them to develop client contact networks yet ensure that employees (whether locally recruited or not) deliver a sufficiently high quality of service to clients:

> *Clearly we expect lawyers in this firm to act in a certain way...[with] a high degree of professionalism. Law requires a high degree of trust...often we are*

dealing with sensitive and of course confidential issues and it is paramount that clients trust both partners and their teams. That is true of any law firm of course, but it is true different firms have different cultures around that... we would be much more understated in our approach than an American firm, for example, and this is why we need secondments and something new trainees have to learn by experience... you can't teach it to them on a course.

(Senior Partner, law firm, Hong Kong / London)

The challenge we have with our international offices is making sure the client-side relationships are well managed... architecture is a lot about keeping the client happy by them understanding the constraints you are working with... so that is about culture, yes, it's a way of dealing with people and you need to be sensitive which is why we need our lead people to be clear on how we would expect things to be dealt with in those relationships...

(Chief Executive, UK architecture / urban design firm, Belfast)

Third, in a range of different business-service industries a growing proportion of managerial practices are becoming concerned with development of recruitment and training strategies that bring about global corporate coherence in relation to employee sense of identity as well as consistent attitudes and behaviour. Senior managers are thus increasingly involved in undertaking and organizing 'global' recruitment and training activities. For example, in investment banking, management consultancy and advertising, managers play a key role in attempts by firms to undertake global-scale training for new recruits and other employees:

I am involved with our global recruitment...each year, every cohort goes out to Chicago to our business school where we put them through our global induction course... like going back to college really: lectures and seminars every day, role-playing exercises, as well as some basic technical and numerical skills... it's also about instilling values though... [about] exposing people to the kind of mindset and ways of doing things we want in our consultants...

(Senior Partner, US management consultancy, London)

Our main offices are here and in New York, although are slowly getting somewhere in Asia... and that is an issue... the way in which people work is different in the US, say, to here [London], but you need people to have common behaviours, deal with clients or pitch in a certain way, yes... so we make sure graduates have experience of other office environments...something I think is likely to be important in the future...

(Partner, UK advertising agency, London)

This kind of global training obviously entails increased mobility for employees at all levels within transnational business-service firms, but managers are again heavily embroiled in these kinds of activities since it is managers who have the capacity and knowledge to communicate and instil the kinds of business behaviours and attitudes that firms need to propagate across a global office network. The research on various business-service industries over the last decade suggests that as firms in these sectors become more globalized, a greater proportion of management practice is being given over to these kinds of activities:

> *Everybody goes to the same place – New York – for the same training; no matter where they're from in the world: London, Hong Kong, Frankfurt...that's how we do it. Part of that, of course, is to get the technical expertise, but probably more important is to build a network. And the strategy behind this is something that has become a major part of my portfolio as this organization's overseas operations get bigger and bigger.*
>
> (Director of Human Resources [Board], US investment bank, New York)

A further aspect to managerial practices associated with global training concerns the need for knowledge-intensive business-service work for employees within firms to have good internal contact networks. Corporate globalization makes it more difficult for business-service employees to create and maintain these essential kinds of internal networks, and in several business-service industries considerable managerial effort is being expended in trying to address this challenge. In legal services, for example, the management of firms have developed overseas training secondment schemes to ensure that professional employees gain experience of working practices in a range of the firm's offices in different countries, in part so that the firm coheres through internal contact networks which would not necessarily develop in a globalizing firm without deliberate managerial intervention to facilitate them.

> *To be honest, these overseas secondments are really just a taster... it is about trainees learning what it is like to be in an office away from London, and how that works and the difficulties and so on...it is also good for the firm overall to have that through-flow of people who have been elsewhere. If everyone just sat here [in London] then I think there would be real problems in maintaining the sense of those offices being an integral part of the firm.*
>
> [paraphrased] [Senior Partner, law firm, London]

Conclusion

The goal of this chapter has been to outline the proposition that management practices are being transformed in the contemporary world and that a management geography approach which takes seriously the new and emerging geographical configuration of such practices has considerable utility in understanding the complexity of these transformations. Such an argument builds on a growing body of work within economic geography that has been concerned with relational and practice-oriented approaches towards economic activity (Yeung 2005a; Jones & Murphy 2011) and has also begun to engage with the complex challenge of conceptualizing corporate globalization in a way that moves beyond simplistic and territorially based models of internationalization of firms (Jones 2005; Dicken 2007; Faulconbridge 2006; 2008). This chapter has therefore outlined a conceptual framework for theorizing new forms of global managerial practice and how they relate to the ongoing evolution of global corporate form and transnational business activity.

However, this framework for understanding the emerging nature of corporate globality opens up a series of further issues. New transnational organizational forms and working practices correspond to two dimensions by which corporate globality might be assessed, but the degree to which firms have become globalized is a more complex and uneven issue. The research discussed considers the aspects of corporate form and managerial practice that provide evidence of the globalization of firms, but equally many aspects of organizational form and operation remain firmly embedded in national and regional contexts. The development of these elements of corporate globality thus represents a partial response by some firms in some sectors to enable them to compete more effectively in international markets. It should be emphasized, however, that these transformations do not necessarily represent the only factors shaping how firms compete at the global level and that national-level practices may remain equally crucial in generating competitive advantage. Seeking to identify and measure new forms of corporate globality thus provides an insight into the balance within transnational firms between 'global integration' and 'local responsiveness' (Bartlett & Ghoshal 2002).

In that sense, a theorization of global managerial practices does not of course represent a final or complete theory of the nature and significance of managerial actors in transnational firms. Rather, it does provide the starting point to begin to think differently about how the working practices of managers are being transformed by the globalization of firms and industries. Such a perspective offers a different set of empirical and conceptual tools to those generally used within management studies in order to understand globalization. Adopting this kind of management geography approach provides a complementary – rather than contradictory – set of conceptual tools for addressing the complex ways in which managers are involved in the globalization (or not) of corporate activity. Whilst the management literature has developed an increasingly sophisticated set of firm- and industry-level models for understanding corporate transnationalization, there has been little engagement with the difference that geographically constituted practices of key actors (i.e. global managers) make below the level of the firm in shaping corporate globality, foreign market entry and international competitiveness.

This chapter has of course developed its theoretical argument on the business-service case study discussed. It provides an illustration of the utility of this approach in understanding how corporate control and corporate culture are both increasingly key attributes of transnational business-service firms in a variety of industries which are (re)produced through a range of globalized working practices undertaken by managers. Within business-service firms, these practices represent a precariously constructed 'transnational social space' with TNCs' ability to globalize successfully via these practices being dependent on how far practices, routines, norms and values are different, transferable, adaptable or resistant to change (cf. Morgan 2001). It is therefore valuable to increasingly understand business-service TNCs as transnational communities maintained and developed by a range of global managerial practices that in some ways exhibit the dynamics of complex social systems.

Yet it is important to emphasize that the research into business-service firms also demonstrates the fragility of these forms of global managerial practice. As Morgan (2001) points out, rather than understanding TNCs as unified rational social actors they are better understood as 'spaces of social relationships that are internally structured in complex ways' (ibid.: 11). I would therefore end on a note of caution with respect to the unresolved issues that further research into global managerial practices needs to address. In particular, this chapter has not considered the degree to which the reliance on global managerial practice within transnational firms is problematic and in some cases contested and resisted (cf. Olcott 2009). Key issues include greater pressures on employees to travel, new configurations of managerial responsibility, the need to work with new transnational communities of practitioners within firms and longer-term pressures to undertake expatriate work away from the home country (cf. Beaverstock 2004; Beaverstock et al. 2010). It also draws on firms in business-service industries, and whilst there is some evidence in the literature that global managerial practices are increasingly important in manufacturing or extractive sectors (cf. Gertler 2004), the nature and significance of these practices will be potentially very different. In that respect, the arguments developed in this chapter need further, empirically based analysis in order to better understand how global managerial practices will shape the trajectories of globalizing firms in various industries in the coming decades.

Note

1   For example, see Ehrenreich's (2002) work on nannies and sex workers or Sampson & Schroeder (2006) on marine crew.

References

Aharoni, Y. (1993) Coalitions and Competition: The Globalization of Professional Business Services. (Oxford: OUP)

Amin, A. (2002) Spatialities of globalisation. *Environment & Planning A* 24: 385–99

Ashkenas, R., Ulrich, D., Jick, T., & Kerr, S. (1995) The Boundaryless Organization: Breaking the Chains of Organizational Structure. (San Francisco: Jossey-Bass)

Bagchi-Sen, S. & Sen, J. (1997) The current state of knowledge in international business in producer services. *Environment & Planning A* 29: 1153–74

Bartlett, C. & Ghoshal, S. (2002) Managing across Borders: The Transnational Solution. 2nd Edition. (Harvard, MA: Harvard University Press)

Beaverstock, J. (2004) 'Managing across borders': Knowledge management and expatriation in professional legal service firms. *Journal of Economic Geography* 4: 1–25

Beaverstock, J., Derudder, B., Faulconbridge, J., & Witlox, F. [eds] (2010) International Business Travel in the Global Economy. (Aldershot: Ashgate)

Beck, U. (2002) The Brave New World of Work. (Cambridge: Polity)

Berggren, C. (1996) Building a truly global organization? ABB and the problems of integrating a multi-domestic enterprise. *Scandinavian Journal of Management* 12 (2): 123–37

Brown, J. & Duguid, P. (2001) Knowledge and organization: A social-practice perspective. *Organization Science* 12 (2): 198–213

Bryson, J., Daniels, P., & Warf, B. (2004) Service Worlds: People, Organizations, Technologies. (London: Routledge)

Carrell, M., Elbert, N., & Hatfield, R. (2000) Human Resource Management: Global Strategies for Managing a Diverse Workforce. 6th Edition. (San Diego: The Dryden Press)

Coe, N., Hess, M., Yeung, H., Dicken, P., & Hendersen, J. (2004) 'Globalizing' regional development: A global production networks perspective. *Transactions of the Institute of British Geographers* 29 (4): 468–84

Coe, N. & Bunnell, T. (2003) 'Spatialising' knowledge communities: Towards a conceptualisation of transnational innovation networks. *Global Networks* 3 (4): 437–56

Cohen, R., Felton, N., Nkosi, M., & van Liere, J. [eds] (1979) The Multinational Corporation: A Radical Approach: Papers by Stephen Herbert Hymer. (Cambridge: CUP)

Comunian, R. (2008) Culture Italian style: Business and the arts. *Journal of Business Strategy* 29 (3): 37–44

Dale, K. & Burrell, G. (2008) The Spaces of Organisation and the Organisation of Space. (Basingstoke: Palgrave Macmillan)

Daniels, P. (1993) Service Industries in the World Economy. (Oxford: Blackwell)

Davidson, W. & De la Torre, J. (1989) Managing the Global Corporation: Case Studies in Strategy and Management. (New York; London: McGraw-Hill)

Debrah, Y. & Smith, I. [eds] (2002) Globalization, Employment and the Workplace: Diverse Impacts. (London: Routledge)

De la Torre, J., Doz, Y., & Devinney, T. (2000) Managing the Global Corporation. (New York: McGraw-Hill)

Depner, H. and Bathelt, H. (2005) Exporting the German model: The establishment of a new automobile industry cluster in Shanghai. *Economic Geography* 81 (1): 53–81.

Dicken, P. (2003) 'Placing' firms: Grounding the debate on the 'global' corporation. In Peck, J. & Wai-cheung, Y. [eds], Remaking the Global Economy, pp. 27–44. (London: Sage)

Dicken, P. (2007) Global Shift: Reshaping the Global Economic Map in the 21st Century. 5th Edition. (London: Sage)

Dicken, P. & Malmberg, A. (2001) Firms in territories: A relational perspective. *Economic Geography* 77: 345–64

Doremus, P., Keller, W., Pauly, L., & Reich, S. (1998) The Myth of the Global Corporation. (Chichester: Princeton University Press)

Dunning, J. (1993) The Globalization of Business. (London: Routledge)

Ehrenreich, B. & Hochschild, A. [eds] (2002) Global Women: Nannies, Maids and Sex Workers in the New Economy. (Cambridge: Granta)

Elger, T. & Smith, C. (2005) Assembling Work: Remaking Factory Regimes in Japanese Multinationals in Britain. (Oxford: OUP)

Enderwick, E. (1989) Multinational Service Firms. (London: Routledge)

Ettlinger, N. (2003) Cultural economic geography and a relational microspace approach to trust, rationalities, networks and change in collaborative workplaces. *Journal of Economic Geography* 3: 145–71

Faulconbridge, J. (2006) Stretching tacit knowledge beyond a local fix? Global spaces of learning in advertising professional service firms. *Journal of Economic Geography* 6: 517–40

Faulconbridge, J. (2008) Negotiating cultures of work in transnational law firms. *Journal of Economic Geography* 8: 497–517

Faulconbridge, J. & Muzio, D. (2009a) Legal education, globalization and cultures of professional practice. *Georgetown Journal of Legal Ethics* 21: 1335–59

Faulconbridge, J. & Muzio, D. (2009b) The financialisation of large law firms: Situated discourses and practices of reorganization. *Journal of Economic Geography* 9: 641–61

Faulconbridge, J.R. & Beaverstock, J.V. (2008) Geographies of international business travel in the professional service economy. In Hislop, D. [ed.], Mobility, Technology and the Workplace, pp. 99–121. (London: Routledge)

Galbraith, J.R. (2000) Designing the Global Corporation. (San Francisco: Jossey-Bass)

Gertler, M. (2003) Tacit knowledge and the economic geography of context, or the indefinable tacitness of being (there). *Journal of Economic Geography* 3: 75–99

Gertler, M. (2004) Manufacturing Culture: The Institutional Geography of Industrial Practice. (Oxford: OUP)

Giddens, A. (1990) Modernity and Self-Identity: Self and Society in the Late Modern Age. (Cambridge: Polity)

Gluckler, J. (2005) Making embeddedness work: Social practice institutions in foreign consulting markets. *Environment and Planning A*, 37 (10): 1727–50

Gluckler, J. & Armbruster, T. (2003) Bridging uncertainty in management consulting: The mechanisms of trust and networked reputation. *Organization Studies* 24: 269–97

Grabher, G. (2006) Trading routes, bypasses, and risky intersections: Mapping the travels of 'networks' between economic sociology and economic geography. *Progress in Human Geography* 30 (2): 163–89

Grabher, G. & Ibert, O. (2006) Bad company? The ambiguity of personal knowledge networks. *Journal of Economic Geography* 6: 251–71

Hall, S. (2006) What counts? Exploring the production of quantitative financial narratives in London's corporate finance industry. *Journal of Economic Geography* 6 (5): 661–78

Hall, S. (2008) Geographies of business education: MBA programmes, reflexive business schools and the cultural circuit of capital. *Transactions of the Institute of British Geographers* 33 (1): 27–41

Harvey, M., Novicevic, M., & Speier, C. (2000) Strategic global human resource management: The role of inpatriate managers. *Human Resource Management Review* 10 (2): 153–75

Held, D., McGrew, A., Goldblatt, D., & Perraton, J. (1999) Global Transformations: Politics, Economics and Culture. (Cambridge: Polity)

Jones, A. (2002) The global city misconceived: The myth of 'global management' in transnational service firms. *Geoforum* 33 (3): 335–50

Jones, A. (2003) Management Consultancy and Banking in an Era of Globalization. (Basingstoke: Palgrave Macmillan)

Jones, A.M. (2005) Truly global corporations? The politics of organizational globalization in business-service firms. *Journal of Economic Geography* 5: 177–200

Jones, A. (2007) More than 'managing across borders?' The complex role of face-to-face interaction in globalizing law firms. *Journal of Economic Geography* 7: 223–46

Jones, A. (2008) The rise of global work. *Transactions of the Institute of British Geographers* 33 (1): 12–26

Jones, A. (2009) Theorising global business space. *Geografisker Annaler B: Human Geography* 91 (3): 203–18

Jones, A. (2010) Understanding mobility in professional business services. In Beaverstock, J., Derudder, B., Faulconbridge, J., & Witlox, F. [eds], International Business Travel in the Global Economy, pp. 195–216. (Aldershot: Ashgate)

Jones, A. & Murphy, J. (2010) Economic geography and practice. *Geography Compass* 4 (4): 303–19

Jones, A. & Murphy, J. (2011) Theorizing practice in economic geography: Foundations, challenges, and possibilities. *Progress in Human Geography* 35 (3): 366–92

Kipping, M. (1999) American Management Consulting Companies in Western Europe, 1920 to 1990: Products, Reputation, and Relationship. *The Business History Review* Vol. 73, No. 2 (Summer, 1999), pp.190-220

Lewis, M. [ed.] (1999) The Globalization of Financial Services. (Cheltenham: Edward Elgar)

Majkgard, A. & Sharma, D. (1998) Client-following and market-seeking strategies in the internationalization of service firms. *Journal of Business-to-Business Marketing* 4 (3): 1–41

Malmberg, A. (2003) Beyond the cluster – local milieus and global connections. In Peck, J. & Yeung, H. [eds], Remaking the Global Economy, pp. 145–59. (London: Sage)

Millar, J. & Salt, J. (2008) Portfolios of mobility: The movement of expertise in transnational corporations in two sectors: aerospace and extractive industries. *Global Networks* 8: 25–50

Miozzo, M. & Miles, I. [eds] (2002) Internationalization, Technology and Services. (Cheltenham: Edward Elgar)

Morgan, G. (2001) The multinational firm: Organizing across institutional and national divides. In Morgan, G., Kristensen, P., & Whitley, R. [eds], The Multinational Firm: Organizing across Institutional and National Divides, pp. 1–26. (Oxford: OUP)

Morgan, G., Kristensen, P., & Whitley, R. [eds] (2001) The Multinational Firm: Organizing across Institutional and National Divides. (Oxford: OUP)

Morrison, A., Ricks, D., & Roth, K. (1991) Globalization versus regionalization: Which way for the multinational? *Organizational Dynamics* 19: 17–19

Mourdoukoutas, P. (1999) The Global Corporation: The Decolonization of International Business. (London: Quorum)

Nachum, L. (1999) The Origins of the International Competitiveness of Firms: The Impact of Location and Ownership in Professional Service Industries. (Cheltenham: Edward Elgar)

Nohria, N. & Ghoshal, S. (1997) The Differentiated Network: Organizing Multinational Corporations for Value Creation. (San Francisco: Jossey-Bass)

Nonaka, I. & Teece, D. [eds] (2001) Managing Industrial Knowledge: Creation, Transfer and Utilization. (London: Sage)

Olcott, G. (2009) Conflict and Change: Foreign Ownership and the Japanese Firm. (Cambridge: CUP)

Pain, K. (2008) Spaces of practice in advanced business services: Rethinking London-Frankfurt relations. *Environment and Planning D: Society and Space* 26 (2): 264–79

Palmer, M. & O'Kane, P. (2007) Strategy as practice: Interactive governance spaces and the corporate strategies of retail transnationals. *Journal of Economic Geography* 7 (4): 515–35

Pauly, L. & Reich, S. (1997) National structures and multinational corporate behaviour: Enduring differences in the age of globalization. *International Organization* 51: 1–30

Preston, A. & Young, J. (2002) Constructing the global corporation and corporate constructions of the global: A picture essay. *Accounting, Organisations and Society* 25: 427–49

Roberts, J. (1998) Multinational Business Service Firms: The Development of Multinational Organisational Structures in the UK Business Services Sector. (Aldershot: Ashgate)

Roberts, J. (2006) Internationalization of management consultancy services: Conceptual issues concerning the cross-border delivery of knowledge intensive services. In Harrington, J. & Daniels, P. [eds], Knowledge-Based Services, Internationalization and Regional Development, pp. 101–24. (Aldershot: Ashgate)

Sadler, D. (1997) The role of supply chain management strategies in the 'Europeanization' of the automobile production system. In Lee, R. & Wills, J. [eds], Geographies of Economies, pp. 311–21. (London: Arnold)

Sampson, H. & Schroeder, T. (2006) In the wake of the wave: Globalization, networks, and the experiences of transmigrant seafarers in northern Germany. *Global Networks* 6 (1): 61–80

Schoenberger, E. (1997) The Cultural Crisis of the Firm. (Oxford: Blackwell)

Storper, M. & Venables, A. (2004) Buzz: Face-to-face contact and the urban economy. *Journal of Economic Geography* 4 (4): 351–70

Strom, P. & Mattsson, J. (2005) Japanese professional business services: A proposed analytical typology. *Asia Pacific Business Review* 11 (1): 49–68

Strom, P. & Mattsson, J. (2006) Internationalization of Japanese professional business service firms. *Service Industries Journal* 26 (3): 249–65

Taylor, M. (2000) Enterprise, power and embeddedness: An empirical exploration. In Vatne, E. & Taylor, M. [eds], The Networked Firm in a Global World, pp. 199–233. (Ashgate: Aldershot)

Taylor, P. & Bain, P. (2005) 'India calling to the far away towns': The call centre labour process and globalization. *Work, Employment and Society* 19 (2): 261–82

Thrift, N. (1997) The rise of soft capitalism. *Cultural Values* 1: 29–57

Thrift, N. (2000) Performing cultures in the new economy. *Annals of the Association of American Geographers* 90 (4): 674–92

Tomlinson, J. (1999) Globalization and Culture. (Cambridge: Polity)

Warf, B. (2001) Global dimensions of US legal services. *Professional Geographer* 53: 398–406

Wenger, E. (1998) Communities of Practice: Learning, Meaning and Identity. (Cambridge: CUP)

Wortzel, H. & Wortzel, L. [eds] (1997) Strategic Management in the Global Economy. (Chichester: Wiley)

Yeung, H. (1998) The social-spatial constitution of business organizations: A geographical perspective. *Organization* 5: 101–28

Yeung, H. (2002) Entrepreneurship and the Internationalization of Asian Firms. (Cheltenham: Edward Elgar)

Yeung, H. (2005a) Rethinking relational economic geography. *Transactions of the Institute of British Geographers* 30: 37–51

Yeung, H. (2005b) The firm as social networks: An organizational perspective. *Growth & Change* 36 (3): 307–28

Yeung, H. (2009) Transnationalizing entrepreneurship: A critical agenda for economic geography. *Progress in Human Geography* 32 (2): 210–35

16
Location-Based Service Innovation Technologies in Japan: A Survey and Critical Analysis

Nathaniel O. Agola

Location-based service innovation technologies have the distinctive characteristic of unrivaled lifting of limitations of time and geographical distance not only within nations, but across national borders. Little extant research has focused on providing a critical analysis of location-based service innovation technologies with regard to the sources of the innovations, associated value creation impact and perhaps bottlenecks to further progress and innovations. This chapter provides a survey and a critical analysis of location-based service innovation technologies in Japan to further understanding of the technologies. The findings of this research are that whereas the location-based service innovation technologies have great economic value creation potential, the lack of major platforms on which services falling under similar categories can be launched and sustained limits the progress of these technologies. Thus the ineffective, fractious nature of both services and markets remains as the most critical inhibition to further progress in location-based service innovations in Japan. In addition, social, legal and institutional bottlenecks are highlighted as barriers to progress of the location-based service innovation technologies.

Introduction

First and foremost, a clear understanding of location-based service technologies requires defining what location-based services (LBS) mean. Little research has been done in the area of location-based services with a focus on what drives the innovations, the value creation impact and inhibitions to further expansion. In essence, a business model for understanding these innovations is generally lacking. On the other hand, much research has focused on information technology and communications media with a bias on the technical aspects and software applications that are behind development of location-based services (see Bricombe and Li 2009, Kupper 2005, Kolodziej and Hjelm 2006, Gartner et al. 2009, Hjelm 2002, Schiller and Voisard 2004). Various alternating reference terms such as 'location-based services', 'location-aware services' and 'location-related services' have been used by different service developer and user communities, thus making a succinct understanding difficult. The main communities behind these service descriptions have been the telecommunications and ubiquitous computing communities.

Perhaps a clear definition and description of location-based services can emerge only out of reference to ordinary business initiatives. Kupper (2005: 2–4) gives a simplified and comprehensive perspective to location-based services premised on business initiatives. As such, location-based services can be understood in terms of the context-awareness nature of these services. Therefore, LBS can be defined as those services that are based on adapting service attributes based on the context of potential service user or target. It is therefore notable that even though information and communication services technologies are responsible for bringing location-based services to the forefront, such services have been in existence since mass mobility of people became a reality, albeit on a limited basis.

An example of location-based services that have been in use even before the onset and wide use of information and communication technologies is the advertising announcements in city-commuter buses in Japan. Information about specific service providers are given based on their location. This is such that just before arriving at a particular bus stop, an announcement is made about for instance a restaurant, a shop or any other service in the vicinity of the bus stop. In terms of value addition of this context-aware service, informational awareness is its main contribution. The value addition magnitude in this case is contingent on relevance chance and memory positioning. Therefore coincidence of timely need for service proposed in the voice advertisement and possible future need are the variables critical to the value addition role of such basic LBS. Chances are quite high that very few people pay attention to the announcements even when alighting at a stop right next to the advertised service provider.

On the other hand, information and telecommunication technologies use context-awareness by exploiting the location of the target to give presumably a wide range of service selections such as traffic jam information for drivers, temperature information, and sales offerings from nearby merchandisers. The contrast with the earlier variety of location-based service in the Japanese city buses lies mainly in scope, though limitation still exists with regard to value addition. This is mainly because the accuracy of service offering based on location of target is a very much a generalized concept premised on generalized assumptions of need and accompanying behavior. This is in sync with theory of affordance, which combines location details

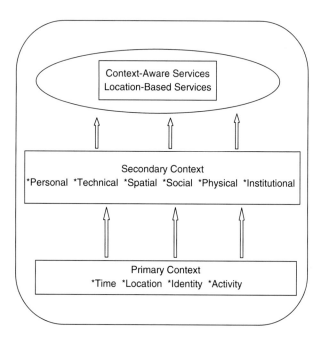

Figure 16.1   Comprehensive model for understanding location-based services as context-awareness value addition services

with possibilities of action by the user (see Hagerstrand 1970, Adams 2000). It is still quite difficult to zero in on the details of the target such as age, gender, personal taste and shopping habits and to combine these with location specifics and precise, timely need. Perhaps the difficulty does not lie only in technical capability limitations, but is rather connected to the wider social values and norms as well. It is therefore important to present a comprehensive model for understanding location-based services as context-awareness value addition services. Figure 16.1 gives an illustration of such a comprehensive model based on a modification of Kupper's (2005: 2) context awareness and location-based services depiction.

It was necessary to add the institutional context as a subset of the secondary context to the model and conception of the context awareness out of recognition of the role and impact of institutional rules and industrial organization systems on any new service innovations. Institutional rules may be related to licensing, regulations and laws required to deliver a service or in certain cases just certain aspects of a service such as personal privacy rules. Industrial organizational systems become relevant where complementary or support services from other businesses are a critical and integral part of service production, intermediation and delivery.

Location-based service technologies in Japan

Little extant research has focused on providing a critical analysis of location-based service innovation technologies in Japan with regard to the sources of the innovation, the value creation impact and perhaps the bottlenecks facing the progress of the technology. Like in other industrialized countries where there has been much progress in the introduction and use of location-based services, research focus in Japan has remained locked on hardware, technical aspects and software applications driving the services. Therefore, this is pioneer research based on literature review focusing on location-based services in Japan as market-oriented innovations and not mere technology innovations. While there are a large variety of location-based services in Japan, the large variety itself makes it hard to vividly understand the nature of the innovations, the value creation impact and any existing inhibitions facing these services. A logical attempt at classification is the first step towards furthering knowledge about the innovations and services. In addition, subjecting these service innovations to a general analytical model of innovations may shed light on the nature of value innovation and any extant inhibition to further progress (note that it is not logical or possible to separate the services and the hardware technologies).

A taxonomy of location-based services in Japan

A logical classification can be based on the nature of the innovations and services and on user/activity categories. Based on the nature of the innovations and services, we can identify *reactive* services, which are activated by users. The users initiate a service session through a mobile device terminal and then get whatever service they are in need of. A case in point is when someone searches for a nearby specific restaurant or gas station. Japanese mobile phone provider Docomo introduced the first such service in Japan and was later followed by other phone carriers. Then, there are the *proactive* location-based services, which use devices such as cellular phones or car navigation systems to automatically trigger a message of service offering at specific locations to the bearer of the electronic device. This is an informational value addition or simply an advertisement of a commercial offering. For instance, tourists can be informed of certain landmarks and sightseeing spots when they draw close to such locations.

Another classification can be based on user/activity categories. This method generates quite a long list of services, which can be confusing. Therefore the previous method is more convenient because it can be used to summarize LBS to a mere two categories of services. Among the services offered are location-based gaming, location-based dating, location-based media services, navigation services, tracking services for both objects and

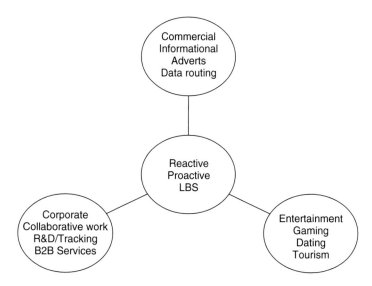

Figure 16.2   A taxonomy of location-based services in Japan

people, location-based coordination of work, location-based advertisements, enquiry and information services, data routing services, and corporate R&D services. Figure 16.2 summarizes the taxonomy of location-based services in Japan.

The most well known LBS are the mobile phone location-based services in Japan. This is partly because of the portability and technical capabilities of mobile phones to efficiently provide timely access to information and to allow users to initiate service sessions. Mobile phone location-based services are widely known, to the point of being synonymous with location-based services, which may be attributed to the various business news media channels' wide coverage of services offered on mobile devices. As such, mobile phone LBS have eclipsed other service offerings via PC and other terminals like car navigation systems with regard to being publicly known. Navigational services were the first to gain much attention, with NTT Docomo's i-mode being the most widely used and known LBS in Japan. Currently such services have been extended to include general train travel, business, entertainment, commercial informational and advertisement services by all the mobile phone carriers. Below is a list of some of the most popular mobile LBS.

1. *Norikae annai* – train/navigational services
2. Eco-navigation – information for daily life
3. Area business informational services – outline of business services, business trends, business plans and user perspective

4. Maps for business-to-business applications – KDDI's GPS map service, iGPS cargo, DoComo's LBS development kit, SAP & KDDI LBS services, LBS revenue control services

Analytical model of location-based services innovations

To understand the nature of innovations, we use the four dimensions space of innovation of Tidd and Bessant (2009: 20–39). The four dimensions space of innovation model is the best analytical tool of choice here due to the comprehensive nature of this model. Through this model, we are able to capture all value addition aspects of the innovations. We are not limited to the variables, actions and innovations within corporate boundaries, but also get the chance to examine variables and developments outside companies that are also quite critical for success of the innovations. It is notable that the innovations in question here are service innovations that are inseparable from the products which are used to deliver the services (devices and applications). Lumping services and products making delivery possible is simply unavoidable and logical; thus no analytical attention is given to the products through which LBS are either delivered or facilitated. Figure 16.3 presents an illustration of the four dimensions of innovation space as applied to LBS.

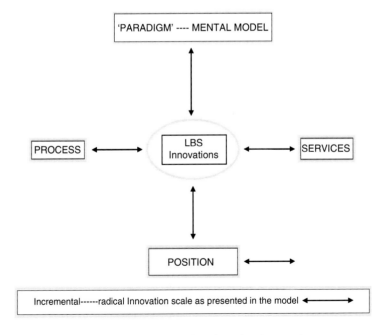

Figure 16.3 Four dimensions of location-based services innovation space

We can map the innovation space of the LBS in Japan based on the above model, premised on the understanding that the innovations may be incremental (providing a service that has been in existence, but only in a better way), platform innovation (an innovation upon which a family of other services can be extended) or radical or discontinuous innovation (game-changing innovations which alter several if not all rules of service offering and mode of operation in the markets (Tidd and Bessant 2009: 26–36).

It is notable that some of the LBS innovations are incremental improvements which represent better ways of doing things than before. The case of informational services of product offerings in a proactive way depending on location represents a better way of doing things than the location-based audio-advertisements in the city buses. So far the mobile device advertisement offerings have not approached the radical innovation level due to both technology limitations and socio-institutional context requirements. It would require a paradigm shift at the individual, social and institutional level to settle privacy issues of concern that stand in the way of personalized commercial informational services. Such a scenario would hold even in the event of technological innovations with technical capabilities affording accurate personalization of commercial informational services.

The corporate services related to R&D collaborative work do represent a radical departure from previous organizational models and ways of thinking. These services are perhaps aided by the paradigm shift in way of thinking about how to organize R&D in some of the major innovative companies. The open innovation movement (see Chesbrough 2003) represents a radical innovative departure which due to its compelling proposition adds to the momentum set by the collaborative R&D LBS initiative. However, as compared to individual end-user LBS such as gaming, dating, tourism and tracking, corporate R&D LBS remain under-used if not outright underdeveloped. The further development and extension of this type of LBS requires not only innovation of services, but also a change in way of thinking (paradigm shift) at the corporate decision-making level, the organizational level and the entire industrial organizational level.

It is notable that a major LBS platform innovation upon which various service innovations and offerings could be developed by emerging industry players has not emerged. Most of the LBS innovations are stand-alone types of innovations, with a single predominant service supplier surrounded by a network of customers. Even in the case of corporate services offered by a major LBS such as NTT Docomo's revenue-collection service to other LBS players, the model tends away from a pure platform to one service offering to different players; thus what appears to be a platform is merely a galaxy of corporate clients and a single supplier. As such, a major player like Docomo has not managed to have its LBS translated into a major platform serving as the launching pad and hub for LBS in Japan.

Conclusion

Though research on business-related LBS is in the infant stage, certain clarities have begun to emerge regarding the nature, taxonomy and pertinent issues facing LBS in Japan. From the LBS taxonomy used in this research, we can further our understanding of LBS innovations in Japan, while the analytical model also furnishes us with clear understanding of the attributes of the innovations and thus we can glean the economic possibilities and limitations. We also note that LBS innovations represent a big economic potential not only by way of doing things better, therefore adding value; but also by creating radically new value if not a totally new industrial category. The lack of innovation platform nature of LBS in Japan is itself a hindrance to the further progress and innovation of services. Creating an LBS platform in itself is a major innovation that requires multidimensional innovation on the four fronts in Figure 16.2. A paradigm shift (as one of the four dimensions) is a requisite condition for LBS innovations to progress further. Such a paradigm shift is mainly related to socio-institutional inhibitions to LBS innovations. From the results of this study we can understand the critical issues in LBS development not only in other Asian countries, but also globally.

References

Adams, P. (2000) Application of a CAD-based accessibility model. In D.G. Janelle and D.C. Hodge (eds), Information, Place and Cyberspace: Issues in Accessibility. Springer, Berlin.

Brimicombe, A., and Li, C. (2009) Location-Based Services and Geo-Information Engineering: Mastering GIS Technology Applications & Management. John Wiley & Sons.

Chesbrough, H. (2003) The Era of Open Innovation. *MIT Sloan Management Review* 44 (3): 35.

Kupper, A. (2005) Location-Based Services: Fundamentals and Operations. John Wiley & Sons.

Hagerstrand, T. (1970) What about people in regional science? *Papers of the Regional Science Association* 24: 7–21.

Kolodziej, K.W., and Hjelm, J. (2006) Local Positioning Systems: LBS Applications and Services. CRC Press.

Gartner, G., Cartwright, W., and Peterson, M.P. (2009) Location Based Services and TeleCartography. Springer, Berlin Heidelberg.

Hjelm, J. (2002) Creating Location Services for the Wireless Web. John Wiley & Sons.

Schiller, J., and Voisard, A. (2004) Location-Based Services. Morgan Kaufmann, San Francisco.

Tidd, J., and Bessant, J. (2009) Managing Innovation: Integrating Technological, Market, and Organizational Change, fourth edition. John Wiley & Sons.

17
Space Oddity – On Managerial Decision Making and Space

Patrik Ström and Roger Schweizer

Introduction and purpose of the study

How managers reason, judge, and decide where to internationalize their businesses – for example, what new market to enter or where to (re)locate production – has been a central question in the literature on internationalization of firms since the early 1970s. As argued in the research review below, the disciplines of international business and economic geography offer various streams of research, all of which focus on different elements of this complex assessment and thereby also propose different explanations for firms' decisions related to geographical space and context. In this paper, space and context will be used interchangeably. A similar jigsaw exists regarding the question of how a firm's local geographical context influences the above-mentioned decisions. Despite 40 years of research, this complexity in decision making has not been adequately mirrored in the prevailing research streams dealing with various aspects relating to a firm's international expansion in geographic space. We still grope about in the dark. We still lack studies that attempt to provide a holistic view on what is important for managers making these decisions. For example, when managers decide to establish a subsidiary in the United States, Asia, or Europe, what do they prioritize? What are they consciously and/or unconsciously considering in this decision-making process and why?

The overall purpose of the study is to increase our knowledge on how managers reason and judge when making international venture decisions. In the process, we emphasize the impact of the geographical context – both in terms of the environment in which the decision is made and in terms of the institutional setting in which the potential international venture is located. More specifically, using anecdotal case evidence of Japanese and Swedish firms' decision making related to their internationalization, the study aims to confront examples of reality with various streams of research in international business and economic geography. This study thereby intends to develop a conceptualization that mirrors the complexity decision makers face when they decide on subjects related to geographic space.

While the study contributes to, and participates in, various ongoing discourses on decision making related to international ventures (e.g. how does institutional embeddedness influence decisions? And why do knowledge-intensive clusters or regional innovation systems occur/exist?), most important, the study promises to work as an important bridge between the hitherto still relatively separated research disciplines of international business and economic geography.

The rest of the paper is structured as follows. First, the literature review provides an overview of the different theoretical streams of research. Second, a conceptual approach is proposed as a way of categorizing the different theories. Third, the paper consists of an empirical part wherein data on internationalization of knowledge-intensive firms in Sweden and Japan show the complexity of issues influencing decisions. The next section elaborates on the conceptual framework and empirical examples and offers potential areas for further study. The final section offers a conclusion.

Literature review

The *economic approach* to the internationalization process puts much emphasis on explaining why internationalization takes place. This approach has its base in mainstream economics; examples are internalization theory (INT) (Buckley and Casson, 1976), transaction-cost theory (TC) (Hennart, 1982), and the eclectic paradigm (Dunning, 1988). INT theory shares some roots with TC theory. The monopoly advantage a firm enjoys is taken abroad to foreign markets with the aim of ultimately controlling competition in that market. The route to such control is through internalization of a firm's resources (Bhowmick, 2004). Hence, advocates of these approaches define internationalization as the internalization of resources in optimal foreign locations selected by minimum transaction cost considerations. The eclectic paradigm is best regarded as a framework to explain the extent, form, and pattern of international production (Dunning, 1988). This approach is founded on the juxtaposition of the ownership-specific advantages of firms contemplating foreign production, the propensity to internalize cross-border markets for these, and the attractions of a foreign market for the production. Therefore, internationalization is seen as a rational decision to enter into a new market based on an analysis of the costs involved, depending on the interplay between ownership-specific advantages, locational attractions of countries, and internalization advantages.

In contrast, rather than explaining the reasons behind internationalization decisions, the concern of researchers within the *behavioral approach* has been to understand the forces underlying the internationalization process of firms. In other words, they put emphasis on what forms and/ or how internationalization takes place. Within the behavioral approach, internationalization can be defined as "the process of increasing involvement in international operations" (Welch and Luostarinen, 1988: 36). The most important behavioral approach to internationalization is the Uppsala model by Johanson and Vahlne (1977). Johanson and Vahlne proposed a view on the internationalization of firms by anticipating that a firm's accumulated knowledge influences its ability to recognize foreign business opportunities. This implies that a firm's lack of market knowledge hampers its ability to detect foreign market opportunities. Therefore, the firm tends to adopt an incremental internationalization process in which it chooses to enter countries displaying similar characteristics. Gradually, a firm will develop knowledge from its experiences supporting the firm in its further internationalization. Johanson and Vahlne's (1977) model has been the starting point for several studies on the internationalization of firms (e.g. Hohenthal, 2001; Choi, 2001). The focus of these more recent studies has been mainly on the barriers a firm encounters when entering new markets as well as on how to overcome these barriers.

The *network approach* is closely interlinked with the behavioral approach and shares several common assumptions about the firm. The network perspective on internationalization focuses on the long-term business relationships that exist between firms in industrial markets (Björkman and Forsgren, 2000). Advocates of the network approach focus on how a firm's business network influences the firm's entry into a foreign market. This is in contrast to the Uppsala model, which focuses on the individual firm as the driving force to internationalization. The network perspective draws attention to the social and cognitive ties formed between firms as well as other actors engaged in business relationships, and it emphasizes how interactions between the firms and actors improve our understanding of the factors behind the internationalization process.

A more recent effort to explain firms' internationalization process is generally referred to as *born globals* (Rennie, 1993) or *international new ventures* (Oviatt and McDougall, 1994). This stream of research has its origin in empirical observations that many firms today – not at least particularly in high-tech niche industries – increasingly internationalize, and do so rapidly, not as gradually and on a step-by-step basis as the Uppsala internationalization model suggests. In contrast, in today's business environment, many firms choose a swifter, dramatic strategy for their international expansions, using a range of market entry modes in multiple markets. McDougall and Oviatt (2000) described such behavior as entrepreneurial, thereby identifying *international entrepreneurship* as an emerging field of study positioned at the intersection of international business and the literature on entrepreneurship. McDougall and Oviatt (2000: 903) define the concept of international entrepreneurship as the "... combination of innovative, proactive and risk-seeking behavior that crosses national borders and is intended to create value in organizations." The latest trend in the literature is to see internationalization not merely as the action of crossing borders, but rather as an outcome of the efforts of entrepreneurs or managers performing entrepreneurial activities to improve their companies' operations and investments (Schweizer et al., 2010). Johanson and Vahlne (2009) also claim that internationalization is best understood as a by-product of efforts taken to improve a company's position in its network(s). They further point out that problems and opportunities of firms involved in international ventures are less a matter of country specificity than of relationship specificity. Accordingly, they suggest future research focus on the liability of outsidership rather than liability of foreignness.

Research in *economic geography* provides insights regarding where and why investments are made at certain locations. This approach connects with much of the research discussed above but broadens the scope through discussions about clusters, embeddedness, organization within space, and national or regional competitiveness (e.g. Scott, 1988; Porter, 1990, 2000; Cooke, 2001; Bathelt et al., 2004; Dicken, 2007; Crevoisier and Jeannerat, 2009). In economic geography, the focus has been on the locational characteristics enabling economic growth, regional economic development, and knowledge sharing. Internal organization and strategy of the firm seem to play a lesser role in many of the geographically based studies. Rather, the focus is often on the regional or industry level and the various impacts of innovations systems or clusters (e.g. Malmberg and Marskell, 2002; Asheim and Coenen, 2005). Studies have also focused on the development of global and regional production systems (Coe et al., 2004; Yeung, 2009). Increasing interest in the interrelation between firm strategy and locational decision making has generated a stream of literature within economic geography (e.g. Ivarsson and Alvstam, 2005; Bryson and Rusten, 2008; Pellenbarg and Wever, 2008; Ström and Wahlqvist, 2010). This literature tries to connect the importance of place with how firms develop their strategy.

Furthermore, firms in various sectors may perceive the attractiveness of a location differently. Externalities, knowledge spillovers, and scale are more important for knowledge-intensive firms, whereas transaction cost and transportation cost are limited. Unstable business relationships in the global economy are localized at "metro economies" where firms seek to be close to customers and qualified labor. These advantages are difficult to quantify because high-end knowledge production is dependent on image and reputation for the recruitment of staff and building relationships in the market. Sometimes it is a question of "being there" that enables firms to tap into localized knowledge clusters. This form of relationship capitalism connects various locations around the globe, often in hierarchical structures (e.g. Bryson, 2000; Taylor et al., 2002). Studies of clusters and agglomeration economies have shown the sectoral differences that exist and how different clusters cope with change. Advantages that have developed through col-location might change over the course of time and eventually lose their competitiveness. This phenomenon proves that change and flexibility are inevitable and that firms continuously shape and reshape industrial land-scapes. These changes might differ in speed over time, but production of goods and services comprising a high level of knowledge content in the val-ue-adding process can transform more rapidly than traditional manufactur-ing. Studies show that the complex institutional setting can help explain the actions of firms (Ström et al., 2005). Localized networks comprising firms, educational institutions, and government support functions take time to develop, and if they facilitate competitiveness, there are clear advantages over pure cost reductions that can be found in other locations. Regional innovation systems and learning capabilities within regions are also exam-ples of the formation of these spatially developed competitive advantages (Rutten and Boekema, 2007). The institutional setting has also been called the "social economy" (Hayter, 2004: 97) in economic geography to cap-ture the underlying economic structure. The debate in relation to economic geography tries to take the analysis further by connecting networks of per-sonal and business relationships, but later also the underlying spatial power structure that exists (Bathelt and Glückler, 2003; Yeung, 2005). Firms can also be seen and studied as temporary coalitions that respond to the chal-lenges of, and adapt to, changing environments. In this way, firms utilize the possibility to build, exploit, and determine value from different forms of special relations (Begley et al., 2009). These kinds of localized advantages help to reduce transaction costs and create flexibility in production net-works. Studies on the company level that try to understand and connect locational characteristics to the decision-making process are often difficult. Companies need close dialogue with the industry and firms that are to be studied, and case studies are often the most commonly used method (e.g. Clark, 1998; Ivarsson and Alvstam, 2005). The challenge for studies in eco-nomic geography has been to combine firm-level analysis with more macro-oriented studies of industry transformation and location.

Ström and Wahlqvist (2010) show that there are clear possibilities of con-necting studies of international business and economic geography. A con-ceptual model is developed to catch the different factors that are covered respectively in the different disciplines. A combination of people, place, production, pace, and power all impact the practices for the development of economic growth and internationalization. Competition and speed in the economic transformation of regions and firms has created a new spatial set-ting. Knowledge and untraded interdependencies can flow freely, and firms can take advantage of different institutional environments. At the same time, competition for talent grows stronger as knowledge content increases in global production networks. This development toward a relational economic geography has also strengthened the possibilities for firms to internationalize. The process is faster, and the geographical scope is bigger. Companies can be active on the global market almost at once, and their main counterparts and relations can be with people on other continents. Thus, the combinatory effects of integrating the study of location in business studies and geography can enhance the understanding of the processes that will shape the future business environment, in which rapid growth and internationalization of firms are vital. The challenge lies in identifying the relationship that exists between locational advantages, such as institutions and innovation systems, and the executive management decision-making process on the firm's level.

Conceptual framework

As mentioned in the introduction, this chapter argues that the complexity in decision making related to a firm's international expansion in space has hitherto not been adequately mirrored in the prevailing research streams. The reason for this lack of a passable framework capturing this intricacy is that until now very few attempts (e.g. Ström and Wahlqvist, 2010) have been made to combine the variety of existing explanatory frameworks. Not only are there almost watertight bulkheads between research in the fields of economic geography and international business, but also within the two disciplines, various competing streams of literature exist. These conceptualizations depicted in the literature review – all of them heavily discussed, developed, and empirically tested – have lived as neighbors for ages; however, they have rarely visited each other.

Figure 17.1 aims at conceptualizing the different levels that exist in firms' internationalization. This is an attempt to show that firms will face different challenges at different geographical and regulatory levels. In some cases, the company encounters problems on one level, and in other cases there are problems on multiple levels. Differences also exist in relation to specific industries. Often studies tend to focus on one of these levels rather than trying to connect them in a more holistic approach. The conceptual framework should be considered as a tool and a structure to study new forms of international ventures and the connections to different levels of geographical space. A number of theoretical explanations exist on the process of internationalization. Over time, the respective theories have become more specialized. However, if they are put together, they contribute to the overall understanding of internationalization and agglomeration. We see a structure of limited perspectives based on the literature review. Referring to the above literature review, we distinguish among three main perspectives on internationalization and space: (1) a neoclassical perspective; (2) a spatially anchored perspective; and (3) a managerial level–based perspective. In other words, using our introductory argument once more, the proposed

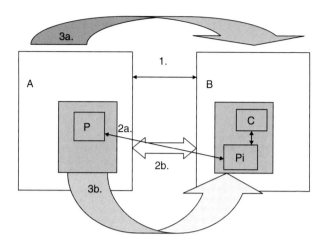

Figure 17.1 Ilustration of theoretical angles explaining internationalization
Source: Ström, 2004

conceptualization identifies three main perspectives, emphasizing different main factors managers consider when they make decisions related to internationalization and space.

The traditional *neoclassical perspectives* on internationalization and space deal with the relationship that exists between two countries A and B, when exchanging goods or services (1). A number of likely outcomes are possible due to factor endowments and comparative advantages. Additionally, measures such as tariffs and non-tariff barriers affect the possibility of trade taking place. This becomes an issue on the macroeconomic level. World trade has been liberalized and deregulated in several steps, but problems still impact international operations. The recent financial crisis shows that free trade is constantly under threat by protectionist measures. Apart from tariffs, the threat from more complicated and subtle non-tariff barriers is also present. Together, these measures might facilitate or hinder movement of activities across borders.

Founded in the neoclassical perspective, studies of the firm and the issue of *foreign direct investment* connect both the corporate (2a) and national levels (2b). Government actions, along with purely firm-specific considerations, are driving forces within the parent company (P) that may lead it to set up operations in a host country (Pi). There are a number of plausible explanations as to why firms choose to move abroad, and also as to how they are best managed in a host market to supply a client (C). Firms must handle various regulatory frameworks, but at the same time they must also be able to evaluate the best strategic fit based on incentives to foreign direct investment such as tax breaks and regionally supported knowledge agglomerations.

Spatially anchored perspectives explain the factors surrounding the firm in the home market and the eventual location in the host market. Spatial theories can be split into two areas. The first is national embeddedness (3a). This level tries to explain a successful industry or company on the basis of the national business structure and factor conditions. National initiatives such as industrial policy or innovations programs can facilitate this space. The second is local agglomeration embeddedness (3b), which focuses primarily on the close surroundings and how these generate a possible environment for specific companies. Through internationalization, this space becomes even more important since it is close to the operation of the firm. Regional initiatives to support innovation and knowledge creation can help to create locational advantages. Sectors dominated by high-knowledge-content production of goods and services rely on connections or "pipelines" among these local spaces to facilitate their company competitiveness (Bathelt et al., 2004). Within and between agglomerations are ongoing transactions of information, both on the industry level and on the personal level. For firms to take advantage of this information flow, just being there is important to tap into these knowledge pools (Gertler, 2003). Internationalization theory, whether it is more economically or behaviorally oriented, studies the process of internationalization. That is, how do firms internationalize, and what incentives or networks are important?

In relation to the discussions on embeddedness (3b), the *managerial level–based perspective* becomes a vital part of understanding the process of internationalization. The focus here is on how managers try to make informed decisions in relation to company strategy. This decision making can be purely rational or involve other factors, such as personal connections. The Nordic scholars within the behavioral approach in general, and Johanson and Vahlne (1977 and later works) in particular, have challenged the economic literature's picture of the decision maker as a *homo oeconomicus* – that is, as a rational, perfectly informed, and self-interested actor who desires wealth and has the ability to make judgments toward those ends. Cyert and March (1963) see decision makers and organizations as subject to limited rationality, conflicting goals, and aspirations. Furthermore, they experience a certain lack of knowledge about alternative actions and their outcomes, and they attempt to avoid uncertainty. Also, more recent studies on international entrepreneurship have incorporated the behavioral perspective's view on how decisions during a firm's internationalization process are made. Overall, when trying to understand managers' decisions related to internationalization and space, the focus is on the decision maker's identity (including value systems, beliefs, intentions, and aspirations), knowledge base, and social network.

The next part of this chapter shows the complexity of internationalization in the knowledge-intensive industry. Examples from Sweden and Japan are used to present issues facing firms in relation to the various conceptual perspectives presented above. These examples should not be seen as case studies in the conventional sense. Rather, they are presented to capture the different layers of the conceptual model. They cover both products and services to show similarities between sectors that share the common ground of knowledge-intensive production and rapid internationalization. Additionally, they show how various structures impact the development of firms. The empirical examples show that issues of management and economic geography have different layers, from the micro-environment of a personal decision to the broader macroeconomic structures that help to form competitiveness. On all layers, linkages within networks are important. Using the examples in this particular way has limitations, but for the purpose of this study it shows how different business environments still can share similarities in terms of paths for internationalization and building of competitive advantage.

Internationalization of the Swedish knowledge-intensive industry: Q-Sense

The episode of Q-Sense's internationalization process below, taken from Schweizer (2009), serves as an example of how businesses – not least small and medium-sized enterprises (SMEs) – make decisions related to space, deciding on issues such as where to internationalize, what mode of entry to use, and when to embark on the international venture.

In 2001, five years after its inception, Q-Sense (a Swedish small and medium-sized supplier of acoustic resonator-based instruments for molecular binding events taking place on various surfaces) established a subsidiary in the US market. The idea to have its own subsidiary in the United States and to deal with the European and Asian markets with the help of distributors the firm had already engaged in 2001 had emerged very early at Q-Sense. A manager at Q-Sense explains why it has always been obvious to have an organization in the United States: "First of all, it is the size of the market, but then again, it has also been hype. We visited other companies; ... [that] managed to build their own organization in the US. We were inspired by their and others' success. Also, despite of the various differences in different states, the US market is relatively homogeneous. Large parts of a huge market could be served with one office. Also we spoke the language." In 2001, a manager moved to the United States to build up a Q-Sense office and to tighten contacts with opinion leaders at Stanford, Harvard, and Rutgers universities. Q-Sense's US adventure, however, had already started one year earlier through a contact that Q-Sense's first CEO had with a company named SWEDLink in California. This company, owned by two Swedish women, worked like an export council, distributing marketing material and visiting potential customers. Once there were enough leads, someone from Q-Sense Sweden came to the United States to make official visits. However, after a while, there were so many leads that it was not judicious to go on like that. Also, Q-Sense understood that US partners did not take them seriously without an office in the country; it was a question of trust – as has been argued: "You need an American address." Q-Sense consulted a local lawyer concerning the legal aspects of establishing the US office. The reasons California was the ultimate choice of location in the United States were that at that time, most US leads were on the West Coast, and the established contacts were with SWEDLink in California. However, Q-Sense also seriously considered the East Coast. Leads existed there too; potential customers could be found; and it had the advantage of a better time zone for communication with the home office. The one-person subsidiary worked well, and in 2003, six (out of a total of 15) were sold in the United States. In 2004, the decision was made to move the US office to the East Coast. In 2007, there were six employees, including salespeople –on both the East and the West Coast – and certain sales support, technical support applications, and administration.

The story of Q-Sense's establishment on the US market also illustrates the complexity involved in decision making related to a firm's journey in space. To take up only a few interesting issues: (1) Q-Sense chose to establish a subsidiary – a highly committed mode on a large and important market relatively early in its evolution; (2) interestingly, the decision fits well with existing beliefs in the firm – the decision was always "obvious"; (3) the decision was also influenced by an existing hype; that is, Q-Sense mimicked other seemingly successful firms; (4) the actual nature of the US market – its size, homogeneity, and importance – justified the decision to establish a subsidiary; (5) Q-Sense felt it had the right competence (e.g. language) and existing contacts/networks; (6) the personal contact of the former CEO with the personnel at SWEDLink opened doors to the United States and later also encouraged Q-Sense to locate the subsidiary in California and not elsewhere; (7) in order to be successful in the United States, a firm needs to be physically present; (8) being present in the United States/California, Q-Sense got better access to relevant scientific clusters. Hence, when trying to understand space-related decision making, we must ask (in the above case), what is important for the managers making the decisions to establish a subsidiary in the United States? What do they prioritize? What are they consciously and unconsciously considering when making the decision and why?

All of the different schools of thought dealing with firms' relation to geographical space would interpret the decision made in this case (i.e. to establish a subsidiary on the US market) differently. The focus would possibly be on factor endowments; ownership-specific advantages of Q-Sense; potential transaction costs; Q-Sense's ability to internalize resources; Q-Sense's development prior to the decision; Q-Sense's overall (incremental) internationalization process; the importance of access to networks and relationships; the importance of the decision maker; the attraction of clusters; or national or regional competiveness. Whereas this list can be extended with many additional topics covered in the above-mentioned research streams, the case of Q-Sense clearly shows that, in reality, when managers make their decisions, this clear-cut division does not exist.

Internationalization of Japanese knowledge-intensive firms:

The examples in this section aim to show how factors on industry or macroeconomic levels impact growth and internationalization of firms. By using Japan and knowledge-intensive sectors, this section contrasts the micro level of more personal decision-making processes shown in the Swedish example. We do not want to uncover specific decisions, but rather show the complex settings in which international networks and competitiveness evolve. Studies of internationalization among professional business firms in Japan reveal a very complex process (Ström, 2004, 2005). The result shows that Japanese firms within this knowledge- intensive sector have traditionally been internationalized to a lesser extent than similar firms in other Organisation for Economic Cooperation and Development (OECD) economies. The Japanese firms have usually followed their Japanese clients into new markets. This process is similar to what has been the case among Western service providers. However, the Japanese firms have not been as successful in developing their client base in foreign markets. The main reason is that the business environment for services has favored internalization in larger companies or *keiretsu* groups (Ström and Mattsson, 2005). In changing market conditions, the networks and potential of leveraging resources among firms have proven to be valuable platforms for the internationalization process.

Comparative studies of Japanese firms in the UK and Singapore show a similar pattern of internationalization (Ström and Mattsson, 2006; Ström, 2006). Only after a long presence in the host markets has the client base started to increase. This has often happened when traditional Japanese clients have come under pressure to restructure their operations. The other alternative has been to establish representative offices with a limited possibility to act in the host market. According to the firms, there are several reasons for entering foreign markets in which the long-term potential is seen to be great. The issue of competence and knowledge absorption was put forward by all firms irrespective of their service activities. This shows the importance of the so-called untraded interdependencies that are discussed in economic geography theory. These locational advantages are difficult to quantify, and Japanese firms have found it difficult to tap into, and connect with, local clusters of knowledge production (Morgan et al., 2002). It seems the traditional business structure of these knowledge-producing firms create hurdles in their internationalization.

Within the knowledge-driven and service-based economy, the importance of international contacts has been a driving force behind rapid internationalization. These relations are more important than geographical distance and cultural similarities. Larger corporations such as the *sogo shosha* have tried to develop new service areas to take advantage of new possibilities in the market. Examples are the growth of Japan's venture industry and increasing interest in the biotechnology industry. Recent studies show that Japanese firms are trying to utilize international relationships to develop their market potential in Asia and globally (Alvstam et al., 2009). The combination of relations to larger Japanese business groups and contact points at international knowledge hubs is vital in building new business relationships. Results also show the complexity of locational decision making and how these knowledge-producing firms need to find a strategic fit for their long-term development. In Asia the connection to established spatial production networks is important to evaluate the location strategy among knowledge-intensive firms (Ström and Yoshino, 2009).

Over the years, Japan has tried to develop national innovation systems for supporting the formation of new firms and industries (Holroyd, 2008). These efforts have been implemented to strengthen the institutional setting needed for knowledge-producing firms. The program has been initiated by the national government, and various regional activities have been launched. Initiatives in the area of information technology, R&D, and biotech have seen strong support on regional levels. Cluster initiatives to support platforms for information sharing and knowledge creation have been established. Universities and other research and educational institutions have also been involved in upgrading the innovation systems (Holroyd, 2008). Large sums of money have been spent, but it has been difficult to achieve sustained results over the long run. Sapporo is one example of a city region that has worked hard to develop its attractiveness to high-tech and service-producing industries but thus far has had only limited national and international success. Regional initiatives in the Kyoto area have instead shown sustained success in the field of life and bio-sciences (Ibata-Arens, 2008). Well-functioning social networks among people and firms, together with long-term strategies, have helped a large number of firms gain strong momentum in innovation and international R&D. In a detailed case study, Ibata-Arens (2008) analyzes the key success factors behind one of these successful firms, Peptide. The local institutional setting, together with international contacts the founder established in Germany, China, and elsewhere proved to be vital. By interacting with researchers at conferences and by joining universities abroad, a network for internationalization evolved. Additionally, the openness and entrepreneurial spirit within firms is important. These are also aspects regarded as vital in attracting talented employees (Florida, 2002; Ström and Wahlqvist, 2010).

These examples show the many challenges that exist within the discussion of internationalization of Japanese firms. In general, two categories are present. The first category includes firms that are already on the international market but need to develop their connection to the local relational or institutional business environment. Second, there are rapidly growing firms that take advantage of regional or national growth initiatives. These firms rely more on personal contacts around the world, and the speed and geography of their internationalization process is very different.

The data on Japanese firms show that the different conceptual perspectives are all present. Firms need to handle more neoclassical aspects of internationalization along with issues related to space and management. It seems questions of locational advantages and embeddedness are vital along with the managerial capability of the firms. However, it is the combination of these perspectives that can help us understand the internationalization process.

Company challenges and conceptual propositions

The literature review, together with the empirical examples, shows the interconnectedness that exists between the internationalization process and the question of locational advantage. Combining firm-level analysis in relation to decision making with the more macro-oriented analysis of the national and regional levels facilitates a better understanding of the decision-making process in relation to long-term strategic considerations. The literature review and the empirical data show it is possible to find explanations for internationalization based on all three perspectives: neoclassical, spatially anchored, and managerial. A holistic view is needed that takes into account the different perspectives and tries to use their respective explanatory power. In relation to the conceptual model introduced in Figure 17.1, a number of challenges exist for firms in rapidly internationalizing sectors. These sectors are characterized by high knowledge content, R&D-driven internationalization, entrepreneurship, and strong spatial concentration in urban areas with complex, untraded interdependencies. Trade relations on the macro level as well as incentive structures for attracting foreign direct investment seem to be less of a problem for these firms. They do not seek locations that are low-cost bases; rather they seek locations that require special competences. With diminishing trade barriers and investment restrictions, locational advantages become a question of strategic complexity for these firms. Instead, it is their position in the institutional setting and their relations with clients, business partners, and employees that are paramount. These relationships are heavily dependent on trust and commitment.

As the importance of the neoclassical perspective declines due to an increased liberalization of world trade and investment, this calls for new explanations for internationalization in relation to space and management. Embeddedness in the special context of national or regional surroundings can only partly help to explain the spatial distribution and relations that are established. Instead, the micro-environment and close surroundings seem to be more important. The empirical examples also point toward the difficulty of specifically attracting these knowledge-intensive firms. Cause and effect is very difficult to establish. The firms need a strong knowledge base and close proximity to capital, but successful internationalization seems to depend more on factors of serendipity. The creation of knowledge clusters through national and regional innovation systems is yet to be evaluated as the engines for growth creation and internationalization. Most advanced countries are pushing these agendas, but it has been difficult to analyze the locational attractiveness of such ventures from comparative global perspectives. This also requires new methodological approaches to catch the longitudinal development; that is, knowledge biographies (Larsson, 2007). Two issues in particular remain to be analyzed in relation to embeddedness and internationalization of firms. Firstly, location advantages can only partly explain the underlying rationale of taking a venture out on to the global market. Secondly, the policy connection is not clear. Nations and regions are working with different policy schemes to build competitiveness, but how this will fit into the strategic decision-making process of firms is far from clear.

The other area that requires additional studies in relation to location and strategy is the notion of *people-dependent internationalization* as an increasingly important part of the managerial perspective. In a global economy dominated by relationships and institutional embeddedness, it seems that newly established firms and firms within knowledge-intensive industries depend to a much larger extent on specific people for their internationalization. These networks can have the form of individual relationships, but also broader coalitions connecting firms (Begley et al., 2009). Additional studies are needed to disaggregate the specific roles played by individuals and their link to the overall theory of internationalization and locational advantage.

Conclusion

Starting with the question of what space factors managers consider when making decisions concerning the internationalization of their firms – an important question both for researchers and practitioners – the chapter has tried to show the complexity of internationalization among firms in knowledge-intensive industries. On the basis of a literature review comprising theories in both international business and economic geography, a conceptual model proposed the holistic approach for the study of internationalization in general and decision making in particular. The conceptualization argues that it is possible to find explanations based on various theoretical streams, but it is the combination of these that could help to uncover more complex relations and reasons for venturing out to the global market. The anecdotal examples presented above show there are different layers impacting decision making. The different data were used to present challenges found in relation to conceptual perspectives. Macroeconomic aspects create the broader setting, but when a decision is considered, very personal considerations impact the managerial level.

An obvious question to be asked is, of course, why have there been few, if any, attempts to construct a more holistic and thereby a more realistic concept of firms' decision making related to space? As mentioned previously, one obvious explanation might be the watertight bulkheads between the various research streams. We believe a second important explanation is the difficulties involved to empirically implement a study that applies the proposed holistic perspective. We believe the complexity outlined above can be captured by employing a case-study approach. Employing an abductively inspired research approach, the conceptualization presented in this chapter can serve as an initial conceptual framework that can then be confronted with the evidence from cases studied (cf. Denzin, 1978). As mentioned by Yin (1994), case studies are rich, empirical descriptions of particular instances of a phenomenon that are typically based on a variety of data sources. In this study, the case-study approach's ability to retain a holistic perspective of the issue studied especially is perceived to be important. Whereas such a confrontation might result in the confirmation of certain assumptions made, unanticipated empirical observations can also be expected, which in turn result in new theoretical insights. These can then be confronted by new cases. Following this process, an eventual final conceptualization can be offered explaining the impact of space on managerial decision making related to international ventures; it should be understood as the result of a successive interaction between relevant theoretical framework(s) at hand and empirical evidence of the case studies. We further suggest that the case studies should be selected by convenience sampling (Merriam, 1998) due to the need for good access. The cases thereby can be understood as instrumental case studies that provide insight into an issue and the refinement of a theory (Stake, 1994).

As discussed above, we believe it makes sense to conduct case studies on knowledge- intensive industries. We further believe a comparative approach–for example, studying Swedish and Japanese firms – offers a sound base for developing a holistic view. Traditionally, most studies on the internationalization process of firms within knowledge-intensive and fast-growing industries have been anchored in theoretical frameworks based on empirical evidence of Western firms. Hence, the proposed comparative study offers the opportunity to study firms from different geographical contexts, and in so doing to try to understand how the strategic decision-making process related to international ventures is influenced by the surrounding economic geography. The two countries share a variety of commonalities that are of importance for the proposed comparative study. Both Sweden and Japan are advanced OECD economies in which knowledge-intensive firms not only face the challenge of increasing international competition, but also internationalize at a rapid pace. Furthermore, these firms are highly dependent on getting access to various geographical locations, resulting in complex international production networks. Finally, regarding data collection, we propose that besides collecting secondary data, such as firm-internal documents and industry data, the main focus should be on interviewing the actual decision makers. One way to structure such an interview would be to first identify various decisions made relating to internationalization and space and then ask the managers to detail the factors on which the decisions were based. We would also need to have a good understanding of the decision maker's personal traits in order to include the third dimension of our proposed framework. In all, this would enable future empirical studies to better unveil the underlying explanations for internationalization and choice of location that are connected to the different perspectives discussed in the conceptual model.

References

Alvstam, C., Ström, P., Yoshino, N. (2009). On the economic interdependence between China and Japan: Challenges and possibilities. *Asia Pacific Viewpoint*, 50(2), 198–214.

Asheim, B., Coenen, L. (2005). Knowledge bases and regional innovation systems: Comparing Nordic clusters. *Research Policy*, 34(8), 1173–90.

Bathelt, H., Glückler, J. (2003). Toward a relational economic geography. *Journal of Economic Geography*, 3(2), 117–44.

Bathelt, H., Malmberg, A., Maskell, P. (2004). Clusters and knowledge: Local buzz, global pipelines and the process of knowledge creation. *Progress in Human Geography*, 28(1), 31–56.

Begley, S., Taylor, M., Bryson, J. (2009). Firms as connected, temporary coalitions: Organisational forms and the exploitation of intellectual capital. *Electronic Journal of Knowledge Management*, 7(1), 11–20.

Bhowmick, S. (2004). Towards understanding small firm internationalization – Technology based SME focus. *Frontiers of E-Business Research*, 758–70.

Björkman, I., Forsgren, M. (2000). Nordic international business. *International Studies of Management and Organization*, 30(1), 6–25.

Bryson, J.R. (2000). Spreading the message: Management consultants and the shaping of economic geographies in time and space. In Bryson, J., Daniels, P.W., Henry, N., Pollard, J. (eds), *Knowledge, Space, Economy*. Routledge, London.

Bryson, J.R., Rusten, G. (2008). Transnational corporations and spatial divisions of 'service' expertise as a competitive strategy: The example of 3M and Boeing. *Service Industries Journal*, 28(3), 307–23.

Buckley, P.J., Casson, M.C. (1976). *The Future of the Multinational Enterprise*. London.

Choi, Y.R., Shepherd, D.A. (2004). Entrepreneurs' decisions to exploit opportunities. *Journal of Management*, 30(3), 377–95.

Clark, G.L. (1998). Stylized facts and close dialogue: Methodology in economic geography. *Annals of the Association of American Geographers*, 88(1), 73–87.

Coe, N.M., Hess, M., Yeung, H.W-C., Dicken, P., Henderson, J. (2004). 'Globalizing' regional development: A global production networks perspective. *Transactions of the Institute of British Geographers*, 29, 468–84.

Crevoisier, O., Jeannerat, H. (2009). Territorial knowledge dynamics: From the proximity paradigm to multi-location milieus. *European Planning Studies*, 17(8), 1223–41.

Denzin, N.K. (1978). The logic of naturalistic inquiry. In Denzin, N.K. (ed.), *Sociological Methods – A Source Book*, pp. 54–73. McGraw-Hill, New York.

Dicken, P. (2007). *Global Shift: Mapping the Changing Contours of the World Economy*. 5th edition. SAGE, London.

Dunning, J.H. (1988). The eclectic paradigm of international production: A restatement and some possible extensions. *Journal of International Business Studies*, 19(1), 1–31.

Florida, R. (2002). *The Rise of the Creative Class: And How It's Transforming Work, Leisure, Community, and Everyday Life*. Basic Books, New York.

Gertler, M. (2003). Tacit knowledge and the economic geography of context, or The undefinable tacitness of being (there). *Journal of Economic Geography*, 3(1), 75–99.

Hayter, R. (2004). Economic geography as dissenting institutionalism: The embeddedness, evolution and differentiation of regions. *Geografiska Annaler*, 86B(2), 95–115.

Hennart, J.-F. (1982). *A Theory of the Multinational Enterprise*. University of Michigan, Ann Arbor.

Hohenthal, J. (2001). *The Creation of International Business Relationships*. Doctoral thesis. Uppsala University.

Holroyd, C. (2008). Reinventing Japan Inc.: Twenty-first century innovation strategies in Japan. *Prometheus*, 26(1), 21–38.

Ibata-Arens, K. (2008). The Kyoto model of innovation and entrepreneurship: Regional innovation systems and cluster culture. *Prometheus*, 26(1), 90–109.

Ivarsson, I., Alvstam, C-G. (2005). The effect of spatial proximity on technology transfer from TNCs to local suppliers in developing countries: The case of AB Volvo's truck and bus plants in Brazil, China, India and Mexico. *Economic Geography*, 81(1), 83–111.

Johanson, J.J., Vahlne, J.-E. (1977). The internationalization process of the firm: A model of knowledge development and increasing foreign market commitment. *Journal of International Business Studies*, 4, 20–9.

Johanson, J.J., Vahlne, J.-E. (2009). The Uppsala internationalization process model revisited – From liability of foreignness to liability of outsidership. *Journal of International Business Studies*, 40(9), 1411–31.

Larsson, A. (2007). *Proximities and Knowledge Flows: A Micro-Level Biographical Approach*. Paper presented at the 2nd Nordic Geographers Meeting, 15–17 June, Bergen, Norway.

Malmberg, A., Maskell, P. (2002). The elusive concept of localization economies: Towards a knowledge-based theory of spatial clustering. *Environment and Planning A*, 34(3), 429–49.

Mathews, J.A., Zander, I. (2007). The international entrepreneurial dynamics of accelerated internationalisation. *Journal of International Business Studies*, 38(3), 387–403.

Merriam, S.B. (1998). *Qualitative Research and Case Study Applications in Education*. Jossey-Bass, San Francisco.

Mcdougall, P.P., Oviatt, B.M. (2000). International entrepreneurship: The intersection of two research paths. *Academy of Management Journal*, 43(5), 902–6.

Morgan, G., Sharpe, D.R., Kelly, W., Whitley, R. (2002). The future of Japanese manufacturing in the UK. *Journal of Management Studies*, 39(8), 1023–44.

Oviatt, B.M., Mcdougall, P.P. (1994). Toward a theory of international new ventures. *Journal of International Business Studies*, 25, 45–64.

Porter, M.E. (1990). *The Competitive Advantage of Nations*. Macmillan, London.

Porter, M.E. (2000). Locations, clusters, and company strategy. In Clark, G.L., Feldman, M.P., Gertler, M.S. (eds), *The Oxford Handbook of Economic Geography*. Oxford University Press, Oxford.

Porter, M., Sölvell, Ö. (1998). The role of geography in the process of innovation and the sustainable competitive advantages of firms. In Chandler, A.D., Hagström, P.,

Sölvell, Ö. (eds), *The Dynamic Firm: The Role of Technology, Strategy, Organizations and Regions.* Oxford University Press, Oxford.

Rennie, M.W. (1993). Born global. *McKinsey Quarterly,* 4, 45–52.

Rutten, R., Boekema, F. (2007). The learning region: Foundations, state of the art, future. In Rutten, R., Boekema, F. (eds), *The Learning Region: Foundations, State of the Art, Future.* Edward Elgar, Cheltenham.

Schweizer, R. (2009). *The Relationship between SME's Business and Internationalization Strategies.* Paper presenterad på Företagsekonomiska Föreningens konferens i Åbo, Finland.

Schweizer, R., Vahlne, J.-E., Johanson, J. (2010). Internationalization as an entrepreneurial process. *Journal of International Entrepreneurship,* 8(4), 343–70.

Scott, A. (1988). Flexible production systems and regional development: The rise of new industrial spaces in North America and Western Europe. *International Journal of Urban and Regional Research,* 12, 171–86.

Stake, R.E. (1994). Case studies. In Denzin, N.K., Lincoln, Y.S. (eds), *Handbook of Qualitative Research,* pp. 236–47. Sage Publications, Thousand Oaks, CA.

Ström, P. (2004). *The 'Lagged' Internationalization of Japanese Professional Business Service Firms: Experiences from the UK and Singapore,* Department of Human and Economic Geography, School of Business, Economics and Law, Göteborg University, Series B, no. 107.

Ström, P. (2005). The Japanese service industry: An international comparison. *Social Science Japan Journal,* 8(2), 253–66.

Ström, P. (2006). Internationalisation of Japanese professional business service firms: Dynamics of competitiveness through urban localization in Southeast Asia. In Harrington, J.W., Daniels, P.W. (eds), *Knowledge-Based Services: Internationalisation and Regional Development.* Ashgate, Aldershot.

Ström, P., Zaring, O., Egels, N., Eriksson, M., Wolff, R. (2005). Företagen som aktörer i den regionala tillväxtstrategin – ur ett företagsledarperspektiv (Chalmers University of Technology and School of Business, Economics and Law, Göteborg University).

Ström, P., Mattsson, J. (2005). Japanese professional business services: A proposed analytical typology. *Asia Pacific Business Review,* 11(1), 49–68.

Ström, P., Mattsson, J. (2006). Internationalisation of Japanese professional business service firms: Client relations and business performance in the UK. *Service Industries Journal,* 26(3), 249–65.

Ström, P., Wahlqvist, E. (2010). Regional and firm competitiveness in the service-based economy: Combining economic geography and international business theory. *Tijdschrift voor Economische en Sociale Geografie,* 101(3), 287–304.

Ström, P., Yoshino, N. (2009). Japanese financial service firms in East and Southeast Asia: Location pattern and strategic response in changing economic conditions. *Asian Business and Management,* 8(1), 33–58.

Taylor, P.J., Walker, D.R.F., Beaverstock, J.V. (2002). Firms and their global service networks. In Sassen, S. (ed.), *Global Networks, Linked Cities.* Routledge, New York.

Welch, L.S., Luostarinen, R.(1988). Internationalization: Evolution of a concept. *Journal of General Management,* 14, 35–55.

Yeung, H.W-C. (2005). Rethinking relational economic geography. *Transactions of the Institute of British Geographers,* 30, 37–51.

Yeung, H.W-C. (2009). Transnational corporations, global production networks, and urban and regional development: A geographer's perspective on multinational enterprises and the global economy. *Growth and Change,* 40(2), 197–226.

Yin, R. (1994). *Case Study Research: Design and Methods.* Sage Publications, Thousand Oaks, CA.

18
Internationalization of Business Networks: How Do Managers with Divergent Cultural Norms Contribute?

Michael Plattner

1. Introduction

Within the context of multinational corporations (MNC) and their multiunit organizational structure, the manager's work is increasingly located in different cultural environments. A hybrid type of international manager has recently appeared in host countries. The hybrid manager can be understood as a newcomer to a MNC. As newcomers they are supposed to have a positive impact on transaction cost between the expatriate managers dispatched from headquarters on the one side and the local staff at subsidiary location on the other side (Almeida and Kogut 1999, Granovetter 2005, Morrison 2002: 1156, Fussel et al. 2006: 158).

A host country's culture is for the local staff the place of social embeddedness. On the other hand, the host country's culture is initially most distant for expatriate managers. Nonetheless, expatriates are relocated by MNC head offices with the aim of implementing headquarters' goals in the host locations. Linking local staff and expatriates, the new hybrid manager is the product of intensive in-culture experience in a host country that matches the depth of his or her home-culture knowledge. Hybrid managers' excellent access to local and international knowledge resources is of advantage. Since the accelerating internationalization of the 1980s, the division of labor has been intensified. However, local staff, hybrid managers and expatriate managers are charged with the same scope of assignment: building productivity and performance in the workplace. Attune to the social advantages unique to a culturally distant location, the key question is can hybrid managers employ their special skills to select and broker appropriate information between expatriates and locals?

Recent theoretical considerations support this question and have been discussed but not yet empirically tested. Via formal learning as well as informal socializing, local staff, hybrid managers and expatriate managers acquire a complementary selection of pervasive and complex information, based on their cultural, managerial and work skills. Regarding knowledge creation and socializing in networks, research has until now focused on the dimension of trust. As a result, the dimension of cultural norms has long been unattended (Coleman 1993, Granovetter 1985, 1992, Nooteboom 2006, Putnam 2002, Lin and Erickson 2008: 7). The ability to adapt to culturally distant norms at a foreign workplace is a precondition for successfully utilizing informal information sources over time (Jun et al. 2001: 375, Toh and DeNisi 2005: 138). When it comes to managerial work between certain cultures, different norms provide dissimilar guidelines for the members of the social network. Thus, norms become an endogenous variable in the process of business internationalization. Trust can emerge from the understanding of norms and the adjustment to norms. This is supported by the observation that "managers establish and maintain strong expressive ties with peers who come from similar cultures" (Manev and Stevenson 2001: 296).

If the managers become more compatible during internationalization, then the homophily – the similarity of related actors – should increase, reflecting the shrinking cultural distance between expatriate and hybrid managers and local staff. To measure similarity due to the assumed bridging function of the hybrid manager, three conditions need to be fulfilled. A panel analysis is appropriate to measure the dynamics of a comprehensible process of MNCs' internationalization (Levi-Strauss 1978, Nadel 1957). Furthermore, business networks need at least some years to become established in a specific economic context. Thus the periods in which the networks evolve should be clearly distinguishable. Finally, the observed managers' cultural distance should be widest (Manev and Stevenson 2001: 285).

Japanese managers in an MNC with activities in North America, Europe, East Asia and South-East Asia can meet the need of the cultural distance. Moreover, within the past three decades in Japan (1987–2012) three periods of economic development can be distinguished clearly: the Bubble Economy (until 1992), the Lost Decade (between 1993 and 2001), and the New Century (since 2002). Furthermore, this evolution has been precisely traced by the narratives authored by Kenji Hirokane focusing on the business network of the multinational electronics company Hatsushiba – a name derived from the company names of Matsushita and Toshiba (Hirokane 1999, 2002, 2004, 2005). Hirokane, a former manager at Matsushita, employed the genre of business manga to describe the work and life of expatriate manager Kosaku Shima and his business partners. Even if Hirokane's stories are fictional, due to the continuous writing and weekly publishing format, the business narrative is always up to date with respect to the current economic situation.

Specific business communities of expatriate manager, hybrid manager and local staff can be codified along with other network attributes. Thus, testable hypotheses evolve out of social capital and social network approaches in the next section of this chapter. The applied methods and the database utilized are described in Section 3. The result of the survey is contained in Section 4, subdivided into the economic context and the three above-mentioned periods. In Section 5 the results will be discussed in a summary leading to the conclusion in Section 6.

2. Social capital, communities and business networks

This chapter acknowledges social capital theory and research but adds collocation of intermediary individuals and groups as a core concept in which cultural norms deploy their socialization effects. Regarding the relational constructivism approach of the social network analysis, it is crucial to know in which comprehensive social structure local staff, hybrid managers and expatriate managers create knowledge and how that may change over time.

The hybrid managers have to be seen as social capital in an international context in which cultural values and norms have a crucial impact on the social networks (Borgatti and Foster 2003, McGrath and Krackhardt 2003, Mitchell 1969). The international manager's social capital is situated around specific business communities. The manager's work is performed within and between those communities. Newcomer hybrid managers contribute as a core group to the social capital of an MNC. Those managers' work is embedded in a local and global web of industrial and social activities (Amin and Cohendet 2005, Håkansson and Johanson, 1993: 40, White 2002). Capable of exercising global action, these hybrid agents can be seen as gatekeepers in the circulation of information on intra- and inter-firm levels because of their multiple activity dependencies between locals and expatriates. According to the knowledge transfer model, transaction occurs as socializing and internalization from explicit to tacit in collocation, or at least co-presence, of trusted managers (Nonaka and Konno 1998: 43). The hybrid manager provides an otherwise missing link in the vertical business network between head office and subsidiary. Transaction cost may be reduced by the phenomenon that like-minded people build influence bearing links to each other, blending attitudes and norms. This can be best expressed by the concept of *homophily* (Kandel 1979). Recent surveys on collocation and co-presence point out that homophily is an appropriate indicator for measuring the impact of interaction on transaction cost (Glückler 2007: 624, Grabher 2006: 179, Sorenson 2003: 515, McPherson et al. 2001: 419). In sum it can be inferred that the socialization refers to culture norms as a precondition for the manager's interaction in distinguished communities: epistemic community and community of practice.

Regarding their deep expertise, the expatriate managers are members of an epistemic community with "a mutually recognized subset of knowledge issues" (Grabher 2004: 16). They need to do local and global business in a network of professionals with expertise and competence in a particular domain. Each manager need therefore consult with one or more local as well as global experts, who have deep knowledge of the cross-national issues involved. As "fast subjects" the expatriate managers span a variety of networks as knowledge-rich in-groups (Haas 1992: 2, Storper and Venables 2003: 356, Thrift 2000). This epistemic community is characterized by a procedural authority exemplified as leading positions in business circles. Contributing members are expatriate managers with a standardized MBA background which gives them similar codes for implementing global management strategies. For the MNC, these individuals form a predictable social capital supporting the coordination between headquarters and subsidiaries, and therefore minimizing headquarters' uncertainty. On the one hand, expatriate managers possess a global personal network. On the other hand, they depend heavily on local subordinates in the host country's subsidiary. Additionally they have a need for support to prevent premature repatriation (McCaughey and Bruning 2005: 23, Tan and Mahoney 2006: 477). The high risk of expatriate failure stems from low ability to absorb new behavior and information and to adapt to the host culture (Lee 2007: 410).

Even if the expatriate managers have the necessary know-what and know-how, communication with local subordinates often functions poorly. One barrier to transferring work goals from the global to the local level is the expatriate manager's often missing adaptation to cultural norms in the lack of know-who and know-where. This gap can be partly filled by the contributions of host-country nationals. They act as local staff within a community of practice. Focusing on individual practices, they help to increase the firm's absorptive capacity at the local level of the subsidiaries. On the downside, their ability to conduct global business interactions is limited (Vance and Paik 2005: 590, Wenger 2004). The predominant studies focus on expatriate managers, and local staff fails to value the assistance that can be made by hybrid managers already working and living in the host country. However, the normative character of socialization has not been taken into account sufficiently. As a result, recent research is lacking a main point.

Hybrid managers constitute a missing link between the expatriate manager and the local staff. Their temporary assignment can bypass the strong of partners and increase the ability to transfer knowledge and reduce transaction cost (Lesser and Storck 2001: 833, Minbaeva and Michailova 2004: 665, Schlunze and Plattner 2007: 80). Their socialization in the home and host countries leads to strong cultural adjustment skills. They are able to make decisions on a local level, keeping in mind the national and international levels of the host and home countries. Additionally the hybrid manager is embedded within a local information network and has the ability to work in the host country as a local. Nonetheless, some threat remains, as the hybrid manager needs to stay in touch with headquarters while the MNC is shifting its global strategies from centralized to decentralized and distributed (Bartlett and Ghoshal 1998). Is there, as Enns et al. (2008) suggest, a shrinking gap of cultural distance and proximity in international business networks? Which effects does the changing economic context have on the influence of intermediary actors, such as hybrid managers?

Social network analysis serves here as an appropriate tool, but most empirical work considering network rules in the sense of the "small-world" phenomenon has been done under the mathematical approach of relational determinism (Watts and Strogatz 1998, Watts 1999, 2004) and actor- and resource-based relational instrumentalism (Gould 1993, Bathelt and Glückler 2005, Braun 2004). Both approaches have their disadvantages regarding their quantitative bias. Relational determinism focuses on the general description of the network to draw descriptive and static formulas. On the downside, the dynamics of a network are not well incorporated. The disadvantages of relational instrumentalism are the focus on the attributes of actors and their contexts while neglecting the measures of relations in between actors. With respect to the initial question: Has the interaction of local staff with the expatriate manager and the newly co-located hybrid manager lead to more interaction and to a reduction of transaction costs? It is crucial to know both in which comprehensive social structure the collocation takes place and how the relational interaction of local staff, hybrid managers and expatriate managers may change over time. Thus, this paper applies the relational constructivism approach of the social network analysis (Watts 2003: 113, White 1992). The approach takes the temporal dynamics into account with focus on the relational aspects of the interaction rather than the structural. Further pros result from the ability to measure

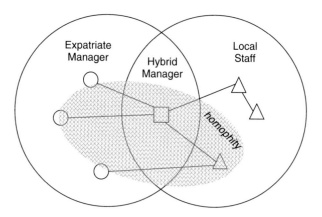

Figure 18.1   Model of homophily

co-presence between the actors in spatial, cultural, institutional and organizational entities.

The previous arguments yield a model in which hybrid managers are intermediary agents who are part of the expatriates' epistemic community as well as the community of local staff practice (see Figure 18.1). Regarding the aggregation of global networks and the multi-market focus of the managers, does a partial cultural assimilation take place, leading to similarity of related actors? To what extent is the shrinking cultural distance among expatriate and hybrid managers and local staff leading to increased homophily? To answer that question, the following hypotheses need to be tested:

First, expatriate managers, hybrid managers and local staff were organized in a hierarchically dependent and unilateral way during the market-driven internationalization period of the MNC. As a result, homophily was low (H1). Second, as a mechanism to assure reliance in dependent relations, the accelerating internationalization led to increased interdependency among expatriate managers, hybrid managers and local staff. They needed to coordinate activities more than follow directives. As a result, homophily was higher than before (H2). Third, the ongoing internationalization with operations internalizing networks of material and knowledge resources led to the flexible multi-actor dependency and further increased interdependency of expatriate managers, hybrid managers and local staff. They needed to work more or less in mutual similarity. As a result, homophily has reached its highest value (H3).

3. Methods and data

Based on the previous discussion, it can be hypothesized that culture norms are the key attribute that shape interactions among local staff, hybrid managers and expatriate managers. Those norms differ in an actor-specific way and, they change over time regarding the development of the general economic context. The source of the survey is the narrative of Kosaku Shima enfolding a network of 267 expatriate and hybrid managers as well as local staff around the Japanese MNC Hatsushiba (N = 267). In order to codify the actor network and the actor attributes (see Table 18.1), 512 business stories (9712 pages) starting from 1983 and extending to 2005 have been analyzed with a non-reactive text analysis. The author, Kenji Hirokane, bases his work on real-world business activity using interviews with businesspeople and academic informants (Matanle et al. 2008, *The Economist* 2008). The overlapping business interaction of expatriates in their epistemic community with locals in their community of practice is precisely described. Additionally the hybrid managers appear when the business of Hatsushiba becomes more and more internationally integrated. Currently, government and business use the Kosaku Shima material, because of its realism, for internal training and to explain Japanese business to foreigners. As the manager interactions

Table 18.1   Actor Attributes

Variables	Values
Economic Context	Bubble Economy, Lost Decade, New Century
Business Context	local business, national business, international business
Employment Status	local staff, hybrid manager, expatriate manager
Trust in Interaction	strong negative, negative, neutral, positive, strong positive
Hierarchical Dependency	below, same, above
Reputation	below average, average, above average
Type of Contact	personal, phone, letter (email, mail), no direct contact
Frequency of Contact	several times a week, once a week, s.t. a month, once a month, s.t. a year, once a year, only once
Duration of Contact	less than one year, up to three years, more than three years
Place of Personal Contact	city

are modeled on real-life Japanese salarymen, validity is effectual. Due to the full-scale survey layout, the results of the analysis are representative for a panel analysis of the three economic periods of the Bubble Economy (Wood 1993), the Lost Decade (Saxonhouse and Stern 2004) and the New Century (Abegglen 2006). For the first period, of economic growth, a network of 61 actors emerges (n = 61). The second period, of economic shrinking, consists of 130 nodes (n = 130). The last period, during economic regeneration, spans a network of n=117 actors.

4. Results

Social network analysis serves in this chapter as a tool to measure the homophily indicators, such as the constitution of cohesive subgroups of cliques, the brokerage of intermediary actors and their centralization (Costenbader and Valente 2003, Nooy et al. 2007). According to the test of the hypothesis mentioned in section 2, section 4 will show for each period how expatriate managers, hybrid managers and local staff shape collocation and the co-presence of the network. First, I will describe the networks' strong and weak ties. Second, I will characterize the cliquishness, the constitution of cohesive subgroups. Third, I will point out the intermediary hybrid managers who bridge those groups at the host and home locations, describing brokers (accelerators) and gatekeepers (filters) of transaction. Thereafter, I will analyze the average tie strength and the ratio of each subgroup of expatriate manager, hybrid manager and local staff. Finally, network centralization measures show the development of the network context. I will measure degree, the centrality measure that counts the number of ties to other actors in the network, as well as betweenness, the centrality measure indicating which actors are found between other individuals in the network. Lastly, I will measure closeness, the degree to which actors are close to each other taking into account all links, and reciprocity, the degree of reciprocal relationships.

The Bubble Economy – strong ties network

Network ties

During the Bubble Economy, the expatriate managers acted within the multinational firm's organization as well as on a market level. Within the *keiretsu* network of Hatsushiba, managers' agendas were filled with personnel affairs, recruitment matters, membership in intra-organizational groups, structural dependencies, and extensive executive meetings. The managers tried to maintain good relations with managers of other *keiretsu* companies whether they liked those people or not. When there was friction between the head office in Tokyo and regional branches in Kyoto, Osaka and other locations, they smoothed things over.

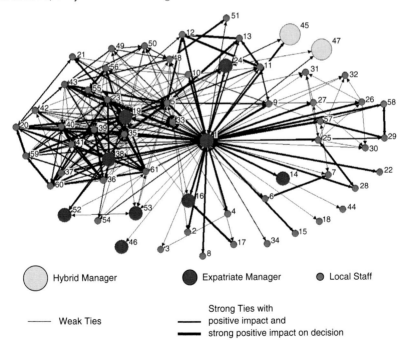

Figure 18.2 Manager network during the Bubble Economy
Source: Own survey 2008; n = 61

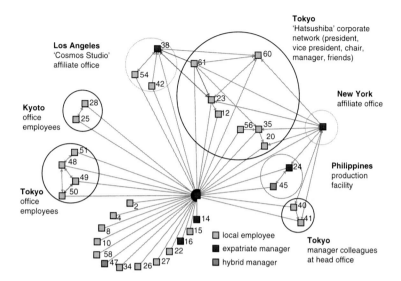

Figure 18.3 Core network and cliques during the Bubble Economy (strong positive impact on decisions)

Source: Own survey 2008; n = 35

Regarding internationalization of the expanding economy in the 1980s, mainly an exclusive group of mobile expatriate managers created synergy in cooperation and spatial proximity with other expatriates and their local employees (see Figure 18.2). Strong ties existed between expatriates' epistemic group and between local staff members' community of practice. Mainly expatriates linked those groups. The relations between the expatriates were long-term in nature, lasting more than five years. Even so, they were top-down in a strongly career manner and based on individuals' reputations. The ties were reliable and highly redundant. In an early stage of internationalization, expatriate managers dominated a hierarchically dependent and unilateral network. During the Bubble Economy, an exclusive group of expatriate managers created synergy in collocation mainly within their own epistemic community. Their local employees were mainly blocked from this community.

Cliquishness

At the level of market interaction, negotiations with customers and suppliers or the cleanup of *yakuza* (organized crime) problems were issues from which subgroups emerged. The aim of the cliques was, for example, market growth, which they achieved through product innovations such as high-definition TV and bread makers while capturing international value chain advantages such as offshore manufacturing (see Figure 18.3). Other efforts

Table 18.2   Network homophily measures

	Bubble Economy (n = 61)	Lost Decade (n = 130)	New Century (n = 117)
Avg. Tie Strength	2.80 %	1.40 %	1.10 %
Local with Local*	1.70 %	0.80 %	0.40 %
Hybrid with Local*	0	1.40 %	0.70 %
Expatriate with Local*	8.40 %	8.50 %	1.70 %
Hybrid with Hybrid*	0	0	1.50 %
Hybrid with Expatriate *	0	25.00 %	3.50 %
Expatriate with Expatriate *	9.70 %	20.00 %	0.80 %
Hybrid per Clique	0	10.35 %	55.00 %
Ratio Expat:Hybrid:Local	9 : 2 : 50	5 : 4 : 121	24 : 26 : 67
Degree Mean	4.21 %	1.69 %	1.25 %
Betweenness	27.60 %	44.20 %	23.70 %
Closeness	5.67 %	13.47 %	9.29 %
Reciprocity	32.47 %	68.31 %	75.29 %
Network Centralization	54.24 %	39.22 %	34.69 %
Network Homophily	3.92 %	2.93 %	55.7 %

Source: Own survey 2008; *Clique Density/Avg. Tie Strength

included specific sales strategies and sponsoring offers. Thus, expatriates were sent to supervise equity holdings in the US entertainment industry or an acquisition such as that of the fictional Cosmos Studios, in Hollywood.

Regarding the constitution of cohesive subgroups, the ratio of density and average tie strength during the Bubble Economy was highest for expatriate-expatriate interaction (9.7%), followed by expatriate-local (8.4%) and local-local interaction (1.7%). That mirrors the binding force of the expatriates' directing force controlling local staff (see Table 18.2). Expatriate managers were sent from the Hatsushiba head office in Tokyo to manage their temporary business assignments with help of local office staff at North American affiliates in Los Angeles and New York. In a further example, a hybrid manager was much needed in a Philippine manufacturing facility to improve the efficiency of the local production staff in collaboration with an expatriate manager.

Brokerage

During the Bubble Economy expatriates and locals interacted in collocation within cliques while expatriates linked these cliques. The strong ties of intermediary expatriate managers were the bridges between these cliques. When local staff was fulfilling the same function, the relations were temporary and the ties lost when the project finished (see Figure 18.3). Expatriates

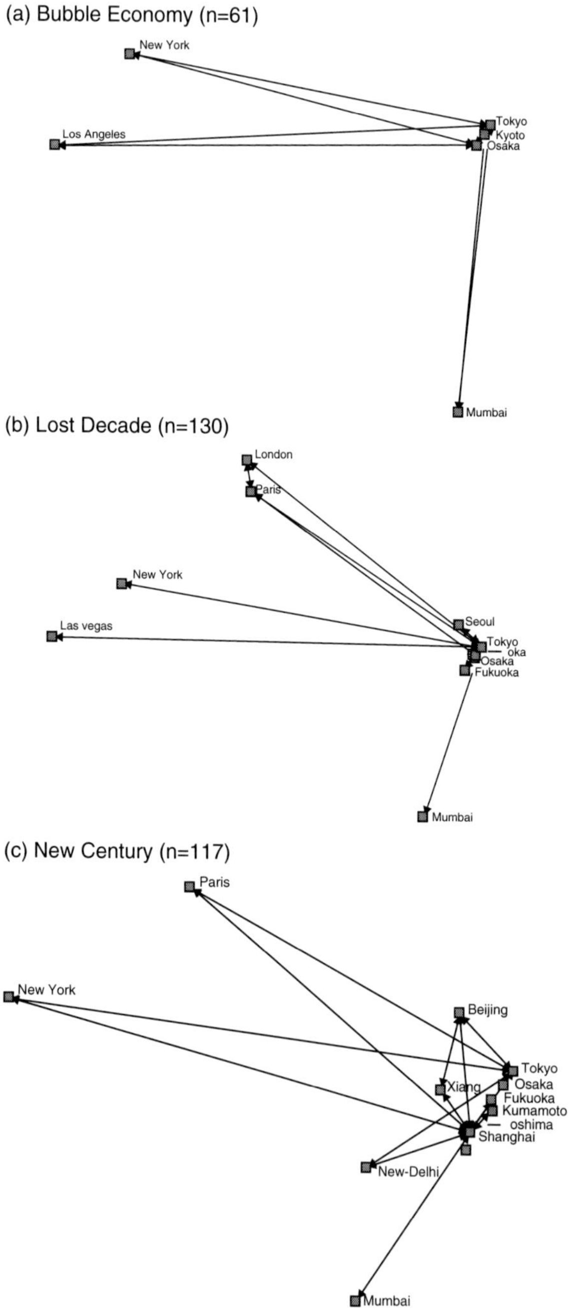

(a) Bubble Economy (n=61)

New York

Tokyo
Kyoto
Osaka

Los Angeles

Mumbai

(b) Lost Decade (n=130)

London
Paris

New York

Las vegas

Seoul
Tokyo
oka
Osaka
Fukuoka

Mumbai

(c) New Century (n=117)

Paris

New York

Beijing

Tokyo
Osaka
Xiang
Fukuoka
Kumamoto
oshima
Shanghai

New-Delhi

Mumbai

Figure 18.4 Spatial shift of the network

Source: Own survey 2008

were usually situated in complete subnetworks containing a minimum of three actor relationships (clique). They brokered access to local staff provided that the local staff members were not directly connected. Thus, the intermediate expatriate managers were gatekeepers, primarily brokers of information both within their epistemic group and at the interface with local staff. Only in the Philippines did a hybrid manager take an important position in negotiating between expatriated management and local staff. Generally hybrid managers were placed in the periphery of the decision-making processes. Weak ties could not emerge, as they were excluded due to the dominant position of the expatriate managers. From the spatial point of view, expatriates in the Bubble Economy interacted mainly in collocation at foreign locations and the head office. Managers at locations in foreign countries had only direct links to the head office (see Figure 18.4a).

Centrality

During the Bubble Economy, interaction was based on market conditions, hierarchical top-down corporate interactions and other interactions negotiated between customers and suppliers. The measures of degree, centralization, betweenness and closeness showed a clear pattern regarding the network between the epistemic community of the expatriated Kosaka Shima and the local staff's community of practice (see Table 18.2). A distinctive hierarchy characterized the manager network of the Bubble Economy. The proportion of the shortest path between pairs of relations that include Kosaku Shima was very low (betweenness: 27.6%). There were only some few expatriate managers with a similar position to the central actor, Kosaku Shima. Thus, the number of relations divided by the sum of all distances between Kosaku Shima and all others was very low (closeness: 5.7%). As a result, the number of relations incident only with Kosaku Shima was low (degree: 4.2%). Therefore, on the one hand, alongside Kosaku Shima there were many other expatriate managers and local staff sharing access to each other. On the other hand, more than every second interaction had a relationship with Kosaku Shima; thus reciprocity was only about one-third (32.5%). Thus, overall network centralization reached 54.2 percent. Nonetheless, local staff depended strongly on expatriate managers. Interaction of similar actors remained very low (homophily: 3.9%).

The Lost Decade – network in transition

Network ties

Between 1993 and 2001, the Lost Decade, the agenda of Japanese international managers in the Kosaku Shima novel series consisted mainly of personnel affairs, downsizing, and structural change. Good relationships with local employees and good customer relations became vital, while the relations with managers of other *keiretsu* companies remained important and were maintained. The managers had to promote sales on national and

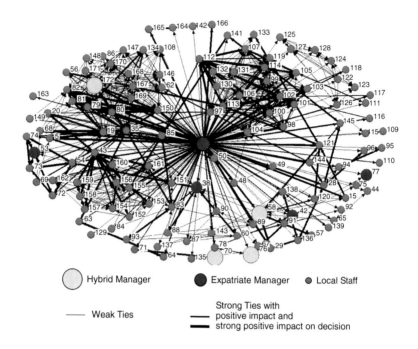

Figure 18.5   Manager network during the Lost Decade
Source: Own survey 2008; n = 130

international levels and needed to clear up issues between the head office and regional branches in Osaka and Kyoto.

During the shrinking of the economy in the 1990s, expatriate managers created synergy in cooperation with local employees. Those managers acted mainly on national and regional levels. On the international level, in each foreign market a sole hybrid manager was involved (see Figure 18.5). Strong ties with a strong positive impact on actors' decisions arose among the local staff at eye level of the community of practice. Only a limited number of expatriate and hybrid managers stood in between. The relations between the managers and the local employees were mid-term in nature, focusing on solving problems at that location. They are top-down in a strongly structured manner. Reputation was of less importance as long as the individuals completed their work. As a mechanism to assure reliance in dependent relations, the accelerating internationalization led to increased interdependency between expatriate managers, hybrid managers and local staff. Mainly expatriate managers created synergy in co-presence as well as in collocation with local employees during the Lost Decade. On the international level, a new actor, the hybrid manager, appeared.

Cliquishness

At the level of market interaction, negotiations with partners cooperating in the value chain to promote sales with innovative products came to form the centre of the manager's effort. The first aim was to develop the Japanese domestic market and open market niches. Therefore alternative sales strategies developed. Instead of downsizing and concentrating on core competencies, the company shifted to trade in products atypical for an electronics firm. Thus cohesive subgroups emerged at global-city locations such as New York, London and Paris (see Figure 18.6). For example, at the Paris branch, wine from the Bordeaux region helped to develop the wine market in Japan. With the help of *keiretsu* partners, managers and local employees moved into other industries, such as the recording business. The second aim was to optimize Hatsushiba's global production system. The greenfield investment of Hatsushiba Semiconductors in an export-processing zone in Vietnam and the emerging triad of hybrid, expatriate and local managers was intended to mirror this globalization goal.

In foreign markets, the managers tried to attract investments to compensate for the domestic downturn. In the home market, activities such as management buyout, employee outplacement and the search for new products

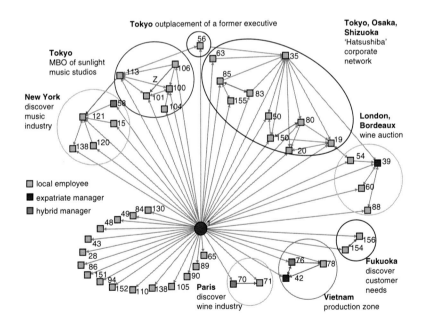

Figure 18.6　Core network and cliques during the Lost Decade (strong positive impact on decisions)

Source: Own survey 2008; n = 48

and customers led business activities. An increasing number of cliques and more hybrid managers appeared. Within the cliques the expat-local ratio held stable (8.5%) but hybrid-expatriate interaction increased strongly (25%) as well as expatriate-expatriate interaction (20%) (see Table 18.2). Hybrid managers were needed in manufacturing facilities in South-East Asia as well as in Western markets such as Paris and New York.

Brokerage

Local staff members became intermediate actors building bridges between their community of practice and the epistemic community of expatriates (see Figure 18.6). Expatriates and locals interacted in collocation within and between cliques. In addition to the strong ties, the weak ties of intermediary local staff became the backbone of the cliques. Locals brokered connections with expatriates in different cliques. Thus, the expatriate managers lost their gatekeeper function as primarily brokers of information within their epistemic group. Additionally hybrid managers took more positions in collocation negotiating between expatriate management and the local staff in foreign locations. From the spatial point of view, expatriates interacted more closely in collocation in foreign workplaces. Managers at locations in foreign countries had only direct links to the head office. During the Lost Decade the first dyadic trinational interaction with co-presence took place when the primary figures in the network had to negotiate business in London and Paris (see Figure 18.4b).

Centrality

During the Lost Decade, the network falls into reconfiguration. Interaction was based on new market conditions. Hierarchical top-down corporate interactions and other interactions did not work the way they were supposed to. Fragmentation of the expatriates' epistemic community could be observed, while the local staff members' community of practice demanded a stronger position in the network in relation to the expatriates (see Figure 18.5). Aside from Kosaku Shima, there were mostly local staff members sharing access. Distinctive heterarchy characterized subgroups of the manager network. The proportion of the shortest path between pairs of relations that include Kosaku Shima increased to almost 50 percent (betweenness: 44.2%) (see Table 18.2). Thus, the number of relations divided by the sum of all distances between Kosaku Shima and all others increased as well (closeness: 13.5%). As a result, the number of relations incident only with Kosaku Shima fell to a minimum (degree: 1.7%) and overall network centralization reached less than 40 percent (centralization: 39.2%). Reciprocity increased to over two-thirds (68.3%), but local staff, expatriate managers and hybrid managers collaborated in a fragmented way. Thus, the interaction of similar actors reached its lowest level (homophily: 2.9%).

The New Century – flexible ties network

Network ties

In the New Century, Japanese international managers in Kosaku Shima's network extended their relations into China and India. At the domestic level, internal personnel affairs mattered regarding how well the individual manager handled the integration of Chinese and Indian production facilities into Hatsushiba's global network. Problems arose regarding copyright and piracy in emerging markets.

In this period, integration of the South and East Asia plants and markets into the global economy helped create a new network. The new network was of hybrid managers growing vigorously to create necessary local as well as international synergies. The hybrid network was parallel to the transnational expatriate network. Hybrid managers and their intermediary activities were vital to maintaining good relationships with local employees in foreign locations. As a result, coordination and control through strong ties with a strong positive impact on the decisions of the actors emerged mainly between expatriate and hybrid managers as well as between local staff and hybrid managers. Parallel multiple strong ties with positive impact

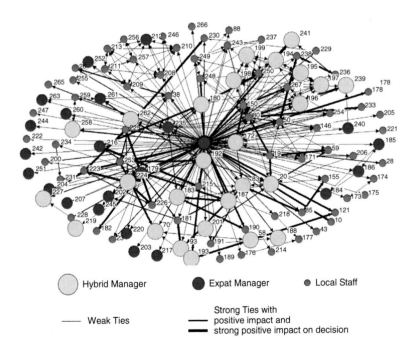

Figure 18.7 Manager network in the New Century
Source: Own Survey 2008; n = 117

and neutral weak ties emerged as well. These multiple ties were seen as alternative routes allowing flexible use (see Figure 18.7). Dispersed internationalization led to multilateral dependency and further increased the interdependency of expatriate managers, hybrid managers and local staff. In the New Century, the network of hybrid managers began growing parallel to the co-presence of expatriate managers. Those hybrid managers were able to create, in addition to expatriate managers, local as well as international synergies. Their skills and abilities created a complementary resilient circulation between expatriate and hybrid managers, reducing transaction cost significantly.

Cliquishness

Internationally, good relations between the expatriate managers sent from the head office in Tokyo and the hybrid managers and local staff at production facilities in Shanghai, Beijing, Mumbai and Delhi became a must. Domestically, factory automation provided a chance for Hatsushiba and the affiliated *keiretsu* companies to increase productivity. Thus, cohesive subgroups emerged in Tokyo, Beijing and Shanghai (see Figure 18.8). Within the cliques, the managers interacted with great autonomy with respect to

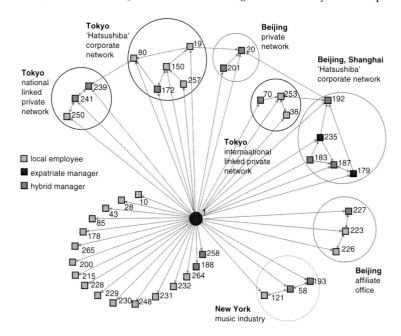

Figure 18.8 Core network and cliques during the New Century (strong positive impact on decisions)

Source: Own Survey 2008; n = 41.

the head office. Within the cliques, no single relational ratio is dominant (see Table 18.2). At this time, an increasing number of hybrid managers appeared. Only the hybrid-expatriate ratio is a bit higher than in the other time periods (3.5%). Importantly, hybrid managers became a valuable interacting member in the network (see Figure 18.8).

Brokerage

Hybrid managers became intermediate actors building bridges between the community of practice of locals and the epistemic community of expatriates (see Figure 18.8). Hybrid and expatriate managers interacted in co-presence within and between cliques. Expatriate managers were generally mobile between the foreign locations, whereas the hybrid managers had a prolonged residential time within the host location. The hybrid managers allocated weak ties as intermediaries, while the local staff completed business procedures (see Figure 18.8). At this time, the hybrid managers blended in as gatekeepers of information between the epistemic community and the community of practice. Additionally hybrid managers took more positions in co-presence in order to negotiate between cliques. Dyadic interaction became common during the New Century, with co-presence developing in Paris-Shanghai-Tokyo, New York-Shanghai-Tokyo and New Delhi-Shanghai-Tokyo (see Figure 18.4c).

Centrality

During the New Century, the network started to consolidate. An emerging market – that of China as discovered in the 1990s – became the target of intensive investment. Hierarchical top-down corporate interactions became more frequent. The fragmentation of the expatriate managers' epistemic community stopped, while the hybrid managers gained ground throughout the whole network (see Figure 18.7). Besides Kosaku Shima and other expatriates there were many hybrid managers sharing access. The proportion of the shortest path between pairs of relations that include Kosaku Shima fell to less than one-fourth (betweenness: 23.7%) (see Table 18.2). Thus, the number of relations divided by the sum of all distances between Kosaku Shima and all others (closeness: 9.3%) as well as the number of relations incident only with Kosaku Shima (degree: 1.3%) was decreasing. In summary, ongoing fragmentation led to a centralization index of one-third (centralization: 34.7%). Reciprocity increased to over three-fourths (75.3%), Thus, local staff, expatriate managers and hybrid managers collaborated as complementary entities. Interaction of similar actors is exceeded 50 percent (homophily: 55.7%).

5. Discussion

Can hybrid managers employ their special skills to select and broker appropriate information between expatriates and locals? To answer that key question, homophily as the degree to which similar actors share cultural norms has been analyzed.

During the Bubble Economy, expatriate and hybrid managers shared resources on a give-and-take basis. This is a strong force guiding the cohesion of the whole network. More than half of the network actors relate only to Kosaku Shima (54.2%). He is the focal point of the network. Thus, during the Bubble Economy overall homophily was very low (3.9%). The managers were hierarchically dependent and unilateral (see Figure 18.9). Hybrid managers are almost non-existent. Regarding the three types – local staff, expatriate managers and hybrid managers – the network was clearly centered on the expatriate epistemic community. Two hybrid managers play a non-integrated role in the periphery of the network. During that time, hierarchical transaction was a form of guidance based on directives to fulfill specific requests. There was close control over the constituent actions of the process. The parties involved sought to provide competitive advantages in order to maintain a high standard of useful interaction over the long run. These were formal, binding contracts leading to reliable relationships; therefore the ties among network nodes were usually strong. For example, within the network, legally dependent partners followed a given strategy. Therefore

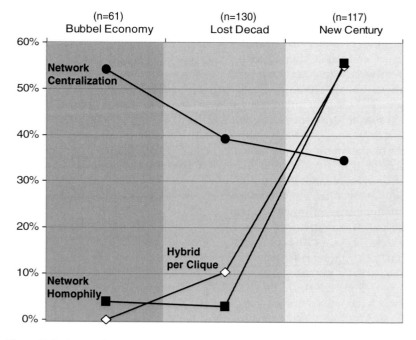

Figure 18.9   Homophily, cliquishness, centrality

Source: Own survey 2008.

collaboration in an alliance was formally solicited and the partners were not able to make decisions on their own. Interdependency regulated access to resources such as experience and know-how and even personnel recommendations, all of which were managed through mutual interactions among the network participants. Thus, achievements involving more than one site required time-consuming iterative consultations along hierarchical levels.

During the Lost Decade, the ties between the managers and local staff were usually strong and rigid linkages. Due to reorganizations and cost-saving measures, hybrid managers appeared and started to interact between expatriate managers and local staff. Along those ties, legally dependent partners made dependent decisions. Additional weak ties arose out of the cyclic communication at the interface of customer and supplier interaction. At those interfaces, the international managers and the local staff built a community based on shared knowledge, available to the involved partners. Here is where access to resources such as experience and know-how were managed. The resulting joint achievements generated mutual understanding in further joint projects. The homophily in the Lost Decade increased as a mechanism to assure reliance, and the international managers became dependent on a greater number of actors (H2). Regarding the three types of managers – local, expatriate and hybrid – during the Lost Decade, the network remained centered around the epistemic community of the controlling expatriate managers. Homophily of the network increased due to the new input of hybrid managers, and the local staff partly took over coordination functions (see Figure 18.9).

During the New Century, homophily increased due to market conditions, hierarchical top-down corporate interactions and other network interactions. The ultimate providers or recipients of information are unclear, in some instances. Control over the constituent actions of the process has become limited due to the flexible division of labor related to any given project. International managers, expatriate managers and hybrid managers can rely on each other and are confident that a partner in the network will gain some benefit in the long term. An informal, non-regulated "give and take" relationship in which the managers and local staff involved seek to give mutual advantage in order to maintain a high standard of useful interaction over the long run has developed. Parallel to legal contracts, informal, non-binding contracts generally lead to faithful and reliable relations. Due to the new input of hybrid managers, the epistemic community of expatriates and the local staff members' community of practice converged. Thus, the ties have become gradually weaker, with less rigid linkages. Collaboration in such a network may be unsolicited, with the partners deciding on their own whether to continue or stop. This kind of flexible organization leads to an accumulation of ideas and know-how allowing the manager network to react quickly to a fast-changing, competitive foreign market. Due to further cost-saving measures, hybrid managers substitute for the expatriate managers in some locations. The hybrid managers have brought in weak ties, which are the communal access to a shared knowledge base, available to all network partners. The New Century network is accessible to new managers and staff in a project. Hybrid managers can contribute and themselves become integrated into the team of expatriate international managers. Evolving redundancies provide a safety net that allows continuity in instances when a manager drops out of the network. Joint achievements generated increasing interdependency and mutual understanding within the network. Network participants became bilaterally and multilaterally dependent.

The internationalization of the network and the multi-market focus of the managers led to partial cultural assimilation. But, cultural distance between expatriate and hybrid managers and local staff did not shrink. In summary, there are three processes in play: the loss of the control monopoly by the expatriate managers, the transformation of hierarchies into heterarchies and the hybrid managers' link the epistemic expatriate and local communities of practice.

Expatriate managers lose monopoly of control

The power of the expatriate managers – that is, their ability to control business processes – comes mainly from degree. The higher the degree, the more centrally a network is organized around the main decision maker. In the network under investigation, degree of the main managers decreases over time. Accordingly, these managers lose their monopoly of power and control. As a result the network centrality decreases from the Bubble Economy (54.2%) through the Lost Decade (39.2%) and into the New Century (34.7%) (see Table 18.2). As a result, more managers have influence on the decision-making process. During the Lost Decade, due to restructuring, heterogeneity decreased. As a result the business network became spatially diversified and organizationally less hierarchic. The results include more interaction in temporary co-presence.

Cutting down of hierarchies

The extent to which the actors are in between other actors has decreased over time. Betweenness was initially low (27.6%) in the Bubble Economy regarding main actors who had direct links. Betweenness increased substantially in the Lost Decade (44.2%) (see Table 18.2). Accommodating the challenging economic situation of the 1990s, management had to cut down hierarchy levels. As a result managers had to deal more than before with intermediates such as local employees, suppliers and customers. Thereafter, in the New Century the network has begun to consolidate, and betweenness has decreased to the lowest level (23.7%). Direct permanent relationships in collocation and interaction within the co-presence of the epistemic community of expatriates and hybrid managers increased.

Convergence of communities

The same up-down pattern can be seen in the closeness measure. The degree to which actors are close to all others regarding all links was very low (5.7%) during the Bubble Economy (see Table 18.2). Only managers with a high degree of centrality were close to each other taking gatekeeper positions in the network. During the transition period represented by the Lost Decade, closeness increased sharply (13.5%). Managers and employees interacted freely in search of business opportunities in the face of a shrinking market. By contrast, in the New Century a novel stable business network has evolved and, in parallel, the closeness has decreased (9.3%). It has become one of multiple linked networks on an international level. Leading expatriate and hybrid managers have come to share permanent linkages in co-presence, keeping the convergent balance of networks' in-centrality and out-centrality. Strong ties have become less important; weak ties have increased their relative ability to adapt to a changing business environment internally as well as externally to the network communities.

6. Conclusion

To what extent the hybrid managers as translators of knowledge between expatriate managers and local staff contribute to the reduction of transaction cost has been tested during three periods of structural change: the Bubble Economy, the Lost Decade, and the New Century.

On the one hand, expatriate managers' spatial mobility and vertical career mobility in culturally distant working and living environments enables them to utilize specific cultural codes. On the other hand, they share similar norms that strengthen their epistemic community internally while nevertheless creating barriers along social lines. However, expatriate managers contribute and adjust by interacting on specific tasks, creating co-presence permanently and temporarily with similar guidelines.

As seen by the changing network degree, the business network has become spatially diversified and organizationally less hierarchic, evincing the shaping power of Japanese international managers. At the same time, the Japanese business network has become one of multiple linked networks on an international level. From the Bubble Economy to the New Century, the influence of hybrid managers increased as a complement to the existing expatriate network. Hybrid managers therefore do have advantages in collocation, sharing similar cultural norms with local staff and with other expatriate managers, while expatriate managers also have advantages as a result of their co-presence in their global community. In dispersed internationalization, hybrid managers find their place in functional cliques linking the epistemic communities and communities of practice. Hybrid managers break through the barriers of cultural distance while pursuing the active management of globalized production systems. They utilize their advantages to become significant translators of knowledge between the local and the global levels of business. Thus, in comparison with expatriate managers, the hybrid manager is able to create synergies at foreign locations of an MNC.

Acknowledgments

The first draft version of this paper was presented at the session "Changing Geographies of Japan" at the 2008 conference of the American Association of Geographers, in Boston. During discussion the author benefitted from the helpful suggestions of Prof. Dr David Edgington, Prof. Dr Tim Reiffenstein and Prof. Dr Shii Okuno. Moreover, thanks are due to William W. Baber, who carefully read and helped to improve the clarity of this research article. The usual disclaimers apply, however, and responsibility for the paper's content rest solely with the author.

References

Abegglen, J.C. (2006) *21st Century Japanese Management: New Systems, Lasting Values.* New York: Palgrave.

Almeda, P., and B. Kogut (1999) Localization of Knowledge and the Mobility of Engineers in Regional Networks, *Management Science*, 45, 905–17.

Amin, A., and P. Cohendet (2005) Geographies of Knowledge Formation in Firms, *Industry and Innovation*, 12, 465–86.

Bartlett, C.A., and S. Ghoshal (1998) *Managing across Borders: The Transnational Solution.* New York: Random House.

Bathelt, H., and J. Glückler (2005) Resources in Economic Geography: From Substantive Concepts towards a Relational Perspective, *Environment and Planning A*, 37, 1545–63.

Borgatti, S.P., and P.C. Foster (2003) The Network Paradigm in Organizational Research: A Review and Typology, *Journal of Management*, 29, 991–1013.

Braun, N. (2004) Tausch in Netzwerken, in A. Diekmann and T. Voss (eds), *Rational Choice Theorie in den Sozialwissenschaften: Anwendung und Probleme*, 129–41. München: Oldenbourg.

Coleman, J.S. (1993) *Foundations of Social Theory.* Cambridge, MA: Harvard University Press.

Costenbader, E., and T.W. Valente (2003) The Stability of Centrality Measures When Networks Are Sampled, *Social Networks*, 25, 283–307.

Enns, S., T. Malinick, and R. Matthews (2008) It's Not Only Who You Know, It's Also Where They Are: Using the Position Generator to Investigate the Structure of Access to Embedded Resources, in Lin, N., and B.H. Erickson (eds), *Social Capital: An International Research Program*, 255–81. Oxford: Oxford University Press.

Fussell, H., J. Harrison-Rexrode, W.R. Kennan, and V. Hazleton (2006) The Relationship between Social Capital, Transaction Costs, and Organizational Outcomes: A Case Study, *Corporate Communications: An International Journal*, 11/2, 148–61.

Glückler, J. (2007) Economic Geography and the Evolution of Networks, *Journal of Economic Geography*, 7, 619–34.

Gould, R.V. (1993) Collective Action and Network Structure, *American Sociological Review*, 58, 182–96.

Grabher, G. (2004) Learning in Projects, Remembering in Networks? Communality, Sociality, and Connectivity in Project Ecologies, *European Urban and Regional Studies*, 11, 99–119.

Grabher, G. (2006) Trading Routes, Bypasses, and Risky Intersections: Mapping the Travels of 'Networks' between Economic Sociology and Economic Geography, *Progress in Human Geography*, 30, 163–89.

Granovetter, M. (1985) Economic Action and Social Structure: Implications for Strategic Choice and Performance, *Administrative Science Quarterly*, 42, 654–81.

Granovetter, M. (1992) Problems of Explanation in Economic Sociology, in Nohria, N., and R.G. Eccles (eds), *Networks and Organization: Structure, Form and Action*, 25–56. Boston: HBS Press.

Granovetter, M. (2005) The Impact of Social Structure on Economic Outcomes, *Journal of Economic Perspectives*, 19, 33–50.

Haas, P. (1992) Introduction: Epistemic Communities and International Policy Coordination, *International Organization*, 46, 1–37.

Håkansson, H., and J. Johanson (1993) The Network as a Governance Structure: Interfirm Cooperation beyond Markets and Hierarchies, in Grabher, G. (ed.), *The Embedded Firm: On the Socioeconomics of Industrial Networks*, 35–51. Routledge.

Hirokane, K. (1999) *General Manager Shima Kosaku*「部長島耕作」, 1–13. Koudansha.

Hirokane, K. (2002) *Managing Director Shima Kosaku*「取締役島耕作」, 1–8. Koudansha.

Hirokane, K. (2004) *Manager Shima Kosaku*「課長島耕作」, 1–8. Koudansha.

Hirokane, K. (2005) *Executive Managing Director Shima Kosaku* 「常務島耕作」, 1–6. Koudansha.

Jun, S., J.W. Gentry, and Y.J. Hyun (2001) Cultural Adaptation of Business Expatriates in the Host Marketplace, *Journal of International Business Studies*, 32, 369–77.

Kandel, D.B. (1979) Homophily, Selection, and Socialization in Adolescent Friendships, *American Journal of Sociology*, 84, 427–36.

Lee, H.-W. (2007) Factors that Influence Expatriate Failure: An Interview Study, *International Journal of Management*, 24, 403–13.

Lesser, E.L., and J. Storck (2001) Community of Practice and Organizational Performance, *IBM Systems Journal*, 40, 831–41.

Levi-Strauss, C. (1978) *Strukturelle Anthropologie 1*. Frankfurt/Main: Suhrkamp.

Lin, N., and B.H. Erickson (eds) (2008) *Social Capital: An International Research Program*. Oxford: Oxford University Press.

Manev, I.M., and W.B. Stevenson (2001) Nationality, Cultural Distance, and Expatriate Status: Effects on the Managerial Network in a Multinational Corporation, *Journal of International Business Studies*, 32, 285–303.

Matanle, P., L. McCann, and D. Ashmore (2008) Men under Pressure: Representations of the 'Salaryman' and His Organization in Japanese Manga, *Organization*, 15, 639–64.

McCaughey, D., and N.S. Bruning (2005) Enhancing Opportunities for Expatriate Job Satisfaction: HR Strategies for Foreign Assignment Success, *Human Resource Planning*, 28, 21–9.

McGrath, C., and D. Krackhardt (2003) Network Conditions for Organizational Change, *Journal of Applied Behavioral Science*, 39, 324–36.

McPherson, M., L. Smith-Lovin, and J.M. Cook (2001) Birds of a Feather: Homophily in Social Networks, *Annual Review of Sociology*, 27, 415–44.

Minbaeva, D.B., and S. Michailova (2004) Knowledge Transfer and Expatriation in Multinational Corporations: The Role of Disseminative Capacity, *Employee Relations*, 26, 663–79.

Mitchell, J.C. (1969) The Concept and Use of Networks, in J.C. Mitchell (ed.), *Social Networks in Urban Situations*, 1–50. Manchester: Manchester University Press.

Morrison, E. (2002) Newcomers' Relationships: The Role of Social Network Ties during Socialization, *Academy of Management Journal*, 45, 1149–60.

Nadel, S.F. (1957) *The Theory of Social Structure*. London: Cohen & West.

Nonaka, I., and N. Konno (1998) The Concept of Ba: Building for Knowledge Creation, *California Management Review*, 40/3, 40–54.

Nooteboom, B. (2006) Social Capital, Institutions and Trust, *CentER Discussion Paper*, 35, 1–22.

Nooy, de W., A. Mrvar, and V. Batagelj (2007) *Exploratory Social Network Analysis with Pajek*. Cambridge: Cambridge University Press.

Putnam, R.D. (2002) *Democracies in Flux: The Evolution of Social Capital in Contemporary Society*. Oxford: Oxford University Press.

Saxonhouse, G., and R. Stern (eds) (2004) *Japan's Lost Decade: Origins, Consequences and Prospects for Recovery*. Oxford: Blackwell.

Schlunze, R.D., and M. Plattner (2007) Evaluating International Managers' Practices and Locational Preferences in the Global City, *The Ritsumeikan Business Review*, 46, 63–89.

Sorenson, O. (2003) Social Networks and Industrial Geography, *Journal of Evolutionary Economics*, 13, 513–27.

Storper, M., and A.J. Venables (2003) Buzz: Face-to-Face Contact and the Urban Economy, *Journal of Economic Geography*, 4, 351–70.

Tan, D., and J.T. Mahoney (2006) Why a Multinational Firm Chooses Expatriates: Integrating Resource-Based, Agency and Transactions Cost Perspective, *Journal of Management Studies*, 43, 457–84.

The Economist [London] (2008, 7 Aug.) Face Value: A Question of Character. What Kosaku Shima, Japan's Most Popular Salaryman, Says about Japanese Business.

Thrift, N. (2000) Performing Cultures in the New Economy, *Annals of the Association of American Geographers*, 90, 674–92.

Toh, S.M., and A.S. DeNisi (2005) A Local Perspective to Expatriate Success, *Academy of Management Executive*, 19, 132–46.

Vance, C.-M., and Y. Paik (2005) Forms of Host-Country National Learning for Enhanced MNC Absorptive Capacity, *Journal of Management Psychology*, 20, 590–606.

Watts, D.J. (1999) Networks, Dynamics and the Small-World Phenomenon, *American Journal of Sociology*, 105, 493–527.

Watts, D.J. (2003) *Six Degrees: The Science of a Connected Age*. New York: W.W. Norton & Company.

Watts, D.J. (2004) The 'New' Science of Networks, *Annual Review of Sociology*, 30, 243–70.

Watts, D.J., and S.H. Strogatz (1998) Collective Dynamics of 'Small World' Networks, *Nature*, 393, 440–2.

Wenger, E. (2004). Communities of Practice: A Brief Introduction. Retrieved October 2008 from: http://www.ewenger.com/theory/index.htm.

White, H.C. (1992) *Identity and Control: A Structural Theory of Social Action*. Princeton/NY: Princeton University Press.

White, H.C. (2002) *Markets from Networks: Socioeconomic Models of Production*. Princeton/NY: Princeton University Press.

Wood, C. (1993) *The Bubble Economy: Japan's Extraordinary Speculative Boom of the '80s and the Dramatic Bust of the '90s*. London: Macmillan.

Index